Bibliographies for Biblical Research

New Testament Series

in Twenty-One Volumes

General Editor

Watson E. Mills

Bibliographies for Biblical Research

New Testament Series

in Twenty-One Volumes

Volume III

The Gospel of Luke

Compiled by

Watson E. Mills

MELLEN BIBLICAL PRESS
Lewiston/Queenston/Lampeter

Library of Congress Cataloging-in-Publication Data
(Revised for vol. 3)

Bibliographies for biblical research. New Teseament
  series.

  Includes indexes.
  Contents: v. 1. The Gospel of Matthew / compiled by
Watson E. Mills --   -- v. 3. The Gospel of Luke /
compiled by Watson E. Mills.
  1. Bible. N.T.--Criticism, interpretation, etc.--
Bibliography. I. Mills, Watson E.
Z7772.L1B4 1993   016.225   93-30864
[BS2341.2]
ISBN 0-7734-2347-8 (v. 1)

ISBN 0-7734-2385-0 (v. 3)

This is volume 3 in the continuing series
Bibliographies for Biblical Research
New Testament Series
Volume 3 ISBN 0-7734-2385-0
Series ISBN 0-7734-9345-X

A CIP catalog record for this book is available from the British Library.

The Edwin Mellen Press
Box 450
Lewiston, New York
USA 14092

The Edwin Mellen Press
Box 67
Queenston, Ontario
CANADA L0S 1L0

Edwin Mellen Press, Ltd.
Lampeter, Dyfed, Wales
UNITED KINGDOM SA48 7DY

Printed in the United States of America

Dedication

In Memory of
Ray Summers
teacher, friend
with much appreciation and affection

Contents

Introduction to the Series

This volume is the first of a series of bibliographies on the books of the Hebrew and Christian Bibles as well as the deutero-canonicals. This ambitious series calls for some 35-40 volumes over the next 4-6 years complied by practicing scholars from various traditions.

Each author (compiler) of these volumes is working within the general framework adopted for the series, i.e., citations are to works published within the twentieth century that make important contributions to the understanding of the text and backgrounds of the various books.

Obviously the former criterion is more easily quantifiable than the latter, and it is precisely at this point that an individual compiler makes her/his specific contribution. We are not intending to be comprehensive in the sense of definitive, but where resources are available, as many listings as possible have been included.

The arrangement for the entries, in most volumes in the series, consists of three divisions: scriptural citations; subject citations; commentaries. In some cases the first two categories may duplicate each other to some degree. Multiple citations by scriptural citation are also included where relevant.

Those who utilize these volumes are invited to assist the compilers by noting textual errors as well as obvious omissions that ought to be taken into account in subsequent printings. Perfection is nowhere more elusive than in the citation of bibliographic materials. We would welcome your assistance at this point.

We hope that these bibliographies will contribute to the discussions and research going on in the field among faculty as well as students. They should serve a significant role as reference works in both research and public libraries.

I wish to thank the staff and editors of the Edwin Mellen Press, and especially Professor Herbert Richardson, for the gracious support of this series.

Watson E. Mills, Series Editor
Mercer University
Macon GA 31211 USA
August 1994

Preface

This Bibliography on the Gospel of Luke provides an index to the journal articles, essays in collected works, books and monographs, dissertations, commentaries, and various encyclopedia and dictionary articles published in the twentieth century through 1993 (a few titles for the early months of 1994 are included when these were available for verification). Technical works of scholarship, from many differing traditions constitute the bulk of the citations though I have included some selected works that intend to reinterpret this research to a wider audience.

Three extant bibliographies on the Gospel of Luke proved most helpful in the preparation of this text: Günter Wagner, *An Exegetical Bibliography of the New Testament. 2: Luke and Acts* (Macon GA: Mercer University Press, 1985); F. Van Segbroeck, *The Gospel of Luke: A Cumulative Bibliography 1973-1988* (BETL #88; Louvain, Peeters Press, 1989); and the exhaustive three-volume work by Paul-Émile Langevin, *Bibliographie biblique* (Les Presses de l'Université Laval, 1972, 1978, 1985).

Building the database necessary for a work of this magnitude was a tedious and time-consuming task. I acknowledge the administration of Mercer University for granting me a sabbatical leave during the 1991-1992 academic year. Also, I acknowledge with gratitude the Education Commission of the Southern Baptist Convention which provided funds for travel to overseas libraries. I acknowledge the support provided by the Edwin D. Johnston Faculty Research Fund which underwrote the purchase of technical materials needed for this project.

I want to express my gratitude to the staff librarians at the following institutions: Baptist Theological Seminary (Rüschlikon, Switzerland); Oxford University (Oxford, UK); Emory University (Atlanta, GA); Duke University (Durham, NC); University of Zürich (Zürich, Switzerland); Southern Baptist Theological Seminary (Louisville, KY).

I wish especially to thank Ms. Virginia Cairns, Reference Librarian, Mercer University Library and Paul Debusman, Reference Librarian at the Southern Baptist Theological Seminary Library for their considerable help in verifying citations in this work. I am grateful to Ms. Nancy Stubbs who assisted with data-entry and to my colleague, Rollin S. Armour, who assisted with the tagging of foreign titles. Finally, I gratefully acknowledge the invaluable assistance given me in technical aspects of this work by my long-time associate Ms. Irene Palmer.

Watson E. Mills
Mercer University
Macon GA 31211 USA
August 1994

Abbreviations

ABQ	American Baptist Quarterly (Valley Forge, PA)
ABR	Australian Biblical Review (Melbourne)
AbrN	Abr-Nahrain (Louvain)
ACEBT	Amsterdanse Cahiers voor exegese en bijbelse theologie (Kampen)
AfTJ	African Theological Journal (Tanzania)
AJBI	Annual of the Japanese Biblical Institute (Tokyo)
AJT	The Asia Journal of Theology
AmER	American Ecclesiastical Review (Washington, DC)
ANRW	Aufstieg und Niedergang der römischen Welt (Berlin)
Ant	Antonianum (Rome)
Asprenas	Asprenas: Rivista di Scienze Teologische (Naples, Italy)
AsSeign	Assemblees du Seigneur (Paris)
ASTI	Annual of the Swedish Theological Institute (Leiden)
ATB	Ashland Theological Bulletin (Ashland OH)
ATJ	Asbury Theological Journal (Wilmore, KY)
ATR	Anglican Theological Review (New York)
AugR	Augustinianum (Rome)
AUSS	Andrews University Seminary Studies (Berrien Springs, MI)
BA	Biblical Archaeologist (New Haven, CN)
BAR	Biblical Archaeology Review (Washington, DC)
BASOR	Bulletin of American Schools of Oriental Research (Ann Arbor, MI)
BB	Bible Bhashyam: An Indian Biblical Quarterly (Vadavathoor)

Bib	Biblica (Rome)
BibFe	Biblia y fe: Revista de teologia bíblica (Madrid)
BibL	Bibel und Leben (Düsseldorf)
BibN	Biblische Notizen: Beiträge zur exegetischen Diskussion (Bamberg)
BibO	Bibbia e Oriente (Milan)
BibTo	Bible Today (Colegeville, MN)
Bij	Bijdragen (Nijmegen)
BJRL	Bulletin of the John Rylands University Library (Manchester)
BK	Bibel und Kirche (Stuttgart)
BL	Bibel und Liturgie (Vienna)
BLOS	Bulletin de liaison sur l'origine des Synoptiques (Orléans)
BR	Biblical Research (Chicago)
BSac	Bibliotheca Sacra (Dallas, TX)
BSS	Bulletin of Saint Sulpice (Paris)
BT	Bible Translator (London)
BTB	Biblical Theology Bulletin (Jamaica NY)
BTF	Bangalore Theological Forum (Bangalore)
Bur	Burgense: Collectanea Scientifica (Burgos)
BVC	Bible et Vie Chretienne (Paris)
BZ	Biblische Zeitschrift (Paderborn)
CahÉv	Cahiers Évangile (Paris)
CalTJ	Calvary Theological Journal (Grand Rapids, MI)
Carth	Carthaginensia
Cath	Catholica: Vierteljahresschrift für ökumenische Theologie (Münster)
CBG	Collationes Brugenses et Gandavenses (Gent)
CBQ	Catholic Biblical Quarterly (Washington, DC)
CBTJ	Calvary Baptist Theological Journal (Lansdale, PA)
CC	Christian Century (Chicago)
CCER	Cahiers du cercle Ernest Renan pour libres recherches d'historie du christianisme (Paris)
Chr	Christus (Paris)
ChrM	Christian Ministry (Chicago, IL)
ChS	Church and Society (New York)

CJ	Concordia Journal (St. Louis, MO)
CJT	Canadian Journal of Theology (Toronto)
CL	Communautés et liturgies (Ottignies)
CollV	Collationes: Vlaams tijdschrift voor theologie en pastoraal (Gent)
Commonweal	Commonweal: A Review of Public Affairs, Literature and the Arts (New York)
Communio	Communio: Commentarii internationales de ecclesia et theologia (Seville)
Communion	Communion (France)
Comp	Compostellanum (Santiago)
ConRel	Conoscenza Religiosa (Firenze)
Crit	Criterion (Chicago, IL)
CrNSt	Cristianesimo nella Storia (Bologna)
Crux	Crux (Vancouver)
CS	Chicago Studies (Chicago)
CT	Christianity Today (Washington, DC)
CThM	Currents in Theology and Mission (St. Louis, MO)
CTM	Concordia Theological Monthly (St. Louis, MO)
CTQ	Concordia Theological Quarterly (Fort Wayne, IN)
CuBí	Cultura Bíblica (Madrid)
CumSem	The Cumberland Seminarian (Memphis, TN)
CVia	Communio Viatorum (Prague)
DBS	DBS
Dia	Dialog (Minneapolis, MN)
Diakonia	Diakonia (Vienna)
Div	Divinitas (Rome)
DR	Downside Review (Bath)
E-I	Eretz-Israel (Jerusalem)
EAJT	East Asia Journal of Theology (Singapore)
EB	Estudios Bíblicos (Madrid)
EcumRev	Ecumenical Review (Geneva)
EE	Estudios Eclesiásticos (Madrid)
EGLMBS	Eastern Great Lakes and Midwest Biblical Society
ÉgT	Église et théologie: A Review of the Faculty of Theology, Saint Paul University, Ottawa (Ottawa, Ontario)

EJ	Evangelical Journal (Myerstown, PA)
Emmanuel	Emmanuel (New York)
Enc	Encounter (Indianapolis, IN)
Epi	Epiphany
EpRev	The Epworth Review (London)
EQ	Evangelical Quarterly (London)
Er	Eranos: Acta Philologica Suecana (Stockholm)
ErAu	Erbe und Auftrag (Beuron)
EstAg	Estudios agustiniano (Valladolid)
EstT	Estudios Teológicos (Guatemala City)
ET	Expository Times (Edinburgh)
ETL	Ephemerides Theologicae Lovanienses (Louvain)
ÉTR	Études Théologiques et Religieuses (Montpellier)
EV	Esprit et Vie (Langres)
EvErz	Der Evangelische Erzieher (Frankfurt)
EvT	Evangelische Theologie (Munich)
FilN	Filologia Neotestamentaria (Cordoba)
FM	Faith and Mission (Wake Forest, NC)
Forum	Forum (Sonoma, CA)
FT	La foi et le temps (Tournai)
FundJ	Fundamentalist Journal (Lynchburg, VA)
Fur	Furrow (Maynooth, Kildare, Ireland)
FV	Foi et Vie (Paris)
FZPT	Freiburger Zeitschrift für Philosophie und Theologie (Freiburg)
GeistL	Geist und Leben (Würzburg)
Greg	Gregorianum (Rome)
GTJ	Grace Theological Journal (Winona Lake, IN)
HBT	Horizons in Biblical Theology (Pittsburg, PA)
HD	Heiliger Dienst (Salzburg)
HeyJ	Heythrop Journal (Oxford)
Hokhmah	Hokhmah: Revue de Réflexion Théologique (Lausanne)
Horizons	Horizons (Villanova PA)
HTR	Harvard Theological Review (Cambridge, MA)
HTS	Hervormde Teologiese Studies (Pretoria)
HUCA	Hebrew Union College Annual (Cincinnati, OH)

IBMR	International Bulletin of Missionary Research (Ventnor, NJ)
IBS	Irish Biblical Studies (London)
IJT	Indian Journal of Theology (Serampore)
IKaZ	Internationale Katholische Zeitschrift (Communio: Rodenkirchen)
IKZ	Internationale Kirchliche Zeitschrift (Bern)
Immanuel	Immanuel: A Bulletin of Religious Thought and Research in Israel (Jerusalem)
Int	Interpretation (Richmond, VA)
IRM	International Review of Mission (London)
ITQ	Irish Theological Quarterly (Maynooth)
ITS	Indian Theological Studies (Bangalore)
JAAR	Journal of the American Academy of Religion (Atlanta)
JASA	Journal of the American Scientific Affiliation (Ipswich, MA)
JBL	Journal of Biblical Literature (Atlanta, GA)
JBR	Journal of Bible and Religion (Boston)
Je	Jeevadhara (Kerala, India)
JeruP	Jerusalem Perspective
JES	Journal of Ecumenical Studies (Philadelphia, PA)
JETS	Journal of the Evangelical Theological Society (Wheaton, IL)
JewBibQ	Jewish Biblical Quarterly
JMP	The Journal of the Moscow Patriarchate (Moscow)
JP	Journal for Preachers (Decatur, GA)
JPC	Journal of Pastoral Care (New York)
JPsyC	Journal of Psychology and Christianity: Official Publication of the Christian Association for Psychological Studies (Farmington Hills, MI)
JPT	Journal of Psychology and Theology (La Mirada, CA)
JQR	Jewish Quarterly Review (Philadelphia PA)
JRH	Journal of Religious History (Sydney, Australia)
JRPR	Journal of Religion and Psychical Research (Bloomfield, CN)
JSNT	Journal for the Study of the New Testament (Sheffield)
JSS	Journal of Semitic Studies (Manchester, UK)

JTS	Journal of Theological Studies (Oxford)
JTSA	Journal of Theology for Southern Africa (Rondebosch)
Jud	Judaica (Zürich)
K	Kairos: Zeitschrift für Religionswissenschaft und Theologie (Salzburg)
KatB	Katechetische Blätter (Münich)
KCTR	King's College Theological Review (London)
KD	Kerygma and Dogma (Göttingen)
KerkT	Kerk en theologie (Den Haa)
Laur	Laurentianum (Rome)
LB	Linguistica Biblica (Bonn)
LexTQ	Lexington Theological Quarterly (Lexington, KY)
List	Listening: Journal of Religion and Culture (Romeoville, IL)
LouvS	Louvain Studies (Louvain)
LQ	Lutheran Quarterly (Gettysburg, PA)
LRSOCE	Lumen: Revista de Sintesis y Orientación de Ciencias Eclesásticas (Vitoria, Spain)
LT	Literature and Theology (Oxford)
LV	Lumen Vitae (Washington, DC)
LVie	Lumière et Vie (Lyon)
MarSt	Marian Studies (Dayton, OH)
May	Mayéutica (Marcilla)
MC	Modern Churchman (Herefordshire, England)
MeliT	Melita Theologia (La Valetta)
MillS t	Milltown Studies (Dublin)
MisCom	Miscelanea Comillas: Revista de Estudios Históricos (Madrid)
Miss	Missiology: An International Review (Scottsdale, PA)
MM	Modern Ministries (Dayton, OH)
MSR	Mélanges de Science Religieuse (Lille Cedex)
NBlack	New Blackfriars (London)
NedTT	Nederlands theologisch tijdschrift ('s-Gravenhage)
Neo	Neotestamentica (Pretoria, South Africa)
NESTTR	Near East School of Theology Theological Review (Beirut, Lebanon)
NGTT	Nederduiste Gereformeerde Teologiese Tijdskrif (Kaapstad)

NovT	Novum Testamentum (Leiden)
NovVet	Nova et Vetera (Fribourg)
NRT	La Nouvelle revue théologique (Louvain)
NTS	New Testament Studies (Cambridge, England)
NTT	Norsk teologisk tidsskrift (Oslo)
OCP	Orientalia christiana periodica: Commentarii de re Orientali Aetatis Christianae Sacra et Profana (Rome)
OLoP	Orientalia Lovaniensia Periodica (Louvain)
OrChr	Oriens Christianus: Hefte für die Kunde des Christlichen Oriens (Wiesbaden)
Orient	Orientierung: Katholische Blüatter für Weltanschauliche Information (Zürich)
OSide	The Other Side (Philadelphia, PA)
Pacifica	Pacifica: Australian Theological Studies (Brunswick East, Victoria, Australia)
Para	Paraclete
ParSpirV	Parola, spirito e vita: Quaderni di lettura biblica (Bologna)
PatByzR	Patristic and Byzantine Review (Kingston, NY)
PerT	Perspectiva Teológica (Brazil)
PIBA	Proceedings of the Irish Biblical Association (Dublin)
PJ	Perkins Journal (Dallas, TX)
Pneuma	Pneuma: The Journal of the Society for Pentecostal Studies (Chicago, IL)
Point	Point (Papua, New Guinea)
PrakT	Praktische Theologie: nederlands Tijdschrift voor Pastorale Wetenschappen (Netherlands)
PRS	Perspectives in Religious Studies (Macon, GA)
PV	Parole di vita (Torino)
QR	Quarterly Review: A Scholarly Journal for Reflection on Ministry (Nashville, TN)
RB	Revue biblique (Paris)
RBén	Revue Bénédictine: De Critique, d'Histoire et de Littérature Religieuse (Belgium)
RBib	Rivista Biblica (Bologna)
RevExp	Review and Expositor: A Baptist Theological Journal (Louisville, KY)

RevQ	Revue de Qumran (Paris)
RevRef	Revue Reformée (France)
RevRel	Review for Religious (Duluth, MN)
RevSR	Revue des Sciences religieuses (Strasbourg)
RHPR	Revue d'historie et de philosophie religieuses (Paris)
RHR	Revue de l'historie des Religions (Paris)
RIL	Religion and Intellectual Life
RivBib	Rivista Biblica (Brescia)
RQ	Restoration Quarterly (Abilene, TX)
RS	Religion and Society: Bulletin of the Christian Institute for the Study of Religion and Society (Bangalore, India)
RSB	Religious Studies Bulletin (Calgary)
RSPT	Revue des Sciences Philosophiques et Thélogiques
RT	Revue Thomiste (Paris)
RTL	Revue théologique de Louvain (Brabant, Belgium)
RTP	Revue de Théologie et de Philosophie (Switzerland)
RTR	Reformed Theological Review (Melbourne, Australia)
SacD	Sacra Doctrina: Rivista Quadrimestrale di Scienze Religiose (Bologna, Italy)
Sale	Salesianum
Salm	Salmanticensis
SBFLA	Studii Biblici Franciscani Liber Annuus (Jerusalem)
SBLSP	Society of Biblical Literature Seminar Papers
SBT	Studia Biblica et Theologica: Essays by Students of Fuller Theological Seminary and Other Theological Institutions (Pasadena, CA)
ScC	Scuola cattolica: Rivista di scienze religiose (Milan)
ScE	Science et Esprit (Montreal)
Schrift	Schrift
Scr	Scripture: Quarterly of Catholic Biblical Association (Edinburgh)
ScrB	Scripture Bulletin (Strawberry Hill, UK)
ScripT	Scripta theologia (Pamplona, Spain)
SE	Sciences Ecclésiastiques
SEÅ	Svensk Exegetisk Årsbok (Lund)
SelTeol	Selecciones de teología (Barcelona)

Semeia	Semeia
Servitium	Servitium, quaderni de spiritualità (Casale Monferrato)
SJT	Scottish Journal of Theology (Edinburgh)
SLJT	Saint Luke's Journal of Theology (Sewanee, TN)
SM	Studia Missionalia: Annual Publication of the Faculty of Missiology, Gregorian University (Rome)
SNTU-A	Studien zum Neuen Testament und Seiner Umwelt: Serie A (Linz, Austria)
Soj	Sojourners (Washington, DC)
SouJT	Southwestern Journal of Theology (Ft. Worth, TX)
Soundings	Soundings: An Interdisciplinary Journal (Nashville, TN)
SpirTo	Spirituality Today (Chicago)
SR	Studies in Religion/Sciences religieuses (Ontario)
ST	Studies in Theology (London)
StJudLAnt	Studies in Judaism in Late Antiquity (Leiden)
StPa	Studia Patavina: Revista di Scienze Religiose (Padova, Italy)
StudB	Studia biblica (Berlin)
StudC	Studii Clasice
StudE	Studia evangelica (Berlin)
StudL	Studium Legionense (León)
SVTQ	St. Vladimir's Theological Quarterly
TBe	Theologische Beiträge (West Germany)
TexteK	Texte und Kontexte: Exegetische Zeitschrift (Berlin)
TGeg	Theologie der Gegenwart (Münster)
TGl	Theologie und Glaube (Paderborn, Germany)
Themelios	Themelios (England)
Theology	Theology (London)
TheoV	Theologische Versuche (Berlin)
ThEv	Theologia evangelica (Pretoria, South Africa)
TijT	Tijdschrift voor Theologie (Nijmegen)
TLZ	Theologische Literaturzeitung
TPQ	Theologische-praktische Quartalschrift (Linz)
TQ	Theologische Quartalschift (Tübingen)
TR	Theologische Rundschau (Tübingen)

Trans	Transformation: An International Evangelical Dialogue on Mission and Ethics (Exeter)
TriJ	Trinity Journal (Deerfield, IL)
TS	Theological Studies (Baltimore, MD)
TSR	Trinity Seminary Review (Columbus, OH)
TT	Theology Today (Princeton, NJ)
TTZ	Trierer Theologische Zeitschrift (Rhineland, West Germany)
TynB	Tyndale Bulletin (England)
TZ	Theologische Zeitschrift (Basel, Switzerland)
UBR	United Brethren Review
UnSa	Una Sancta: Zeitschrift für Ökumenische Begegnung (Brooklyn, NY)
USQR	Union Seminary Quarterly Review (New York, NY)
VC	Vigiliae Christianae
VD	Verbum Domine: Commentarii de re Biblica (Rome)
VoxE	Vox evangelica: Biblical and Historical Essays from the London Bible College (London)
VS	La vie spirituelle (Paris)
VT	Vetus Testamentum
WesTJ	Wesleyan Theological Journal
WoAnt	Wort und Antwort (West Germany)
Worship	Worship (Collegeville, MN)
WS	Word and Spirit
WTJ	Westminster Theology Journal (Philadelphia, PA)
WW	Word and World (St. Paul, MN)
ZAW	Zeitschrift für die alttestamentliche Wissenschaft (Berlin)
ZDPV	Zeitschrift des Deutschen Palästina-Veriens (Wiesbaden)
ZKT	Zeitschrift für Katholische Theologie (Innsbruck)
ZMiss	Zeitschrift für Mission (Basel)
ZNW	Zeitschrift für die neutestamentliche Wissenschaft
ZPE	Zeitschrift für Papyrologie und Epigraphik (Bonn)
ZST	Zeitschrift für systematische Theologie
ZTK	Zeitschrift für Theologie und Kirche (Tübingen)
Zwing	Zwingliana (Zürich)

PART ONE

Citations by Chapter and Verse

1-12

0001 K. Aland, "Eine neue Ausgabe des griechischen Neuen Testaments: Zur Oxforder Ausgabe von Luk. 1-12," *TR* 80 (1984): 441-48.

1-9

0002 Roland Meynet, *Quelle est donc cette Parole? Lecture 'rhétorique' de l'évangile de Luc (1-9, 22-24).* Lectio divina #99. Paris: Cerf, 1979.

1-4

0003 Gilberto Marconi, "Il Bambino da Vedere: l'Estetica Lucana Nel Cantico di Simeone e Dintorni," *Greg* 72/4 (1991): 629-54.

1:1-4:44

0004 Feargus O'Fearghail, "The Introduction to Luke-Acts: A Study of the Role of Lk 1,1-4,44 in the Composition of Luke's Two-Volume Work," doctoral dissertation, Pontifical Biblical Institute, Rome, 1987. 2 vols. See *Introduction to Luke-Acts: A Study of the Role of Luke 1:1-4:44 in the Composition of Luke's Two-Volume Work.* Rome: Biblical Institute Press, 1991.

1:1-4:30

0005 John M. Gibbs, "Mk 1,1-15, Mt 1,1-4,16, Lk 1,1-4,30, Jn 1,1-51: The Gospel Prologues and Their Function," *StudE* 4 (1968): 154-88.

1:1-4:22

0006 Thomas L. Brodie, "A New Temple and a New Law," *JSNT* 5 (1979): 21-45.

1-3

0007 J. H. Davies, "The Lucan Prologue (1-3): An Attempt at Objective Redaction Criticism," *StudE* 4 (1968): 78-85.

0008 M. Völkel, "Exegetische Erwägungen zum Verständnis des Begriffs κατεκσῆς im Lukanischen Prolog," *NTS* 20 (1973-1974): 289-99.

1:1-3:22

0009 Joseph G. Kelly, "Lucan Christology and the Jewish-Christian Dialogue," *JES* 21 (1984): 688-708.

0010   G. Eerdman, *Die Vorgeschichten des Lukas- und Matthäus-Evangeliums und Vergils vierte Ekloge*. Göttingen: Vandenhoeck & Ruprecht, 1932.

0011   J. Casper, "Und Jesus nahm zu," *BL* 11 (1939-1940): 9-12.

0012   E. Burrows, "The Gospel of the Infancy: The Form of Luke. Chapters 1 and 2," in E. Burrows, ed., *The Gospel of Infancy and Other Biblical Essays*. London: Burns, Oates & Washbourne, 1940. Pp. 1-58.

0013   Harald Sahlin, "Die protolukanische Gestaltung von Lk 1-2," in *Der Messias und das Gottesvolk*. Uppsala: Almquist, 1945. Pp. 63-69.

0014   H. T. Kuist, "Sources of Power in the Nativity Hymns. An Exposition of Luke 1 and 2," *Int* 2 (1948): 288-98.

0015   Martin Dibelius, "Jungfrauensohn und Krippenkind: Untersuchungen zur Geburtsgeschichte Jesu im Lukas-Evangelium," in Martin Dibelius, ed., *Botschaft und Geschichte*. Tübingen: Mohr, 1953. Pp. 1-78.

0016   T. Maertens, *Le Messie est la!* Brugges: Abbaye de Saint-André, 1954.

0017   J. S. Pedro, "Valor apologético de la infancia de Jesús," *CuBí* 11 (1954): 39-40.

0018   Paul Winter, "Two Notes on Luke 1-2 with Regard to the Theory of 'Imitation Hebraisms'," *ST* 7 (1954): 158-65.

0019   Paul Winter, "Some Observations on the Language in the Birth and Infancy Stories of the Third Gospel," *NTS* 1 (1954-1955): 111-21.

0020   Nigel Turner, "The Relation of Luke i and ii to Hebraic Sources and to the Rest of Luke-Acts," *NTS* 2 (1955-1956): 100-109.

0021   Paul Winter, " 'Nazareth' and 'Jerusalem' in Luke i and ii," *NTS* 3 (1956-1957): 136-42.

0022 Michael D. Goulder and M. L. Sanderson, "St. Luke's Genesis," *JTS* 8 (1957): 12-30.

0023 P. Gaechter, "Die literarische Geschichte von Lk 1-2," in *Maria im Erdenleben*. Innsbruck: Tyrolia Verlag, 1958. Pp. 9-77.

0024 S. Muñoz Iglesias, "Los Evangelios de la infancia y las infancias de los héroes," in *Géneros literanos en los Evangelios*. Madrid: Científica Medinaceli, 1958. Pp. 83-113.

0025 Paul Winter, "Lukanische Miszellen," *ZNW* 59 (1958): 65-77.

0026 Paul Winter, "The Main Literary Problem of the Lucan Infancy Story," *ATR* 40 (1958): 257-64.

0027 S. Muñoz Iglesias, "El Evangelio de la infancia en San Lucas y las infancias de los héroes biblicos," in *Teología bíblica sobre el pecado: La teología bíblica*. Madrid: Libería Científica Medinaceli, 1959. Pp. 325-74.

0028 P. J. Thompson, "The Infancy Gospels of St. Matthew and St. Luke Compared," *StudE* 1 (1959): 217-22.

0029 R. McLean Wilson, "Some Recent Studies in the Lucan Infancy Narratives," *StudE* 1 (1959): 235-53.

0030 Frans Neirynck, *L'Évangile de Noël selon S. Luc*. Brussels: La Pensée Catholique, 1960.

0031 H. H. Oliver, "The Lucan Birth Stories and the Purpose of Luke-Acts," *NTS* 10 (1963-1964): 202-26.

0032 Paul S. Minear, "Luke's Use of the Birth Stories," in Leander Keck and J. L. Martyn, eds., *Studies in Luke-Acts* (festschrift for Paul Schubert). Nashville: Abingdon Press, 1966. Pp. 111-30.

0033 H. Schürmann, "Aufbau Eigenart und Geschichtswert von Lukas 1-2," *BK* 21 (1966): 106-11.

0034 A. Smitmans, "Die Hymnen der Kindheitsgeschichte nach Lukas," *BK* 21 (1966): 115-18.

0035   G. Voss, "Die Christusverkündigung der Kindheitgeschichte im
       Rahmen des Lukasevangeliums," *BK* 21 (1966): 112-15.

0036   W. B. Tatum, "The Epoch of Israel: Luke i-ii and the Theological
       Plan of Luke-Acts," *NTS* 13 (1966-1967): 184-95.

0037   G. Danieli, "Vangeli dell'infanzia," in *Il Messaggio della salvezza*.
       5 vols. Torino: Leumann, 1966-1970. 4:150-203.

0038   K. H. Schelkle, "Die Kindheitsgeschichte Jesu," in *Bibel und
       Zeitgemässer Glaube*. Band II: *Neues Testament*. Klosterneuberg:
       Kunstverlag, 1967. II:11-36.

0039   Walter Wink, "John the Baptist in the Lukan Infancy Narratives,"
       in *John the Baptist in the Gospel Tradition*. Cambridge: University
       Press, 1968. Pp. 58-82.

0040   C. Duquoc, "Les enfances du Christ," in *Christologie*. 2 vols.
       Paris: Cerf, 1968-1972. 1:23-41.

0041   U. E. Lattanzi, "Il vangelo dell'infanzia è verità o mito?" in *De
       primordiis cultus marian. 4. De cultu B. V. Mariae respectu habito
       ad mythologiam et libros apocryphos*. Rome: Mariana
       Internationalis, 1970. 4:31-46.

0042   A. Malet, *Les évangiles de Noël: Mythe ou réalité?*. Lausanne:
       Éditions l'Âge d'Homme, 1970.

0043   C. T. Ruddick, "Birth Narratives in Genesis and Luke," *NovT* 12
       (1970): 343-48.

0044   H. Schürmann, "Aufbau, Eigenart und Geschichtswert der
       Vorgeschichte Lk 1-2," in *Traditionsgeschichtliche
       Untersuchungen zu den synoptischen Evangelien*. Düsseldorf:
       Patmos, 1970. Pp. 198-208.

0045   A. Smitmans, "Die synoptischen Kindheitsgeschichten," in *Maria
       im Neuen Testament*. Stuttgart: Katholisches Bibelwerk, 1970. Pp.
       13-34.

0046   A. Vögtle, "Offene Fragen zur lukanischen Geburts- und
       Kindheitsgeschichte," *BL* 11 (1970): 51-67.

0047 K. Gutbrod, *Die "Weihnachtsgeschichten" des Neuen Testaments.* Stuttgart: Calwer, 1971.

0048 André Feuillet, "Observations sur les recits de l'enfance chez S. Luc," *EV* 82 (1972): 721-24.

0049 S. Muñoz Iglesias, "Midráš y Evangelios de la Infancia," *EE* 47 (1972): 331-59.

0050 A. V. Cernuda, "El paralelismo de γεννω y τικτω en Lc 1-2," *Bib* 55 (1974): 260-64.

0051 André Feuillet, *Jésus et sa mère d'après les récits lucaniens de l'enfance et d'après saint Jean.* Paris: Gabalda, 1974.

0052 Réne Laurentin, "Les evangiles de l'enfance," *LV* 119 (1974): 84-105.

0053 M. Sinoir, "Jesus et sa Mere d'apres les recits lucaniens de l'enfance," *EV* 84 (1974): 625-34.

0054 F. Gryglewicz, "Die Herkunft der Hymnen des Kindheitsevangeliums des Lucas," *NTS* 21 (1974-1975): 265-73.

0055 Gerhard Lohfink, "Israel in Lk 1-2," in *Die Sammlung Israels.* Münich: Kösel, 1975. Pp. 17-32.

0056 J. M. Ford, "Zealotism and the Lukan Infancy Narratives," *NovT* 18 (1976): 280-92.

0057 C. Perrot, "Les récits de l'enfance de Jésus," *CahÉv* 18 (1977): 72.

0058 C. Escudero Freire, *Devolver el Evangelio a los pobres: A proposito de Lc 1-2.* Salamanca: Sigueme, 1978.

0059 Reginald H. Fuller, "The Conception/Birth of Jesus as a Christological Moment," *JSNT* 1 (1978): 37-52.

0060 J. Galot, "Riflessioni sul primo atto di fede cristiana. Maria la prima credente," *CC* 1 (1978): 27-39.

0061   G. De Rosa, "Storia e teologia nei racconti dell'infanzia di Gesù,"
        CC 4 (1978): 521-37.

0062   D. S. Tam, "The Literary and Theological Unity Between Luke
        1-2 and Luke 3-Acts 28," doctoral dissertation, Duke University,
        Durham NC, 1978.

0063   Tavares A. Augusto, "Infancy Narratives and Historical
        Criticism," *TD* 28 (1980): 53-54.

0064   S. C. Farris, "On Discerning Semitic Sources in Luke 1-2," in
        Robert T. France and David Wenham, eds., *Gospel Perspectives II*.
        Sheffield: JSOT Press, 1981. Pp. 201-37.

0065   G. Jankowski, "In jenen Tagen: Der politische Kontext zu Lukas
        1-2," *TexteK* 12 (1981): 5-17.

0066   Leopold Sabourin, "Recent Views on Luke's Infancy Narratives,"
        RSB 1/1 (1981): 18-25.

0067   Charles Thomas Davis, "The Literary Structure of Luke 1-2," in
        D. J. A. Clines, et al., eds., *Art and Meaning: Rhetoric in Biblical
        Literature*. Sheffield: JSOT Press, 1982. Pp. 215-29.

0068   Agnès Gueuret, "Luc 1-2: Analyse sémiotique," *SémBib* 25
        (1982): 35-42.

0069   Réne Laurentin, "Vérité des Évangiles de l'enfance," *NRT* 105
        (1983): 691-710.

0070   Alberto Casalegno, *Gesù e il tempio: Studio redazionale su
        Luca-Atti*. Brescia: Morcelliana, 1984.

0071   A. J. B. Higgins, "Luke 1-2 in Tatian's *Diatessaron*," *JBL* 103
        (1984): 193-222.

0072   Réne Laurentin, "La speranza dei giusti in Lc 1-2," *ParSpirV* 9
        (1984): 123-36.

0073   Stephen C. Mott, "The Use of the Bible in Social Ethics: 2. The
        Use of the New Testament [2 pts.]," *Trans* 1/2 (1984): 21-26; 3
        (1984): 19-26.

0074   M. Boyd, "The Search for the Living Text of the Lukan Infancy
       Narrative," in D. E. Groh and Robert Jewett, eds., *The Living Text*
       (festschrift E. W. Saunders). Lanham MD: University Press of
       America, 1985. Pp. 123-40.

0075   S. C. Farris, *The Hymns of Luke's Infancy Narratives: Their
       Origin, Meaning and Significance*. Sheffield: JSOT Press, 1985.

0076   P. Boyd Mather, "The Search for the Living Text of the Lukan
       Infancy Narrative," in Dennis Groh and Robert Jewett, eds., *The
       Living Text* (festschrift for Ernest Saunders). Lanham MD:
       University Press of America, 1985. Pp. 123-40.

0077   Raymond E. Brown, "Gospel Infancy Narrative Research From
       1976 to 1986: Part II (Luke)," *CBQ* 48/4 (1986): 660-80.

1:1-5

0078   Eugene Seraphin, "The Edict of Caesar Augustus," *CBQ* 7 (1945):
       91-96.

1:1-4

0079   P. Alfaric, "Les Prologues de Luc," *RHR* 115 (1937): 37-52.

0080   W. C. van Unnik, "Remarks on the Purpose of Luke's Historical
       Writing (Luke 1:1-4)," *NedTT* 9 (1955): 323-31.

0081   D. E. Nineham, "Eyewitness Testimony and the Gospel
       Tradition," *JTS* 9 (1958): 13-25, 243-52.

0082   H. Schürmann, "Evangelienschrift und kirchliche Unterweisung:
       Die repräsentative Funktion der Schrift nach Lk 1,1-4," in E.
       Kleineidam and H. Schürmann, eds., *Miscellanea Erfordiana*.
       Leipzig: St. Benno-Verlag, 1962. Pp. 48-73.

0083   Günter Klein, "Lukas 1,1-4 als theologisches Programm," in E.
       Dinkler, ed., *Zeit und Geschichte* (festschrift for Rudolf Bultmann).
       Tübingen: Mohr, 1964. Pp. 193-216.

0084   D. J. Sneed, "An Exegesis of Luke 1:1-4 with Special Regard to
       Luke's Purpose as a Historian," *ET* 83 (1971-1972): 40-43.

0085   É. Samain, "L'Évangile de Luc: un témoignage ecclésial et
       missionnaire," *AsSeign* N.S. 34 (1973): 60-73.

0086   Schuyler Brown, "The Prologues of Luke-Acts in Their Relation to the Purpose of the Author," *SBLSP* 5 (1975): 1-14.

0087   L. Alexander, "Luke-Acts in its Contemporary Setting with Special Reference to the Prefaces (Luke 1:1-4 and Acts 1:1)," doctoral dissertation, Oxford University, UK, 1977.

0088   G. Menestrina, "L'incipit dell'espitola 'Ad Diognetum,' Luca 1:1-4 et Atti 1:1-2," *BibO* 19 (1977): 215-18.

0089   Schuyler Brown, "The Role of the Prologues in Determining the Purpose of Luke-Acts," in Charles H. Talbert, ed., *Perspectives on Luke-Acts*. Macon GA: Mercer University Press, 1978. Pp. 99-111.

0090   Vernon K. Robbins, "Prefaces in Greco-Roman Biography and Luke-Acts," *SBLSP* 8/2 (1978): 193-208.

0091   Roger L. Omanson, "A Note on Luke 1.1-4," *BT* 30 (1979): 446-47.

0092   R. J. Dillon, "Previewing Luke's Project from his Prologue (Luke 1:1-4)," *CBQ* 43 (1981): 205-27.

0093   Peter Fiedler, "Geschichten als Theologie und Verkündigung: Die Prologe des Matthäus- und Lukas-Evangeliums," in Rudolf Pesch, ed., *Zur Theologie der Kindheitsgeschichten: Der heutige Stand der Exegese*. Münich: Schnell, 1981. Pp. 11-26.

0094   Franz Mussner, "Die Gemeinde des Lukasprologs," *SNTU-A* 6/7 (1981-1982): 113-30.

0095   Erhardt Güttgemanns, "In welchem Sinne ist Lukas 'Historiker'? Die Beziehungen von Luk 1,1-4 und Papias zur antiken Rhetotik," *LB* 54 (1983): 9-26.

0096   Robert H. Stein, "Luke 1:1-4 und Traditionsgeschichte," *JETS* 26 (1983): 421-30.

0097   Franz Mussner, "Die Gemeinde des Lukasprologs," in William C. Weinrich, ed., *The New Testament Age*. 2 vols. Macon GA: Mercer University Press, 1984. 2:201-206.

0098 Terrance Callan, "The Preface of Luke-Acts and Historiography," *NTS* 31 (1985): 576-81.

0099 P. Gibert, "Les évangiles et l'histoire (Luc 1,1-4; Jean 20,30-31)," *LVie* 175 (1985): 19-26.

100 Jaroslav B. Stanek, "Lukas: Theologie der Heilgeschichte," *CVia* 28/1-2 (1985): 9-31.

0101 Roland Kany, "Der Lukanische Bericht von Tod und Auferstehung Jesu aus der Sicht eines hellenistischen Romanlesers," *NovT* 28/1 (1986): 75-90.

0102 J. W. Scott, "Luke's Preface and the Synoptic Problem," doctoral dissertation, St. Andrews University, UK, 1986.

0103 James M. Dawsey, "The Origin of Luke's Positive Perception of the Temple," *PRS* 18 (1991): 5-22.

1:1

0104 J. Bauer, "*Polloi* Lk 1,1," *NovT* 4 (1960-1961): 263-66.

0105 F. W. Goodman, "Ἐπειδήπερ πολλοὶ ἐπεχείρησαν (Luke 1,1): A Proposed Ementation," *StudE* 4 (1968): 205-208.

1:2

0106 André Feuillet, "Témoins oculaires et serviteurs de la parole," *NovT* 15 (1973): 241-59.

0107 Vladimir Ivanov, "The Spiritual Foundations of Ecclesiastical Art, Pt. 1," *JMP* 8 (1984): 74-78.

1:3

0108 J. Kurzinger, "Lk 1,3: . . . ἀκριβῶς καθεξῆς σοι γράψαι," *BZ* 18 (1974): 249-55.

0109 Brigitte Kahl, "Armenevangelium und Heidenevangelium: 'Sola Scriptura' und die ökumenische Traditions Problematik," *TLZ* 110 (1985): 779-81.

1:5-4:15

0110   Charles H. Talbert, "Prophecies of Future Greatness: The
       Contribution of Greco-Roman Biographies to an Understanding of
       Luke 1:5-4:15," in James L. Crenshaw and Samuel Sandmel, eds.,
       The Divine Helmsman (festschrift for L. Silberman). New York:
       KTAV, 1980. Pp. 129-41.

1:5-2:52

0111   Mario Galizzi, "Vangelo dell'infanzia (Lc 1,5-2,52)," *PV* 21
       (1976): 455-64.

1:5-2:20

0112   H. L. MacNeill, "The *Sitz im Leben* of Luke 1,5-2,20," *JBL* 65
       (1946): 123-30.

1:5-80

0113   Harald Sahlin, "Lk 1:5-80," in *Der Messias und das Gottesvolk*.
       Uppsala: Almquist, 1945. Pp. 70-189.

1:5-55

0114   John J. Kilgallen, "A Consideration of Some of the Women in the
       Gospel of Luke," *SM* 40 (1991): 27-55.

1:5-38

0115   G. Saldarini, "Le due annunciazioni (Lc 1,5-38)," in L. Moraldi
       and S. Lyonnet, eds., *I Vangelini (Introduzione alla Bibbia)*.
       Torino: Marietti, 1960. Pp. 426-76.

1:5-23

0116   Giovanni Berlingieri, *Il lieto annuncio della nascita e del
       concepimento del Precursore di Gesù (Lu 1,5-23.24-25) nel quadro
       dell'opera luanan: uno studio tradizionale e redazionale*. Roma:
       Gregoriana, 1991.

1:5-15

0117   R. F. Collins, "Jesus' Ministry to the Deaf and Dumb," *MeliT*
       35/1 (1984): 12-36.

1:5-6

0118   Gordon MacDonald, "John the Baptizer and Obedience," in
       John E. Kyle, ed., *The Unfinished Task*. Ventura CA: Regal Books,
       1984. Pp. 39-47.

1:5

0119 David L. Jones, "Luke's Unique Interest in Historical Chronology," *SBLSP* 19 (1989): 378-87.

0120 Abramo Levi, "Esempi di vocazione net NT," *Servitium* 3/61 (1989): 24-34.

0121 Günther Schwarz, "Ἐξ ἐφημερίας 'Αβιά?" *BibN* 53 (1990): 30-31.

1:8-2:7

0122 A. Brenner, "Female Social Behaviour: Two Descriptive Patterns Within the 'Birth of the Hero' Paradigm," *VT* 36 (1986): 257-73.

1:12-15

0123 F. Smyth-Florentin, "Jésus, le Fils du Père, vainqueur de Satan," *AsSeign* 14 (1973): 56-75.

1:13-34

0124 Harold L. Willmington, "The Twelve Questions of Christmas," *FundJ* 1/4 (1982):

1:14

0125 J. Ryckmans, "Un parallèle sud-arabe à l'imposition du nom de Jean-Baptiste et de Jésus," in R. G. Stiegmer, ed., *Al-Hudhud* (festschrift for M. Höfner). Graz: Franzens University Press, 1981. Pp. 28-94.

0126 L. Alexander, "Luke's Preface in the Context of Greek Preface-Writing," *NovT* 28/1 (1986): 48-74.

1:15

0127 B. Sussarellu, "De praevia sanctificatione Praecursoris," *SBFLA* 3 (1952-1953): 37-110.

1:17

0128 J. Peters, "In de geest en de kracht van Elia (Lucas 1,17)," *Schrift* 88 (1983): 148-52.

0129 Carlos Mesters, "Restabelecer a Justiça de Deus No Meio Do Povo: Vida e Luta Do Profeta Elias: Sobre a Missao Profética," *EstT* 24/2 (1984): 129-47.

14

1:22

0130 Heinrich Baarlink, "Friede im Himmel: die Lukanische Redaktion von Lk 19,38 und Ihre Deutung," *ZNW* 76/3 (1985): 170-86.

1:24-25

0131 Giovanni Berlingieri, *Il lieto annuncio della nascita e del concepimento del Precursore di Gesù (Lu 1,5-23.24-25) nel quadro dell'opera luanan: uno studio tradizionale e redazionale.* Roma: Gregoriana, 1991.

1:24

0132 G. Graystone, *Virgin of All Virgins: The Interpretation of Luke 1:24.* Rome: Pontifical Biblical Commission, 1968.

1:25

0133 Paul Winter, "ʺΟτι Recitativum in Luke 1:25, 61; 2:23," *HTR* 48 (1955): 213-18.

1:26-56

0134 K. Butting, "Eine Freundin Gottes: Luk. 1,26-56," *TexteK* 21 (1984): 42-49.

0135 Roland Meynet, "Dieu Donne Son Nom à Jésus: Analyse Rhétorique de Lc. 1:26-56 et de 1 Sam. 2:1-10," *Bib* 66/1 (1985): 39-72.

0136 Raymond E. Brown, "The Annunciation to Mary, the Visitation and the Magnificat (Luke 1:26-56)," *Worship* 62 (1988): 249-59.

1:26-45

0137 H. Vermeyen, "Mariologie als Befreiung. Luke 1:26-45, 56 im Kontext," *ZKT* 105 (1983): 168-83.

0138 Marie Assaad, "Reversing the Natural Order," in J. S. Pobee and Bärbel von Wartenberg-Potter, eds., *New Eyes for Reading: Biblical and Theological Reflections by Women from the Third World.* Geneva: WCC Publications, 1986. Pp. 25-27.

1:26-38

0139 Reginald H. Fuller, "The Virgin Birth: Historical Fact or Kerygmatic Truth?" *BR* 1 (1957): 1-8.

0140   I. Rodriguez, "Consideración filológica sobre el mensaje de la Anunciación (Luc 1,26-38)," in *Géneros literanos en los Evangelios*. Madrid: Científica Medinaceli, 1958. Pp. 221-49.

0141   O. A. Piper, "The Virgin Birth. The Meaning of the Gospel Accounts," *Int* 18 (1964): 131-48.

0142   H. Langkammer, "The Soteriological Character of Mary's Fiat," *SBFLA* 15 (1964-1965): 293-301.

0143   M. D. Johnson, "The Genealogy of Jesus in Luke," in *The Purpose of the Biblical Genealogies*. Cambridge: University Press, 1969. Pp. 229-52.

0144   Pierre Benoit, "L'Annonciation (Lc 1)," *AsSeign* N.S. 8 (1972): 39-50.

0145   B. Prete, "Il racconto dell'Annunziazione di Luca 1,26-38," *BibO* 15 (1973): 75-88.

0146   André Feuillet, "L'Annonciation (1,26-38)," in *Jesus et sa mère*. Paris: Gabalda, 1974. Pp. 17-24.

0147   D. Moody Smith, "Luke 1:26-38," *Int* 29 (1975): 411-17.

0148   A. Orbe, *Anunciación: Meditaciones sobre Lucas 1,26-38*. Biblioteca de autores cristianos #42. Madrid: Editorial catolica, 1976.

0149   A. Stöger, " 'Wir sind Gottes Volk!' Bibelmeditation über Luke 1:26-38," *BL* 50 (1977): 250-52.

0150   A. Knockaert and C. Van Der Plancke, "Catéchèse de l'annonciation," *LV* 34 (1979): 79-121.

0151   A. M. Serra, "L'annunciazione a Maria (Lc 1,26-38), un formulario di alleanza?" *PV* 25 (1980): 164-71.

0152   K. Stock, "Die Berufung Marias (Luke 1:26-38)," *Bib* 61 (1980): 457-91.

0153   K. Stock, "Lo Spirito su Maria (Lc 1,26-38)," *ParSpirV* 4 (1981): 88-98.

0154 U. Wilckens, "Empfangen vom Heiligen Geist geboren aus der Jungfrau Maria, Lk 1,26-38," in Rudolf Pesch, ed., *Zur Theologie der Kindheitsgeschichten: Der heutige Stand der Exegese.* Münich: Schnell, 1981. Pp. 49-73.

0155 E. A. LaVerdiere, "Be It Done to Me," *Emmanuel* 90 (1984): 184-90.

0156 Willem S. Vorster, "The Annunciation of the Birth of Jesus in the Protoevangelium of James," in J. H. Petzer and P. J. Hartin, eds., *A South African Perspective on the New Testament* (festschrift for Bruce Metzger). Leiden: Brill, 1986. Pp. 33-53.

1:26-31
0157 Charles H. Talbert, "Luke 1:26-31," *Int* 39 (1985): 288-91.

1:26-28
0158 Martin Conway, "Your Will Be Done: Mission in Christ's Way," *IRM* 75 (1986): 423-59.

1:27
0159 C. H. Dodd, "New Testament Translation Problems," *BT* 27/3 (1976): 301-305; 28 (1977): 101-16.

0160 J. Carmignac, "The Meaning of παρθένος in Lk 1,27: A Reply to C. H. Dodd," *BT* 28 (1977): 327-30.

1:28-42
0161 A. Salas, ed., "El Avemaria (Lc 1,28.42)," *BibFe* 10 (1984): 1-103.

1:28
0162 F. Stummer, "Beitrage zur Exegese der Vulgata," *ZAW* 62 (1949-1950): 152-67.

0163 P. Franquesa, "Sugerencias en torno a Luke 1:28," *CuBí* 11 (1954): 320-22.

0164 J. Leal, "El saludo del Angel a la Virgen," *CuBí* 11 (1954): 293-301.

0165 Raimund Köbert, "Lc. 1:28, 42 in den Syrischen Evangelien," *Bib* 42/2 (1961): 229-30.

0166   F. A. Strobel, "Der Gruss an Maria (Lc 1:28): Eine Philologische Betrachtung Zu Seinem Sinngehalt," *ZNW* 53/1-2 (1962): 86-110.

0167   D. Yubero, "Maria, 'el Señor es contigo'," *CuBí* 31 (1974): 91-96.

0168   G. M. Verd, " 'Gratia plena' (Lc 1,28). Sentido de una traduccion," *EE* 50 (1975): 357-89.

0169   Leopold Sabourin, "Recent Views on Luke's Infancy Narratives," *RSB* 1/1 (1981): 18-25.

0170   Carlo Buzzetti, "Κεχαριτωμένη, 'Favoured' (Lk 1:28), and the Italian Common Language New Testament," *BT* 33 (1982): 243.

0171   Silverio Zedda, "Il Χαῖρε di Lc 1,28 in luce di un triplice contesto anticotestamentario," in C. Marcheselli Casale, ed., *Parola e Spirito* (festschrift for S. Cipriani). Brescia: Paideia, 1982. Pp. 273-92.

0172   Édouard Delebecque, "Sur la salutation de Gabriel à Marie (Lc 1,28)," *Bib* 65 (1984): 352-55.

0173   Reginald H. Fuller, "A Note on Luke 1:28 and 38," in William C. Weinrich, ed., *The New Testament Age* (festschrift for Bo Reicke). 2 vols. Macon GA: Mercer University Press, 1984. 1:201-206.

0174   Carlo Buzzetti, "Traducendo Κεχαριτωμένη Lc 1,28)," in M. Angelini, et al., eds., *Testimonium Christi* (festschrift for Jacques Dupont). Brescia: Paideia, 1985. Pp. 111-16.

0175   Ignace de la Potterie, "Κεχαριτωμένη en Lc 1,28: Étude philologique," *Bib* 68 (1987): 357-82.

<u>1:31-33</u>

0176   Rudolf Schnackenburg, "Davidsspross und Krippenkind (Lk 1,31-33)," in *Glaubensimpulse aus dem Neuen Testament.* Düsseldorf: Patmos, 1972. Pp. 34-38.

<u>1:31</u>

0177   B. Schellenberger, "Die Jungfrau wird schwanger werden," *GeistL* 53 (1980): 38-40.

1:32-35
    0178 Raymond E. Brown, "Luke's Method in the Annunciation Narratives of Chapter One," in J. W. Flangan, ed., *No Famine in the Land* (festschrift for J. L. McKenzie). Missoula MT: Scholars Press, 1975. Pp. 179-94.

1:32-34
    0179 G. Richter, "Zu den Tauferzahlungen Mk 1:9-11 und Joh 1:32-34," *ZNW* 65 (1974): 43-56.

1:32-33
    0180 J. G. Sobosan, "Completion of Prophecy: Jesus in Lk 1:32-33," *BTB* 4 (1974): 317-23.

1:32
    0181 J. Ryckmans, "Un parallèle sud-arabe à l'imposition du nom de Jean-Baptiste et de Jésus," in R. G. Stiegmer, ed., *Al-Hudhud* (festschrift for M. Höfner). Graz: Franzens University Press, 1981. Pp. 28-94.

    0182 Frederick W. Danker, "Politics of the New Age According to St. Luke," *CThM* 12 (1985): 338-45.

    0183 Lucien Legrand, "The Angel Gabriel and Politics: Messianism and Christology," *ITS* 26 (1989): 1-21.

1:33
    0184 David H. C. Read, "Recognizing Jesus as King Today," *ET* 92 (1980-1981): 81-82.

1:34-38
    0185 M. Villanueva, "Nueva controversia en torno al voto de virginidad de Nuestra Señora," in *Géneros literanos en los Evangelios*. Madrid: Científica Medinaceli, 1958. Pp. 251-72.

1:34-35
    0186 Gerhard Schneider, "Lk 1,34.35 als redaktionelle Einheit," *BZ* 15 (1971): 255-59.

1:34
    0187 H.-J. Vogel, "Zur Textgeschichte von Lc 1,34ff.," *ZNW* 43 (1950-1951): 256-60.

1:34

0188 N. L. Martinez, "Porque no conozco varón," *CuBí* 11 (1954): 333-35.

0189 Josef Gewiess, "Die Marienfrage, Lk. 1:34," *BZ* 5/2 (1961): 221-54.

0190 Hans Quecke, "Lk. 1:34 in Den Alten Ubersetzungen und im Protevangelium des Jakobus," *Bib* 44/4 (1963): 499-520.

0191 J. Bauer, "Philologische Bemerkungen zu Lk. 1:34," *Bib* 45/4 (1964): 535-40.

0192 Hans Quecke, "Lk. 1:34 im Diatessaron," *Bib* 45/1 (1964): 85-88.

0193 M. Orsatti, "Verso la decodificazione di un insolita espressione (Luke 1:34)," *RBib* 29 (1981): 343-57.

1:35

0194 Tjitze Baarda, "Dionysios Bar Salibi and the Text of Luke 1:35," *VC* 17 (1963): 225-29.

0195 S. Muñoz Iglesias, "Lucas 1,35b," in *La idea de Dios en la Biblia.* Madrid: Consejo Superior de Investigaciones Científicas, 1971. Pp. 303-24.

0196 Pierre Grelot, "La naissance d'Issac et celle de Jésus," *NRT* 104 (1972): 462-87, 561-85.

0197 F. W. Schlatter, "The Problem of John 1:3b-4a," *CBQ* 34/1 (1972): 54-58.

0198 A. V. Cernuda, "La presunta sustantivacion de *gennōmenon* en Lc 1,35b," *EB* 33 (1974): 265-73.

0199 C. Escudero Freire, "Alcance christológico de Lc 1,35 y 2,49," *Communio* 8 (1975): 5-77.

0200 Leopold Sabourin, "Two Lukan Texts (1:35; 3:22)," *RSB* 1 (1981): 29-32.

0201 S. Brock, "Passover, Annunciation and Epiclesis: Some Remarks on the Term *Aggen* in the Syriac Versions of Luke 1:35," *NovT* 24 (1982): 222-33.

0202   Silverio Zedda, "Lc 1,35b, 'Colui che nascerà santo sarà chiamato Figlio di Dio': I. Breve storia dell'esegesi recente," *RBib* 33 (1985): 29-43.

0203   Silverio Zedda, "Lc 1,35b, 'Colui che nascerà santo sarà chiamato Figlio di Dio': II. Questioni sintattiche ed esegesi," *RBib* 33 (1985): 165-89.

0204   Gerald Bostock, "Virgin Birth or Human Conception?" *ET* 97/9 (1986-1987): 260-63.

0205   S. Brock, "Maggnanuta: A Technical Term in East Syrian Spirituality and Its Background," in R. Coquin, ed., *Mélanges Antoine Guillaumont.* Genève: P. Cramer, 1988. Pp. 121-29.

0206   S. Brock, "The Lost Old Syriac at Luke 1:35 and the Earliest Syriac Terms for the Incarnation," in William L. Petersen, ed., *Gospel Traditions in the Second Century: Origins, Recensions, Text and Transmission.* Notre Dame IN: University Press, 1989. Pp. 117-31.

1:38

0207   S. del Paramo, "El Fiat de la Virgen en la Anunciación, punto de enlace entre el Antiguo y Nuevo Testamento en la historia de la salvación," in *Jalones de la Historia de la Salvación en el Antiguo y Nuevo Testamento.* 2 vols. Madrid: Científica Medinaceli, 1969. 2:101-19.

0208   Reginald H. Fuller, "A Note on Luke 1:28 and 38," in William C. Weinrich, ed., *The New Testament Age* (festschrift for Bo Reicke). 2 vols. Macon GA: Mercer University Press, 1984. 1:201-206.

1:39-56

0209   J. G. Cepeda, "La Virgen, poetisa Sagrada," *CuBí* 11 (1954): 391-94.

0210   André Feuillet, "La Visitation (1,39-56): Marie et la Fille de Sion," in *Jesus et sa mère.* Paris: Gabalda, 1974. Pp. 25-29.

0211   C. L'Eplattenier, "Une série pour l'Avent," *ETL* 57 (1982): 569-82.

0212 P. Raffin, "L'Annonciation et l'espérance (Luke 1:39-56)," *EV* 83 (1983): 241-42.

0213 Tina Pippin, "The Politics of Meeting: Women and Power in the New Testament," in Michael Downey, ed., *That They Might Live: Power, Empowerment, and Leadership in the Church.* New York: Crossroad, 1991. Pp. 13-24.

1:39-47
0214 J. P. Martin, "Luke 1:39-47," *Int* 36 (1982): 394-99.

1:39-45
0215 P.-E. Jacquemin, "La Visitation (Lc 1)," *AsSeign* N.S. 8 (1972): 64-75.

0216 J. M. Salgado, "La visitation de la Sainte Vierge Marie: exercice de sa Maternité Spirituelle," *Div* 16 (1972): 445-52.

0217 H. B. Beverly, "Luke 1:39-45," *Int* 30 (1976): 396-400.

1:41-50
0218 E. Galbiati, "La Visitazione (Luke 1:41-50)," *BibO* 4 (1962): 139-44.

1:42
0219 Raimund Köbert, "Lc. 1:28, 42 in den Syrischen Evangelien," *Bib* 42/2 (1961): 229-30.

1:45-46
0220 W. Vischer, "Luke 1:45-46," *ÉTR* 30 (1955): 17-19.

0221 Randall Buth, "Hebrew Poetic Tenses and the Magnificat," *JSNT* 21 (1984): 67-83.

1:46-56
0222 J. R. Harris, "Mary or Elisabeth?" *ET* 41 (1929-1930): 266-67.

0223 J. R. Harris, "Again the Magnificat," *ET* 42 (1930-1931): 188-90.

0224 P. Gaechter, "Das Magnificat," in P. Gaechter, ed., *Maria im Erdenleben.* 2nd ed. Innsbruck: Marianischen Verlag, 1954. Pp. 127-54.

0225   Paul Winter, "Magnificat and Benedictus: Maccabaean Psalms?"
       BJRL 37 (1954-1955): 328-47.

0226   J. G. Davies, "The Ascription of the Magnificat to Mary," *JTS* 15
       (1964): 307-308.

0227   D. R. Jones, "The Background and Character of the Lukan
       Psalms," *JTS* 19 (1968): 19-50.

0228   P.-E. Jacquemin, "Le Magnificat (Lc 1)," *AsSeign* N.S. 66 (1973):
       28-40.

0229   P. Schmidt, "Maria in der Sicht des Magnifikat," *GeistL* 46
       (1973): 417-30.

0230   Robert C. Tannehill, "The Magnificat as Poem," *JBL* 93 (1974):
       263-75.

0231   P. Schmidt, "Maria und das Magnificat," *Cath* 29 (1975): 230-46.

0232   Walter Vogels, "Le Magnificat, Marie et Israel," *ÉgT* 6 (1975):
       279-96.

0233   L. Schottroff, "Das Magnificat und die älteste Tradition über Jesus
       von Nazareth," *ET* 38 (1978): 298-313.

1:46-55
0234   G. Castellino, "Osservazioni sulla struttura letteraria del
       'Magnificat," in *Studi dedicati alla memoria di Paolo Ubaldi*.
       Milano: Società editrice, 1937. Pp. 413-30.

0235   V. Hamp, "Der alttestamentliche Hintergrund des Magnifikat," *BK*
       8/3 (1953): 17-23.

0236   Kathryn Sullivan, "His Lowly Maid," *Worship* 36 (1962): 374-79.

0237   Stephen Benko, "The Magnificat: A History of the Controversy,"
       JBL 86 (1967): 263-75.

0238   J. Duncan M. Derrett, "Il significato della mangiatoia," *ConRel* 1
       (1973): 439-44.

0239 K. E. Bailey, "The Song of Mary: Vision of a New Exodus (Luke 1,46-55)," *NESTTR* 2 (1979): 29-35.

0240 M. Tréves, "Le Magnificat et le Benedictus (Lc 1,46-55.68-79)," *CCER* 27 (1979): 105-10.

0241 D. Minguez, "Poética generativa del Magnificat," *Bib* 61 (1980): 55-77.

0242 Jacques Dupont, "Il cantico della Vergine Maria (Lc 1,46-55)," *ParSpirV* 3 (1981): 89-105.

0243 Leopold Sabourin, "Recent Views on Luke's Infancy Narratives," *RSB* 1/1 (1981): 18-25.

0244 I. Gomá Civit, *El Magnificat: Cántico de la salvación.* Madrid: Editorial católica, 1982.

0245 Theo Bell, "Das Magnificat vorteutschet und ausgelegt, 1521: een kommentaar bij het voorwoord," in J. T. Bakker and J. P. Boendermaker, eds., *Luther na 500 jaar.* Kampen: Kok, 1983. Pp. 78-98.

0246 Robert J. Karris, "Mary's Magnificat and Recent Study," *RevRel* 42 (1983): 903-908.

0247 X. Pikaza, "Engrandece mi alma al Señor," *BibFe* 9 (1983): 238-48.

0248 A. Salas, "Magnificat," *BibFe* 9 (1983): 1-98.

0249 P.-M. Bogaert, "Épisode de la controverse sur le 'Magnificat': À propos d'un article inédit de Donatien de Bruyne," *RBén* 94 (1984): 38-49.

0250 B. Grigsby, "Compositional Hypotheses for the Lucan 'Magnificat': Tensions for the Evangelical," *EQ* 56 (1984): 159-72.

0251 Patricia A. Harrington, "Mary and Femininity: A Psychological Critique," *JRH* 23 (1984): 204-17.

0252   T. Ossanna, *Il Magnificat progetto di vita: Analisi etico-strutturale di Lc 1,46b-55*. Rome: Borla, 1984.

0253   E. R. Obbard, *Magnificat: The Journey and the Song*. Mahwah NJ: Paulist Press, 1985.

0254   Gail R. O'Day, "Singing Woman's Song: A Hermeneutic of Liberation," *CThM* 12 (1985): 203-10.

0255   Alberto Valentini, "Magnifcat e lopera lucana," *RBib* 33 (1985): 395-423.

0256   P. Bemile, *The Magnificat within the Context and Framework of Lukan Theology: An Exegetical Theological Study of Luke 1:46-55*. Bern: Lang, 1986.

0257   Helmer Ringgren, "Luke's Use of the Old Testament," in George W. E. Nickelsburg and George W. MacRae, eds., *Christians among Jews and Gentiles* (festschrift for Krister Stendahl). Philadelphia: Fortress, 1986. Pp. 227-35.

0258   David M. Scholer, "The Magnificat (Luke 1:46-55): Reflections on its Hermeneutical History," in Mark I. Branson and C. René Padilla, eds., *Conflict and Context*. Grand Rapids MI: Eerdmans, 1986. Pp. 210-19.

0259   C. Hugo Zorrilla, "The Magnificat: Song of Justice," in Mark I. Branson and C. René Padilla, eds., *Conflict and Context*. Grand Rapids MI: Eerdmans, 1986. Pp. 220-37.

0260   Jean Delorme, "Le Magnificat: Laforme et le sens," in H. Cazelles, ed., *La vie de la parole* (festschrift for P. Grelot). Paris: Desclée, 1987. Pp. 175-94.

0261   Alberto Valentini, *Il Magnificat, Genere letterario, struttura, esegesi*. Bologna: Dehoniane, 1987.

0262   Heribert Schützeichel, "Das berühmte und denkwürdige Lied der heiligen Jungfrau: Calvins Auslegung des Magnificat," in Thomas Franke, et al., eds., *Creatio ex amore: Beiträge zu einer Theologie der Liebe* (festschrift for Alexandre Ganoczy). Würzburg: Echter, 1989. Pp. 300-11.

0263 Willem S. Vorster, "Die Lukaanse Liedere," *HTS* 1 (1989): 17-34.

0264 Christoph Burger, "Luthers Predigten über das Magnifikat (Lk 1,46-55)," in *Théorie et pratique de l'exégèse: actes du troisième colloque international sur l'historie de l'exégèse biblique au XVIe siècle.* Genève: Droz, 1990. Pp. 273-86.

0265 Gail R. O'Day, "The Praise of New Beginnings: The Infancy Hymns in Luke," *JP* 14/1 (1990): 3-8.

1:47-55
0266 Maurya P. Horgan and Paul J. Kobelski, "The Hodayot (1QH) and New Testament Poetry," in M. P. Horgan and P. J. Kobelski, eds., *To Touch the Text: Biblical and Related Studies in Honor of Joseph A. Fitzmyer.* New York: Crossroad, 1989. Pp. 179-93.

1:49
0267 Paul Winter, "Lc 1,49 und Targum Yerushalmi Again," *ZNW* 46 (1955): 140-41.

0268 A. Manrique, "El poderoso ha hecho maravillas," *BibFe* 9 (1983): 259-64.

1:51-55
0269 Rudolf Schnackenburg, "Umsturzplane Gottes (Lk 1,51-55)," in *Glaubensimpulse aus dem Neuen Testament.* Düsseldorf: Patmos, 1972. Pp. 39-43.

1:51
0270 P. L. Schoonheim, "Der alttestamentliche Boden der Vokabel *uperêphanos,* Lukas i,51," *NovT* 8 (1966): 235-46.

0271 M. C. Crespo, "Dios dispersó a los soberbios," *BibFe* 9 (1983): 265-78.

1:52-53
0272 V. Casas, "Dios colmó a los hambrientos," *BibFe* 9 (1983): 288-99.

1:52
0273 E. G. Rupp, "A Great and Mighty Wonder!" *ET* 89 (1977-1978): 81-82.

0274 A. Salas, "Dios derribó a los poderosos," *BibFe* 9 (1983): 274-87.

1:54-55
0275 E. Gallego, "Dios acogió a Israel. La fidelidad del amor," *BibFe* 9 (1983): 300-11.

1:56
0276 H. Vermeyen, "Mariologie als Befreiung. Luke 1:26-45, 56 im Kontext," *ZKT* 105 (1983): 168-83.

1:57-59
0277 Gordon MacDonald, "John the Baptizer and Obedience," in John E. Kyle, ed., *The Unfinished Task*. Ventura CA: Regal Books, 1984. Pp. 39-47.

1:57
0278 V. Soria, "El nacimiento de Juan el Bautista," *CuBí* 16 (1959): 120-23.

1:59-63
0279 Gerard Mussies, "Vernoemen in de antieke wereld: De historische achtergrond van Luk. 1,59-63," *NTT* 42 (1988): 114-25.

1:61
0280 Paul Winter, "Ὅτι Recitativum in Luke 1:25, 61; 2:23," *HTR* 48 (1955): 213-18.

1:67-79
0281 Joachim Gnilka, "Der Hymnus des Zacharias [Lk. 1:67-79]," *BZ* 6/2 (1962): 215-38.

0282 C. L'Eplattenier, "Une série pour l'Avent," *ETL* 57 (1982): 569-82.

1:68-79
0283 P. Vielhauer, "Das Benedictus des Zacharias (Lk 1,68-79)," *ZTK* 49 (1952): 255-72.

0284 Paul Winter, "Magnificat and Benedictus: Maccabaean Psalms?" *BJRL* 37 (1954-1955): 328-47.

0285 G. Saldarini, "Il cantico Benedictus," in L. Moraldi and S. Lyonnet, eds., *I Vangelini (Introduzione alla Bibbia)*. Torino: Marietti, 1960. Pp. 477-92.

0286 M. Gertner, "Midrashim in the New Testament," *JSS* 7 (1962): 267-92.

0287 A. Vanhoye, "Structure du 'Benedictus'," *NTS* 12 (1965-1966): 382-89.

0288 O. Haggenmüller, "Der Lobgesang des Zacharias (Luke 1:68-79)," *BibL* 9 (1968): 249-60.

0289 D. R. Jones, "The Background and Character of the Lukan Psalms," *JTS* 19 (1968): 19-50.

0290 P. Auffret, "Note sur la structure littéraire de Luke 1:68-79," *NTS* 24 (1977-1978): 248-58.

0291 J. Reuss, "Studien zur Lukas-Erklärung des Presbyters Hesychius von Jerusalem," *Bib* 59 (1978): 562-71.

0292 M. Tréves, "Le Magnificat et le Benedictus (Lc 1,46-55.68-79)," *CCER* 27 (1979): 105-10.

0293 M. del Oro, "Benedictus de Zacarias (Luc 1,68-79) ¿Indicios de una cristologia arcaica?" *RevB* 45 (1983): 145-77.

0294 J. Severino Croatto, "El 'Benedictus' Como Memoria de la Alianza: Estructura y Teología de Lucas 1:68-79," *RevB* 47/4 (1985): 207-19.

0295 Helmer Ringgren, "Luke's Use of the Old Testament," *HTR* 79/1-3 (1986): 227-35.

0296 François Rousseau, "Les Structures du Benedictus (Luc 1:68-79)," *NTS* 32/2 (1986): 268-82.

0297 W. Carter, "Zechariah and the Benedictus (Luke 1,68-79): Practicing What He Preaches," *Bib* 69 (1988): 239-47.

0298   Maurya P. Horgan and Paul J. Kobelski, "The Hodayot (1QH) and New Testament Poetry," in M. P. Horgan and P. J. Kobelski, eds., *To Touch the Text: Biblical and Related Studies in Honor of Joseph A. Fitzmyer.* New York: Crossroad, 1989. Pp. 179-93.

1:80

0299   A. S. Getser, "The Youth of John the Baptist: A Deduction from the Break in the Parallel Account of the Lucan Infancy Story," *NovT* 1 (1956): 70-75.

2-3

0300   A. R. C. Leaney, "The Birth Narratives in St. Luke and St. Matthew," *NTS* 8 (1961-1962): 158-66.

2:1-52

0301   Harald Sahlin, "Lk 2:1-52," in *Der Messias und das Gottesvolk.* Uppsala: Almquist, 1945. Pp. 190-311.

2:1-21

0302   J. Riedl, "Zur lukanischen Weihnachtsbotschaft," *BL* 39 (1966): 341-50.

0303   H. Tsuchiya, "The History and the Fiction in the Birth Stories of Jesus: An Observation on the Thought of Luke the Evangelist," *AJBI* 1 (1975): 73-90.

0304   Rudolf Pesch, "Das Weihnachtsevangelium (Lk 2,1-21): Literarische Kunst—Politische Implikationen," in Rudolf Pesch, ed. *Zur Theologie der Kindheitsgeschichten: Der heutige Stand der Exegese.* Münich: Schnell, 1981. Pp. 97-118.

2:1-20

0305   E. Galbiati, "Il Natale (Luke 2:1-20)," *BibO* 2 (1960): 214-19.

0306   F. Kamphaus, " 'Es geschah in jenen Tagen . . . ' Besinnung zum Weihnachtsevangelium Luke 2:1-20," *BibL* 9 (1968): 299-302.

0307   H. Schürmann, " 'Sie gebar ihren erstgeborenen Sohn . . . ' Lk 2,1-20 als Beispiel homologetischer Geschichtsschreibung," in *Ursprung und Gestalt.* Düsseldorf: Patmos, 1970. Pp. 217-21.

0308   C. Westermann, "Alttestamentliche Elemente in Lukas 2,1-20," in
        G. Jeremias, et al., eds., *Tradition und Glaube: Das frühe
        Christentum in seiner Unwelt* (festschrift for Karl Georg Kuhn).
        Göttingen: Vandenhoeck & Ruprecht, 1971. Pp. 317-27.

0309   J. Duncan M. Derrett, "The Manger at Bethlehem: Light on St.
        Luke's Technique from Contemporary Jewish Religious Law,"
        StudE 6 (1973): 86-94.

0310   W. Schmithals, "Die Weihnachtsgeschichte Lukas 2,1-20," in G.
        Ebeling, E. Jungel and G. Schunack, eds., *Festschrift für Ernst
        Fuchs.* Tübingen: Mohr, 1973. Pp. 281-97.

0311   André Feuillet, "Quelques observations sur la structure de Luc 1,2:
        La naissance de Jésus et l'hommage des bergers (2,1-20)," in *Jesus
        et sa mère.* Paris: Gabalda, 1974. Pp. 47-58.

0312   Jan Lambrecht, "The Child in the Manger: A Meditation on Luke
        2:1-20," *LouvS* 5 (1974-1975): 331-35.

0313   L. Hermans, "Lucas' Pastorale: Exegetische kanttekeningen bij
        Lucas 2,1-20," in J. J. A. Kahmann and H. G. Manders, eds., *De
        weg van ha woord.* Hilversum: Gooi & Sticht, 1975. Pp. 16-43.

0314   Raymond E. Brown, "The Meaning of the Manger: The
        Significance of the Shepherds," *Worship* 50 (1976): 528-38.

0315   H. Schüngel-Straumann, "Cäsar oder Christus? Christologische und
        politische Anliegen im Weihnachtsevangelium des Lukas," *KatB*
        101 (1976): 796-803.

0316   M.-A. Chevallier, "L'analyse littéraire des textes du Nouveau
        Testament," *RHPR* 57 (1977): 367-78.

0317   A. Vögtle, *Was Weihnachten bedeutet: Meditation zu Lukas 2,1-20.*
        Freiburg: Herder, 1977.

0318   Vittorio Fusco, "Il messaggio e il segno: Riflessioni esegehche sul
        racconto lucano della natività. (Lc 2,1-20)," in Marcheselli Casale,
        ed., *Parola e Spirito* (festschrift for S. Cipriani). Brescia: Paideia,
        1982. Pp. 293-333.

0319   Birgit Stolt, "Poesie und Mythos: Ubersetzungstheoretische und
rezeptionsästhetische Studien zu Luthers Bibelübersetzung im
Wandel der Zeiten," in H. Becker and R. Kaczynski, eds., *Liturgie*
und Dichtung: Ein interdisziplin ares Kompendium. St. Ottilien:
EOS Verlag, 1983. Pp. 1-40.

0320   Charles T. Knippel, "The Nativity of Our Lord," *CJ* 11 (1985):
228-29.

0321   G. Bouwman, "Het geboorteverhaal van Lucas (Lc 2,1-20)," in W.
Weren, ed., *Geboorteverhalen van Jesus.* Brugge: Tabor, 1988. Pp.
75-87.

2:1-14

0322   W. J. Hollenweger, *Besuch bei Lukas: 4 narrative Exegesen zu 2*
Mose 14, Lukas 2,1-14, 2 Kor 6,4-11 und Lukas 19,1-10. Münich:
Kaiser, 1981.

0323   Fritz Büsser, "Weihnachtspredigten über Lk 2,1-14," in *Théorie*
et pratique de l'exégèse: actes du troisième colloque international
sur l'historie de l'exégèse biblique au XVIe siècle. Genève: Droz,
1990. Pp. 127-40.

2:1-12

0324   E. Galbiati, "L'adorazione dei Magi (Luke 2:1-12)," *BibO* 4
(1962): 20-29.

2:1-10

0325   B. Trémel, "Le signe du nouveau né dans la mangeoie: À propos
de Lc 2,1-10," in P. Casetti, et al., eds., *Mélanges Dominique*
Barthélemy. Göttingen: Vandenhoeck, 1981. Pp. 593-612.

0326   A. M. Wolff, "Der Kaiser und das Kind: Ein Auslegung von Luk
2,1-10," *TexteK* 12 (1981): 18-31.

2:1-7

0327   G. Ogg, "The Quirinius Question Today," *ET* 79 (1967-1968):
231-36.

0328   J. Duncan M. Derrett, "Further Light on the Narratives of the
Nativity," *NovT* 17 (1975): 81-108.

2:1-5

0329 F. Stauffer, "Die Dauer des Census Augusti - Neue Beiträge zum lukanischen Schatzungsbericht," in *Studien zum Neuen Testament und zur Patristik* (festschrift for Erich Klostermann). Berlin: Akademie-Verlag, 1961. Pp. 9-34.

0330 P. W. Barnett, "Ἀπογραφή and ἀπογράφεσθαι in Luke 2:1-5," *ET* 85 (1973-1974): 377-80.

0331 Pierre Benoit, "Quirinius," *DBS* 9 (1977): 693-720.

2:1-2

0332 Horst R. Moehring, "The Census in Luke as an Apologetic Device," in David E. Aune, ed., *Studies in New Testament and Early Christian Literature* (festschrift Allen Wikgren). Leiden: Brill, 1972. Pp. 144-60.

0333 R. H. Smith, "Caesar's Decree (Luke 2:1-2): Puzzle or Key," *CThM* 7 (1980): 343-51.

2:1

0334 E. Neuhäusler, "Die Herrlichkeit des Herrn," *BibL* 8 (1967): 233-35.

0335 T. P. Wiseman, " 'There Went Out a Decree from Caesar Augustus . . . ,'" *NTS* 33 (1987): 497.

0336 Royce L. B. Morris, "Why Αὐγοῦστος? A Note to Luke 2:1," *NTS* 38 (1992): 142-44.

2:2-24

0337 Patrick P. Saydon, "Some Biblico-Liturgical Passages Reconsidered," *MeliT* 18/1 (1966): 10-17.

2:2

0338 G. Ogg, "The Quirinius Question Today," *ET* 79/8 (1967-1968): 231-36.

0339 W. Brindle, "The Census and Quirinius: Luke 2:2," *JETS* 27 (1984): 43-52.

0340 J. Daoust, "Le recensement de Quirinius," *EV* 94 (1984): 366-67.

0341 K. Haacker, "Erst unter Quirinius? Ein Übersetzungsvorschlag zu Lk 2,2," *BibN* 38/39 (1987): 39-43.

2:4-5

0342 George D. Kilpatrick, "Luke 2:4-5 and Leviticus 25:10," *ZNW* 80/3-4 (1989): 264-65.

2:7

0343 D. Yubero, "Una opinión original del 'Brocense'," *CuBí* 11 (1954): 3-6.

0344 E. Pax, "Denn sie fanden keinen 'Platz in der Herberge'. Jüdisches und frühchristliches Herbergswesen," *BibL* 6 (1965): 285-98.

0345 K. E. Bailey, "The Manger and the Inn: The Cultural Background of Luke 2,7," *NESTTR* 2 (1979): 33-44.

0346 John R. Rice, "No Room for Jesus," *FundJ* 1/4 (1982): 30-32.

0347 E. A. LaVerdiere, "Jesus the First-Born," *Emmanuel* 89 (1983): 544-48.

0348 E. A. LaVerdiere, "Wrapped in Swaddling Clothes," *Emmanuel* 90 (1984): 542-46.

0349 E. A. LaVerdiere, "No Room for them in the Inn," *Emmanuel* 91 (1985): 552-57.

0350 Hildegard Must, "A Diatessaric Rendering in Luke 2:7," *NTS* 32/1 (1986): 136-43.

0351 J. L. Ottey, "In a Stable Born Our Brother," *ET* 98/3 (1986-1987): 71-73.

0352 L. P. Trudinger, "No Room in the Inn: A Note on Luke 2:7," *ET* 102 (1990-1991): 172-73.

2:8-39

0353 C. L'Eplattenier, "Une série pour l'Avent," *ETL* 57 (1982): 569-82.

2:8-14

0354   F. J. Steinmetz, "Nachtwache. Eine Betrachtung zu Luke 2:8-14,"
GeistL 55 (1982): 465-67.

2:10-14

0355   Gyllenberg Rafael, "Till julevangelists exeges," in *Erling Eidem:
Theologiae doctori, summo suo praedidi, sexagenario, pie ac
reverenter obtulit hunc fasciculum societas exegetica upsaliensis.*
Uppsala: Wretmans, 1940. Pp. 83-94.

2:10

0356   F. J. Heggen, "Vrees niet want zie, ik verkondig u een blijde
boodschap die bestemd is voor heel het volk," *PrakT* 16 (1989):
553-58.

2:11

0357   F. Wulf, "Gott im Menschen Jesus. Auslegung und Meditation von
Johannes 1:14; Phil 2:7; Lk 2:11," *GeistL* 42 (1969): 273-73.

0358   Robert R. Hann, "*Christos Kyrios* in PsSol 17:32: 'The Lord's
Anointed' Reconsidered," *NTS* 31 (1985): 620-27.

0359   B. Prete, " 'Oggi vi è nato . . . il Salvatore che è il Cristo Signore'
(Lc 2,11)," *RBib* 34 (1986): 289-325.

2:12

0360   A. Pritchard, "Our True Selves," *ET* 94 (1982-1983): 81-82.

0361   John Killinger, "Christmas and Abortion," *ChrM* 16/6 (1985):
26-27.

2:13-14

0362   Ioann Wendland, "On the Nativity of Christ," *JMP* 1 (1985): 37.

2:14

0363   G. Von Rad, "Noch einmal Lc 2:14 *anthrōpoi eudokias*," *ZNW* 29
(1930): 111-15.

0364   E. R. Smothers, "*En anthrôpois eudokias*," *RechSR* 24 (1934):
86-93.

0365   C. C. Tarelli, "An Interpretation of Luke 2,14." *ET* 48
(1936-1937): 322.

0366   A. L. Williams, "Men of Good-Will (Lk 2,14)," *ET* 50 (1938-1939): 283-84.

0367   A. Goetze, "Peace on Earth," *BASOR* 93 (1944): 17-20.

0368   C.-H. Hunzinger, "Neues Licht auf Lc 2,14," *ZNW* 44 (1952-1953): 85-90.

0369   E. Vogt, " 'Peace among Men of God's Good Pleasure' Lk. 2,14," in K. Stendahl, ed., *The Scrolls and the New Testament*. New York: Harper & Brothers, 1957. Pp. 114-17.

0370   Joseph A. Fitzmyer, "Peace upon Earth among Men of His Good Will (Lk 2:14)," *TS* 19 (1958): 225-27.

0371   C.-H. Hunzinger, "Ein weiterer Beleg zu Lc 2,14 *anthrōpoi eudokias*," *ZNW* 49 (1958): 129-30.

0372   Reinhard Deichgräber, "Lc. 2:14: *anthrōpoi eudokais*," *ZNW* 51/1-2 (1960): 132.

0373   Raimund Köbert, "Sabrâ Tabâ Im Syrischen Tatian Luc 2:14," *Bib* 42/1 (1961): 90-91.

0374   H. Rusche, " 'Et in terra pax hominibus bonae voluntatis', Erklärung, Deutung and Betrachtung zum Engelchor in Luke 2:14," *BibL* 2 (1961): 229-34.

0375   D. Flusser, "Sanktus und Gloria," in O. Betz, M. Hengel, and P. Schmidt, eds., *Abraham unser Vater: Juden un Christen im Gespräch über die Bibel* (festschrift for Otto Michel). Leiden: Brill, 1963. Pp. 129-52.

0376   E. F. F. Bishop, "Men of God's Good Pleasure," *ATR* 48 (1966): 63-69.

0377   J. Riedl, " 'Ehre sei Gott in der Höhe'. Meditation über Lukas 2:14," *BK* 21 (1966): 119-22.

0378   H. Schürmann, " 'Es wurde ihm der Name Jesus gegeben . . . ' (Lk 2,21): Zum biblischen Verständnis eines liturgischen Festes," in *Ursprung und Gestalt*. Düsseldorf: Patmos, 1970. Pp. 222-26.

0379   Günther Schwarz, "Der Lobgesang der Engel (Lk 2,14)," *BZ* 15 (1971): 260-64.

0380   C. H. Dodd, "New Testament Translation Problems," *BT* 27/3 (1976): 301-305; 28 (1977): 101-16.

0381   J. C. O'Neill, "Glory to God in the Highest, and on Earth?" in J. R. McMay, ed., *Biblical Studies* (festschrift for William Barclay). London: Collins, 1976. Pp. 172-77.

0382   E. Hansack, "Luke 2:14: 'Friede den Menschen auf Erden, die guten Willens sind'?" *BZ* 21 (1977): 117-18.

0383   F. V. Mills, "The Christmas Music of St. Luke," *ET* 93 (1981-1982): 49.

0384   Paul R. Berger, "Luke 2:14: ἀνθρώποις εὐδοκίας. Die auf Gottes Weisung mit Wohlgefallen beschenkten Menschen," *ZNW* 74 (1983): 129-44.

0385   Günther Schwarz, " . . . '*anthropoi eudokias*'," *ZNW* 75 (1984): 136-37.

0386   Paul R. Berger, "Menschen Ohne 'Gottes Wohlgefallen' Lk. 2:14," *ZNW* 76/1-2 (1985): 119-22.

0387   K. Smyth, " 'Peace on Earth to Men . . . ' (Luke 2,14)," *IBS* 9 (1987): 27-34.

0388   Manuel Guerra Gómez, "Análisis filológico-teológio y traducción del himno de los ángeles en Belén," *Bur* 30 (1989): 31-86.

0389   Manuel Guerra Gómez, "Hominibus Bonae Voluntatis: Análisis Filológico-Teológico y Traducción," *ScripT* 21/3 (1989): 755-75.

2:15-20
0390   G. Zananiri, "Les bergers de Noël (Luke 2:15-20)," *EV* 81 (1981): 340-41.

0391   Kikuo Matsunaga, "Pondering Mary," *EAJT* 4/2 (1986): 14-17.

2:15

0392   Christoph Burchard, "Fußnoten zum neutestamentlichen Griechisch
II," *ZNW* 69 (1978): 143-57.

0393   Christoph Burchard, "A Note on ῥῆμα in JosAs 17:1f.; Luke 2:15,
17; Acts 10:37," *NovT* 27 (1985): 281-95.

2:17

0394   P. Ellingworth, "Luke 2:17: Just Who Spoke to the Shepherds?"
BT 31 (1980): 447.

0395   Christoph Burchard, "A Note on ῥῆμα in JosAs 17:1f.; Luke 2:15,
17; Acts 10:37," *NovT* 27 (1985): 281-95.

2:19-51

0396   B. Buby, "The Biblical Prayer of Mary," *RevRel* 39 (1980):
577-81.

2:19

0397   Ben F. Meyer, "But Mary Kept All These Things," *CBQ* 26
(1964): 31-49.

0398   F. Meyer, "Tradition und Meditation. Meditation über Luke 2:19,"
BibL 12 (1971): 285-87.

0399   D. Ogston, "A Time for Pause," *ET* 89 (1977-1978): 50-52.

0400   G. Bellia, " 'Confrontando nel suo cuore.' Custodia sapienziale di
Maria in Luke 2:19b," *BibO* 25 (1983): 215-28.

0401   Werner Bieder, "Das Volk Gottes in Erwartung von Licht und
Lobpreis," *TZ* 40/2 (1984): 137-48.

2:21-40

0402   Bo Reicke, "Jesus, Simeon and Anna (Lk 2:21-40)," in J. I. Cook,
ed., *Saved by Hope* (festschrift for R. C. Oudersluys). Grand
Rapids MI: Eerdmans, 1978. Pp. 96-108.

2:21

0403   E. Galbiati, "La Circoncisione di Gesù (Luke 2:21)," *BibO* 8
(1966): 37-45.

0404 H. Schürmann, " 'Es wurde ihm der Name Jesus gegeben . . . '
(Lk 2,21): Zum biblischen Verständnis eines liturgischen Festes,"
in *Ursprung und Gestalt.* Düsseldorf: Patmos, 1970. Pp. 222-26.

0405 Lucien Legrand, "On l'appela du nom de Jésus (Luke 2:21)," *RB*
89 (1982): 481-91.

0406 T. Stramare, "La circoncisione di Gesù: Signifcato esegetico e
teologico," *BibO* 26 (1984): 193-203.

2:22-52
0407 K. Stock, "Maria nel tempio (Lc 2,22-52)," *ParSpirV* 6 (1982):
114-25.

2:22-40
0408 E. Galbiati, "La Presentazione al tempio (Luke 2:22-40)," *BibO*
6 (1964): 28-37.

0409 A. George, "La présentation de Jésus au Temple (Lc 2)," *AsSeign*
N.S. 11 (1971): 29-39.

0410 André Feuillet, "La presentation de Jésus au Temple et la
transfixion de Marie (2,22-40)," in *Jesus et sa mère.* Paris:
Gabalda, 1974. Pp. 58-69.

0411 Raymond E. Brown, "The Presentation of Jesus (Luke 2:22-40),"
Worship 51 (1977): 2-11.

0412 T. Stramare, "La presentazione di Gesu al tempio (Luke
2:22-40)," *BibO* 25 (1983): 63-71.

0413 Marion L. Soards, "Luke 2:22-40," *Int* 44 (1990): 400-405.

2:22-38
0414 P. Figueras, "Syméon et Anne, ou le témoignage de la loi et des
prophètes," *NovT* 20 (1978): 84-99.

0415 M. Miyoshi, "Jesu Darstellung oder Reinigung im Tempel unter
Berücksichtigung von 'Nunc Dimittis' Luke 2:22-38," *AJBI* 4
(1978): 85-115.

2:22-35

0416 J. Sudbrack, "Gesetz und Geist: Jesu Darstellung im Tempel (Lk 2,22-35)," *GeistL* 48 (1975): 462-66.

2:22-32

0417 G. Ravini, "Esegesi degli Evangeli festivi," *BibO* 1 (1959): 17-19.

2:22

0418 T. Stramare, "Compiuti i giorni della loro purificazione (Luke 2:22): gli avvenimenti del Nuovo Testamento conclusivi di un disegno," *BibO* 24 (1982): 199-205.

0419 A. R. C. McLellan, "What the Law Required," *ET* 94 (1982-1983): 82-83.

2:23

0420 Paul Winter, "Ὅτι Recitativum in Luke 1:25, 61; 2:23," *HTR* 48 (1955): 213-18.

0421 T. Stramare, " 'Sanctum Domino vocabitur' (Luke 2:23): Il crocevia dei riti è la Santità," *BibO* 25 (1983): 21-34.

2:25-39

0422 P. Figueras, "Syméon et Anne, ou le témoignage de la loi et des prophètes," *NovT* 20 (1978): 84-99.

2:25-35

0423 A. Culter, "Does the Simeon of Luke 2 Refer to Simeon the Son of Hillel?" *JBR* 34 (1966): 29-35.

2:25

0424 J. T. Coakley, "The Old Man Simeon (Lk 2.25) in Syriac Tradition," *OCP* 47 (1981): 189-212.

2:27-33

0425 Pierre Grelot, "Le Cantique de Siméon," *RB* 93/4 (1986): 481-509.

2:29-32

0426 J. Reuss, "Studien zur Lukas-Erklärung des Presbyters Hesychius von Jerusalem," *Bib* 59 (1978): 562-71.

0427 Klaus Berger, "Das Canticum Simeonis (Lk. 2:29-32)," *NT* 27 (1985): 27-39.

0428 Robert C. Tannehill, "Israel in Luke-Acts: A Tragic Story," *JBL* 104 (1985): 69-85.

2:29-30

0429 Tjitze Baarda, "Nunc dimittis: Annotaties bij Lucas 2,29-30," in J. M. van der Linde, et al., eds., *Zending op weg naar de toekomst* (festschrift for J. Verkuyl). Kampen: Kok, 1978. Pp. 59-79.

2:29

0430 B. Prete, "Il senso della formula ʾen eirēnē in Luca 2,29," in *Chiesa per il mondo* (festschrift for M. Pellegrino). Bologna: Dehoniane, 1974. Pp. 39-60.

0431 Ioann Pokrovsky, "Faith and Eternity," *JMP* 4 (1984): 32.

2:31

0432 George D. Kilpatrick, "*Laoi* at Luke ii.31 and Acts iv.25, 27," *JTS* 16 (1965): 127.

2:32

0433 A. Smitmans, " 'Ein Licht zur Erleuchtung der Völker' (Luke 2:32). Meditation über das *Nunc dimittis*," *BK* 24 (1969): 138-39.

0434 W. Richey Hogg, "Vatican II's *Ad Gentes:* A Twenty-Year Retrospective," *IBMR* 9 (1985): 146-54.

0435 A. Simon-Muñoz, "Cristo, luz de los gentiles: Puntualizationes sobre Lc 2,32," *EB* 46 (1988): 27-44.

2:34-35

0436 W. Wiskirchen, "Das Zeichen des Widerspruchs. Homilie über Luke 2:34b-35," *BibL* 4 (1963): 138-42.

2:34

0437 Harold A. Guy, "The Virgin Birth in St. Luke," *ET* 68 (1956-1957): 157-58.

2:35

0438 Pierre Benoit, "Et Toi-Même, Un Glaive Te Transpercera L'âme! (Luc 2:35) [Ezek. 14:7]," *CBQ* 25 (1963): 251-61.

0439   I. Bailey, "Parental Heart-Break," *ET* 89 (1977-1978): 85-86.

2:36-37
0440   M. P. John, "Luke 2,36-37: How Old Was Anna?" *BT* 26 (1975): 247.

0441   A. T. Varela, "Luke 2:36-37: Is Anna's Age What is Really in Focus?" *BT* 27 (1976): 446.

0442   J. K. Elliott, "Anna's Age," *NovT* 30 (1988): 100-102.

2:39
0443   J. A. Bain, "Did Joseph Belong to Bethlehem or to Nazareth?" *ET* 47 (1935-1936): 93.

2:40-52
0444   Otto Glombitza, "Der Zwölfjährige Jesus, Luk 2:40-52: Ein Beitrag zur Exegese der Lukanischen Vorgeschichte," *NovT* 5 (1962): 1-4.

2:40
0445   J. Guillet, "Croissance de Jésus," in *Jésus Christ dans notre monde*. Paris: Desclée de Brouwer, 1974. Pp. 29-38.

2:41-52
0446   J. K. Elliott, "Does Luke 2:41-52 Anticipate the Resurrection?" *ET* 83 (1971-1972): 87-89.

0447   André Feuillet, "Le recouvrement de Jésus au Temple (2,41-52)," in *Jesus et sa mère*. Paris: Gabalda, 1974. Pp. 69-79.

0448   G. Schmahl, "Luke 2:41-52 und die Kindheitserzählung des *Thomas* 19:1-5. Ein Vergleich," *BibL* 15 (1974): 249-58.

0449   J. F. Jansen, "Luke 2:41-52," *Int* 30 (1976): 400-404.

0450   Raymond E. Brown, "The Finding of the Boy Jesus in the Temple: A Third Christmas Story," *Worship* 51 (1977): 474-85.

0451   P. W. Van Der Horst, "Notes on the Aramaic Background of Luke 2:41-52," *JSNT* 7 (1980): 61-66.

0452 Lucas van Rompay, "De ethiopische versie van het Kindsheidsevangelie volgens Thomas de Israeliet," in A. Théodoridès, et al., eds., *L'enfant dans les civilisations*. Louvain: Peeters Press, 1980. Pp. 119-32.

0453 E. Schüssler Fiorenza, "Luke 2:41-52," *Int* 36 (1982): 399-403.

2:41-51
0454 B. M. F. van Iersel, "Finding of Jesus in the Temple: Some Observations on the Original Form of Luke 2:41-51a," *NovT* 4 (1960): 161-73.

0455 H. J. de Jonge, "Sonship, Wisdom, Infancy: Luke 2:41-51a," *NTS* 24 (1977-1978): 317-54.

2:41-50
0456 John J. Kilgallen, "Luke 2:41-50: Foreshadowing of Jesus, Teacher," *Bib* 66/4 (1985): 553-59.

0457 Lucien Legrand, "Deux voyages: Lc 2,41-50; 24,13-33," in Françios Refoulé, ed., *à cause de l'Evangile: Etudes sur les synoptiques et les Actes* (festschrift for Jacques Dupont). Paris: Cerf, 1985. Pp. 409-29.

2:42-52
0458 E. Galbiati, "Gesù giovinetto nel tempio (Luke 2:42-52)," *BibO* 2 (1960): 21-25.

2:43-46
0459 J. R. Gray, "Was Our Lord an Only Child?" *ET* 71 (1959-1960): 53.

2:49
0460 Patrick J. Temple, " 'House' or 'Business' in Luke 2:49?" *CBQ* 1 (1939): 342-52.

0461 E. R. Smothers, "A Note on Luke ii,49," *HTR* 45 (1952): 67-69.

0462 Paul Winter, "Lc 2,49 and Targum Yerushalmi," *ZNW* 45 (1954): 145-79.

0463 W. C. Robinson, "The Virgin Birth—A Broader Base," *CT* 17/5 (1972): 238-40.

0464   J. Bishop, "The Compulsion of Love," *ET* 85 (1973-1974): 371-73.

0465   C. Escudero Freire, "Alcance christológico de Lc 1,35 y 2,49," *Communio* 8 (1975): 5-77.

0466   F. D. Weinert, "The Multiple Meanings of Luke 2:49 and their Significance," *BTB* 13 (1983): 19-22.

0467   Juan M. Lozano, "Jesucristo en la Espiritualidad de San Antonio María Claret," *EE* 60 (1985): 157-79.

0468   Dennis D. Sylva, "The Cryptic Clause ἐν τοῖς τοῦ πατρός μου δεῖ εἶναί με in Luke," *ZNW* 78 (1987): 132-40.

2:50

0469   S. M. Harris, "My Father's House," *ET* 94 (1982-1983): 84-85.

2:51

0470   Ben F. Meyer, "But Mary Kept All These Things," *CBQ* 26 (1964): 31-49.

2:52

0471   Patrick J. Temple, "Christ's Holy Youth According to Luke 2:52," *CBQ* 3 (1941): 243-50.

0472   B. Couroyer, "À propos de Luke 2:52," *RB* 86 (1979): 92-101.

3-24

0473   Silverio Zedda, "La croce nella cristologia della kénosis di Luca 3-24," in B. Rinaldi, ed., *La sapienza della croce oggi*. Torino (Leumann): ElleDiCi, 1976. 1:86-94.

3-4

0474   Walt Russell, "The Anointing With the Holy Spirit in Luke-Acts," *TriJ* 7/1 (1986): 47-63.

3:1-4:30

0475   Mark McVann, "Rituals of Status Transformation in Luke-Acts: The Case of Jesus the Prophet," in Jerome H. Neyrey, ed., *The Social World of Luke-Acts*. Peabody MA: Hendrickson Publishers, 1991. Pp. 333-60.

3:1-22
0476 Ben Witherington, "Jesus and the Baptist: Two of a Kind?" *SBLSP* 18 (1988): 225-44.

3:1-20
0477 Ivor Buse, "St. John and 'The First Synoptic Pericope'," *NovT* 3 (1959-1960): 57-61.

3:1-18
0478 William D. Howden, "Good News: Repent," *ChrM* 16/6 (1985): 28.

3:1-14
0479 Martin Forward, "Pilgrimage: Luke-Acts and the World of Religions," *KCTR* 8 (1985): 9-11.

3:1-12
0480 B. Marconcini, "La predicazione del Battista in Marco e Luca confrontata con la redazione di Matteo," *RBib* 20 Suppl. (1972): 451-66.

3:1-6
0481 E. Galbiati, "Esegesi degli Evangeli festivi. Preparate la via del Signore," *BibO* 5 (1963): 213-15.

0482 J. Mas, "Domingo 2. de Adviento. Ciclo C.: 1. lectura, Baruc 5:1-9; 2. lectura, Filipenses 1:4-6, 8-11; 3. lectura, Lucas 3:1-6," *CuBí* 27 (1970): 343-46.

0483 Albert Fuchs, "Die Überschneidungen von Mk und 'Q' nach B. H. Streeter und E. P. Sanders und ihre wahre Bedeutung (Mk 1,1-8 par.)," in W. Haubeck and M. Bachmann, eds., *Wort in der Zeit* (festschrift for K. H. Rengstorf). Leiden: Brill, 1980. Pp. 28-81.

3:1-4
0484 W. Brueggemann, "Luke 3:1-4," *Int* 30 (1976): 404-409.

3:1-2
0485 Robert M. Grant, "The Occasion of Luke 3:1-2," *HTR* 33 (1940): 151-54.

0486 V. E. McEachern, "Dual Witness and Sabbath Motif in Luke," *CJT* 12 (1966): 267-80.

3:1

0487   D. R. Fotheringham, "Bible Chronology," *ET* 48 (1936-1937): 234-35.

0488   E. Neuhäusler, "Nach mir kommt, der stärker ist als ich. Homilie zum Evangelium des 4. Adventssonntags (Luke 3:1)," *BibL* 4 (1963): 277-81.

3:2-22

0489   Ellen Juhl Christiansen, "Taufe Als Initiation in der Apostelgeschichte," *ST* 40/1 (1986): 55-79.

3:2-3

0490   Gerd Theissen, "Lokalkoloritforschung in den Evangelien: Plädoyer für die Erneuerung Einer Alten Fragestellung," *EvT* 45 (1985): 481-99.

3:2

0491   Gerhard Lohfink, " 'Da erging das Wort des Herrn . . . ' Homilie zum 4. Adventssonntag," *BibL* 5 (1964): 271-74.

3:3-22

0492   Harry Fleddermann, "The Beginning of Q," *SBLSP* 15 (1985): 153-59.

3:3-14

0493   H. Gollwitzer, "Predigt uber Lukas 3,3-14," *EvT* 11 (1951-1952): 145-51.

3:3

0494   Hartwig Thyen, "Baptisma metanoias eis aphesin amartiōn," in E. Dinkler, ed., *Zeit und Geschichte* (festschrift for Rudolf Bultmann). Tübingen: Mohr, 1964. Pp. 97-125.

0495   M. Bachmann, "Johannes der Täufer bei Lukas: Nachzügler oder Vorläufer?" in W. Haubeck and M. Bachmann, eds., *Wort in der Zeit* (festschrift for K. H. Rengstorf). Leiden: Brill, 1980. Pp. 123-55.

0496   Homer Heater, "A Textual Note on Luke 3:33," *JSNT* 28 (1986): 25-29.

3:7-9

0497   C. R. Kazmierski, "The Stones of Abraham: John the Baptist and the End of Torah (Matt 3,7-10 par. Luke 3,7-9)," *Bib* 68 (1987): 22-40.

3:10-18

0498   B. L. Robertson, "Luke 3:10-18," *Int* 36 (1982): 404-409.

3:10-14

0499   S. V. McCasland, " 'Soldiers on Service': The Draft among the Hebrews," *JBL* 62 (1943): 59-71.

0500   Harald Sahlin, "Die Früchte der Umkehr," *ST* 1 (1948): 54-68.

0501   Paul W. Hollenbach, "Social Aspects of John the Baptizer's Preaching Mission in the Context of Palestinian Judaism," *ANRW* II.19.1 (1979): 850-75.

3:14-30

0502   D. Seccombe, "Luke and Isaiah," *NTS* 27 (1980-1981): 252-59.

3:15-17

0503   Mark E. Wangerin, "The Baptism of Our Lord," *CJ* 11 (1985): 231-32.

3:15

0504   J. A. Bailey, "Speculation about John the Baptist: Luke 3.15, John 1.19,27," in *The Traditions Common to the Gospels of Luke and John*. Leiden: Brill, 1963. Pp. 9-11.

0505   Edmond Jacquemin, "Le baptême du Christ. Mt 3,13-17; Mc1,6b-11; Lc 3,15s.21s.," *AsSeign* 12 (1969): 48-66.

3:16-17

0506   Paul W. Hollenbach, "Social Aspects of John the Baptizer's Preaching Mission in the Context of Palestinian Judaism," *ANRW* II.19.1 (1979): 850-75.

0507   Harry Fleddermann, "John and the Coming One (Matt 3:11-12//Luke 3:16-17)," *SBLSP* 14 (1984): 377-84.

0508   J. D. Charles, " 'The Coming One'/'Stronger One' and His Baptism: Matthew 3:11-12, Mark 1:8, Luke 3:16-17," *Pneuma* 11 (1989): 37-50.

3:16

0509   T. F. Glasson, "Water, Wind and Fire (Luke iii.16): An Orphic Initiation," *NTS* 3 (1956-1957): 69-71.

0510   L. W. Barnard, "A Note on Matt. iii.11 and Luke iii.16," *JTS* 8 (1957): 107.

0511   P. Proulx and L. Alonso Schokel, "Las Sandalias del Mesías Esposo," *Bib* 59 (1978): 1-37.

0512   Simon Légasse, "L'autre 'baptême' (Mc 1,8; Mt 3,11; Lc 3,16; Jn 1,26.31-33)," in F. van Segbroeck, et al., eds., *The Four Gospels 1992* (festschrift for Frans Neirynck). 3 vols. BETL #100. Louvain: Peeters Press, 1992. 1:257-73.

3:17

0513   James S. Alexander, "A Note on the Interpretation of the Parable of the Threshing Floor at the Conference at Carthage of A.D. 411," *JTS* 24/2 (1973): 512-19.

0514   Günther Schwarz, "Τὸ δὲ ἄχυρον κατακαύσει," *ZNW* 72 (1981): 272-76.

3:18-23

0515   R. F. Collins, "Jesus' Ministry to the Deaf and Dumb," *MeliT* 35/1 (1984): 12-36.

3:21-38

0516   J. Rius-Camps, "Constituye Lc 3,21-38 un solo periodo? Propuesta de un cambio de puntuación," *Bib* 65 (1984): 189-209.

3:21-22

0517   M. Dutheil, "Le Baptême de Jésus. Éléments d'interprétation," *SBFLA* 6 (1955-1956): 85-124.

0518   Placide Roulin and Giles Carton, "Le Bapteme du Christ," *BVC* 25 (1959): 39-48.

0519 G. H. P. Thompson, "Called-Proved-Obedient: A Study in the Baptism and Temptation Narratives of Matthew and Luke," *JTS* 11 (1960): 1-12.

0520 Pietro Zarella, "Il battesimo di Gesù nei Sinottici (Mc. 1,9-14; Mt. 3,13-17; Lc. 3,21-22)," *ScC* 97 (1969): 3-29.

0521 R. F. Collins, "Luke 3:21-22: Baptism or Anointing?" *BibTo* 84 (1976): 821-31.

0522 M.-A. Chevallier, "L'analyse littéraire des textes du Nouveau Testament," *RHPR* 57 (1977): 367-78.

0523 C. Dennison, "How Is Jesus the Son of God? Luke's Baptism Narrative and Christology," *CalTJ* 17 (1982): 6-25.

0524 Mark E. Wangerin, "The Baptism of Our Lord," *CJ* 11 (1985): 231-32.

3:21

0525 Edmond Jacquemin, "Le baptême du Christ. Mt 3,13-17; Mc 1,6b-11; Lc 3,15s.21s.," *AsSeign* 12 (1969): 48-66.

3:22

0526 Leopold Sabourin, "Two Lukan Texts (1:35; 3:22)," *RSB* 1 (1981): 29-32.

3:23-38

0527 G. Bolsinger, "Die Ahnenreihe Christi nach Matthäus und Lukas," *BK* 12 (1957): 112-17.

0528 G. Saldarini, "La genealogia di Gesù," in L. Moraldi and S. Lyonnet, eds., *I Vangelini (Introduzione alla Bibbia)*. Torino: Marietti, 1960. Pp. 411-25.

0529 K. H. Schelkle, "Die Frauen im Stammbaum Jesu," *BK* 18 (1963): 113-15.

0530 M. J. Moreton, "The Genealogy of Jesus," *StudE* 3 (1964): 219-24.

0531 M. Byskov, "Verus Deus - verus homo, Luc 3:23-28," *ST* 26 (1972): 25-32.

0532   P. Seethaler, "Eine kleine Bemerkung zu den Stammbäumen Jesu nach Matthaus und Lukas," *BZ* 16 (1972): 256-57.

0533   E. L. Abel, "The Genealogies of Jesus *o Khristos*," *NTS* 20 (1973-1974): 203-10.

0534   O. Da Spinetoli, "Les généalogies de Jésus et leur signification: Mt 1,1-25; Lc 3,23-38," *AsSeign* 9 (1974): 6-19.

0535   J. Neville Birdsall, "Some Names in the Lukan Genealogy of Jesus in the Armenian Biblical Tradition," in M. E. Stone, ed., *Armenian and Biblical Studies*. Jerusalem: St. James, 1976. Pp. 13-16.

0536   George E. Rice, "Luke 3:22-38 in Codex Bezae: The Messianic King," *AUSS* 17 (1979): 203-208.

0537   E. Lerle, "Die Ahnenverzeichnisse Jesu. Versuch einer christologischen Interpretation," *ZNW* 72 (1981): 112-17.

0538   William S. Kurz, "Luke 3:23-38 and Greco-Roman and Biblical Genealogies," in Charles H. Talbert, ed., *Luke-Acts: New Perspectives from the Society of Biblical Literature*. New York: Crossroad, 1984. Pp. 169-87.

0539   André Feuillet, "Observations sur les deux généalogies de Jésus-Christ de saint Matthieu (1,1-17) et de saint Luc (3,23-38)," *EV* 98 (1988): 605-608.

0540   M. D. Johnson, *The Purpose of the Biblical Genealogies with Special Reference to the Setting of the Genealogies of Jesus*. 2nd ed. Cambridge: University Press, 1988.

3:23

0541   G. Ogg, "The Age of Jesus When He Taught," *NTS* 5 (1958-1959): 291-98.

0542   G. M. Lee, "Luke iii,23," *ET* 79 (1967-1968): 310.

0543   A. Salas, "José, el padre," *BibFe* 6 (1980): 304-32.

0544   John W. Miller, "Jesus' 'Age Thirty Transition': A Psychohistorical Probe," *SBLSP* 15 (1985): 45-56.

0545 Jerry Vardaman, "Jesus' Life: A New Chronology," in Jerry Vardaman and Edwin M. Yamauchi, eds., *Chronos, Kairos, Christos* (festschrift for Jack Finegan). Winona Lake: Eisenbrauns, 1989. Pp. 55-82.

3:33

0546 Homer Heater, "A Textual Note on Luke 3:33," *JSNT* 28 (1986): 25-29.

3:36

0547 Gert J. Steyn, "The Occurrence of 'Kainam' in Luke's Genealogy," *ETL* 65 (1989): 409-11.

4:1-13

0548 G. S. Freeman, "The Temptation," *ET* 48 (1936-1937): 45.

0549 J. M. Bover, "Diferente género literario de los evangelistas en la narración de las tentaciones de Jesus en el Desierto," in *En torno al problema de la escatología individual del Antiguo Testamento*. Madrid: Científica Medinaceli, 1955. Pp. 213-19.

0550 André Feuillet, "Le récit lucanien de la tentation (Lc 4,1-13)," in *Studia Biblica et Orientalia*. 3 vols. Rome: Pontifical Institute, 1959. 2:45-63.

0551 G. H. P. Thompson, "Called-Proved-Obedient: A Study in the Baptism and Temptation Narratives of Matthew and Luke," *JTS* 11 (1960): 1-12.

0552 Jacques Dupont, "Les Tenations de Jésus dans le Récit de Luc," *SE* 14/1 (1962): 7-29.

0553 B. Gerhardsson, *The Testing of God's Son (Matt 4:1-11, Par.): An Analysis of an Early Christian Midrash*. Lund: Gleerup, 1966.

0554 H. Swanston, "The Lukan Temptation Narrative," *JTS* 17 (1966): 71.

0555 F. Smyth-Florentin, "Jésus, le Fils du Père, vainqueur de Satan," *AsSeign* 14 (1973): 56-75.

0556 P. Pokorný, "The Temptation Stories and Their Intention," *NTS* 20 (1973-1974): 115-27.

0557 Wilhelm Wilkens, "Die Versuchungsgeschichte, Luk. 4,1-13, und die Komposition des Evangeliums," *TZ* 30 (1974): 262-72.

0558 D. C. Hester, "Luke 4:1-13," *Int* 31 (1977): 53-59.

0559 Dieter Zeller, "Die Versuchungen Jesu in der Logienquelle," *TTZ* 89 (1980): 61-73.

0560 J. A. Davidson, "The Testing of Jesus," *ET* 94 (1982-1983): 113-15.

0561 Paul J. Achtemeier, "Enigmatic Bible Passages: It's the Little Things that Count," *BA* 46 (1983): 30-31.

0562 S. C. Glickman, "The Temptation Account in Matthew and Luke," doctoral dissertation, University of Basel, Switzerland, 1983.

0563 F. Gerald Downing, "Cynics and Christians," *NTS* 30/4 (1984): 584-93.

0564 Albert Fuchs, "Versuchung Jesu," *SNTU-A* 9 (1984): 95-159.

0565 Elliott J. Bush, "A Fruitful Wilderness," *ChrM* 16/2 (1985): 24-26.

0566 Bill Kellermann, "A Confusion Before the Cross: Confronting Temptation [Pt. 2 of 6]," *Soj* 14/2 (1985): 32-35.

0567 William R. Stegner, "Early Jewish Christianity—A Lost Chapter?" *ATJ* 44/2 (1989): 17-29.

4:1-12

0568 R. Yates, "Jesus and the Demonic in the Synoptic Gospels," *ITQ* 44 (1977): 39-57.

4:1-11

0569 A. Knockaert and C. Van Der Plancke, "Catéchèses de la tentation," *LV* 34 (1979): 123-53.

4:1-3

0570 Klaus-Peter Koppen, "The Interpretation of Jesus' Temptations by the Early Church Fathers," *PatByzR* 8/1 (1989): 41-43.

4:1

0571 Philippe Rolland, "L'arrière-fond sémitique des évangiles synoptiques," *ETL* 60 (1984): 358-62.

4:4

0572 Robert Hodgson, "On the *Gattung* of Q: A Dialogue with James M. Robinson," *Bib* 66/1 (1985): 73-95.

4:5-8

0573 R. Morgenthaler, "Roma - Sedes Satanae. Röm, 13,1ff. im Lichte von Luk. 4,5-8," *TZ* 12 (1956): 289-304.

4:7-8

0574 D. Flusser, "Die Versuchung Jesu und ihr jüdischer Hintergrund," *Jud* 45 (1989): 110-28.

4:9-12

0575 N. Hyldahl, "Die Versuchung auf der Zinne des Tempels," *ST* 15 (1961): 113-27.

0576 J.-M. Odero, "El debate de Jesús con Satán (Mt 4,5-7; Lc 4,9-12)," in J. M. Casciaro, et al., eds., *Biblia y hermeneútica*. Pamplona: Universidad de Navarra, 1986. Pp. 241-55.

0577 David R. Catchpole, "Temple traditions in Q," in William Horbury, ed., *Templum amicitiae*. Sheffield: JSOT Press, 1991. Pp. 305-29.

4:9

0578 J. Jeremias, "Die Zinne des Tempels (Mt. 4,5; Lk. 4,9)," *ZDPV* 59 (1936): 195-208.

4:13-30

0579 Bo Reicke, "Jesus in Nazareth Lk 4,13-30," in H. Balz, ed., *Das Wort und die Wörter* (festschrift for G. Friedrich). Stuttgart: Kohlhammer, 1973. Pp. 47-55.

4:13

0580 Heinrich Baarlink, "Friede im Himmel: die Lukanische Redaktion von Lk 19,38 und Ihre Deutung," *ZNW* 76/3 (1985): 170-86.

4:14-44
0581   C. Escudero Freire, "Jesús profeta, libertador del hombre: Visión lucana de su ministerio terrestre," *EE* 51 (1976): 463-96.

0582   A. del Agua Perez, "El cumplimiento del Reino de Dios en la misión de Jesús: Programa del Evangelico de Lucas (Luke 4:14-44)," *EB* 38 (1979-1980): 269-93.

4:14-30
0583   Jacob W. Elias, "The Beginning of Jesus' Ministry in the Gospel of Luke: A Redaction-Critical Study of Luke 4:14-30," doctoral dissertation, Toronto School of Theology, Toronto, 1978.

0584   Edna Brocke, "Die Hebräische Bibel im Neuen Testament: Fragen anhand von Lk 4,14-30," in Edna Brocke and Jürgen Seim, eds., *Gottes Augapfel: Beiträge zur Erneuerung des Verhältnisses von Christen und Juden.* Neukirchen-Vluyn: Neukirchener Verlag, 1986. Pp. 113-19.

4:14-22
0585   William W. Klein, "The Sermon at Nazareth (Luke 4:14-22)," in Kenneth W. M. Wozniak and Stanley J. Grenz, eds., *Christian Freedom* (festschrift for Vernon C. Grounds). Lanham MD: University Press of America, 1986. Pp. 153-72.

4:14-16
0586   H. Schürmann, "Der 'Bericht vom Anfang': Ein Rekonstruktionsversuch auf Grund von Lk. 4,14-16," *StudE* 3 (1964): 242-58.

0587   Joël Delobel, "La rédaction de Lc. IV,14-16a et le 'Bericht vom Anfang'," in *L'Évangile de Luc: Problèmes littéraires et théologiques.* Gembloux: Duculot, 1973. Pp. 203-23.

4:14-15
0588   É. Samain, "L'Évangile de Luc: un témoignage ecclésial et missionnaire," *AsSeign* 34 (1973): 60-73.

4:16-5:11
0589   Michael D. Goulder, "On Putting Q to the Test," *NTS* 24 (1977-1978): 218-34.

4:16-44
0590   Sharon H. Ringe, "Luke 4:16-44: A Portrait of Jesus as Herald of God's Jubilee," *EGLMBS* 1 (1981): 73-84.

4:16-30
0591   Bruno Violet, "Zum rechten Verständnis der Nazarethperikope Lc 4,16-30," *ZNW* 37 (1938): 251-71.

0592   Asher Finkel, "Jesus' Sermon at Nazareth (Luk 4,16-30)," in O. Betz, M. Hengel, and P. Schmidt, eds., *Abraham unser Vater: Juden un Christen im Gespräch über die Bibel* (festschrift for Otto Michel). Leiden: Brill, 1963. Pp. 106-15.

0593   A. Strobel, "Die Ausrufung des Jobeljahres in der Nazarethpredigt Jesu; zur apokalyptischen Tradition Lc 4:16-30," in Erich Grässer, et al., eds., *Jesus in Nazareth*. Berlin: de Gruyter, 1972. Pp. 38-50.

0594   Hugh Anderson, "Broadening Horizons: The Rejection at Nazareth Pericope of Luke 4:16-30 in Light of Recent Critical Trends," *Int* 18 (1964): 259-75.

0595   C. H. Cave, "The Sermon at Nazareth and the Beatitudes in the Light of the Synagogue Lectionary," *StudE* 3 (1964): 231-35.

0596   A. Strobel, "Das apokalyptische Terminproblem in der sogenannten Antrittspredigt Jesu," *TLZ* 92 (1967): 251-54.

0597   David Hill, "The Rejection of Jesus at Nazareth: Luke 4:16-30," *NovT* 13/3 (1971): 161-80.

0598   Robert C. Tannehill, "The Mission of Jesus according to Luke 4:16-30," in Erich Grässer, et al., eds., *Jesus in Nazareth*. Berlin: de Gruyter, 1972. Pp. 51-75.

0599   H. J. B. Combrink, "The Structure and Significance of Luke 4:16-30," *Neo* 7 (1973): 27-47.

0600   C. Perrot, "Luc, 4,16-30 et la lecture biblique de l'ancienne Synagogue," *RevSR* 47 (1973): 324-40.

0601   J. J. A. Kahmann, "Het woord van bevrijding: Redactie en interpretatie in Lucas 4,16-30," in J. J. A. Kahmann and H. G. Manders, eds., *De weg van het woord* (festschrift for F. van Trigt). Hilversum: Gooi en Sticht, 1975. Pp. 44-63.

0602   Robert B. Sloan, *The Favorable Year of the Lord: A Study of Jubilary Theology in the Gospel of Luke.* Austin TX: Scholars Press, 1977.

0603   Ulrich Busse, *Das Nazareth-Manifest Jesu: Eine Einführung in das lukanische Jesusbild nach Lk 4,16-30.* Stuttgart: Katholisches Bibelwerk, 1978.

0604   Donald R. Miesner, "The Circumferential Speeches of Luke-Acts: Patterns and Purpose," *SBLSP* 8/2 (1978): 223-37.

0605   D. W. Blosser, "Jesus and the Jubilee, Luke 4,16-30: The Significance of the Year of the Jubilee in the Gospel of Luke," doctoral dissertation, St. Andrews University, UK, 1979.

0606   M. Rodgers, "Luke 4:16-30: A Call for a Jubilee Year?" *RTR* 40 (1981): 72-82.

0607   Christopher M. Tuckett, "Luke 4,16-30, Isaiah and Q," in J. Delobel, ed., *Logia: Les paroles de Jésus (The Sayings of Jesus).* BETL #59. Louvain: Peeters Press, 1982. Pp. 343-54.

0608   R. Albertz, "Die 'Antrittspredigt' Jesu im Lukasevangelium auf ihrem alttestamentlichen Hintergrund," *ZAW* 74 (1983): 182-206.

0609   J. Kodell, "Luke's Gospel in a Nutshell (Luke 4:16-30)," *BTB* 13 (1983): 16-18.

0610   Paul Löffer, "Jesus und die Nicht-Juden," *ZMiss* 10/2 (1984): 66-69.

0611   Joseph B. Tyson, "The Jewish Public in Luke-Acts," *NTS* 30/4 (1984): 574-83.

0612   Jean N. Aletti, "Jésus à Nazareth (Lc 4,16-30): Prophétie, écriture et typologie," in *À cause de l'Évangile: Études sur les synoptiques et les Actes* (festschrift for Jacques Dupont). Paris: Cerf, 1985. Pp. 431-51.

0613 S. Coutinha, "The Rejection of Jesus at Nazareth (Lk 4,16-30): An Analysis of the Synoptic Tradition and Redaction," doctoral dissertation, Pontifical University Gregorium, Rome, 1985.

0614 M. Alvarez-Barredo, "Discurso Inaugural de Jesús en Nazareth (Lc 4,16-30): Clave teológica de Evangelio de Lucas," *Carth* 2 (1986): 23-34.

0615 B.-J. Koet, " 'Today this Scripture Has Been Fulfilled in Your Ears': Jesus' Explanation of Scripture in Luke 4,16-30," *Bij* 47 (1986): 368-94.

0616 T. V. Walker, "Luke 4:16-30," *RevExp* 85 (1988): 321-24.

0617 Judette M. Kolasny, "An Example of Rhetorical Criticism: Luke 4:16-30," in Earl Richard, ed., *New Views on Luke and Acts.* Collegeville MN: Liturgical Press, 1990. Pp. 67-77.

0618 Eben H. Scheffler, "Reading Luke from the Perspective of Liberation Theology," in Patrick J. Hartin and J. H. Petzer, eds., *Text and Interpretation: New Approaches in the Criticism of the New Testament.* Leiden: Brill, 1991. Pp. 281-98.

0619 Jeffrey S. Siker, "First to the Gentiles: A Literary Analysis of Luke 4:16-30," *JBL* 111 (1992): 73-90.

4:16-22
0620 Thomas W. D. Baird, "Epiphany," *JPC* 39 (1985): 286.

4:16-21
0621 É. Samain, "Le discours-programme de Nazareth (Lc 4)," *AsSeign* N.S. 20 (1973): 17-27.

0622 Patrick D. Miller, "Luke 4:16-21," *Int* 29 (1975): 417-21.

0623 É. Samain, "Projeto evangélico e direitos humanos," *REB* 37 (1977): 76-90.

0624 John Momis, "Renew the Face of the Earth," *Point* 9 (1980): 7-15.

0625 G. Casalis, "Un Nouvel An. Luke 4:16-21," *ÉTR* 56 (1981): 148-58.

0626   B. D. Chilton, "Announcement in Nazara: An Analysis of Luke 4,16-21," in Robert T. France and David Wenham, eds., *Gospel Perspectives II*. Sheffield: JSOT Press, 1981. Pp. 147-72.

0627   K. H. Schelkle, "Jesus und Paulus lesen die Bibel," *BK* 36 (1981): 277-79.

0628   G. Garlatti, "Evangelización y liberación de los pobres," *RevB* 49 (1987): 1-15.

0629   Dirk Monshouwer, "The Reading of the Prophet in the Synagogue at Nazareth," *Bib* 72 (1991): 90-99.

4:16-20

0630   W. Eltester, "Israel im lukanischen Werk und die Nazareth perikope," in Erich Grässer, et al., eds., *Jesus in Nazareth*. Berlin: de Gruyter, 1972. Pp. 76-147.

4:16

0631   J. Bishop, "The Place of Habit in the Spiritual Life," *ET* 91 (1980-1981): 374-75.

0632   Hans Hübner, "The Holy Spirit in Holy Scripture," *EcumRev* 41 (1989): 324-38.

4:17

0633   Tjitze Baarda, "Anoixas - Anaptyxas: Over de Vaststelling van de Tekst van Lukas 4,17 in het Diatessaron," *NedTT* 40/3 (1986): 199-208.

4:18-19

0634   J. E. Murray, "The Beatitudes," *Int* 1 (1947): 374-76.

0635   Heinrich Baarlink, "Ein gnädiges Jahr des Hern und Tage der Vergeltung," *ZNW* 73 (1982): 204-20.

0636   Franciszek Blachnicki, "A Theology of Liberation in the Spirit," *RCL* 12 (1984): 157-67.

0637   Robert Hodgson, "On the *Gattung* of Q: A Dialogue with James M. Robinson," *Bib* 66/1 (1985): 73-95.

0638 Priscilla Padolina, "Our Presence among the Poor," in J. S. Pobee and Bärbel von Wartenberg-Potter, eds., *New Eyes for Reading: Biblical and Theological Reflections by Women from the Third World*. Geneva: WCC Publications, 1986. Pp. 37-40.

4:18

0639 B. Rinaldi, "Proclamare ai prigionieri la liberazione (Luke 4:18)," *BibO* 18 (1976): 241-45.

0640 E. Peretto, "Evangelizare pauperibus (Lk 4,18; 7,22-23) nella lettura patristica dei secoli II-III," *AugR* 17 (1977): 71-100.

0641 S. Dawson, "The Spirit's Gift of Sight," *ET* 90 (1978-1979): 241-42.

0642 Leopold Sabourin, "Evangelize the Poor (Luke 4:18)," *RSB* 1 (1981): 101-109.

0643 Gerhard Sauter, "Leiden und 'Handeln'," *EvT* 45 (1985): 435-58.

0644 James A. Berquist, "Good News to the Poor: Why Does This Lucan Motif Appear to Run Dry in the Book of Acts?" *BTF* 18/1 (1986): 1-16.

4:21-30

0645 É. Samain, "Aucun prophète n'est bien reçu dans sa patrie (Lc 4)," *AsSeign* 35 (1973): 63-72.

4:22-30

0646 Donald G. Miller, "Luke 4:22-30," *Int* 40/1 (1986): 53-58.

4:22

0647 John L. Nolland, "Impressed Unbelievers as Witnesses to Christ (Luke 4:22a)," *JBL* 98 (1979): 219-29.

0648 John L. Nolland, "Words of Grace (Luke 4,22)," *Bib* 65 (1984): 44-60.

0649 Feargus O'Fearghail, "Rejection in Nazareth: Lk 4,22," *ZNW* 75 (1984): 60-72.

4:23-24
    0650 John J. Kilgallen, "Provocation in Luke 4:23-24," *Bib* 70/4 (1989): 511-16.

4:23
    0651 John L. Nolland, "Classical and Rabbinic Parallel to 'Physician, heal yourself' (Luke 4:23)," *NovT* 21 (1979): 193-209.

    0652 S. J. Noorda, " 'Cure Yourself, Doctor!' (Luke 4,23): Classical Parallels to an Alleged Saying of Jesus," in J. Delobel, ed., *Logia: Les paroles de Jésus (The Sayings of Jesus)*. BETL #59. Louvain: Peeters Press, 1982. Pp. 459-67.

4:25-27
    0653 L. C. Crockett, "Luke 4:25-27 and Jewish-Gentile Relations in Luke-Acts," *JBL* 88 (1969): 177-83.

    0654 Günther Schwarz, "Versuch Einer Wiederherstellung des Geistigen Eigentums Jesu," *BibN* 53 (1990): 32-37.

4:25
    0655 B. E. Thiering, "The Three and a Half Years of Elijah," *NovT* 23 (1981): 41-55.

4:27
    0656 Gerald Bostock, "Jesus as the New Elisha," *ET* 92 (1980-1981): 39-41.

4:28-30
    0657 Jacob W. Elias, "The Furious Climax in Nazareth (Luke 4:28-30)," in W. Klassen, ed., *The New Way of Jesus* (festschrift for H. Charles). Newton KS: Faith and Life, 1980. Pp. 87-99.

4:29-30
    0658 Tjitze Baarda, "The Flying Jesus: Luke 4:29-30 in the Syriac Diatessaron," *VC* 40/4 (1986): 313-41.

4:29
    0659 M.-A. Chevallier, "À propos de Nazareth," *CCER* 32 (1984): 75-76.

4:31-9:50

0660 Frans Neirynck, " 'Traditio marciana pura' dans Lc., IV,31-IX,50," in Frans Neirynck, ed., *L'Évangile de Luc: Problèmes littéraires et théologiques* (festschrift for Lucien Cerfaux). BETL #32. Gembloux: Duculot, 1973. Pp. 162-66.

4:36

0661 E. Käsemann, "Die Heilung der Besessenen," *Reformatio* 28 (1979): 7-18.

4:38-39

0662 Rudolf Pesch, "Die Heilung der Schwiegermutter des Simon-Petrus," in *Neuere Exegese - Verlust oder Gewinn?* Freiburg: Herder, 1968. Pp. 143-75.

0663 Albert Fuchs, "Entwicklungsgeschichtliche Studie zu Mark 1:29-31 par Matthew 8:14-15 par Luke 4:38-39: Macht über Fieber und Dämonen," *SNTU-A* 6/7 (1981-1982): 21-76.

0664 E. Jane Via, "Women, the Discipleship of Service, and the Early Christian Ritual Meal in the Gospel of Luke," *SLJT* 29 (1985): 37-60.

4:42

0665 Gregory Murray, "Did Luke Use Mark?" *DR* 104 (1986): 268-71.

4:43

0666 Günther Schwarz, "Auch den anderen Städten?" *NTS* 23 (1976-1977): 344.

4:44

0667 D. R. Fotheringham, "St. Luke 4:44," *ET* 45 (1933-1934): 237.

5:1-6:19

0668 M. Theobald, "Die Anfänge der Kirche: Zur Struktur von Lk. 5:1-6:19," *NTS* 30 (1984): 91-108.

5:1-11

0669 Rudolf Bultmann, "Lukas 5,1-11," in Rudolf Bultmann, ed., *Marburger Predigten*. Tübingen: Mohr, 1956. Pp. 137-47.

0670   J. A. Bailey, "Miraculous Catch of Fish: Luke 5.1-ll, John 21.1-14," in *The Traditions Common to the Gospels of Luke and John.* Leiden: Brill, 1963. Pp. 12-17.

0671   H. Schürmann, "Die Verheissung an Simon Petrus. Auslegung von Luke 5:1-11," *BibL* 5 (1964): 18-24.

0672   K. Zillessen, "Das Schiffdes Petrus und die Gefährten vom andern Schiff (Lc 5,1-11)," *ZNW* 57 (1966): 137-39.

0673   Günter Klein, "Die Berufung des Petrus," *ZNW* 58 (1967): 1-44.

0674   Rudolf Pesch, *Der Reiche Fischfang. Lk 5,1-11, Jo 21,1-14. Wundergeschichte - Berufungserzählung - Erscheinungsbericht.* Düsseldorf: Patmos, 1969.

0675   Jean Delorme, "Luc v.1-11: Analyse Structurale et Histoire de la Rédaction," *NTS* 18 (1971-1972): 331-50.

0676   K.-H Crumbach, "Der 'reiche Fischzug' als Berufungsgeschichte. Eine Meditation zu Lk 5,1-11," *GeistL* 47 (1974): 228-31.

0677   H. Schürmann, "La promesse à Simon-Pierre: Lc 5,1-11," *AsSeign* 36 (1974): 63-70.

0678   Jean Delorme, "Linguistique, Sémiotique, Exégèse: à propos du Séminaire de Durham," *SémBib* 6 (1977): 35-59.

0679   A. Viard, "La Parole de Dieu et la mission de Pierre," *EV* 87 (1977): 8.

0680   J. Duncan M. Derrett, "Ἦσαν γὰρ ἁλεῖς (Mark 1:16). Jesus' Fisherman and the Parable of the Net," *NovT* 22/2 (1980): 108-37.

0681   George E. Rice, "Luke's Thematic Use of the Call to Discipleship," *AUSS* 20 (1981): 51-58.

0682   C. Rene Padilla, "Bible Studies," *Miss* 10/3 (1982): 319-38.

0683   Samuel O. Abogunrin, "The 3 Variant Accounts of Peter's Call: Critical, Theological Examination of the Texts," *NTS* 31 (1985): 587-602.

0684   Claude Coulot, "Les figures du maître et de ses disciples dans les premières communautés chrétiennes," *RevSR* 59/1 (1985): 1-11.

0685   G. Bouwman, "De wonderbare visvangst (Lc 5,1-11). Een proeve van integrale exegese," in W. Weren and N. Poulssen, eds., *Bij de put van Jakob* (festschrift for M. Rijkhoff). Tilburg: University Press, 1986. Pp. 109-29.

0686   W. Schlichting, " 'Auf dein Wort hin' (Lukas 5,1-11)," *TBe* 17 (1986): 113-17.

<u>5:1</u>

0687   George D. Kilpatrick, "Three Problems of New Testament Text," *NovT* 21 (1979): 289-92.

0688   J. Rius-Camps, "El καὶ αὐτὸς en los encabezamientos lucanos, ¿una fórmula anadórica?" *FilN* 2 (1989): 187-92.

<u>5:4-6</u>

0689   F. Wulf and M. Velte, " 'Auf den Wort hin . . .' Meditationen zu Lukas 5,4-6," *GeistL* 44 (1971): 309-12.

<u>5:4</u>

0690   J. A. Fishbaugh, "New Life in the Depths of His Presence," *ET* 90 (1978-1979): 146-48.

<u>5:6</u>

0691   A. Viard, "La Parole de Dieu dans l'Église du Christ," *EV* 87 (1977): 7-11.

<u>5:8</u>

0692   D. P. Davies, "Luke 5:8 (Simon Peter)," *ET* 79 (1967-1968): 382.

0693   Anthony Pope, "More on Luke 5:8," *BT* 41 (1990): 442-43.

<u>5:10</u>

0694   Rudolf Pesch, "La rédaction lucanienne du logion des pêcheurs d'hommes (Lc. V,10c)," in *L'Évangile de Luc: Problèmes littéraires et théologiques*. Gembloux: Duculot, 1973. Pp. 225-44.

0695   J. Duncan M. Derrett, "James and John as Co-rescuers from Peril (Luke 5:10)," *NovT* 22 (1980): 299-303.

0696   F. Deltombe, "Désormais tu rendras la vie à des hommes (Luke 5:10)," *RB* 89 (1982): 492-97.

5:11

0697   K. Barth, "Predigt über Luk. 5,11," *EvT* 1 (1934-1935): 129-37.

5:12-16

0698   Rudolf Pesch, "Die lukanische Fassung der Erzählung Lk 5,12-16," in *Jesu ureigene Taten?* Freiburg: Herder, 1970. Pp. 98-107.

0699   J. K. Elliott, "The Healing of the Leper in the Synoptic Parallels," *TZ* 34 (1978): 175-76.

0700   Frans Neirynck, "Papyrus Egerton 2 and the Healing of the Leper," *ETL* 61 (1985): 153-60.

0701   Dominique Hermant, "La purification du lépreux (Mt 8,1-4; Mc 1,40-45; Lc 5,12-16)," *BLOS* 4 (1990): 12-18.

5:12

0702   Christoph Burchard, "Fußnoten zum neutestamentlichen Griechisch II," *ZNW* 69 (1978): 143-57.

5:17-26

0703   Frans Neirynck, "Les accords mineurs et la rédaction des évangiles: L'épisode du paralytique (Mt. IX,1-8; Lc. V,17-26 par.; Mc. II,1-12)," *ETL* 50 (1974): 215-30.

0704   Bo Reicke, "The Synoptic Reports on the Healing of the Paralytic: Matt. 9,1-8 with Parallels," in J. K. Elliott, ed., *Studies in New Testament Language and Text* (festschrift for G. D. Kilpatrick). Leiden: Brill, 1976. Pp. 319-29.

0705   Hans C. Rublack, "Zwingli und Zürich," *Zwing* 16/5 (1985): 393-426.

0706   Albert Fuchs, "Offene Probleme der Synoptikerforschung: Zur Geschichte der Perikope Mk 2,1-12 par Mt 9,1-8 par Lk 5,17-26," *SNTU-A* 15 (1990): 73-99.

5:17

0707 Christoph Burchard, "Fußnoten zum neutestamentlichen Griechisch II," *ZNW* 69 (1978): 143-57.

5:18

0708 Michael D. Goulder, "On Putting Q to the Test," *NTS* 24 (1977-1978): 218-34.

5:24

0709 José O'Callaghan, "Tres casos de armonización en Mt 9," *EB* 47 (1989): 131-34.

5:26

0710 A. T. Rich, "Luke 5,26," *ET* 44 (1932-1933): 428.

0711 J. H. M. Dabb, "Luke 5:26," *ET* 45 (1933-1934): 45.

5:27-32

0712 B. M. F. van Iersel, "La vocation de Lévi 5 Mc II,13-17; Mt IX,9-13; Lc V,27-32)," in *De Jésus aux Évangiles: Tradition et Rédaction dans les Évangiles synoptiques. Donum natalicum Iosepho Coppens septuagesimum annum complenti D.D.D. collegae et amici*, I. de la Potterie, ed. Bibliotheca ephemeridum theologicarum lovaniensium 25. Gembloux/Paris: Duculot/Lethielleux, 1967. Pp. 212-32.

5:27-28

0713 Juan Fernández, "Vocacion de Mateo 'el publicano'," *CuBí* 19 (1962): 45-50.

5:28

0714 Philippe Rolland, "L'arrière-fond sémitique des évangiles synoptiques," *ETL* 60 (1984): 358-62.

5:29-35

0715 C. B. Cousar, "Luke 5:29-35," *Int* 40 (1986): 58-63.

5:33-6:11

0716 George E. Rice, "Luke 5:33-6:11: Release for the Captives," *AUSS* 20 (1982): 23-28.

0717 George E. Rice, "Luke 5:33-6:11: Release from Cultic Tradition," *AUSS* 20 (1982): 127-32.

5:33-39

0718   Juan Fernández, "La cuestion de ayuno (Mt 9,14-17; Mc 2,18-22; Lu 5,33-39)," *CuBí* 19 (1962): 162-69.

0719   Bo Reicke, "Die Fastenfrage nach Luk. 5,33-39," *TZ* 30 (1974): 321-28.

0720   D. Flusser, "Do You Prefer New Wine?" *Immanuel* 9 (1979): 26-31.

0721   Philippe Rolland, "Les Predecesseurs de Marc: Les Sources Presynoptiques de Mc II,18-22 et Paralleles," *RB* 89/3 (1982): 370-405.

0722   R. S. Good, "Jesus, Protagonist of the Old, in Luke 5:33-39," *NovT* 25/1 (1983): 19-36.

5:33-35

0723   André Feuillet, "La controverse sur le jeûne (Mc 2,18-20; Mt 9,14-15; Lc 5,33-35)," *NRT* 90 (1968): 113-36, 252-77.

5:33

0724   José O'Callaghan, "Tres casos de armonización en Mt 9," *EB* 47 (1989): 131-34.

5:35

0725   F. G. Cremer, *Die Fastenansage Jesu.: Mk 2,20 und Parallelen in der Sicht der patristischen und scholastischen Exegese.* Bonn: Hanstein, 1965.

5:36-39

0726   A. Kee, "The Old Coat and the New Wine," *NovT* 12 (1970): 13-21.

0727   L. P. Trudinger, "The Word on the Generation Gap: Reflexions on a Gospel Metaphor," *BTB* 5 (1975): 311-15.

5:36

0728   J. M. Bover, "La parábola del Remiendo (Mt. 9,16; Mc. 2,21; Lc. 5,36)," in A. Metzinger, ed., *Miscellanea Biblica et Orientalia.* Rome: Orbis Catholicus, 1951. Pp. 327-39.

5:39

0729   Jacques Dupont, "Vin Vieux, Vin Nouveau (Luc 5:39)," *CBQ* 25 (1963): 286-304.

0730   G. Brooke, "The Feast of New Wine (Qumran Temple Scroll 19,11-21) and the Question of Fasting," *ET* 95 (1983-1984): 175-76.

6-7

0731   W. K. Grossouw, "La morale du Sermon sur la montagne," in *Spiritualité du Nouveau Testament*. Paris: Cerf, 1964. Pp. 45-58.

6:1-13

0732   Dennis J. Ireland, "A History of Recent Interpretation of the Parable of the Unjust Steward," *WTJ* 51 (1989): 293-318.

6:1-5

0733   Hermann Aichinger, "Quellenkritische Untersuchung der Perikope vom Ährenraufen am Sabbat. Mk 2,23-28 par Mt 12,1-8 par Lk 6,1-5," *SNTU-A* 1 (1976): 110-53.

0734   W. Dietrich, " '. . . den Armen das Evangelium zu verkünden': Vom befreienden Sinn biblischer Gesetze," *TZ* 41 (1985): 31-43.

6:1

0735   B. Cohen, "The Rabbinic Law Presupposed by Matthew 12:2 and Luke 6:1," *HTR* 23 (1930): 91-92.

0736   E. Mezger, "Le Sabbat 'second-premier' de Luc," *TZ* 32 (1976): 138-43.

0737   J. T. Buchanan, "The 'Second-First Sabbath' (Luke 6:1)," *JBL* 97 (1978): 259-62.

0738   E. Isaac, "Another Note on Luke 6:1," *JBL* 100 (1981): 96-97.

0739   T. C. Skeat, "The 'Second-First' Sabbath (Luke 6:1): The Final Solution," *NovT* 30 (1988): 103-106.

6:3ff.

0740   W. Grundmann, "Die Bergpredigt nach der Lukasfassung," *StudE* 3 (1964): 180-89.

6:4

0741 Ernst Bammel, "The Cambridge Pericope: The Addition to Luke 6:4 in Codex Bezae," *NTS* 32/3 (1986): 404-26.

6:5-15

0742 P. Courthial, "La Parabole du Semeur en Luke 6:5-15," *ÉTR* 47 (1972): 397-420.

6:5

0743 Joël Delobel, "Luke 6,5 in Codex Bezae: The Man Who Worked on Sabbath," in Françios Refoulé, ed., *à cause de l'Evangile: Études sur les synoptiques et les Actes* (festschrift for Jacques Dupont). Paris: Cerf, 1985. Pp. 453-77.

0744 Joël Delobel, "Extra-canonical Sayings of Jesus: Marcion and Some 'Non-received' Logia," in William L. Petersen, ed., *Gospel Traditions in the Second Century: Origins, Recensions, Text and Transmission.* Notre Dame: University Press, 1989. Pp. 105-16.

6:7

0745 J. A. L. Lee, "A Non-Aramaism in Luke 6:7," *NovT* 33 (1991): 28-34.

6:12-9:50

0746 J. Rius-Camps, "Estructura i funció signif cativa del tercer cicle o secció de les recognicions (Lc 6,12-9,50)," *RCT* 9 (1984): 269-328.

6:14

0747 Michael D. Goulder, "On Putting Q to the Test," *NTS* 24 (1977-1978): 218-34.

6:16

0748 Johannes Beutler, "Lk 6:16: Punkt Oder Komma?" *BZ* 35/2 (1991): 231-33.

6:17-49

0749 Raymond E. Brown, "Le 'Beatitudini' secondo Luca," *BibO* 7 (1965): 3-8.

0750 L. J. Topel, "The Lukan Version of the Lord's Sermon," *BTB* 11 (1981): 48-53.

6:17-26

0751 P.-E. Jacquemin, "Les Béatitudes selon saint Luc (Lc 6)," *AsSeign* N.S. 37 (1971): 80-91.

0752 David L. Tiede, "Luke 6:17-26," *Int* 40 (1986): 63-68.

6:17-25

0753 H. Kahlefeld, "Selig ihr Armen," *BibL* 1 (1960): 55-61.

0754 J. Salguero, "Las Bienaventuranzas evangélicas," *CuBí* 29 (1972): 73-90.

0755 A. Viard, "Les Béatitudes et leur contre-partie," *EV* 87 (1977): 8-10.

6:17

0756 J. Manek, "On the Mount, On the Plain (Mt. 5:1, Lk. 6:17)," *NovT* 9 (1967): 124-31.

6:18

0757 E. Käsemann, "Die Heilung der Besessenen," *Reformatio* 28 (1979): 7-18.

6:20-49

0758 A. M. Perry, "The Framework of the Sermon on the Mount," *JBL* 54 (1935): 103-15.

0759 H. Schürmann, "Die Warnung des Lukas vor der Falschlehre in der 'Predigt am Berge'," in *Traditionsgeschichtliche Untersuchungen zu den synoptischen Evangelien.* Düsseldorf: Patmos, 1970. Pp. 290-309.

0760 Ronald D. Worden, "A Philological Analysis of Luke 6,20b-49 and Parallels," doctoral dissertation, Princeton Theological Seminary, Princeton NJ, 1973.

0761 G. Menestrina, "Matteo 5-7 e Luca 6:20-49 nell'Evangelo di Tommaso," *BibO* 18 (1976): 65-67.

0762 David R. Catchpole, "Jesus and the Community of Israel: The Inaugural Discourse in Q," *BJRL* 68 (1985-1986): 296-316.

0763 Leif E. Vaage, "Composite Texts and Oral Myths: The Case of the 'Sermon' (6:20b-49)," *SBLSP* 19 (1989): 424-39.

6:20-38
>   0764   W. Weren, "Kinderen van de Allerhoogste: Struktuur en
>   samenhang in Lucas 6,20-38," *Schrift* 68 (1980): 57-63.

6:20-31
>   0765   H. Deim, "Predigt über Lukas 6,20-31," *EvT* 14 (1954): 241-46.

6:20-29
>   0766   J. Guillet, "Le discours sur la montagne," in *Jésus devant sa vie
>   et sa mort.* Paris: Aubier, 1971. Pp. 83-93.

6:20-27
>   0767   Alberto Ablondi, "Meditando il Magnificat," in P. Visentin, et al.,
>   eds., *L'annuncio del regno ai poveri: b atti della XV Sessione di
>   formazione ecumenica organizzata dal Segretariato attivit'a
>   ecumeniche.* Leumann: Elle Di Ci, 1978. Pp. 147-57.

>   0768   Valdo Vinay, "Beati voi - Guai a voi," in P. Visentin, et al., eds.,
>   *L'annuncio del regno ai poveri: b atti della XV Sessione di
>   formazione ecumenica organizzata dal Segretariato attivit'a
>   ecumeniche.* Leumann: Elle Di Ci, 1978. Pp. 159-67.

6:20-26
>   0769   Wilhelm Pesch, "Lohn und Strafe in Jesu Volks- und
>   Jüngerpredigt," in *Der Lohnpedanke in der Lehre Jesu.* Münich:
>   Zink, 1955. Pp. 53-80.

>   0770   E. Neuhäusler, "Die Seligpreisungen," in *Anspruch und Antwort
>   Gottes.* Düsseldorf: Patmos, 1962. Pp. 141-69.

>   0771   Raymond E. Brown, "The Beatitudes According to Luke," in
>   R. E. Brown., ed., *New Testament Essays.* Milwaukee: Bruce, 1965.
>   Pp. 265-71.

>   0772   H.-J. Degenhardt, "Seligpreisungen und Weherufe: Lk 6,20-26,"
>   in *Lukas Evangelist der Armen.* Stuttgart: Katholisches Bibelwerk,
>   1965. Pp. 43-53.

>   0773   R. Kieffer, "Wisdom and Blessing in the Beatitudes of St.
>   Matthew and St. Luke," *StudE* 6 (1968): 291-95.

>   0774   G. Strecker, "Die Makarismen der Bergpredigt," *NTS* 17
>   (1970-1971): 255-75.

0775   R. Kieffer, "Un exemple concret, les béatitudes (Mt 5,1-12; Lc 6,20-26)," in *Essais de méthodologie néo-testamentáire*. Lund: Gleerup, 1972. Pp. 26-50.

0776   J. Coppens, "Les Béatitudes," *ETL* 50 (1974): 256-60.

0777   D. Flusser, "Some Notes to the Beatitudes (Matthew 5:3-12, Luke 6:20-26)," *Immanuel* 8 (1978): 37-47.

0778   Valdo Vinay, "Le beatitudini secondo il Vangelo di Luca," in P. Visentin, et al., eds., *L'annuncio del regno ai poveri: b atti della XV Sessione di formazione ecumenica organizzata dal Segretariato attivit' a ecumeniche*. Leumann: Elle Di Ci, 1978. Pp. 339-51.

0779   N. J. McEleney, "The Beatitudes of the Sermon on the Mount/Plain," *CBQ* 43 (1981): 1-13.

0780   Christopher M. Tuckett, "The Beatitudes: A Source-Critical Study, with a Reply by M. D. Goulder," *NovT* 25 (1983): 193-216.

0781   William R. Domeris, "Biblical Perspectives on the Poor," *JTSA* 57 (1986): 57-61.

6:20-23
0782   E. Percy, "Die Seligpreisungen der Berspredigt (Mt 5,3-12; Lk 6,20-23)," in *Die Botschaft Jesu*. Lund: Gleerup, 1953. Pp. 40-108.

0783   H. Frankemölle, "Die Makarismen (Mt 5,1-12; Lk 6,20-23)," *BZ* 15 (1971): 52-75.

0784   M. Eugene Boring, "Criteria of Authenticity: The Lucan Beatitudes as a Test Case," *Forum* 1 (1985): 3-38.

0785   Edgar Wirt, "What Do the Beatitudes Say: A Literal Study," *JRPR* 8 (1985): 81-87.

0786   M. Eugene Boring, "The Historical-Critical Method's Criteria of Authenticity: The Beatitudes in Q and Thomas as a Test Case," *Semeia* 44 (1988): 9-44.

0787   Josef Heer, "Freut euch, ihr Armen . . . Herausforderung zum Glaubenshumor durch Jesus," in Johannes J. Degenhardt, ed., *Die Freude an Gott: Unsere Kraft* (festschrift for Otto B. Knoch). Stuttgart: Verlag Katholisches Bibelwerk, 1991. Pp. 432-38.

70

BIBLIOGRAPHIES FOR BIBLICAL RESEARCH

<u>6:20-21</u>

0788 Eduard Schweizer, "Formgeschichtliches zu den Seligpreisungen Jesu," *NTS* 19 (1972-1973): 121-26.

<u>6:20</u>

0789 M. Knepper, "Die 'Armen' der Bergpredigt Jesu," *BK* 8/1 (1953): 19-27.

0790 Piero Bensi, "Beati voi, poveri, perché Dio vi chiama a essere il suo popolo," in P. Visentin, et al., eds., *L'annuncio del regno ai poveri: b atti della XV Sessione di formazione ecumenica organizzata dal Segretariato attivit'a ecumeniche*. Leumann: Elle Di Ci, 1978. Pp. 177-96.

0791 Mario Galizzi, "Beati voi, poveri, perché vostro è il Regno di Dio," in P. Visentin, et al., eds., *L'annuncio del regno ai poveri: b atti della XV Sessione di formazione ecumenica organizzata dal Segretariato attivit'a ecumeniche*. Leumann: Elle Di Ci, 1978. Pp. 169-75.

<u>6:21</u>

0792 Gianni Capra, "Beati voi, che ora piangete: Dio vi darà gioia," in P. Visentin, et al., eds., *L'annuncio del regno ai poveri: b atti della XV Sessione di formazione ecumenica organizzata dal Segretariato attivit'a ecumeniche*. Leumann: Elle Di Ci, 1978. Pp. 205-16.

0793 Luigi Sartori, "Beati voi, che ora avete fame: Dio vi sazierà," in P. Visentin, et al., eds., *L'annuncio del regno ai poveri: b atti della XV Sessione di formazione ecumenica organizzata dal Segretariato attivit'a ecumeniche*. Leumann: Elle Di Ci, 1978. Pp. 197-203.

<u>6:22-23</u>

0794 John S. Kloppenborg, "Blessing and Marginality: The 'Persecution Beatitude' in Q, Thomas, and Early Christianity," *Forum* 2 (1986): 36-56.

0795 W. R. Stenger, "Die Seligpreisungen der Geschmähtem (Mt 5,11-12; Lk 6,22-23)," *K* 28 (1986): 33-60.

<u>6:22</u>

0796 Patrick P. Saydon, "Some Biblico-Liturgical Passages Reconsidered," *MeliT* 18/1 (1966): 10-17.

0797 Günther Schwarz, "Lukas 6,22a.23c.26. Emendation, Rückübersetzung, Interpretation," *ZNW* 66 (1975): 269-74.

0798 Renzo Bertalot, "Beati voi, quando gli altri vi odieranno - e vi disprezzeranno - perché Dio vi darà la sua grande ricompensa," in P. Visentin, et al., eds., *L'annuncio del regno ai poveri: b atti della XV Sessione di formazione ecumenica organizzata dal Segretariato attivit'a ecumeniche.* Leumann: Elle Di Ci, 1978. Pp. 217-24.

6:23
0799 Günther Schwarz, "Lukas 6,22a.23c.26. Emendation, Rückübersetzung, Interpretation," *ZNW* 66 (1975): 269-74.

6:24-26
0800 P. Klein, "Die lukanischen Weherufe Luke 6:24-26," *ZNW* 71 (1980): 150-59.

6:26
0801 Günther Schwarz, "Lukas 6,22a.23c.26. Emendation, Rückübersetzung, Interpretation," *ZNW* 66 (1975): 269-74.

6:27-38
0802 A. Viard, "L'amour des ennemis," *EV* 87 (1977): 10-11.

0803 Gerd Theissen, "Gewaltverzicht und Feindesliebe (Mt 5,38-48 / Lk 6,27-38) und deren sozialgeschichtlichen Hintergrund," in *Studien zur Soziologie des Urchristentums.* WUNT #19. Tübingen: Mohr, 1979. Pp. 160-97.

6:27-36
0804 D. Lührmann, "Liebet eure Feinde (Lk 6,27-36; Mt 5,39-48)," *ZTK* 69 (1972): 412-38.

0805 Paul S. Minear, "Love and Lend," in *Commands of Christ.* Nashville: Abingdon Press, 1972. Pp. 69-82.

0806 L. Schottroff, "Non-Violence and the Love of One's Enemies," in L. Schottroff, et al., eds., *Essays on the Commandment of Love.* Philadelphia: Fortress, 1978. Pp. 9-39.

0807 Fritz Neugebauer, "Die dargebotene Wange und Jesu Gebot der Feindesliebe: Erwägungen zu Lk. 6:27-36; Matt. 5:38-48," *TLZ* 110/12 (1985): 865-75.

0808 J. Sauer, "Traditionsgeschichtliche Erwägungen zu den synoptischen und paulinischen Aussagen über Feindesliebe und Wiedervergeltungsverzicht," *ZNW* 76 (1985): 1-28.

0809 D. Gill, "Socrates and Jesus on Non-Retaliation and Love of Enemies," *Horizons* 18 (1991): 246-62.

6:27-29

0810 Marcus J. Borg, "A New Context for Romans XIII," *NTS* 19/2 (1972-1973): 205-18.

6:27-28

0811 O. Seitz, "Love your Enemies," *NTS* 16 (1969-1970): 39-54.

0812 Gerhard Schneider, "Imitatio Dei als Motiv der Ethik Jesu," in Helmut Merklein, ed., *Neues Testament und Ethik* (festschrift for Rudolf Schnackenburg). Freiburg: Herder, 1989. Pp. 71-83.

6:27

0813 Günther Schwarz, "ἀγαπᾶτε τοὺς ἐχθροὺς ὑμῶν: Mt 5,44a / Lk 6,27a (35a)," *BibN* 12 (1980): 32-34.

0814 V. J. Jahnke, " 'Love Your Enemies': The Value of New Perspectives," *CThM* 15 (1988): 267-73.

6:29

0815 J. T. Cummings, "The Tassel of His Cloak: Mark, Luke, Matthew, and Zechariah," *StudB* 2 (1980): 47-61.

0816 Gerhard Lohfink, "Der ekklesiale Sitz im Leben der Aufforderung Jesu zum Gewaltverzicht (Matt. 5:39-42/Luke 6:29)," *TQ* 162 (1982): 236-53.

0817 Robert W. Funk, "The Beatitudes and Turn the Other Cheek: Recommendations and Polling," *Forum* 2 (1986): 103-28.

0818 J. W. Harris, "Lawyers and Forgiveness: Until Seventy Times Seven?" *MC* 28/2 (1986): 32-41.

6:31

0819 Hans Werner Bartsch, "Traditionsgeschichtliches zur 'goldenen Regel' und zum Aposteldekret," *ZNW* 75 (1984): 128-32.

0820 P. Ricoeur, "The Golden Rule: Exegetical and Theological Perplexities," *NTS* 36 (1990): 392-97.

6:32-35
0821 W. C. van Unnik, "Die Motivierung der Feindesliebe in Lukas vi,32-35," *NovT* 8 (1966): 284-300.

6:32
0822 Marcus J. Borg, "A New Context for Romans XIII," *NTS* 19/2 (1972-1973): 205-18.

6:35-36
0823 Gerhard Schneider, "Imitatio Dei als Motiv der Ethik Jesu," in Helmut Merklein, ed., *Neues Testament und Ethik* (festschrift for Rudolf Schnackenburg). Freiburg: Herder, 1989. Pp. 71-83.

6:35
0824 Marcus J. Borg, "A New Context for Romans XIII," *NTS* 19/2 (1972-1973): 205-18.

0825 Günther Schwarz, "ἀγαπᾶτε τοὺς ἐχθροὺς ὑμῶν: Mt 5,44a / Lk 6,27a (35a)," *BibN* 12 (1980): 32-34.

0826 Günther Schwarz, "Μηδὲν ἀπελπίζοντες," *ZNW* 71 (1980): 133-35.

0827 P. Ricoeur, "The Golden Rule: Exegetical and Theological Perplexities," *NTS* 36 (1990): 392-97.

6:36
0828 M. McNamara, " 'Be You Merciful as Your Father is Merciful,' Lk 6,36 and TJI Lv 22,28," in *The New Testament and the Palestinian Targum to the Pentateuch*. Rome: Pontifical Biblical Institute, 1966. Pp. 133-38.

0829 R. Koch, "L'appello alla sanlità di Lv 19,2 alla luce di Mt 5,48 e Lc 6,36," in M. Napela and T. Kennedy, eds., *La coscienza morale oggi* (festschrift for D. Capone). Quaestiones morales #3. Rome: Ed. Acad. Alphonsianae, 1988. Pp. 25-38.

6:37-45

0830 Jacob Kremer, "Mahnungen zum innerkirchlichen Befolgen des Liebesgebotes: textpragmatische Erwägungen zu Lk 6,37-45," in Hubert Frankemölle, ed., *Vom Urchristentum zu Jesus* (festschrift for Joachim Gnilka). Freiburg: Herder, 1989. Pp. 231-45.

6:37-43

0831 Randel Helms, "Fiction in the Gospels," in R. Joseph Hoffmann and Gerald A. Larue, eds., *Jesus in History and Myth*. Buffalo: Prometheus Books, 1986. Pp. 135-42.

6:37-42

0832 J. Duncan M. Derrett, "Christ and Reproof (Matthew 7:1-5/Luke 6:37-42)," *NTS* 34/2 (1988): 271-81.

6:38

0833 Gordon D. Fee, "A Text-Critical Look at the Synoptic Problem," *NovT* 22/1 (1980): 12-28.

0834 D. Bivin, "A Measure of Humility," *JeruP* 4 (1991): 13-14.

6:39-45

0835 A. George, "Le disciple fraternel et efficace (Lc 6)," *AsSeign* N.S. 39 (1972): 68-77.

6:41-42

0836 G. B. King, "A Further Note on the Mote and the Beam (Matt. 7:3-5; Luke 6:41-42)," *HTR* 26 (1933): 73-76.

6:43-46

0837 M. Krämer, "Hütet euch vor den falschen Propheten. Eine überlieferungsgeschichtliche Untersuchung zu Mt 7:15-23/Lk 6:43-46/Mt 12:33-37," *Bib* 57 (1976): 349-77.

6:43-45

0838 H. B. Green, "Matthew 12,22-50 and Parallels: An Alternative to Matthean Conflation," in C. M. Tuckett, ed., *Synoptic Studies*. Sheffield: JSOT Press, 1984. Pp. 157-76.

6:43

0839 M. Simonetti, "Mt 7,17-18 (= Lc 6,43) dagli gnostici ad Agostino," *AugR* 16 (1976): 271-90.

6:46

0840   Gerhard Schneider, "Christusbekenntnis und christliches Handeln.
Lk 6,46 und Mt 7,21 im Kontext der Evangelien," in Rudolf
Schnackenburg, et al., eds., *Die Kirche des Anfangs* (festschrift for
H. Schürmann). Leipzig: St. Benno, 1978. Pp. 9-24.

6:47-49

0841   K. Abou-Chaar, "The Two Builders: A Study of the Parable in
Luke 6:47-49," *NESTTR* 5 (1982): 44-58.

0842   Michael D. Goulder, "A House Built on Sand," in A. E. Harvey,
ed., *Alternative Approaches to New Testament Study*. London:
SPCK, 1985. Pp. 1-24.

6:48-7:5

0843   Edouard Massaux, "Deux Fragments d'un Manuscrit Oncial de la
Vulgate [Lc. 6:48-7:5, 11-13; Jo. 12:39-49; 13:6-15]," *ETL* 37
(1961): 112-17.

7:1-19

0844   F. Schnider and W. Stenger, "Der Hauptmann von Kapharnaum:
Die Heilung des Sohnes des a 'Königlichen'," in *Johannes und die
Synoptiker*. Münich: Kösel, 1971. Pp. 54-88.

7:1-10

0845   H. F. D. Sparks, "The Centurion's *pais*," *JTS* 42 (1941): 179-80.

0846   E. Haenchen, "Faith and Miracle," *StudE* 1 (1959): 496-98.

0847   E. F. Siegman, "St. John's Use of the Synoptic Material," *CBQ*
30/2 (1968): 182-98.

0848   J. Duncan M. Derrett, "Law in the New Testament: The
Syro-Phoenician Woman and the Centurion of Capernaum," *NovT*
15 (1973): 161-86.

0849   A. George, "Guérison de l'esclave d'un centurion (Lc 7)," *AsSeign*
N.S. 40 (1973): 66-77.

0850   A. Weiser, "Eine Heilung und ihr dreifacher Bericht (Matthäus
8,5-13; Lukas 7,1-10; Johannes 4,43-54)," in *Werkstatt
Bibelauslegung: Bilder, Interpretationen, Texte*. Stuttgart:
Katholisches Bibelwerk, 1976. Pp. 64-69.

0851   K. Gatzweiler, "L'exégèse historico-critique: Une guérison à Capharnaum," *FT* 9 (1979): 297-315.

0852   E. Haapa, "Zur Selbsteinschätzung des Hauptmanns von Kapharnaum im Lukasevangelium," in J. Kiilunen, et al., eds., *Glaube und Gerechtigkeit* (festschrift for R. Gyllenberg). Helsinki: Vammalan Kirjapaino, 1983. Pp. 69-76.

0853   A. Dauer, *Johannes und Lukas: Untersuchungen zu den johanneisch-lukanischen Parallel-Perikopen Joh 4,46-54/Lk 7,1-10; Joh 12,1-8/Lk 7,36-50, 10,38-42; Joh 20,19-29/Lk 24,36-49.* Würzburg: Echter, 1984.

0854   J. A. G. Haslam, "The Centurion at Capernaum: Luke 7:1-10," *ET* 96 (1984-1985): 109-10.

0855   Keith Pearce, "The Lucan Origins of the Raising of Lazarus," *ET* 96 (1984-1985): 359-61.

0856   Uwe Wegner, *Der Hauptmann von Kafarnaum (Mt 7.28a; 8.5-10.13 par Lk 7.1-10): Ein Beitrag zur Q-Forschung.* WUNT #II/14. Tübingen: Mohr, 1985.

7:2-8:3

0857   D. A. S. Ravens, "The Setting of Luke's Account of the Anointing: Luke 7.2-8.3," *NTS* 34 (1988): 282-92.

7:8

0858   M. Frost, " 'I Also Am a Man Under Authority'," *ET* 45 (1933-1934): 477-78.

7:11-17

0859   A. Del Riego, "La resurrección del hijo de la viuda de Naín. Commentario-meditación," *CuBí* 22 (1965): 354-59.

0860   P. Ternant, "La résurrection du fils de la veuve de Naïm (Lc 7)," *AsSeign* N.S. 41 (1971): 69-79.

0861   A. Harbarth, "Gott hat sein Volk heimgesucht: Eine form- und redaktionsgeschichtliche Untersuchung zu Lk 7,11-17. Die Erweckung des Jünglings von Naim," doctoral dissertation, University of Freiburg, Germany, 1977.

0862 J. Kluge, " 'Die Auferstehung des Jünglings zu Nain' oder 'Der Auferstehungsglaube und die Frage nach Leben und Tod': Zwei Unterrichtsmodelle zu Lk 7,11-17," in R. Kakuschke, ed., *Auferstehung - Tod und Leben.* Göttingen: Vandenhoeck, 1978. Pp. 202-20.

0863 C. Schnyder, "Zum Leben befreit: Jesus erweckt den einzigen Sohn einer Witwe vom Tode (Lukas 7,11-17). Eine Totenerweckung," in A. Steiner, ed., *Wunder Jesu.* Basel: Reinhardt, 1978. Pp. 78-88.

0864 F. A. J. Macdonald, "Pity or Compassion?" *ET* 92 (1980-1981): 344-46.

0865 Walter Vogels, "A Semiotic Study of Luke 7:11-17," *ÉgT* 14 (1983): 273-92.

0866 Keith Pearce, "The Lucan Origins of the Raising of Lazarus," *ET* 96 (1984-1985): 359-61.

0867 Thomas L. Brodie, "Towards Unravelling Luke's Use of the Old Testament: Luke 7:11-17 as an Imitation of 1 Kings 17:17-24," *NTS* 32/2 (1986): 247-67.

0868 Santos Sabugal, " 'Joven, te lo digo, levántate' (Lc 7,11-17): Análisis histórico," *EstAg* 23 (1988): 469-82.

0869 Sabine Demel, "Jesu Umgang Mit Frauen Nach Dem Lukasevangelium," *BibN* 57 (1991): 41-95.

7:11-16

0870 E. Galbiati, "La risurrezione del giovane di Naim (Lc 7:11-16)," *BibO* 4 (1962): 175-77.

7:11-13

0871 Edouard Massaux, "Deux Fragments d'un Manuscrit Oncial de la Vulgate [Lc. 6:48-7:5, 11-13; Jo. 12:39-49; 13:6-15]," *ETL* 37 (1961): 112-17.

7:12-22

0872 Robert J. Karris, "Luke's Soteriology of With-ness," *CThM* 12 (1985): 346-52.

7:16

0873   Patrick P. Saydon, "Some Biblico-Liturgical Passages Reconsidered," *MeliT* 18/1 (1966): 10-17.

0874   Dorotej Filipp, "The Influence of the Moravian Mission on the Orthodox Church in Czechoslovakia," *IRM* 74 (1985): 219-29.

7:18-35

0875   P. Hoffmann, "Johannes und der Menschensohn Jesus," in *Studien zur Theologie der Logienquelle*. Münster: Aschendorff, 1972. Pp. 190-233.

0876   Ben Witherington, "Jesus and the Baptist: Two of a Kind?" *SBLSP* 18 (1988): 225-44.

7:18-23

0877   A. Vögtle, "Wort und Wunder in der urkirchlichen Glaubenswerbung (Mt 11,2-6, Lk 7,18-23)," in *Das Evangelium und die Evangelien*. Düsseldorf: Patmos, 1971. Pp. 219-42.

0878   S. Sabugal, "La embajada mesiánica del Bautista (Mt 11,2-6 = Lc 7,18-23): Análisis histórico-tradicional," *AugR* 13 (1973): 215-78.

0879   M. Völkel, "Anmerkungen zur lukanischen Fassung der Täuferanfrage Luk 7,18-23," in W. Dietrich, et al., eds., *Festgabe für K. H. Rengstorf*. Leiden: Brill, 1973. Pp. 166-73.

0880   Santos Sabugal, "La embajada mesiánica del Bautista (Mt 11,2-6 = Lc 7,18-23): La redacción lucana," *AugR* 14 (1974): 5-39.

0881   Jan Lambrecht, " 'Are You the One Who is to Come, or Shall We Look for Another?' The Gospel Message of Jesus Today," *LouvS* 8/2 (1980): 115-18.

0882   Martin Cawley, "Health of the Eyes: Gift of the Father: In the Gospel Tradition 'Q'," *WS* 3 (1981): 41-70.

0883   I. Kerr, "The Signs of Jesus," *ET* 94 (1982-1983): 49-51.

0884   Walter Wink, "Jesus' Reply to John: Matt 11:2-6/Luke 7:18-23," *Forum* 5 (1989): 121-28.

7:18

0885 P. Habandi, "Eine wieder aktuelle Frage. Zu Lukas 7,18ff.: 'Bist du es, der kommen soll, oder sollen wir auf einen andern warten'?" *ZMiss* 6 (1980): 195-98.

7:19

0886 A. Strobel, "Die Täuferanfrage (Mt 11,3/Luk 7,19)," in *Untersuchungen zum eschatologischen Verzögerungsproblem auf Grund der spätjüdischurchristlichen Geschichte von Habakuk 2,2ff.* Leiden: Brill, 1961. Pp. 265-77.

7:21

0887 E. Käsemann, "Die Heilung der Besessenen," *Reformatio* 28 (1979): 7-18.

7:22-26

0888 Vyacheslav Reznikov, "On the Day of the Beheading of St. John the Baptist," *JMP* 8 (1984): 48-49.

7:22-23

0889 E. Peretto, "Evangelizare pauperibus (Lk 4,18; 7,22-23) nella lettura patristica dei secoli II-III," *AugR* 17 (1977): 71-100.

7:22

0890 A. George, "Paroles de Jésus sur ses miracles (Mt 11,5.21; 12,27.28 et par.)," in Jacques Dupont, ed., *Jésus aux origines de la christologie.* BETL #40. Louvain: Peeters Press, 1975. Pp. 283-302.

0891 Wolfgang Beinert, "Jesus Christus: das Ursakrament Gottes," *Cath* 38/4 (1984): 340-51.

7:24-25

0892 C. Daniel, "Les Esséniens et 'Ceux qui sont dans les maisons des rois'," *RevQ* 6 (1967): 261-77.

7:27

0893 Michael D. Goulder, "On Putting Q to the Test," *NTS* 24 (1977-1978): 218-34.

0894 W. C. Kaiser, "The Promise of the Arrival of Elijah in Malachi and the Gospels," *GTJ* 3/2 (1982): 221-33.

7:28

0895   J. H. Greenlee, "Some Examples of Scholarly 'Agreement in Error'," *JBL* 77 (1958): 363-64.

0896   Vyacheslav Reznikov, "On the Day of the Beheading of St. John the Baptist," *JMP* 8 (1984): 48-49.

7:29-30

0897   G. Gander, "Notule sur Luc 7,29-30," *VC* 19 (1951): 141-44.

7:31-35

0898   Franz Mussner, "Der nicht erkannte Kairos (Mt 11,16-19 = Lk 7,31-35)," in *Studia Biblica et Orientalia.* 3 vols. Rome: Pontifical Institute, 1959. 2:31-44.

0899   Simon Légasse, "La parabole des enfants sur la place," in *Jésus et l'enfant.* Paris: Gabalda, 1969. Pp. 289-317.

0900   O. Linton, "The Parable of the Children's Game," *NTS* 22/2 (1975-1976): 159-79.

0901   C. Siburt, "The Game of Rejecting God: Luke 7:31-35," *RQ* 19 (1976): 207-10.

0902   Wendy J. Cotter, "The Parable of the Children in the Market-Place, Q (Lk) 7:31-35," *NovT* 29 (1987): 289-304.

0903   Wendy J. Cotter, "Children Sitting in the Agora: Q (Luke) 7:31-35," *Forum* 5 (1989): 63-82.

7:31-32

0904   Dieter Zeller, "Die Bildlogik des Gleichnisses Mt 11,16f. / Lk 7,31f," *ZNW* 68 (1977): 252-57.

7:33-34

0905   Leif E. Vaage, "Q and the Historical Jesus: Some Peculiar Sayings," *Forum* 5 (1989): 159-76.

0906   M. H. Franzmann, "Of Food, Bodies, and the Boundless Reign of God in the Synoptic Gospels," *Pacifica* 5 (1992): 17-31.

7:33

0907   Otto Böcher, "Johannes der Täufer kein Brot (Luk. vii.33)?" *NTS* 18 (1971-1972): 90-92.

0908   S. L. Davies, "John the Baptist and Essene Kashruth," *NTS* 29 (1983): 569-71.

7:34

0909   P. Maurice Casey, "The Son of Man Problem," *ZNW* 67/3 (1976): 147-54.

0910   A. Orbe, "El Hijo del hombre come y bebe (Mt 11,19; Lc 7,34)," *Greg* 58 (1977): 523-55.

0911   M. Völkel, "Freund der Zöllner und Sünder," *ZNW* 69 (1978): 1-10.

0912   Robert J. Karris, "Luke's Soteriology of With-ness," *CThM* 12 (1985): 346-52.

7:35

0913   I. J. Du Plessis, "Contextual Aid for an Identity Crisis: An Attempt to Interpret Lk 7:35," in J. H. Petzer and P. J. Hartin, eds., *A South African Perspective on the New Testament* (festschrift for Bruce M. Metzger). Leiden: Brill, 1986. Pp. 112-27.

7:36-50

0914   R. K. Orchard, "On the Composition of Luke vii,36-50," *JTS* 38 (1937): 243-45.

0915   André Legault, "An Application of the Form-Critique Method to the Anointing in Galilee (Lc 7,36-50) and Bethany (Mt 26,6-13; Mk 14,3-9; Lk 12,1-8)," *CBQ* 16 (1954): 131-45.

0916   J. A. Bailey, "The Anointing of Jesus and the Mary-Martha Stories: Luke 7.36-50; John 12.1-8," in *The Traditions Common to the Gospels of Luke and John*. Leiden: Brill, 1963. Pp. 1-8.

0917   Georg Braumann, "Die Schuldner und die Sünderin Luk. VII.36-50," *NTS* 10/4 (1963-1964): 487-93.

0918 G. Eichholz, "Von den beiden Schuldnern," in *Gleichnissvangelien.* Neukirchen-Vluyn: Neukirchener Verlag, 1971. Pp. 55-64.

0919 K. Löning, "Ein Platz für die Verlorenen. Zur Formkritik zweier neutestamentlicher Legenden (Lk 7,36-50)," *BibL* 12 (1971): 198-208.

0920 L. Ramaroson, "Simon et la pécheresse anonyme (Lc 7,36-50)," *SE* 24 (1972): 379-83.

0921 H. Leroy, "Vergebung und Gemeinde nach Lukas 7,36-50," in *Wort Gottes in der Zeit.* Düsseldorf: Patmos, 1973. Pp. 85-94.

0922 K. Schäfer, *Zu Gast bei Simon: Eine biblische Geschichte langsam gelesen.* Düsseldorf: Patmos, 1973.

0923 U. Wilckens, "Vergebung für die Sünderin (Lk 7,36-50)," in *Orientierung an Jesus: Zur Theologie der Synoptiker* (festschrift for Josef Schmid). Freiburg: Herder, 1973. Pp. 394-424.

0924 J. K. Elliott, "The Anointing of Jesus," *ET* 85 (1973-1974): 105-107.

0925 André Feuillet, "Les deux onctions faites sur Jésus, et Marie-Madeleine," *RT* 75 (1975): 357-94.

0926 R. Holst, "The One Anointing of Jesus: Another Application of the Form-Critical Method," *JBL* 95 (1976): 435-46.

0927 R. Frei, "Die Salbung Jesu durch die Sünderin: Eine redaktionskritische Untersuchung zu Lk 7,36-50," doctoral dissertation, University of Mainz, 1978.

0928 T. McCaughey, "Paradigms of Faith in the Gospel of St. Luke," *ITQ* 45 (1978): 177-84.

0929 M. Völkel, " 'Freund der Zöllner und Sünder'," *ZNW* 69 (1978): 1-10.

0930 Jacques Dupont, "Le pharisien et la pécheresse (Lc 7,36-50)," *CL* 62 (1980): 260-68.

0931 M. Sabbe, "The Footwashing in John 13 and Its Relation to the Synoptic Gospels," *ETL* 58 (1982): 279-308.

0932 E. Springs Steele, "Jesus's Table Fellowship with Pharisees: An Editorial Analysis of Luke 7:36-50, 11:37-54, and 14:1-24," doctoral dissertation, University of Notre Dame, Notre Dame IN, 1982.

0933 Thomas L. Brodie, "Luke 7:36-50 as an Internalization of 2 Kings 4:1-37: A Study in Luke's Use of Rhetorical Imitation," *Bib* 64 (1983): 457-85.

0934 Jacques Dupont, "Jésus et la pécheresse (Lc 7,36-50)," *CL* 65 (1983): 11-17.

0935 C. Légaré, "Jésus et la pécheresse. Analyse de Luc 7:36-50," *SémBib* 29 (1983): 19-45.

0936 J. P. Sauzède, "Une série pour le Carême," *ÉTR* 58 (1983): 59-71.

0937 A. Dauer, *Johannes und Lukas: Untersuchungen zu den johanneisch-lukanischen Parallel-Perikopen Joh 4,46-54/Lk 7,1-10; Joh 12,1-8/Lk 7,36-50, 10,38-42; Joh 20,19-29/Lk 24,36-49.* Würzburg: Echter, 1984.

0938 Victor Saxer, "Anselme et la Madeleine: l'oraison LXXIV, ses sources, son style et son influence," in Raymonde Foreville, ed., *Les mutations socio-Culturelles*. Paris: Editions du Centre national de la recherche scientifique, 1984. Pp. 365-82.

0939 Keith Pearce, "The Lucan Origins of the Raising of Lazarus," *ET* 96 (1984-1985): 359-61.

0940 Christian D. Kettler, "The Vicarious Repentance of Christ in the Theology of John McLeod Campbell and R. C. Moberly," *SJT* 38/4 (1985): 529-43.

0941 John J. Kilgallen, "John the Baptist, the Sinful Woman and the Pharisee," *JBL* 104/4 (1985): 675-79.

0942 J. Louw, "Macro Levels of Meaning in Lk 7:36-50," in J. H. Petzer and P. J. Hartin, eds., *A South African Perspective on the New Testament* (festschrift for Bruce Metzger). Leiden: Brill, 1986. Pp. 128-35.

0943 Bernadine G. McRipley, "Racial-Ethnic Presbyterian Women: In Search for Community," *ChS* 76/4 (1986): 47-53.

0944 J. A. Sanders, "Extravagant Love," *NBlack* 68 (1987): 278-84.

0945 J. T. Coakley, "The Anointing at Bethany and the Priority of John," *JBL* 107 (1988): 241-56.

0946 Mauro Láconi, "Fede e amore: La peccatrice perdonata (Lc 7,36-50)," *ParSpirV* 17 (1988): 143-55.

0947 Jean Delorme, "Récit, parole et parabole," in Jean Delorme, ed., *Les paraboles évangéliques: perspectives nouvelles.* Paris: Cerf, 1989. Pp. 123-50.

0948 Bernard-Marie Ferry, "La pécheresse pardonnée (Lc 7:36-50): pourquoi verse-t-elle des pleurs," *EV* 99 (1989): 174-76.

0949 Antony Hurst, "The Woman with the Ointment," *ET* 101 (1989-1990): 304.

0950 C. M. Martini, *Women in the Gospels.* New York: Crossroad, 1990.

0951 Edmund Beck, "Der syrische Diatessaronkommentar zu der Perikope von der Sünderin, Luc 7,36-50," *OrChr* 75 (1991): 1-15.

0952 Sabine Demel, "Jesu Umgang Mit Frauen Nach Dem Lukasevangelium," *BibN* 57 (1991): 41-95.

0953 John J. Kilgallen, "A Proposal for Interpreting Luke 7:36-50," *Bib* 72/3 (1991): 305-30.

0954 James L. Resseguie, "Automatization and Defamiliarization in Luke 7:36-50," *LT* 5 (1991): 137-50.

0955 James L. Resseguie, "Luke 7:36-50," *Int* 46 (1992): 285-90.

7:36-38
    0956 Simon Légasse, "Jésus et les prostituées," *RTL* 7 (1976): 137-54.

7:37-48
    0957 John Chryssavgis, "The Notion of 'Divine Eros' in the Ladder of St. John Climacus," *SVTQ* 29/3 (1985): 191-200.

7:41-43
    0958 J. Maiworm, "Umgekehrte Gleichnisse," *BK* 10 (1955): 82-85.

    0959 Gerhard Sellin, "Gleichnisstrukturen," *LB* 31 (1974): 89-115.

7:45
    0960 J. Jeremias, "Lukas 7:45: *eisēlthon*," *ZNW* 51/1-2 (1960): 131.

7:46
    0961 K. Weiss, "Der westliche Text von Lc 7,46 und sein Wert," *ZNW* 46 (1955): 241-45.

7:47
    0962 L. Ramaroson, " 'Le premier, c'est l'amour' (Lc 7,47a)," *SE* 39 (1987): 319-29.

7:48
    0963 J. Guillet, " 'Tes péchés sont pardonnés' (Mc 2,5 et Lc 7,48)," in M. Carrez, et al., eds., *De la Tôrah au Messie* (festschrift for H. Cazelles). Paris: Desclée, 1981. Pp. 425-29.

8:1-21
    0964 W. Weren, "Oude en nieuwe wegen in de exegese: De wording en de werking van Lc 8,1-21," in W. Logister, et al., eds., *Twintig jaar ontwikkelingen in de theologie: Tendenzen en perspectieven.* Kampen: Kok, 1987. Pp. 58-72.

    0965 W. Weren, "De parabel van het zaad (Lc 8,1-21)," in B. van Iersel, et al., eds., *Parabelverhalen in Lucas: Van semiotiek naar pragmatiek.* TFT-Studies #8. Tilburg: University Press, 1987. Pp. 22-54.

8:1-3
    0966 Ben Witherington, "On the Road with Mary Magdalene, Joanna, Susanna, and Other Disciples (Luke 8:1-3)," *ZNW* 70 (1979): 243-48.

0967   Sister Philsy, "Diakonia of Women in the New Testament," *IJT* 32 (1983): 110-18.

0968   David C. Sim, "The Women Followers of Jesus: The Implications of Luke 8:1-3," *HeyJ* 30 (1989): 51-62.

8:4-21

0969   W. C. Robinson, "On Preaching the Word of God (Luke 8:4-21)," in Leander Keck and J. L. Martyn, eds., *Studies in Luke-Acts* (festschrift for Paul Schubert). Nashville: Abingdon Press, 1966. Pp. 131-38.

0970   H. Schürmann, "Lukanische Reflexionen über die Wortverkündigung in Lk 8,4-21," in *Ursprung und Gestalt.* Düsseldorf: Patmos, 1970. Pp. 29-41.

0971   S. A. Panimolle, " 'Fate attenzione a come ascoltate!' (Lc 8,4-21," *ParSpirV* 1 (1980): 95-119.

8:4-18

0972   M. Miguéns, "La predicazione di Gesù in parabole," *BibO* 1 (1959): 35-40.

8:4-15

0973   David Wenham, "The Interpretation of the Parable of the Sower," *NTS* 20 (1973-1974): 299-319.

0974   J. Toy, "The Parable of the Sower and its Interpretation," *ET* 92 (1980-1981): 116-18.

0975   Craig Westendorf, "The Parable of the Sower in the Seventeenth Century," *LQ* 3 (1989): 49-64.

8:4

0976   Michael B. Walker, "Luke 8:4," *ET* 75 (1963-1964): 151.

8:5-15

0977   I. Howard Marshall, "Tradition and Theology in Luke 8:5-15," *TynB* 20 (1969): 56-75.

8:7

0978   José O'Callaghan, "La Variante 'Ahogaron' en Mt 13,7," *Bib* 68/3 (1987): 402-403.

8:9-10

0979 E. F. Siegman, "Teaching in Parables," *CBQ* 23 (1961): 161-81.

8:10

0980 L. Cerfaux, "La connaissance des secrets du Royaume d'après Matt. xiii. et par.," *NTS* 2 (1955-1956): 238-49.

0981 Vittorio Fusco, "L'accord mineur Mt 13,11a / Lc 8,10a contre Mc 4,11a," in J. Delobel, ed., *Logia: Les paroles de Jésus (The Sayings of Jesus)*. BETL #59. Louvain: Peeters Press, 1982. Pp. 355-61.

8:12

0982 John Ferguson, "Mary Magdalene," *ET* 97/9 (1985-1986): 275-76.

8:14-15

0983 J. Gervais, "Les épines étouffantes (Luc 8,14-15)," *ET* 84 (1972-1973): 5-40.

8:14

0984 Romano Penna, "Osservazioni sull'anti-edonismo nel Nuovo Testamento in rapporto al suo ambiente culturale [Lk 8:14; 2 Tim 3:4; Tit 3:3; Jas 4:1-3; 2 Pet 2:13]," in M. Angelini, et al., eds., *Testimonium Christi* (festschrift for Jacques Dupont). Brescia: Paideia, 1985. Pp. 351-77.

8:16-18

0985 Jacques Dupont, "La transmission des paroles de Jésus sur la lampe et la mesure dans Marc 4,21-25 et dans la tradition Q," in J. Delobel, ed., *Logia: Les paroles de Jésus (The Sayings of Jesus)*. BETL #59. Louvain: Peeters Press, 1982. Pp. 259-94.

8:18

0986 G. Lindeskog, "Logia-Studien," *ST* 4 (1951-1952): 129-89.

0987 C. Bamberg, " 'Gebt acht, dass ihr gut hört!' (Lk 8:18). Zur christlichen Wortmeditation," *GeistL* 50 (1977): 390-94.

8:19-21

0988 Roger Mercurio, "Some Difficult Marian Passages in the Gospels," *MarSt* 11 (1960): 104-22.

0989   H. B. Green, "Matthew 12,22-50 and Parallels: An Alternative to
Matthean Conflation," in C. M. Tuckett, ed., *Synoptic Studies*.
Sheffield: JSOT Press, 1984. Pp. 157-76.

8:22-25
0990   G. Bornkamm, "Die Sturmstillung im Matthäusevangelium," in G.
Bornkamm, et al., eds, *Überlieferung und Auslegung im
Matthäusevangelium*. 2nd ed. Neukirchen-Vluyn: Neukirchener
Verlag, 1971. Pp. 48-53.

8:22
0991   Christoph Burchard, "Fußnoten zum neutestamentlichen Griechisch
II," *ZNW* 69 (1978): 143-57.

0992   Philippe Rolland, "L'arrière-fond sémitique des évangiles
synoptiques," *ETL* 60 (1984): 358-62.

8:26-39
0993   T. Hawthorn, "The Gerasene Demoniac: A Diagnosis (Marc 5:1-20
and Luke 8:26-39)," *ET* 66 (1954-1955): 79-80.

0994   A. Vögtle, "Die historische und theologische Tragweite de
heutigen Evangelienforschung," *ZKT* 86 (1964): 385-471.

0995   Lee Meyer, "Towards Wholeness: The Christian Ministry of
Health and Healing," *Point* 10/2 (1981): 62-70.

0996   J. M. García Pérez, "El endemoniado de Gerasa (Lc 8,26-39)," *EB*
44 (1986): 117-46.

8:26-37
0997   Tjitze Baarda, "Gadarenes, Gerasenes, Gergesenes and the
'Diatessaron' Traditions," in E. Earle Ellis and M. Wilcox, eds.,
Neotestamentica et Semitica (festschrift for Matthew Black).
London: T. &. T. Clark, 1969. Pp. 181-97.

8:33
0998   C. H. Cave, "The Obedience of Unclean Spirits," *NTS* 11
(1964-1965): 93-97.

8:36
0999   E. Käsemann, "Die Heilung der Besessenen," *Reformatio* 28
(1979): 7-18.

8:40-56
1000   L. Dambrine, "Guérison de la femme hémorroïsse et résurrection de la fille de Jaïre. Un aspect de la lecture d'un texte: Mc 5:21-43; Mt 9:18-26; Lc 8:40-56," *FV* 70 (1971): 75-81.

1001   O. Genest, "De la fille à lafemme à la fille (Luc 8,40-56)," in *De Jésus et des femmes: Lectures sémiotiques.* Paris: Cerf, 1987. Pp. 105-20.

8:41-56
1002   Hieromonk Gavriil, "24th Sunday After Pentecost: Faith and Obedience," *JMP* 11 (1985): 68.

1003   Dominique Hermant, "Le femme au flux de sang et la fille de Jaïre (Mt 9:18-26; Mc 5:22-43; Lc 8:41-56)," *BLOS* 5 (1990): 8-16.

8:41
1004   Rudolf Pesch, "Jarius (Mk 5:22/Lk 8:41)," *BZ* 14/2 (1970): 252-56.

8:42-48
1005   S. T. Kimbrough, "Preachers: Actors in a Drama," *ChrM* 16/2 (1985): 22-24.

8:43-48
1006   T. McCaughey, "Paradigms of Faith in the Gospel of St. Luke," *ITQ* 45 (1978): 177-84.

1007   Jyotsna Chatterji, "Our Struggle for Wholeness: A Bible Study," *RS* 36 (1989): 37-40.

8:52
1008   R. C. Fuller, "The Healing of Jairus' Daughter," *Scr* 3 (1948): 53.

9-10
1009   Michael D. Goulder, "From Ministry to Passion in John and Luke," *NTS* 29 (1983): 561-68.

9:1-50
1010   Wilhelm Wilkens, "Die Auslassung von Mark 6:45-8:26 bei Lukas im Lichte der Komposition Luke 9:1-50," *TZ* 32 (1976): 193-200.

1011 David P. Moessner, "Luke 9:1-50: Luke's Preview of the Journey of the Prophet Like Moses of Deuteronomy," *JBL* 102 (1983): 575-605.

1012 Robert F. O'Toole, "Luke's Message in Luke 9,1-50," *CBQ* 49 (1987): 74-89.

9:1-34

1013 J. G. Davies, "The Prefigurement of the Ascension in the Third Gospel," *JTS* 6 (1955): 229-33.

9:1-6

1014 Gregory Murray, "Did Luke Use Mark?" *DR* 104 (1986): 268-71.

9:1

1015 Michael D. Goulder, "On Putting Q to the Test," *NTS* 24 (1977-1978): 218-34.

9:3

1016 Tijitze J. Baarda, " 'A Staff Only, Not a Stick': Disharmony of the Gospels and the Harmony of Tatian (Matthew 10,9f.; Mark 6:8; Luke 9,3 and 10,4)," in *The New Testament in Early Christianity: La réception des écrits néotestamentaires dans le christianism primitif.* BETL #86. Louvain: University Press/Peeters Press, 1989. Pp. 311-33.

9:5

1017 Édouard Delebecque, "Sur un hellénisme de Saint Luc," *RB* 87 (1980): 590-93.

1018 Édouard Delebecque, " 'Secouez la Poussiere de vos Pieds . . . sur l'Hellenisme de Luc IX,5," *RB* 89/2 (1982): 177-84.

9:7-62

1019 D. A. S. Ravens, "Luke 9:7-62 and the Prophetic Role of Jesus," *NTS* 36 (1990): 119-29.

9:7-9

1020 Vyacheslav Reznikov, "On the Day of the Beheading of St. John the Baptist," *JMP* 8 (1984): 48-49.

1021 Philippe Rolland, "La question synoptique demande-t-elle une response compliquee?" *Bib* 70/2 (1989): 217-23.

9:10-17
1022 William R. Stegner, "Lucan Priority in the Feeding of the Five Thousand," *BR* 21 (1976): 19-28.

1023 J. P. Sauzède, "Une série pour le Carême," *ÉTR* 58 (1983): 59-71.

1024 Jonathan Krogh, "The Trouble With Leftovers: Tupperware Faith," *Crit* 24/2 (1985): 13-14.

1025 Joseph A. Grassi, *Loaves and Fishes: The Gospel Feeding Narratives*. Collegeville MN: Liturgical Press, 1991.

9:10-11
1026 M.-É. Boismard, "The Two-Source Theory at an Impasse," *NTS* 26 (1979-1980): 1-17.

1027 Franz Neirynck, "The Matthew-Luke Agreements in Matt 14:13-14 and Lk 9:10-11 (Par. Mk 6:30-34): The Two Source Theory Behind the Impasse," *ETL* 60/1 (1984): 25-44.

9:11-17
1028 F. Prod'homme, "Le pain qui rassasie les multitudes (Lc 9)," *AsSeign* N.S. 32 (1971): 55-67.

9:11-13
1029 Philippe Rolland, "L'arrière-fond sémitique des évangiles synoptiques," *ETL* 60 (1984): 358-62.

9:13
1030 Joseph A. Grassi, " 'You Yourselves Give Them to Eat': An Easily Forgotten Command of Jesus," *BibTo* 97 (1978): 1704-1709.

9:14
1031 Ernst Bammel, "The Feeding of the Multitude," in E. Bammel and C. F. D. Moule, eds., *Jesus and the Politics of His Day*. Cambridge: University Press, 1984. Pp. 211-40.

9:16
1032 S. Brock, "Note on Luke 9:16 [Codex Bezae Cantabrigiensis]," *JTS* 14 (1963): 391-93.

9:18-45

1033 Oscar H. Hirt, "Interpretation in the Gospels: An Examination of the Use of Redaction Criticism in Mark 8:27-9:32," doctoral dissertation, Dallas Theological Seminary, Dallas TX, 1985.

9:18-27

1034 Hartwig Thyen, "Das Petrusbekenntnis von Caesarea-Philippi: Mk. 8,27-9,1 parr.," in *Studien zur Sündenvergebung.* Göttingen: Vandenhoeck & Ruprecht, 1970. Pp. 218-36.

1035 M. Corbin, "Le Christ de Dieu. Méditation théologique sur Luc 9:18-27," *NRT* 99 (1977): 641-80.

1036 M. J. Kingston, "Suffering," *ET* 94 (1982-1983): 144-45.

9:18-24

1037 D. E. Miller, "Luke 9:18-24," *Int* 37 (1983): 64-68.

9:18-22

1038 B. Willaert, "La connexion litteraire entre la premiere prediction de la passion et la confession de Pierre chez les synoptiques," *ETL* 32 (1956): 24-45.

1039 A. Vögtle, "Messiasbekenntnis und Petrusverheissung. Zur Komposition Mt 16,13-23 par," *BZ* NF 1 (1957): 252-72; 2 (1958): 85-103.

1040 A. Denaux, "Petrusbelijdenis en eerste lijdensvoorspelling. Een exegese van Mc. 8,27-33 par. Lc. 9,18-22," *CBG* 15 (1969): 188-220.

1041 J. Guillet, "La confession de Césaree," in *Jésus devant sa vie et sa mort.* Paris: Aubier, 1971. Pp. 117-35.

9:20

1042 Rudolf Bultmann, "Die Frage nach dem messianischen Bewusstsein Jesu und das Petrus-Bekenntnis," *ZNW* 19 (1919-1920): 165-74.

9:22

1043 John M. Perry, "The Three Days in the Synoptic Passion Predictions," *CBQ* 48/4 (1986): 637-54.

1044 Frans Neirynck and Timothy A. Friedrichsen, "Note on Luke 9:22," *ETL* 65/4 (1989): 390-94.

9:23-24
1045 David H. C. Read, "At the Centre of the Self," *ET* 5 (1986): 142-44.

9:23
1046 D. R. Fletcher, "Condemned to Die. The Logion on Cross-Bearing: What Does It Mean?" *Int* 18 (1964): 156-64.

1047 Josef G. Plöger, "Kreuzesnachfolge: Nachdenkliches zu einem leicht überhörten Herrenwort (Lk 9,23)," in Johannes J. Degenhardt, ed., *Die Freude an Gott: Unsere Kraft* (festschrift for Otto B. Knoch). Stuttgart: Verlag Katholisches Bibelwerk, 1991. Pp. 319-35.

9:24
1048 C. Stephen Finley, "Greater Than Tongue Can Tell: Carlyle and Ruskin on the Nature of Christian Heroism," *CL* 34/4 (1985): 27-40.

9:25
1049 José O'Callaghan, "Nota Critica a Mc 8,36," *Bib* 64/1 (1983): 116-17.

9:27-36
1050 R. H. Gause, "The Lukan Transfiguration Account (Luke 9:27-36): Luke's Pre-Crucifixion Presentation of the Exalted Lord in the Story of the Kingdom of God," doctoral dissertation, Emory University, Atlanta GA, 1975.

9:27
1051 J. D. Kaestli, "Luc 9:27: Certains ne goûteront pas la mort avant d'avoir vu le Royaume de Dieu," in *L'eschatologie dans l'oeuvre de Luc*. Genève: Labor et Fides, 1969. Pp. 17-18.

1052 C. L. Holman, "The Idea of an Imminent Parousia in the Synoptic Gospels," *SBT* 3 (1973): 15-31.

9:28-37

1053   R. Silva, "El relato de la transfiguración. Problemas de crítica
       literaria y motivos teológicos en Mc 9,2-10; Mt 17,1-9; Lc
       9,28-37," *Comp* 10 (1965): 5-26.

9:28-36

1054   Heinrich Baltensweiler, *Die Verklärung Jesu: Historisches Ereignis
       und synoptische Berichte.* Zürich: Zwingli, 1959.

1055   M. Coune, "Radieuse Transfiguration. Mt 17,1-9; Mc 9,2-10; Lc
       9,28-36," *AsSeign* 15 (1973): 44-84.

1056   Frans Neirynck, "Minor Agreements: Matthew-Luke in the
       Transfiguration Story," in *Orientierung an Jesus: Zur Theologie
       der Synoptiker* (festschrift for Josef Schmid). Freiburg: Herder,
       1973. Pp. 253-66.

1057   Daniel H. Pokorny, "The Transfiguration of Our Lord," *CJ* 11
       (1985): 17-18.

1058   Barbara Reid, "The Transfiguration: An Exegetical Study of Luke
       9:28-36," doctoral dissertation, Catholic University of America,
       Washington DC, 1988.

1059   Barbara Reid, "Voices and Angels: What Were They Talking
       About at the Transfiguration? A Redaction-Critical Study of Luke
       9:28-36," *BR* 34 (1989): 19-31.

1060   Michael Rogness, "The Transfiguration of Our Lord: Luke
       9:28-36," *WW* 9 (1989): 71-75.

9:28-31

1061   F. V. Pratt, "The Exodus of Jesus (Lk 9,28-31)," *ET* 41
       (1929-1930): 376-77.

9:31

1062   J. Manek, "The New Exodus of the Books of Luke," *NovT* 2
       (1957-1958): 8-23.

1063   André Feuillet, "L' 'Exode' de Jésus et le déroulement du mystère
       rédempteur d'après S. Luc et S. Jean," *RT* 77 (1977): 181-206.

1064   J. D. Yoder, "The Exodus of Jerusalem," *EJ* 4 (1986): 51-69.

1065 Susan R. Garrett, "Exodus from Bondage: Luke 9:31 and Acts 12:1-24," *CBQ* 52 (1990): 656-80.

9:33
1066 José O'Callaghan, "Discusion Critica en Mt 17,4," *Bib* 65/1 (1984): 91-93.

9:34
1067 Michael D. Goulder, "On Putting Q to the Test," *NTS* 24 (1977-1978): 218-34.

9:37-43
1068 Hermann Aichinger, "Zur Traditionsgeschichte der Epileptiker-Perikope Mk 9,14-29 par Mt 17,14-21 par Lk 9,37-43a," *SNTU-A* 3 (1978): 114-43.

9:44
1069 M. Bastin, "L'annonce de la passion et les critères de l'historicité," *RevSR* 50 (1976): 289-329.

9:46-56
1070 J. Kodell, "Luke and the Children: The Beginning and End of the Great Interpolation (Luke 9:46-56; 18:9-23)," *CBQ* 49 (1987): 415-30.

9:46-50
1071 B. C. Butler, "M. Vaganay and the 'Community Discourse'," *NTS* 1 (1954-1955): 283-90.

1072 David Wenham, "A Note on Mark 9:33-42/Matt. 18:1-6/Luke 9:46-50," *JSNT* 14 (1982): 113-18.

9:46-48
1073 Simon Légasse, "Le debat sur 'le plus grand': Marc, ix,33-37 et paralleles," in *Jésus et l'enfant*. Paris: Gabalda, 1969. Pp. 17-36.

1074 Dominique Hermant, "La première scene d'enfants (Mt 18,1-5; Mc 9,33-37; Lc 9,46-48)," *BLOS* 3 (1990): 7-11.

9:50
1075 Heinrich Baltensweiler, " 'Wer nicht gegen uns (euch) ist, ist für uns (euch)': Bemerkungen zu Mk 9,40 und Lk 9,50," *TZ* 40 (1984): 130-36.

1076　H. B. Green, "Matthew 12,22-50 and Parallels: An Alternative to Matthean Conflation," in C. M. Tuckett, ed., *Synoptic Studies.* Sheffield: JSOT Press, 1984. Pp. 157-76.

9:51-19:48

1077　Helmut L. Egelkraut, *Jesus' Mission to Jerusalem: A Redaction-Critical Study of the Travel Narrative in the Gospel of Luke.* Bern: Lang, 1976.

1078　W. A. Beardslee, "Saving One's Life By Losing It," *JAAR* 47 (1979): 57-72.

9:51-19:46

1079　J. H. Davies, "The Purpose of the Central Section of St. Luke's Gospel," *StudE* 3 (1964): 164-69.

1080　Michael D. Goulder, "The Chiastic Structure of the ·Lucan Journey," *StudE* 3 (1964): 195-202.

1081　Paul Kariamadam, "The Composition and Meaning of the Lucan Travel Narrative (Luke 9,51-19,46)," *BB* 13 (1987): 179-98.

9:51-19:44

1082　James L. Resseguie, "Interpretation of Luke's Central Section (Luke 9:51-19:44) Since 1856," *SBT* 5/2 (1975): 3-36.

1083　James L. Resseguie, "Point of View in the Central Section of Luke (9:51-19:44)," *JETS* 25 (1982): 41-47.

1084　H. K. Farrel, "The Structure and Theology of Luke's Central Section," *TriJ* 7 (1986): 33-54.

9:51-19:28

1085　Gerhard Sellin, "Komposition, Quellen und Funktion des Lukanischen Reiseberichtes," *NovT* 20 (1978): 100-35.

1086　J. L. Espinel, "La vida-viaje ·de Jesús hacia Jerusalén (Luke 9:51-19:28)," *CuBí* 37 (1980): 29-38.

9:51-19:27

1087　H. LaPointe, "L'espace-temps de Lc 9,51-19,27," *ÉgT* 1 (1970): 275-90.

1088 G. Ogg, "The Central Section of the Gospel according to St. Luke," *NTS* 18 (1971-1972): 39-53.

1089 G. W. Trompf, "La section médiane de l'évangile de Luc: L'organisation des documents," *RHPR* 53 (1973): 141-54.

9:51-18:15
1090 W. Grundmann, "Fragen der Komposition des lukanischen 'Reiseberichts'," *ZNW* 50 (1959): 252-70.

9:51-18:14
1091 W. Gasse, "Zum Reisebericht des Lukas," *ZNW* 34 (1935): 293-99.

1092 C. C. McCown, "The Geography of Luke's Central Section," *JBL* 57 (1938): 51-66.

1093 L. Girard, *L'évangile des voyages de Jésus ou la section 9,51-18,14 de saint Luc*. Paris: Gabalda, 1951.

1094 J. Leal, "Los viajes de Jesús a Jerusalén según San Lucas," in *Valoración sobrenatural del "cosmos": La inspiración bíblica*. Madrid: Científica Medinaceli, 1954. Pp. 365-82.

1095 Bo Reicke, "Instruction and Discussion in the Travel Narrative," *StudE* 1 (1959): 206-16.

1096 Mauro Láconi, "Il 'grande inciso' di Luca," in *Il Messaggio della salvezza*. 5 vols. Torino: Leumann, 1966-1970. 4:433-42.

1097 J. Blinzler, "Der Reisebericht im Lukasevangelium," in *Aus der Welt und Um welt des Neuen Testaments*. Stuttgart: Katholisches Bibelwerk, 1969. Pp. 62-93.

1098 D. Gill, "Observations on the Lukan Travel Narrative and Some Related Passages," *HTR* 63 (1970): 199-221.

1099 P. von der Osten-Sacken, "Zur Christologie des lukanischen Reiseberichts," *EvT* 33 (1973): 476-96.

1100 G. W. Trompf, "La section médiane de l'évangile de Luc: L'organisation des documents," *RHPR* 53 (1973): 141-54.

1101   Morton S. Enslin, "The Samaritan Ministry and Mission," *HUCA* 51 (1980): 29-38.

1102   John W. Wenham, "Synoptic Independence and the Origin of Luke's Travel Narrative," *NTS* 27 (1980-1981): 507-15.

1103   A. J. Tankersley, "Preaching the Christian Deuteronomy: Luke 9:51-18:14," doctoral dissertation, Claremont School of Theology, Claremont CA, 1983.

9:51-10:24
1104   M. Miyoshi, *Ler Anfang des Reiseberichts, Lk 9,51-10,24.* Rome: Biblical Institute Press, 1974.

1105   P. Bony, "Les disciples en situation d'envoyés: Une lecture de Lc 9,51-10,24," *BSS* 8 (1982): 130-51.

9:51-62
1106   W. Hülsbusch, "Mit Jesus auf dem Weg nach Jerusalem," *BL* 12 (1971): 121-26.

1107   J. W. Drane, "Simon the Samaritan and the Lucan Concept of Salvation History," *EQ* 47 (1975): 131-37.

1108   B. G. Powley, "Time and Place," *ET* 94 (1983): 371-72.

9:51-56
1109   D. Flusser, "Lukas 9:51-56: ein hebräisches Fragment," in William C. Weinrich, ed., *The New Testament Age* (festschrift for Bo Reicke). 2 vols. Macon GA: Mercer University Press, 1984. 1:165-79.

1110   Thomas L. Brodie, "The Departure for Jerusalem (Luke 9:51-56) as a Rhetorical Imitation of Elijah's Departure for the Jordan (2 Kgs 1:1-2:6)," *Bib* 70/1 (1989): 96-109.

9:51
1111   G. Friedrich, "Lk 9,51 und die Entrückungschristologie des Lukas," in *Orientierung an Jesus: Zur Theologie der Synoptiker* (festschrift for Josef Schmid). Freiburg: Herder, 1973. Pp. 48-77.

1112   André Feuillet, "L' 'Exode' de Jésus et le déroulement du mystère rédempteur d'après S. Luc et S. Jean," *RT* 77 (1977): 181-206.

1113   J. Rius-Camps, "El καὶ αὐτός en los encabezamientos lucanos, ¿una fórmula anadórica?" *FilN* 2 (1989): 187-92.

9:52-11:36
1114   F. Katz, "Luke 9,52-11,36: Beobachtungen zur Logienquelle und ihrer hellenistisch-judenchristlichen Redaktion," doctoral dissertation, University of Mainz, 1973.

9:52-56
1115   C. Kenneth Lysons, "The Seven Deadly Sins Today, Pt. 3: Anger," *ET* 97/10 (1985-1986): 302-304.

9:54-56
1116   J. M. Ross, "The Rejected Words of Luke 9,54-56," *ET* 84 (1972-1973): 85-88.

9:57-62
1117   C. Küven, "Weisung für die Nachfolge. Eine Besinnung über Luke 9:57-62," *BibL* 2 (1961): 49-52.

1118   Otto Glombitza, "Die christologische Aussage des Lukas in seiner Gestaltung der drei Nachfolgeworte Lukas IX,57-62," *NovT* 13 (1971): 14-23.

1119   Thomas L. Brodie, "Luke 9:57-62: A Systematic Adaptation of the Divine Challenge to Elijah (1 Kings 19)," *SBLSP* 19 (1989): 237-45.

1120   Harry Fleddermann, "The Demands of Discipleship. Matt 8,19-22 par. Luke 9,57-62," in F. van Segbroeck, et al., eds., *The Four Gospels 1992* (festschrift for Frans Neirynck). 3 vols. BETL #100. Louvain: Peeters Press, 1992. 1:541-61.

9:57-58
1121   Leif E. Vaage, "Q and the Historical Jesus: Some Peculiar Sayings," *Forum* 5 (1989): 159-76.

9:58
1122   P. Maurice Casey, "The Son of Man Problem," *ZNW* 67/3 (1976): 147-54.

1123   P. Maurice Casey, "The Jackals and the Son of Man (Matt. 8.20//Luke 9.58)," *JSNT* 23 (1985): 3-22.

1124 Peter Lampe, "Fremdsein Als Urchristlicher Lebensaspekt," *Reformatio* 34/1 (1985): 58-62.

1125 Mahlon H. Smith, "No Place for a Son of Man," *Forum* 4/4 (1988): 83-107.

9:60

1126 H. G. Klemm, "Das Wort von der Selbstbestattung der Toten," *NTS* 16 (1969-1970): 60-75.

9:61-62

1127 Michael G. Steinhauser, "Putting One's Hand to the Plow: The Authenticity of Q 9:61-62," *Forum* 5 (1989): 151-58.

9:61

1128 Édouard Delebecque, "Sur un hellénisme de Saint Luc," *RB* 87 (1980): 590-93.

9:62

1129 H. J. Blair, "Putting One's Hand to the Plough," *ET* 79 (1967-1968): 342-43.

1130 Wanis A. Semaan, "Some Are Called; Others Volunteer," *TR* 61 (1985): 3-5.

10:1-24

1131 R. J. Dillon, "Early Christian Experience in the Gospel Sayings," *BibTo* 21 (1983): 83-88.

10:1-20

1132 A. Lignee, "La mission des soixante-douze (Lc 10)," *AsSeign* N.S. 45 (1974): 64-74.

10:1-7

1133 Rudolf Schnackenburg, "Zur Traditionsgeschichte von Joh 4,46-54," *BZ* 8 (1964): 58-88.

10:1

1134 Bruce M. Metzger, "Seventy or Seventy-Two Disciples," *NTS* 5 (1958-1959): 299-306.

1135 S. Jellicoe, "St. Luke and the Seventy(-Two)," *NTS* 6 (1959-1960): 319-21.

10:2-16

1136 Arland D. Jacobson, "The Literary Unity of Q: Lc 10,2-16 and Parallels as a Test Case," in J. Delobel, ed., *Logia: Les paroles de Jésus (The Sayings of Jesus)*. BETL #59. Louvain: Peeters Press, 1982. Pp. 419-23.

1137 Ulrich Luz, "Q 10:2-16; 11:14-23," *SBLSP* 15 (1985): 101-102.

1138 James M. Robinson, "The Mission and Beelzebul: Pap Q 10:2-16; 11:14-23," *SBLSP* 15 (1985): 97-99.

10:2

1139 H.-J. Venetz, "Bitlel den Herrn der Ernte: Überlegungen zu Lk 10,2 // Mt 9,37," *Diakonia* 11 (1980): 148-61.

10:4

1140 A. O'Hagan, "Greet No One on the Way (Lk 10,4b)," *SBFLA* 16 (1965-1966): 69-84.

1141 I. Bosold, *Pazifsmus und prophetische Provokahon: Das Grußverbot Lk 10,4b und sein historischer Kontext.* SBS #90. Stuttgart: Katholisches Bibelwerk, 1978.

1142 Bernhard Lang, "Grussverbot oder Besuchsverbot?" *BZ* 26 (1982): 75-79.

1143 Tijitze J. Baarda, " 'A Staff Only, Not a Stick': Disharmony of the Gospels and the Harmony of Tatian (Matthew 10,9f.; Mark 6:8; Luke 9,3 and 10,4)," in *The New Testament in Early Christianity: La réception des écrits néotestamentaires dans le christianism primitif.* BETL #86. Louvain: University Press/Peeters Press, 1989. Pp. 311-33.

10:6

1144 William Klassen, " 'A Child of Peace' in First Century Context," *NTS* 27 (1980-1981): 488-506.

10:7

1145 Édouard Delebecque, "Sur un hellénisme de Saint Luc," *RB* 87 (1980): 590-93.

1146 A. E. Harvey, " 'The Workman is Worthy of His Hire': Fortunes of a Proverb in the Early Church," *NovT* 2 (1982): 209-21.

1147   Günther Schwarz, "Τῆς τροφῆς αὐτοῦ oder τῆς μισθοῦ αὐτοῦ?" *BibN* 56 (1991): 25.

10:9

1148   F. Schulz, " 'Die Gottesherrschaft ist nahe herbeigekommen': Der kerygmatische Entwurf der Q-Gemeinde Syriens," in H. Balz and S. Schulz, eds., *Das Wort und die Wörter* (festschrift for G. Friedrich). Stuttgart: Kohlhammer, 1973. Pp. 57-68.

10:11

1149   A. Viard, "Eigences de la vie chrétienne," *EV* 87 (1977): 345-48.

10:13

1150   A. George, "Paroles de Jésus sur ses miracles (Mt 11,5.21; 12,27.28 et par.)," in Jacques Dupont, ed., *Jésus aux origines de la christologie*. BETL #40. Louvain: Peeters Press, 1975. Pp. 283-302.

1151   M. Miyoshi, "Das jüdische Gebet Sema und die Abfolge der Traditionsstücke in Luke 10:13," *AJBI* 7 (1981): 70-123.

10:16

1152   H. Helbling, "Hören und Gehörtwerden. Eine biblische Meditation," *FZPT* 24 (1977): 3-6.

1153   A. Houtepen, "Eigentijds Leergezag: Een Oecumenische Discussie," *TijT* 18/1 (1978): 26-47.

10:17-20

1154   David Crump, "Jesus: The Victorious Scribal-Intercessor in Luke's Gospel," *NTS* 38 (1992): 51-65.

10:18

1155   U. B. Müller, "Vision und Botschaft. Erwägungen zur prophetischen Struktur der Verkündigung Jesu," *ZTK* 74 (1977): 416-48.

1156   A. Puig i Tárrech, "Lc 10,18: La visió de la caíguda de Satanàs," *RCT* 3 (1978): 217-43.

1157   Samuel Vollenweider, "Ich Sah Den Satan wie Einen Blitz vom Himmel Fallen (Lk. 10:18)," *ZNW* 79/3-4 (1988): 187-203.

1158 Julian V. Hills, "Luke 10:18—Who Saw Satan Fall?" *JSNT* 46 (1992): 25-40.

10:19
1159 Pierre Grelot, "Étude critique de Luc 10:19," *RechSR* 69 (1981): 87-100.

10:20-24
1160 L. Randellini, "L'inno di giubulo: Mt. 11,25-30; Lc. 10,20-24," *RBib* 22 (1974): 183-235.

10:20
1161 E. Käsemann, "Die Heilung der Besessenen," *Reformatio* 28 (1979): 7-18.

1162 Oda Hagemeyer, " 'Freut euch, dass eure Namen im Himmel verzeichnet sind'!" *HD* 39 (1985): 160-63.

10:21-24
1163 Peter Richardson, "The Thunderbolt in Q and the Wise Man in Corinth," in P. Richardson and J. C. Hurd, eds., *From Jesus to Paul* (festschrift for F. W. Beare). Waterloo: Laurier University Press, 1984. Pp. 91-111.

10:21-22
1164 Harold A. Guy, "Matthew 11,25-27; Luke 10,21-22," *ET* 49 (1937-1938): 236-37.

1165 Simon Légasse, "La révélation aux 'simples' et l'appel aux 'accablés' (Mt., xi,25-30)," in *Jesus et l'enfant*. Paris: Gabalda, 1969. Pp. 231-46.

1166 André Feuillet, "Comparaison avec les synoptiques: L'hymbe de jubilation (Mt 11,25-30; Lc 10,21-22)," in *Le mystère de l'amour divin dans la théologie johannique*. Paris: Gabalda, 1972. Pp. 133-77.

1167 P. Hoffmann, "Die Apokalypsis des Sohnes," in *Studien zur Theologie der Logienquelle*. Münster: Aschendorff, 1972. Pp. 102-42.

1168   R. Garrison, "Matthew 11:25-27, Luke 10:21-22: A Bridge between the Synoptic and Johannine Traditions," doctoral dissertation, Oxford University, 1979.

1169   K. J. Scaria, "Jesus' Prayer and Christian Prayer," *BB* 7 (1981): 160-85, 201-24.

1170   J. Gibert, "La prière d'action de grace de Jésus dans son contexte lucanien (Lc 10,21-22)," in *Qu'est-ce que Dieu? Philosophie-Théologie* (festschrift for D. Coppieters de Gibson). Brussels: Faculty of the University of St. Louis, 1985. Pp. 613-35.

10:21

1171   W. Marchel, "Le terme 'Abba' expression des aspects originaux de la priere de Jésus au Père (Mt 11,25.26; Lc 10,21)," in *Abba, Pere! La prière du Christ et des chrétiens*. Rome: Biblical Institute Press, 1963. Pp. 150-71.

1172   A. Stöger, "Jesu Jubelruf: Quell seiner Freude. Meditation über Lk 10,21f.," *BL* 50 (1977): 187-91.

1173   A. F. J. Klijn, "Matthew 11:25/Luke 10:21," in Elton J. Epp and Gordon D. Fee, eds., *New Testament Textual Criticism* (festschrift for Bruce M. Metzger). Oxford: Clarendon Press, 1981. Pp. 1-14.

10:22

1174   E. Percy, "Der Vater und der Sohn (Mt 11,27; Lk 10,22)," in *Die Botschaft Jesu*. Lund: Gleerup, 1953. Pp. 259-71.

1175   Paul Winter, "Matthew 11:27 and Luke 10:22 from the First to the Fifth Century: Reflections on the Development of the Text," *NovT* 1 (1956): 112-48.

1176   W. Grundmann, "Die *nēpioi* in der Urchristlichen Paranese," *NTS* 5 (1958-1959): 188-205.

1177   Jesse Sell, "Johannine Traditions in Logion 61 of the Gospel of Thomas," *PRS* 7/1 (1980): 24-37.

1178   M. Sabbe, "Can Mt 11,25-27 and Lk 10,22 Be Called a Johannine Logion?" in J. Delobel, ed., *Logia: Les paroles de Jésus (The Sayings of Jesus)*. BETL #59. Louvain: Peeters Press, 1982. Pp. 363-71.

1179 A. Denaux, "The Q-Logion Mt 11,27/Lk 10,22 and the Gospel of John," in Adelbert Denaux, ed., *John and the Synoptics*. BETL #101. Louvain: Peeters Press, 1992. Pp. 163-200.

10:23-37
1180 E. Galbiati, "Esegesi degli Evangeli festivi," *BibO* 1 (1959): 17-19.

10:23-24
1181 W. Grimm, "Selige Augenzeugen, Luk. 10,23f. Alttestamentlicher Hintergrund und ursprünglicher Sinn," *TZ* 26 (1970): 172-83.

1182 Patrick Tishel, "The Parable of the Good Samaritan," *Epi* 6/2 (1985): 6-9.

1183 M. Eugene Boring, "A Proposed Reconstruction of Q: 10:23-24," *SBLSP* 18 (1988): 456-71.

10:24-42
1184 Bruno Corsani, "Ascolto della parola e vita cristiana nell'opera di Luca," in M. Angelini, et al., eds., *Testimonium Christi* (festschrift for Jacques Dupont). Brescia: Paideia, 1985. Pp. 141-49.

10:25-18:30
1185 J. Rius-Camps, "Lc 10,25-18,30: una perfecta estructura concéntrica dins la secció del viatge," *RCT* 8 (1983): 283-357.

10:25-38
1186 Browning Ware, "Preaching to the Power Brokers," *FM* 3/1 (1985): 50-56.

10:25-37
1187 C. H. Lindijer, "Oude en Nieuwe Visies op de Gelijkenis van de Barmhartige Samaritaan," *NedTT* 15 (1960): 11-23.

1188 Robert W. Funk, " 'How Do You Read?' A Sermon on Luke 10:25-37," *Int* 18 (1964): 56-61.

1189 Christoph Burchard, "Das doppelte Liebesgebot in der fruhen christlichen Uberlieferung," in E. Lohse, et al., eds., *Der Ruf Jesu und die Antwort der Gemeinde*. Göttingen: Vandenhoeck & Ruprecht, 1970. Pp. 39-62.

1190   H. Zimmermann, "Das Gleichnis vom barmherzigen Samariter: Lk 10,25-37," in E. Lohse, et al., eds., *Der Ruf Jesu und die Antwort der Gemeinde.* Göttingen: Vandenhoeck & Ruprecht, 1970. Pp. 58-69.

1191   G. Eichholz, "Vom barmherzigen Samariter (Luk. 10,25-37)," in *Gleichnisse der Evangelien.* Neukirchen-Vluyn: Neukirchener Verlag, 1971. Pp. 147-78.

1192   Erhardt Güttgemanns, "Narrative Analyse Synoptischer Texte," *LB* 25/26 (1973): 50-73.

1193   G. Crespy, "The Parable of the Good Samaritan: An Essay in Structural Research," trans. John Kirby, *Semeia* 2 (1974): 27-50.

1194   John Dominic Crossan, "The Good Samaritan: Towards a Generic Definition of Parable," *Semeia* 2 (1974): 82-112.

1195   Robert W. Funk, "The Good Samaritan as Metaphor," *Semeia* 2 (1974): 74-81.

1196   Jan Lambrecht, "The Message of the Good Samaritan," *LouvS* 5 (1974): 121-35.

1197   Daniel Patte, "An Analysis of Narrative Structure and the Good Samaritan," *Semeia* 2 (1974): 1-26.

1198   Daniel Patte, "Comments on the Article of John Dominic Crossan," *Semeia* 2 (1974): 117-21.

1199   Gerhard Sellin, "Lukas als Gleichniserzählen: Die Erzählung vom barmherzigen Samariter (Lk 10,25-37)," *ZNW* 65 (1974): 166-89.

1200   Robert C. Tannehill, "Comments on the Articles of Daniel Patte and John Dominic Crossan," *Semeia* 2 (1974): 113-16.

1201   P. Ternant, "Le bon Samaritain (Lc 10)," *AsSeign* N.S. 46 (1974): 66-77.

1202   Daniel Patte, "Structural Network in Narrative: The Good Samaritan," *Soundings* 58 (1975): 221-42.

1203   Jean Delorme, "Linguistique, Sémiotique, Exégèse: à propos du
        Séminaire de Durham," *SémBib* 6 (1977): 35-59.

1204   Dietfried Gewalt, "Der 'Barmherzige Samariter': Zu Lukas
        10:25-37," *EvT* 38 (1978): 403-17.

1205   Robert H. Stein, "The Interpretation of the Parable of the Good
        Samaritan," in W. W. Gasque, ed., *Scripture, Tradition, and
        Interpretation* (festschrift for E. F. Harrison). Grand Rapids MI:
        Eerdmans, 1978. Pp. 278-95.

1206   R. Kieffer, "Analyse sémiotique et commentaire. Quelques
        réflexions à propos d'études de Luc 10:25-37," *NTS* 25 (1979):
        454-68.

1207   Peter R. Jones, "The Love Command in Parable: Luke 10:25-37,"
        PRS 6 (1979): 224-42.

1208   Walter Wink, "The Parable of the Compassionate Samaritan: A
        Communal Exegesis Approach," *RevExp* 76 (1979): 199-217.

1209   M. J. Kingston, "Love Cannot Be Contained By Rules," *ET* 91
        (1979-1980): 339-40.

1210   André Feuillet, "Le bon Samaritain (Luc 10,25-37): Sa
        signification christologique et l'universalisme de Jésus," *EV* 90
        (1980): 337-51.

1211   N. Heutger, "Die lukanischen Samaritanererzählungen in
        religionspädagogischer Sicht," in W. Haubeck and M. Bachmann,
        eds., *Wort in der Zeit* (festschrift for K. H. Rengstorf). Leiden:
        Brill, 1980. Pp. 275-87.

1212   H. Servotte and L. Verbeek, "De strukturalistische bijbellezing,"
        CollV 10 (1980): 426-41.

1213   Robert W. Funk, "The Prodigal Samaritan," *JAAR* 48 (1981):
        83-97.

1214   H.-J. Venetz, "Theologische Grundstrukturen in der Verkündigung
       Jesu? Ein Vergleich von Mk 10,17-22; Lk 10,25-37 und Mt
       5,21-48," in P. Casetti, et al., eds., *Mélanges Dominique
       Barthélemy*. Orbis Biblicus et Orientalis #38. Göttingen:
       Vandenhoeck, 1981. Pp. 613-50.

1215   P. Jones, "La parabole du fils prodigue: deux méthodes
       d'interprétation," *RevRef* 34 (1983): 122-37.

1216   T. Sorg, "Zwischen Jerusalem und Jericho: Predigt über Lukas
       10,25-37," *TBe* 14 (1983): 1-5.

1217   Dennis M. Sweetland, "The Good Samaritan and Martha and
       Mary," *BibTo* 21 (1983): 325-30.

1218   N. H. Young, "The Commandment to Love Your Neighbour as
       Yourself and the Parable of the Good Samaritan," *AUSS* 21
       (1983): 265-72.

1219   Peter R. Jones, "The Compassionate Samaritan," in James C.
       Barry, ed., *Preaching in Today's World*. Nashville: Broadman
       Press, 1984. Pp. 83-89.

1220   F. S. Spencer, "Chronicles 28:5-15 and the Parable of the Good
       Samaritan," *WTJ* 46 (1984): 317-49.

1221   P. Y. Bourdil, "L'église, un Monde et sa Pensée," *RHPR* 65/3
       (1985): 297-314.

1222   Medardo Gómez, "Forbidden to be a Samaritan," *TSR* 7/1 (1985):
       14-17.

1223   W. R. Stenger, "The Parable of the Good Samaritan and Leviticus
       18:5," in D. E. Groh and Robert Jewett, eds., *The Living Text*
       (festschrift for E. W. Saunders). Lanham MD: University Press of
       America, 1985. Pp. 27-38.

1224   Frederick C. Bauerschmidt, "Doing Theology in Light of Divine
       Aniconicity," *SLJT* 29/2 (1986): 117-35.

1225   William R. Herzog, "The New Testament and the Question of
       Racial Injustice," *ABQ* 5/1 (1986): 12-32.

1226 A. van Schaik, "De barmhartige Samaritaan (Lc 10,25-37)," in B. van Iersel, et al., *Parabelverhalen in Lucas: Van semiotiek naar pragmatiek.* TFT-Studies #8. Tilburg: University Press, 1987. Pp. 55-82.

1227 Stephen F. Noll, "The Good Samaritan and Justification by Faith," *MM* 8 (1990): 36-37.

1228 Pamela Thimmes, "The Language of Community: Metaphors, Systems of Convictions, Ethnic, and Gender Issues in Luke 10:25-37 and 10:38-42," *SBLSP* 21 (1991): 698-713.

10:25-27
1229 J. Duncan M. Derrett, "The Parable of the Good Samaritan," in *Law in the New Testament.* London: Darton, Longman & Todd, 1970. Pp. 208-27.

10:27
1230 J. S. Piper, "Is Self-Love Biblical?" *CT* 21 (1977): 1150-53.

1231 Reginald H. Fuller, "The Double Commandment of Love: Test Case for the Criteria of Authenticity," in L. Schottroff, et al., eds., *Essays on the Love Commandment.* Philadelphia: Fortress Press, 1978. Pp. 41-56.

1232 G. M. Soares-Prahbu, "The Synoptic Love-Commandment: The Dimensions of Love in the Teaching of Jesus," *Je* 13 (1983): 85-103.

10:29-38
1233 J. Duncan M. Derrett, "Law in the New Testament: Fresh Light on the Parable of the Good Samaritan," *NTS* 11 (1964-1965): 22-37.

10:29-37
1234 W. J. Masson, "The Parable of the Good Samaritan," *ET* 48 (1936-1937): 179-81.

1235 F. H. Wilkinson, "Oded: Proto-Type of the Good Samaritan," *ET* 69 (1957-1958): 94.

1236 Bo Reicke, "Der barmherzige Samariter," in O. Böcher and K. Haacker, eds., *Verborum Veritas* (festschrift for Gustav Stählin). Wuppertal: Brockhaus, 1970. Pp. 103-109.

1237   L. Ramaroson, "Comme 'Le Bon Samaritain' ne chercher qu'à aimer (Lc 10,29-37)," *Bib* 56 (1975): 533-36.

1238   D. O. Ellsworth, "Confronting Christian Responsibility: Exegesis and Application of Luke 10:29-37, the Good Samaritan Example Story," doctoral dissertation, Claremont School of Theology, Claremont CA, 1976.

1239   Patrick Tishel, "The Parable of the Good Samaritan," *Epi* 6/2 (1985): 6-9.

1240   M. Gourgues, "L'autre dans le récit exemplaire du Bon Samaritain (Lc 10,29-37)," in M. Gourgues and G.-D. Mailhiot, eds., *L'altérité vivre ensemble differents*. Montréal: Bellarmin, 1986. Pp. 257-68.

1241   R. A. Cooke, "What Is a Person Worth? The Good Samaritan Problem Reconsidered," *List* 23/3 (1988): 198-213.

1242   Jeanne S. Moessner, "A New Pastoral Paradigm and Practice," in Maxine Glaz and Jeanne S. Moessner, eds., *Women in Travail and Transition*. Minneapolis MN: Fortress Press, 1991. Pp. 198-225.

10:29

1243   E. Biser, "Wer ist meiner Nächster?" *GeistL* 48 (1975): 406-14.

1244   L. P. Trudinger, "Once Again, Now, 'Who Is My Neighbour'?" *EQ* 48 (1976): 160-63.

1245   N. H. Young, "Once Again, Now, 'Who Is My Neighbour?' A Comment," *EQ* 49 (1977): 178-79.

10:30-37

1246   B. Gerhardsson, *The Good Samaritan, The Good Shepherd?* Lund: Gleerup, 1958.

1247   H. Binder, "Das Gleichnis vom barmherzigen Samariter," *TZ* 15 (1959): 176-94.

1248   C. Daniel, "Les Esséniens et l'arrière-fond historique de la parabole du Bon Samaritain," *NovT* 11 (1969): 71-104.

1249   Stephen Hoyer and Patrice McDaniel, "From Jericho to Jerusalem: The Good Samaritan From a Different Direction," *JPT* 18 (1990): 326-33.

1250   Wilhelm C. Linss, "Example Stories," *CThM* 17 (1990): 447-53.

1251   Uwe Wegner, "Repensando Uma Velha Pergunta: Quem é Meu Próximo?" *EstT* 30/1 (1990): 59-73.

10:30-35
1252   E. Biser, "Wer ist meiner Nächster?" *GeistL* 48 (1975): 406-14.

1253   James Champion, "The Parable as an Ancient and a Modern Form," *LT* 3 (1989): 16-39.

10:30
1254   H. G. Klemm, "Schillers ethisch-ästhetische Variationen zum Thema Lk 10,30ff.," *KD* 17 (1971): 127-40.

1255   Gerhard Sellin, "Gleichnisstrukturen," *LB* 31 (1974): 89-115.

10:31-32
1256   Christoph Burchard, "Fußnoten zum neutestamentlichen Griechisch II," *ZNW* 69 (1978): 143-57.

10:34
1257   G. Scholz, "Aesthetische Beobachtungen am Gleichnis vom reichen Mann und armen Lazarus und von drei anderen Gleichnissen," *LB* 43 (1978): 67-74.

1258   J. R. Royce, "A Philonic Use of πανδοχεῖον," *NovT* 23 (1981): 193-94.

10:35
1259   Douglas E. Oakman, "The Buying Power of Two Denarii," *Forum* 3 (1987): 33-38.

10:36
1260   R. S. Clucas, "The Neighbour Questions," *ThEv* 17 (1984): 49-50.

10:37

1261   J. W. Drane, "Simon the Samaritan and the Lucan Concept of Salvation History," *EQ* 47 (1975): 131-37.

10:38-42

1262   E. Laland, "Die Martha-Maria-Perikope Lukas 10,38-42," *ST* 13 (1959): 70-86.

1263   A. Knockaert, "Analyse structurale du texte biblique," *LV* 33 (1978): 331-40.

1264   F. Castel, "Luc 10.38-42," *ÉTR* 55 (1980): 560-65.

1265   J. A. Ciordia, "Lecturas biblicas (Lc 10,38-42)," *May* 7 (1981): 73-78.

1266   J. A. Davidson, "Things to be Understood and Things to be Done," *ET* 94 (1982-1983): 306-307.

1267   E. A. LaVerdiere, "The One Thing Required," *Emmanuel* 89 (1983): 398-403.

1268   A. Dauer, *Johannes und Lukas: Untersuchungen zu den johanneisch-lukanischen Parallel-Perikopen Joh 4,46-54/Lk 7,1-10; Joh 12,1-8/Lk 7,36-50, 10,38-42; Joh 20,19-29/Lk 24,36-49.* Würzburg: Echter, 1984.

1269   Jutta Brutscheck, *Die Maria-Marta-Erzählung: Eine redaktionskritische Untersuchung zu Lk 10,38-42.* Frankfurt: Hanstein, 1986.

1270   Elisabeth Schüssler Fiorenza, "A Feminist Critical Interpretation for Liberation: Martha and Mary: Lk 10:38-42," *RIL* 3/2 (1986): 21-36.

1271   J. T. Coakley, "The Anointing at Bethany and the Priority of John," *JBL* 107 (1988): 241-56.

1272   France Beydon, "A Temps Nouveau, Nouvelles Questions: Luc 10:38-42," *FV* 88 (1989): 25-32.

1273   Jutta Brutscheck, "Lukanische Anliegen in der Maria-Marta-Erzählung zu Lk 10:38-42," *GeistL* 62 (1989): 84-96.

1274 Robert W. Wall, "Martha and Mary (Luke 10:38-42) in the Context of a Christian Deuteronomy," *JSNT* 35 (1989): 19-35.

1275 Blake R. Heffner, "Meister Eckhart and a Millennium with Mary and Martha," *LQ* 5 (1991): 171-85.

1276 Adele Reinhartz, "From Narrative to History: The Resurrection of Mary and Martha," in Amy-Jill Levine, ed., *"Women Like This": A New Perspective on Jewish Women in the Greco-Roman World*. Atlanta: Scholars Press, 1991. Pp. 161-84.

1277 Pamela Thimmes, "The Language of Community: Metaphors, Systems of Convictions, Ethnic, and Gender Issues in Luke 10:25-37 and 10:38-42," *SBLSP* 21 (1991): 698-713.

1278 Wendy Robins, "Woman's Place: Jesus Reverses Traditional Understanding," *ChS* 82 (1992): 85-88.

10:42

1279 J. M. Bover, "Porro unum est necessarium (Luc. 10,42)," in *Valoración sobrenatural del "cosmos": La inspiración bíblica*. Madrid: Científica Medinaceli, 1954. Pp. 383-90.

1280 M. Augsten, "Lukanische Miszelle," *NTS* 14 (1967-1968): 581-83.

1281 B. Prete, *Il logion di Gesù: "Una cosa sola è necessaria (Lc. 10,42): Associazione biblica italiana, Fondamenti biblici della teologia morale*. Atti della XXII settimana biblica. Brescia: Paideia, 1973.

1282 Jacques Dupont, "De quoi est-il besoin (Lc 10,42)," in Ernest Best and R. McL. Wilson, eds., *Text and Interpretation* (festschrift for Matthew Black). Cambridge: University Press, 1979. Pp. 115-20.

1283 Gordon D. Fee, " 'One Thing Is Needful'? Luke 10:42," in Elton J. Epps and Gordon D. Fee, eds., *New Testament Textual Criticism* (festschrift for Bruce M. Metzger). Oxford: Clarendon Press, 1981. Pp. 61-75.

11-12

1284 M. Perry, "A Judaeo-Christian Source in Luke," *JBL* 49 (1930): 181-94.

11:1-13

1285 W. Ott, "Die Gebetsunterveisungen in Lk 11,1-13," *Gebet und Heil*. Münich: Kösel, 1965. Pp. 92-123.

1286 P. Ternant, "Le Père exauce la priere filiale (Lc 11)," *AsSeign* N.S. 48 (1972): 61-72.

1287 Roy A. Harrisville, "God's Mercy: Tested, Promised, Done! An Exposition of Genesis 18:20-32; Luke 11:1-13; Colossians 2:6-15," *Int* 3 (1977): 165-78.

11:1-4

1288 P. Dacquino, "La preghiera del cristano," *BibO* 5 (1963): 201-205.

1289 J. K. Elliott, "Did the Lord's Prayer Originate With John the Baptist?" *TZ* 29 (1973): 215.

11:1

1290 R. F. Collins, " 'Lord, Teach Us to Pray': A Reflection on the Prayer of Petition," *LouvS* 10 (1984-1985): 354-71.

1291 Jan Ambaum, "Gemeinsames Oder Persönliches Beten," *IKaZ* 14/4 (1985): 315-18.

11:2-13

1292 E. A. LaVerdiere, "God as Father," *Emmanuel* 88 (1982): 545-50.

11:2-4

1293 O. Schäfer, "Das Vaterunser, das Gebet des Christen," *TGl* 35 (1943): 1-6.

1294 W. Stiller, "Vater unser, Biblische Erwägungen," *TGl* 42 (1952): 49-52.

1295 T. W. Manson, "The Lord's Prayer," *BJRL* 38 (1955-1956): 99-113, 436-48.

1296 R. Leaney, "The Lucan Text of the Lord's Prayer (Lk xi 2-4)," *NovT* 1 (1956): 103-11.

1297 H. Schürmann, *Das Gebet des Herrn aus der Verkündigung Jesu erläutert*. Freiburg: Herder, 1957.

1298   W. Fresenius, "Beobachtungen und Gedanken zum Gebet des Herrn," *EvT* 20 (1960): 235-39.

1299   G. Miegge, "Le 'Notre Père' prière du temps présent," *ÉTR* 35 (1960): 237-53.

1300   Ernst Bammel, "A New Text of the Lord's Prayer," *ET* 73 (1961-1962): 54.

1301   Michael D. Goulder, "The Composition of the Lord's Prayer," *JTS* 14 (1963): 32-45.

1302   G. G. Willis, "The Lord's Prayer in Irish Gospel Manuscript," *StudE* 3 (1964): 282-88.

1303   Raymond E. Brown, "The Pater Noster as an Eschatological Prayer," in R. E. Brown, ed., *New Testament Essays*. Milwaukee: Bruce, 1965. Pp. 217-53.

1304   J. Jeremias, "Das Vater-Unser im Lichte der neuren Forschung," in *Abba*. Göttingen: Vandenhoeck & Ruprecht, 1966. Pp. 152-71.

1305   R. Freudenberger, "Zum Text der zweiten Vaterunserbitte," *NTS* 15 (1968-1969): 419-32.

1306   Günther Schwarz, "Matthaus vi.9-13 = Lukas xi.2-4," *NTS* 15 (1968-1969): 233-47.

1307   J. Carmignac, *Recherches sur le "Notre Pere."* Paris: Letouzey et Ané, 1969.

1308   G. Casalis, "Das Vater Unser und die Weltlage," *EvT* 29 (1969): 357-71.

1309   S. van Tilborg, "A Form-Criticism of the Lord's Prayer," *NovT* 14 (1972): 94-105.

1310   A. Vögtle, "Der 'eschatologische' Bezug der Wir-Binen des Vaterunsers (Lk 11,2c-4; Mt 6, 9b-13)," in E. Earle Ellis and Erich Grässer, eds., *Jesus und Paulus* (festschrift for W. G. Kummel). Göttingen: Vandenhoeck, 1975. Pp. 344-62.

1311   J. Ashton, "Our Father," *Way* 18 (1978): 83-91.

1312   P. Edmonds, "The Lucan 'Our Father': A Summary of Luke's Teaching on Prayer?" *ET* 91 (1979-1980): 140-43.

1313   Pierre Grelot, "L'Arrière-Plan Araméen du 'Pater'," *RB* 91/4 (1984): 531-56.

1314   J. D. Amphoux, "La révision marcionite du 'Notre Père' de Luc (11,2-4) et sa place dans l'histoire du texte," in R. Gryson and P.-M. Bogaert, eds., *Recherches sur l'histoire de la Bible latine.* Louvain-la-Neuve: Publications de la Faculté de Théologie, 1987. Pp. 105-21.

1315   J. C. De Moor, "The Reconstuction of the Aramaic Original of the Lord's Prayer," in P. Van der Meer and J. C. De Moor, eds., *The Structural Analysis of Biblical and Canaanite Poetry.* Sheffield: JSOT Press, 1988. Pp. 397-422.

1316   Robert J. Miller, "The Lord's Prayer and Other Items from the Sermon on the Mount," *Forum* 5 (1989): 177-86.

1317   W. M. Buchan, "Research on the Lord's Prayer," *ET* 100 (1989-1990): 336-39.

1318   Tjitze Baarda, "De Korte Tekst Van Het Onze Vader in Lucas 11:2-4: Een Marcionitische Coruptie?" *NedTT* 44 (1990): 273-87.

1319   H.-M. Barth, "Das Vaterunser als ökumenisches Gebet," *US* 45 (1990): 99-109, 113.

1320   Wiard Popkes, "Die letzte Bitte des Vater-Unser. Formgeschichte Beobachtungen zum Gebet Jesu," *ZNW* 81 (1990): 1-20.

1321   D. Baumgardt, "Kaddish and the Lord's Prayer," *JewBibQ* 19 (1991): 164-69.

1322   R. G. Kratz, "Die Gnade de täglichen Brots: Späte Psalmen auf dem Weg zum Vaterunser," *ZTK* 89 (1992): 1-40.

11:2

1323   W. Marchel, "Les aspects théologiques de la priere chrétienne 'Abba, Pere' (Gal 4, 6; Rom 8,15)," in *Abba, Pere! Le prière du Christ et des chrétiens.* Rome: Pontifical Biblical Institute, 1963. Pp. 213-43.

1324   W. Marchel, "Notre Pere (Mt 6,9; Lc 11,2)," in *Abba, Pere! Le prière du Christ et des chrétiens*. Rome: Pontifical Biblical Institute, 1963. Pp. 191-202.

1325   Gerhard Schneider, "Die Bitte um das Kommen des Geistes im lukanischen Vaterunser," in Wolfgang Schrage, eds., *Studien zum Text und zur Ethik des Neuen Testaments* (festschrift for Heinrich Greeven). New York: de Gruyter, 1986. Pp. 344-73.

11:3

1326   Matthew Black, "The Aramaic of *ton arton ēmōn ton epiousion*: Matt. vi.11, Luke xi.3," *JTS* 42 (1941): 186-89.

1327   A. Baker, "What Sort of Bread Did Jesus Want Us to Pray for?" *NBlack* 54 (1973): 125-29.

1328   Bernard Orchard, "The Meaning of τὸν ἐπιούσιον (Mt 6:11 = Lk 11:3)," *BTB* 3 (1973): 274-82.

1329   F. M. Braun, "Le pain dont nous avons besoin. Matt. 6:11; Luke 11:3," *NRT* 100 (1978): 559-68.

1330   R. ten Kate, "Geef ons Heden ons 'Dagelijks Brood'," *NedTT* 32/2 (1978): 125-39.

1331   Pierre Grelot, "La Quatrième Demande du 'Pater' et son Arrière-Plan Sémitique," *NTS* 25 (1978-1979): 299-314.

1332   H. Bourgoin, "Epiousios expliqué par la notion de préfixe vide," *BibL* 60 (1979): 91-96.

1333   L. M. Dewailly, " 'Donne-nous notre pain': quel pain? Notes sur la quatrième demande du Pater," *RSPT* 64 (1980): 561-88.

1334   D. Alexandre, "En torno a la cuarta petición del padrenuestro," *EB* 45 (1987): 325-36.

1335   S. Schroer, "Konkretionen zum Vaterunser," *US* 45 (1990): 110-13.

1336   L. Ramaroson, " 'Notre part de nourriture'," *ScE* 43 (1991): 87-115.

1337   R. G. Kratz, "Die Gnade de täglichen Brots: Späte Psalmen auf dem Weg zum Vaterunser," *ZTK* 89 (1992): 1-40.

11:4

1338   C. B. Houk, "*Peirasmos*, The Lord's Prayer, and the Massah Tradition," *SJT* 19 (1966): 216-25.

1339   Stanley E. Porter, "Mt 6:13 and Lk 11:4: 'Lead Us Not into Temptation," *ET* 101 (1989-1990): 359-62.

11:5-13

1340   G. Bornkamm, "Bittet, Suchet, Klopfet an," *EvT* 13 (1953): 1-5.

1341   E. Fuchs, "Notes bibliques de prédication: pour les temps de Pâques et de Pentecôte," *VC* 58 (1961): 214-26.

1342   R. R. Rickards, "The Translation of Luke 11,5-13," *BT* 28 (1977): 239-43.

11:5-10

1343   Curtis C. Mitchell, "Why Keep Bothering God: The Case for Persisting in Prayer," *CT* 29/18 (1985): 33-34.

11:5-9

1344   David R. Catchpole, "Q and 'The Friend at Midnight'," *JTS* 34 (1983): 407-24.

11:5-8

1345   W. Ott, "Vergleich mit der Parabel vom mit- ternachts bittenden Freund Lk 11,5-8," in *Gebet und Heil*. Münich: Kösel, 1965. Pp. 23-31.

1346   J. Duncan M. Derrett, "The Friend at Midnight: Asian Ideas in the Gospel of St. Luke," in E. Bammel, ed., *Donum Gentiliaum* (festschrift for David Daube). New York: Clarendon Press, 1978. Pp. 78-87.

1347   E. W. Hubbard, "The Parable of the Friend at Midnight: God's Honor or Man's Persistence?" *RQ* 21 (1978): 154-60.

1348   A. F. Johnson, "Assurance for Man: The Fallacy of Translating *anaideia* by 'Persistence' in Luke 11:5-8," *JETS* 22 (1979): 123-31.

1349 K. Haacker, "Mut zum Bitren: Ein Auslegung von Lukas 11,5-8,"
TBe 17 (1986): 1-6.

1350 Christopher M. Tuckett,"Q, Prayer, and the Kingdom," *JTS* 40
(1989): 367-76.

11:6

1351 J. Duncan M. Derrett, "Moving Mountains and Uprooting Trees,"
BibO 30 (1988): 231-44.

11:9-13

1352 R. A. Piper, "Matthew 7,7-11 par. Luke 11,9-13: Evidence of
Design and Argument in the Collection of Jesus Sayings," in J.
Delobel, ed., *Logia: Les paroles de Jésus (The Sayings of Jesus)*.
BETL #59. Louvain: Peeters Press, 1982. Pp. 419-23.

1353 Dale Goldsmith, "Ask, and It Will Be Given . . . : Toward Writing
the History of a Logion," *NTS* 35/2 (1989): 254-65.

11:9

1354 N. Brox, "Suchen und Finden. Zur Nachgeschichte von Mt 7,7b,
Lk 11,9b," in P. Hoffmann, et al., eds., *Orientierung an Jesus: Zur
Theologie der Synoptiker* (festschrift for Josef Schmid). Freiburg:
Herder, 1973. Pp. 17-36.

11:11-12

1355 J. Vara, "Una sugerencia: κόρπιον lección originaria de σκορπίον
en Lucas 11:11-12," *Salm* 30 (1983): 225-29.

11:13

1356 Édouard Delebecque, "Sur un hellénisme de Saint Luc," *RB* 87
(1980): 590-93.

11:14-36

1357 H. Schürmann, "QLk 11,14-36 kompositionsgeschichtlich befragt,"
in F. van Segbroeck, et al., eds., *The Four Gospels 1992* (festschrift
for Frans Neirynck). 3 vols. BETL #100. Louvain: Peeters Press,
1992. 1:563-86.

11:14-32

1358 H. B. Green, "Matthew 12,22-50 and Parallels: An Alternative to
Matthean Conflation," in C. M. Tuckett, ed., *Synoptic Studies*.
Sheffield: JSOT Press, 1984. Pp. 157-76.

1359   Kerry M. Craig and Margret A. Kristjansson, "Women Reading as Men/Women Reading as Women: A Structural Analysis for the Historical Project," *Semeia* 51 (1990): 119-36.

11:14-28
1360   E. Käsemann, "Lukas 11,14-28," in *Exegetische Versuche und Besinnungen.* 2 vols. Göttingen: Vandenhoeck & Ruprecht, 1960-1965. 1:242-48.

1361   E. Galbiati, "Esegesi degli Evangeli festivi," *BibO* 3 (1961): 58-64.

11:14-26
1362   Roland Meynet, "Qui Donc Esr 'Le Plus Fort'? Analyse Rhetorique de Mc 3,22-30; Mt 12,22-37; Luc 11,14-26," *RB* 90/3 (1983): 334-50.

11:14-23
1363   R. F. Collins, "Jesus' Ministry to the Deaf and Dumb," *MeliT* 35/1 (1984): 12-36.

1364   Ulrich Luz, "Q 10:2-16; 11:14-23," *SBLSP* 15 (1985): 101-102.

1365   James M. Robinson, "The Mission and Beelzebul: Pap Q 10:2-16; 11:14-23," *SBLSP* 15 (1985): 97-99.

11:14-20
1366   I. Hermann, " ' . . . dann ist das Gottesreich zu euch gekommen.' Eine Homilie zu Lk 11:14-20," *BibL* 1 (1960): 198-204.

1367   John S. Kloppenborg, "Q 11:14-20: Work Sheets for Reconstruction," *SBLSP* 15 (1985): 133-51.

1368   Eduard Schweizer, "The Testimony to Jesus in the Early Christian Community," *HBT* 7/1 (1985): 77-98.

11:15-23
1369   B. D. Chilton, "A Comparative Study of Synoptic Development: The Dispute between Cain and Abel in the Palestinian Targums and the Beelzebul Controversy in the Gospel," *JBL* 101 (1982): 553-62.

11:15

1370   W. C. B. MacLaurin, "Beelzeboul," *NovT* 20/2 (1978): 156-60.

11:16

1371   D. Merli, "Il Segno di Giona," *BibO* 14 (1972): 61-77.

1372   David R. Catchpole, "The Law and the Prophets in Q," in G. F. Hawthorne and O. Betz, eds., *Tradition and Interpretation in the New Testament* (festschrift for E. Earle Ellis). Grand Rapids MI: Eerdmans, 1987. Pp. 95-109.

11:17-30

1373   Chrys C. Caragounis, "Kingdom of God, Son of Man and Jesus' Self-Understanding," *TynB* 40 (1989): 3-23.

11:17

1374   H. E. Bryant, "Note on Luke 11:17," *ET* 50 (1938-1939): 525-26.

1375   Frans Neirynck, "Mt 12,25a / Lc 11,17a et la rédaction des évangiles," *ETL* 62 (1986): 122-33.

11:18

1376   W. C. B. MacLaurin, "Beelzeboul," *NovT* 20/2 (1978): 156-60.

11:19-20

1377   A. George, "Paroles de Jésus sur ses miracles (Mt 11,5.21; 12,27.28 et par.)," in Jacques Dupont, ed., *Jésus aux origines de la christologie*. BETL #40. Louvain: Peeters Press, 1975. Pp. 283-302.

11:19

1378   Robert Shirock, "Whose Exorcists Are They? The Referents of οἱ υἱοὶ ὑμῶν at Matthew 12:27/Luke 11:19," *JSNT* 46 (1992): 41-51.

11:20

1379   J. E. Yates, "Luke's Pneumatology and Lk. 11,20," *StudE* 3 (1964): 295-99.

1380   Robert G. Hamerton-Kelly, "A Note on Matthew xii.28 par. Luke xi.20," *NTS* 11 (1964-1965): 167-69.

1381   A. George, "Par le doigt de Dieu (Lc 11:20)," *SE* 18 (1966): 461-66.

1382   T. Lorenzmeier, "Zum Logion Mt 12,28; Lk 11,20," in D. D. Betz
       and L. Schottroff, eds., *Neues Testament und christliche Existenz*
       (festschrift for Herbert Braun). Tübingen: Mohr, 1973. Pp.
       289-304.

1383   J.-M. Van Cangh, " 'Par l'esprit de Dieu, par le doigt de Dieu':
       Mt 12,28 par. Lc 11,20," in J. Delobel, ed., *Logia: Les paroles de
       Jésus (The Sayings of Jesus).* BETL #59. Louvain: Peeters Press,
       1982. Pp. 343-54.

1384   Gerhard Lohfink, "Die Korrelation von Reich Gottes und Volk
       Gottes bei Jesus," *TQ* 165/3 (1985): 173-83.

1385   Robert W. Wall, "The Finger of God: Deuteronomy 9:10 and Luke
       11:20," *NTS* 33 (1987): 144-50.

11:21-22
1386   Simon Légasse, " 'Homme Fort' de Luc XI,21-22," *NovT* 5
       (1962): 5-9.

11:21
1387   L. Michael White, "Sealing the Strongman's 'Court'," *Forum* 3
       (1987): 3-28.

11:26
1388   E. Käsemann, "Die Heilung der Besessenen," *Reformatio* 28
       (1979): 7-18.

11:27-28
1389   R. C. Wahlberg, "Jesus and the Uterus Image (Lc 11,27-28)," *ITQ*
       41 (1974): 235-50.

11:27
1390   M. McNamara, "Blessed is the Womb that Bore You . . . ; Lk
       11,27 and PT Gn 49,25," in *The New Testament and the
       Palestinian Targum to the Pentateuch.* Rome: Pontifical Biblical
       Institute, 1966. Pp. 131-33.

1391   H. Zimmermann, " 'Selig die das Wort Gotres hören und es
       bewahren': Eine exegetische Studie zu Lk 11,27f.," *Cath* 29
       (1975): 114-19.

11:28

1392 J. Riedl, "Selig, die das Wort Gottes hören und befolgen (Lk 11:28). Theologisch-biblische Adventsbesinnung," *BibL* 4 (1963): 252-60.

1393 H. P. Scott, "A Note on the Meaning and Translation of Luke 11:28," *ITQ* 41 (1974): 235-50.

1394 M. Corbin, "Garder la parole de Dieu: Essai sur Luc 11,28," in J. Audinet, et al., eds., *Le déplacement de la théologie.* Paris: Beauchesne, 1977. Pp. 109-18.

11:29-32

1395 John Howton, "The Sign of Jonah," *SJT* 15 (1962): 288-304.

1396 D. Merli, "Il Segno di Giona," *BibO* 14 (1972): 61-77.

1397 G. Schmitt, "Das Zeichen des Jona," *ZNW* 69 (1978): 123-29.

1398 Dietrich Correns, "Jona und Salomo," in W. Haubeck and M. Bachmann, eds., *Wort in der Zeit* (festschrift for K. H. Rengstorf). Leiden: Brill, 1980. Pp. 86-94.

1399 David R. Catchpole, "The Law and the Prophets in Q," in G. F. Hawthorne and O. Betz, eds., *Tradition and Interpretation in the New Testament* (festschrift for E. Earle Ellis). Grand Rapids MI: Eerdmans, 1987. Pp. 95-109.

11:29-30

1400 J. Bowman, "Jonah and Jesus," *AbrN* 25 (1987): 1-12.

1401 A. K. M. Adam, "The Sign of Jonah: A Fish-Eye View," *Semeia* 51 (1990): 177-91.

11:29

1402 R. A. Edwards, *The Sign of Jonah: In the Theology of the Evangelists and Q.* London: SCM, 1971.

1403 James Swetnam, "No Sign of Jonah," *Bib* 66/1 (1985): 126-30.

1404 Dieter Zeller, "Entrückung zur Ankunft als Menschensohn (Lk 13:34f; 11:29f)," in François Refoulé, ed., *à cause de l'Evangile: Etudes sur les synoptiques et les Actes* (festschrift for Jacques Dupont). Paris: Cerf, 1985. Pp. 513-30.

11:30

1405 Santiago Guijarro Oporto, "The Sign of Jonah," *TD* 32/1 (1985): 49-53.

11:33-36

1406 F. Hahn, "Die Worte vom Licht Lk 11,33-36," in *Orientierung an Jesus: Zur Theologie der Synoptiker* (festschrift for Josef Schmid). Freiburg: Herder, 1973. Pp. 107-38.

1407 Marc Philonenko, "La parabole sur la lampe (Luc 11:33-36) et le horoscopes qoumâniens," *ZNW* 79/1-2 (1988): 145-51.

1408 Susan R. Garrett, "Lest the Light in You Be Darkness: Luke 11:33-36 and the Question of Commitment," *JBL* 110 (1991): 93-105.

11:33

1409 E. Alliata, "La κρυπτη di Lc 11,33 e le grotte ripostiglo delle antiche case palestinesi," *SBFLA* 34 (1984): 53-66.

11:34-36

1410 Dale C. Allison, "The Eye Is the Lamp of the Body (Matthew 6.22-23; Luke 11.34-36)," *NTS* 33 (1987): 61-83.

11:34-35

1411 C. Edlung, *Das Auge der Einfalt: Eine Untersuchung zu Matth. 6,22-23 und Luk. 11,34-35*. Lund: Gleerup, 1952.

11:37-54

1412 Wilhelm Pesch, "Drohweissangungen," in *Der Lohngedanke in der Lehre Jesu*. Münster: Zink, 1955. Pp. 45-50.

1413 E. Springs Steele, "Jesus's Table Fellowship with Pharisees: An Editorial Analysis of Luke 7:36-50, 11:37-54, and 14:1-24," doctoral dissertation, University of Notre Dame, Notre Dame IN, 1982.

1414 Werner Bieder, "Das Volk Gottes in Erwartung von Licht und Lobpreis," *TZ* 40/2 (1984): 137-48.

1415 E. Springs Steele, "Luke 11:37-54: A Modifed Hellenistic Symposium?" *JBL* 103 (1984): 379-94.

1416 H. Schürmann, "Die Redekomposition wider 'dieses Geschlecht' und seine Führung in der Redeguelle (vgl. Mt 23,1-39 par Lk 11,37-54)," *SNTU-A* 11 (1986): 33-81.

11:39-52

1417 Leif E. Vaage, "The Woes in Q (and Matthew and Luke): Deciphering the Rhetoric of Criticism," *SBLSP* 18 (1988): 582-607.

11:39-41

1418 Robert J. Miller, "The Inside is (not) the Outside: Q 11:39-41 and GThom 89," *Forum* 5 (1989): 92-105.

11:39

1419 Jacob Neusner, "The Absoluteness of Christianity and the Uniqueness of Judaism: Why Salvation Is Not of the Jews," *Int* 43 (1989): 18-31.

11:41

1420 W. Auer, "Bibeltexte - flasch verstanden," *BK* 13 (1958): 85-88.

11:42

1421 Dietrich Correns, "Die Verzehntung der Raute. Luk XI,42 und M Schebi IX,I," *MeliT* 6/2 (1963): 110-12.

11:44

1422 Günther Schwarz, " 'Unkenntliche Gräber'? (Lukas XI.44)," *NTS* 23/2 (1976-1977): 345-46.

11:47-51

1423 J. Duncan M. Derrett, "You Build the Tombs of the Prophets," *StudE* 4 (1968): 187-93.

11:47

1424 J. Jeremias, *Heiligengräberin Jesu Umwelt (Mt. 23,29; Lk. 11,47): Eine Untersuchung zur Volksreligion der Zeit Jesu.* Göttingen: Vandenhoeck & Ruprecht, 1958.

11:49-51
    1425 E. Earle Ellis, "Luke 11:49-51: An Oracle of a Christian Prophet?" *ET* 74 (1962-1963): 157-58.

    1426 Giuseppe Frizzi, "Carattere originale e rilevanza degli 'apostoli inviati' in Q," *RBib* 21 (1973): 401-12.

11:49
    1427 O. Seitz, "The Commission of Prophets and 'Apostles': A Re-Examination of Matthew 23,34 with Luke 11,49," *StudE* 4 (1968): 236-40.

    1428 Günter Klein, "Die Verfolgung der Apostel: Lukas 11,49," in H. Baltensweiler and Bo Reicke, eds., *Neues Testament und Geschichte* (festschrift for Oscar Cullmann). Zürich: Theologischer Verlag, 1972. 4:113-24.

11:51
    1429 J. Barton Payne, " 'Zechariah Who Perished'," *GTJ* 8/3 (1967): 33-35.

12:1-13:9
    1430 Dennis M. Sweetland, "The Understanding of Discipleship in Lk 12:1-13:9," doctoral dissertation, University of Notre Dame, Notre Dame IN, 1978.

    1431 Wilhelm Wuellner, "The Rhetorical Genre of Jesus' Sermon in Luke 12:1-13:9," in Duane F. Watson, ed., *Persuasive Artistry: Studies in New Testament Rhetoric* (festschrift for George A. Kennedy). Sheffield: JSOT Press, 1991. Pp. 93-118.

12:1-12
    1432 Dennis M. Sweetland, "Discipleship and Persecution: A Study of Luke 12,1-12," *Bib* 65 (1984): 61-80.

12:1-8
    1433 André Legault, "An Application of the Form-Critique Method to the Anointing in Galilee (Lc 7,36-50) and Bethany (Mt 26,6-13; Mk 14,3-9; Lk 12,1-8)," *CBQ* 16 (1954): 131-45.

12:1
    1434 A. Negōitā and C. Daniel, "L'énigme du levain. Ad Mc. viii,15; Mt. xvi,6; et Lc. xii,1," *NovT* 9 (1967): 306-14.

12:2-7
1435 John S. Kloppenborg, "The Q Sayings on Anxiety (Q 12:2-7),"
      Forum 5 (1989): 83-98.

12:6
1436 A. Scattolon, "L'agapêtos sinottico nella luce della tradizione
      guidaica," *RBib* 26 (1978): 2-32.

12:7
1437 Dale C. Allison, "The Hairs on Your Head Are Numbered," *ET*
      102 (1990-1991): 334-36.

12:8-9
1438 G. W. H. Lampe, "St. Peter's Denial," *BJRL* 55/2 (1973): 346-68.

1439 A. J. B. Higgins, " 'Menschensohn' oder 'ich' in Q Lk 12,8-9 / Mt
      10,32-33?" in Rudolf Pesch, et al., eds., *Jesus und der
      Menschensohn* (festschrift for A. Vogtle). Freiburg: Herder, 1975.
      Pp. 117-23.

1440 J. M. McDermott, "Luke 12:8-9: Stone of Scandal," *RB* 84 (1977):
      523-37.

1441 Jan Lambrecht, "Q-influence on Mark 8,34-9,1," in J. Delobel,
      ed., *Logia: Les paroles de Jésus (The Sayings of Jesus)*. BETL #59.
      Louvain: Peeters Press, 1982. Pp. 277-304.

1442 Harry Fleddermann, "The Q Sayings on Confessing and Denying,"
      SBLSP 17 (1987): 606-16.

12:8
1443 Werner Georg Kümmel, "Das Verhalten Jesus gegenüber und das
      Verhalten des Menschensohns. Markus 8,38 par. und Lukas 12,8f.
      par. und Matthäus 10,32f.," in Rudolf Pesch and Rudolf
      Schnackenburg, eds., with Odilo Kaiser, *Jesus und den
      Menschensohn: Für Anton Vögtle*. Freiburg/Vienna/Basel: Herder,
      1975. Pp. 210-24.

1444 Rudolf Pesch, "Über die Autorität Jesu: Eine Rückfrage anhand
      des Bekenner- und Verleugnerspruchs Lk 12,8f par.," in Rudolf
      Schnackenburg, et al., eds., *Die Kirche des Anfangs* (festschrift for
      H. Schürmann). Freiburg: Herder, 1978. Pp. 25-55.

1445 B. Lindars, "Jesus as Advocate: A Contribution to the Christology Debate," *BJRL* 62/2 (1980): 476-97.

1446 David R. Catchpole, "The Angelic Son of Man in Luke 12:8," *NovT* 2 (1982): 255-65.

1447 D. R. Copestake, "Luke 12:8 and 'Silent Witness'," *ET* 94 (1982-1983): 335.

<u>12:10</u>

1448 I. Howard Marshall, "Hard Sayings [Lk. 12:10; 7th in Series]," *Theology* 67 (1964): 65-67.

1449 J. G. Williams, "A Note on the 'Unforgivable Sin' Logion," *NTS* 12 (1965-1966): 75-77.

1450 Jan Lambrecht, "Ware Verwantshasp en Eeuwige Zonde: Onstaan en Structuur van Mc. 3:20-35," *Bij* 29/2 (1968): 114-50.

1451 E. Lövestam, "Logiet om hädelse mot den helige Ande (Mark. 3:28f. par. Matt. 12:31f.; Luk. 12:10)," *SEÅ* 33 (1968): 101-17.

1452 E. Lövestam, *Spiritus Blasphemia: Eine Studie zu Mk 3,82f. par Mt 12,31f., Lk 12,10.* Lund: Gleerup, 1968.

1453 R. Schippers, "The Son of Man in Matt. xii.32/Lk. xii.10, Compared with Mk. iii.28," *StudE* 4 (1968): 231-65.

1454 C. Colpe, "Der Spruch von der Lästerung des Geistes," in E. Lohse, et al., eds., *Der Ruf Jesu und die Antwort der Gemeinde.* Göttingen: Vandenhoeck & Ruprecht, 1970. Pp. 63-79.

1455 M. Eugene Boring, "The Unforgivable Sin Logion Mark 3:28-29/Matt 12:31-32/Luke 12:10: Formal Analysis and History of the Tradition," *NovT* 18/4 (1976): 258-79.

1456 P. Maurice Casey, "The Son of Man Problem," *ZNW* 67/3 (1976): 147-54.

1457 T. H. Wrege, "Zur Rolle des Geisteswortes in frühchristlichen Traditionen (Lc 12,10 parr.)," in J. Delobel, ed., *Logia: Les paroles de Jésus (The Sayings of Jesus).* BETL #59. Louvain: Peeters Press, 1982. Pp. 373-77.

1458   Chrys C. Caragounis, "Kingdom of God, Son of Man and Jesus' Self-Understanding," *TynB* 40 (1989): 3-23.

12:11-12

1459   Bo Reicke, "A Test of Synoptic Relationships: Matthew 10,17-23 and 24,9-14 with Parallels," in William R. Farmer, ed., *New Synoptic Studies*. Macon GA: Mercer University Press, 1983. Pp. 209-29.

1460   William L. Schutter, "Luke 12:11-12/21:12-15 and the Composition of Luke-Acts," *EGLMBS* 10 (1990): 236-50.

12:11

1461   George R. Beasley-Murray, "The Parousia in Mark," *RevExp* 75/4 (1978): 565-81.

1462   Matthew Mahoney, "Luke 21:14-15: Editorial Rewriting or Authenticity?" *ITQ* 47/3 (1980): 220-38.

12:13-34

1463   E. Neuhäusler, "Allem Besitz entsagen," in *Anspruch und Antwort Gottes*. Düsseldorf: Patmos, 1962. Pp. 170-85.

1464   H.-J. Degenhardt, "Die rechte Einstellung zum Besitz: Lk 12,13-34," in *Lukas Evangelist der Armen*. Stuttgart: Katholisches Bibelwerk, 1965. Pp. 68-97.

12:13-21

1465   G. Eichholz, "Vom reichen Kornbauern (Luk. 12,13-21)," in *Gleichnisse der Evangelien*. Neukirchen-Vluyn: Neukirchener Verlag, 1971. Pp. 179-91.

1466   G. Gaide, "Le riche insensé (Lc 12)," *AsSeign* N.S. 49 (1971): 82-89.

1467   H. Sawatzky, "What's Gotten Into Us?" *ET* 91 (1979-1980): 245-47.

1468   J. A. Ciordia, " 'Maestro, di a mi hermano . . . ' (Lc 12,13-21," *May* 10 (1984): 168-73.

1469 H. Welzen, "De parabel van de rijke boer (Lc 12,13-21)," in B. van Iersel, et al., eds., *Parabelverhalen in Lucas: Van semiotiek naar pragmatiek.* TFT-Studies #8. Tilburg: University Press, 1987. Pp. 83-109.

1470 Mauro Láconi, "Ricchi davanti a Dio," *SacD* 34 (1989): 5-41.

12:13-14
1471 Tjitze Baarda, "Lk 12,13-14: Text and Transmission from Marcion to Augustine," *StJudLAnt* 12 (1975): 107-62.

1472 T. Gorringe, "A Zealot Option Rejected? Luke 12:13-14," *ET* 98 (1986-1987): 267-70.

12:14
1473 John Killinger, "On Not Being Everybody's Commodity," *ChrM* 16/3 (1985): 23-25.

12:15-21
1474 George W. E. Nickelsburg, "Riches, the Rich, and God's Judgment in 1 Enoch 92-105 and the Gospel according to Luke," *NTS* 25 (1978-1979): 324-44.

12:15-20
1475 Henry Chadwick, "The Shorter Text of Luke 12:15-20," *HTR* 50 (1957): 249-58.

12:15
1476 C. C. Tarelli, "A Note on Luke xii.15," *JTS* 41 (1940): 260-62.

12:16-21
1477 Erhardt Güttgemanns, "Narrative Analyse Synoptischer Texte," *LB* 25/26 (1973): 50-73.

1478 J. Duncan M. Derrett, "The Rich Fool: A Parable of Jesus Concerning Inheritance," *HeyJ* 18 (1977): 131-51.

1479 E. W. Seng, "Der reiche Tor: Eine Untersuchung von Lk xii,16-21 unter besonderer Berüsichtigung form—und motivgeschichtlicher Aspekte," *NovT* 20 (1978): 136-55.

12:16-20

1480 Günther Schwarz, "Ταύτῃ τῇ νυκτὶ τὴν ψυχήν σου ἀπαιτοῦσιν ἀπὸ σοῦ," *BibN* 25 (1984): 36-41.

12:16

1481 J. Neville Birdsall, "Luke 12:16ff. and the Gospel of Thomas," *JTS* 13 (1962): 332-36.

1482 H. R. Graham, "Once there Was a Rich Man . . . : Five 'Rich Man' Stories in Luke," *BibTo* 26 (1988): 98-103.

12:19

1483 W. Ameling, "Griechische Parallelen zu zwei Stellen aus dem Neuen Testament," *ZPE* 60 (1985): 35-44.

12:20

1484 Günther Schwarz, "λυθῆναι απὸ τοῦ δεσμοῦ τούτου," *BibN* 15 (1981): 47.

1485 Günther Schwarz, "Ταύτῃ τῇ νυκτὶ τὴν ψυχήν σου ἀπαιτοῦσιν ἀπὸ σοῦ," *BibN* 25 (1984): 36-41.

12:22-31

1486 M. F. Olsthoorn, *The Jewish Background and the Synoptic Setting of Matthew 6,25-33 and Lucas 12,22-31.* Jerusalem: Franciscan Printing Press, 1975.

1487 P. Hoffmann, "Der Q-Text det Sprüche wm Sorgen: Mt 6,25-33 / Lk 12,22-31: Ein Rekonstruktionsversuch," in L. Schenke, ed., *Studien zum Matthäusevangelium* (festschrift for W. Pesch). Stuttgart: Katholisches Bibelwerk, 1988. Pp. 128-55.

12:24

1488 E. Fuchs, "Die Verkündigung Jesu: Der Spruch von den Raben," in H. Ristow and K. Matthiae, eds., *Der historische Jesus und der kerygmatische Christus.* Berlin: Evangelische Verlagsanstalt, 1962. Pp. 385-88.

1489 J. F. Healey, "Models of Behavior: Matt 6:26," *JBL* 108 (1989): 497-98.

12:32-48
> **1490** A. George, "L'attente du maître qui vient (Lc 12)," *AsSeign* N.S. 50 (1974): 66-76.

12:32
> **1491** Wilhelm Pesch, "Zur Formgeschichte und Exegese von Lk. 12:32," *Bib* 41/1 (1960): 25-40.

> **1492** Warren Vanhetloo, "The Incarnate Shepherd," *CBTJ* 1/1 (1985): 20-34.

12:35-59
> **1493** C. Küven, "Advent in der Entscheidung nach Lukas 12:35-59," *BK* 16 (1961): 109-12.

12:35-48
> **1494** Paul Marshall, "A Christian View of Economics," *Crux* 21/1 (1985): 3-6.

> **1495** Andries G. van Aarde, "Narrative Point of View: An Ideological Reading of Luke 12:35-48," *Neo* 22 (1988): 235-52.

> **1496** J. Botha, "Isers Wandering Viewpoint: A Reception-Analytical Reading of Luke 12:35-48," *Neo* 22 (1988): 253-68.

> **1497** H. J. B. Combrink, "Readings, Readers and Authors: An Orientation," *Neo* 22 (1988): 189-203.

> **1498** Bernard C. Lategan, "Reading Luke 12:35-48: An Empirical Study," *Neo* 22 (1988): 391-413.

> **1499** J. J. J. van Rensburg, "A Syntactical Reading of Luke 12:35-48," *Neo* 22 (1988): 415-48.

> **1500** Eben H. Scheffler, "A Psychological Reading of Luke 12:35-48," *Neo* 22 (1988): 355-71.

> **1501** C. W. Schnell, "Historical Context in Parable Interpretation: A Criticism of Current Tradition-Historical Interpretations of Luke 12:35-48," *Neo* 22 (1988): 269-82.

> **1502** W. Sebothoma, "Luke 12:35-48: A Reading by a Black South African," *Neo* 22 (1988): 325-35.

1503 D. J. Smit, "Responsible Hermeneutics: A Systematic Theologian's Response to the Readings and Readers of Luke 12:35-48," *Neo* 22 (1988): 441-84.

1504 P. van Staden, "A Sociological Reading of Luke 12:35-48," *Neo* 22 (1988): 337-53.

1505 S. van Tilborg, "An Interpretation from the Ideology of the Text," *Neo* 22 (1988): 205-15.

1506 Claus P. März, "Zur Vorgeschichte von Lk 12,35-48: Beobachtungen zur Komposition der Logientradition in der Redequelle," in Karl Kertelge, ed., *Christus bezeugen* (festschrift for Wolfgang Trilling). Leipzig: St. Benno-Verlag, 1989. Pp. 166-78.

12:35-40
1507 Richard J. Bauckham, "Synoptic Parousia Parables and the Apocalypse," *NTS* 23 (1976-1977): 162-76.

1508 P. Deterding, "Eschatological and Eucharistic Motifs in Luke 12,35-40," *CJ* 5 (1979): 85-94.

1509 Richard J. Bauckham, "Synoptic Parousia Parables Again," *NTS* 29 (1983): 129-34.

12:35-39
1510 H. Spaemann, "Advent der Christen im Gleichnis. Eine Meditation über Lk 12:35-39," *BibL* 1 (1960): 266-70.

12:35-38
1511 A. Weiser, "Das Gleichnis von den wachenden Knechten Lk 12,35-38," in *Die Knechtsgleichnisse der synoptischen Evangelien*. Münich: Kösel, 1971. Pp. 161-77.

12:35-37
1512 E. Lövestam, "The Parable of the Waiting Servants," in *Spiritual Wakefulness in the New Testament*. Lund: Gleerup, 1963. Pp. 92-95.

12:39-46
1513 Harry Fleddermann, "The Householder and the Servant Left in Charge," *SBLSP* 16 (1986): 17-26.

12:39-40
1514　A. Smitmans, "Das Gleichnis vom Dieb," in H. Feld and J. Nolte, eds., *Wort Gottes in der Zeit* (festschrift for Karl Hermann Schelkle). Düsseldorf: Patmos, 1973. Pp. 43-68.

12:41-48
1515　Patrick J. Hartin, "Angst in the Household: A Deconstructive Reading of the Parable of the Supervising Servant," *Neo* 22 (1988): 373-90.

12:42-46
1516　A. Weiser, "Das Gleichnis vom treuen und untreuen Knecht Mt 24,45-51 par Lk 12,42-46.47f.," in *Die Knechtsgleichnisse der synoptischen Evangelien.* Münich: Kösel, 1971. Pp. 178-225.

1517　H. Schürmann, "Die zwei unterschiedlichen Berufungen, Dienste und Lebensweisen im Presbyterium," in *In libertatem vocati estis (Gal 5,13)* (festschrift for B. Häring). Studia Moralia #15. Rome: Academia Alfonsiana, 1977. Pp. 401-20.

1518　Arthur J. Dewey, "A Prophetic Pronouncement: Q 12:42-46," *Forum* 5 (1989): 99-108.

12:46
1519　P. Ellingworth, "Luke 12:46: Is There an Anti-Climax Here?" *BT* 31 (1980): 242-43.

12:47
1520　A. Weiser, "Das Gleichnis vom treuen und untreuen Knecht Mt 24,45-51 par Lk 12,42-46.47f.," in *Die Knechtsgleichnisse der synoptischen Evangelien.* Münich: Kösel, 1971. Pp. 178-225.

12:49-59
1521　J.-D. Kaestli, "Luc 12:49-59: Diverses paroles eschatologiques," in *L'eschatologie dans l'oeuvre de Luc.* Genève: Labor et Fides, 1969. Pp. 19-23.

12:49-53
1522　A. George, "La venue de Jésus, cause de division entre les hommes (Lc 12)," *AsSeign* N.S. 51 (1972): 62-71.

12:49
1523　P. Kutter, "Eine 'biblische' Ansprache," *BK* 5 (1950): 48-50.

1524   Claus P. März, "Feuer auf die Erde zu werfen, bin ich gekommen: Zum Verständnis und zur Entstehung von Lk 12,49," in Françios Refoulé, ed., *à cause de l'Evangile: Etudes sur les synoptiques et les Actes* (festschrift for Jacques Dupont). Paris: Cerf, 1985. Pp. 479-511.

1525   Stephen J. Patterson, "Fire and Dissension: *Ipsissima Vox Jesu* in Q 12:49, 51-53?" *Forum* 5 (1989): 121-39.

12:50

1526   G. Delling, "*Baptisma baptisthēnai*," *NovT* 2 (1957-1958): 92-115.

1527   André Feuillet, "La coupe et le baptême de la Passion (Mc x,35-40; cf. Mt xx,20-23; Lc xii,50)," *RB* 74 (1967): 356-91.

1528   J. Duncan M. Derrett, "Christ's Second Baptism (Lk. 12:50; Mk. 10:38-40)," *ET* 100 (1988-1989): 294-95.

12:51-53

1529   T. A. Roberts, "Some Comments on Matthew x.34-36 and Luke xii.51-53," *ET* 69 (1957-1958): 304-306.

1530   Stephen J. Patterson, "Fire and Dissension: *Ipsissima Vox Jesu* in Q 12:49, 51-53?" *Forum* 5 (1989): 121-39.

12:51

1531   Matthew Black, " 'Not Peace but a Sword: Matt 10:34-55; Luke 12:51ff.," in Ernst Bammel and C. F. D. Moule, eds., *Jesus and the Politics of His Day*. Cambridge: University Press, 1984. Pp. 287-94.

12:54-56

1532   Jan Nicolaas Sevenster, "Geeft den Keizer, Wat des Keizers is, en Gode, Wat Gods is," *NedTT* 17 (1962): 21-31.

1533   Günter Klein, "Die Prüfung der Zeit (Lukas 12:54-56)," *ZTK* 61/4 (1964): 373-90.

12:57-59

1534   L. J. Topel, "Aquittal: A Redaction-Critical Study of Luke 12:57-59," doctoral dissertation, Marquette University, Milwaukee WI, 1973.

1535   G. Strecker, "Die Antithesen der Bergpredigt (Mt 5,21-48 par),"
           ZNW 69 (1978): 36-72.

13:1-9

1536   P. Ternant, "Le dernier délai de la conversion (Lc 13)," *AsSeign*
           N.S. 16 (1971): 59-72.

1537   F. W. Young, "Luke 13:1-9," *Int* 31 (1977): 59-63.

1538   A. van Schaik, "De vijgeboom met kans op vruchten (Lc 13,1-9),"
           in B. van Iersel, et al., eds., *Parabelverhalen in Lucas: Van
           semiotiek naar pragmatiek.* TFT-Studies #8. Tilburg: University
           Press, 1987. Pp. 110-32.

1539   Mauro Láconi, "La pazienza di Dio," *SacD* 34 (1989): 437-72.

13:1-5

1540   Sherman E. Johnson, "A Note on Luke 13:1-5," *ATR* 17 (1935):
           91-95.

1541   J. Blinzler, "Die Niedermetzelung von Galiläern durch Pilatus,"
           NovT 2 (1957-1958): 24-49.

1542   Günther Schwarz, "Lukas xiii.1-5—Eine Emendation," *NovT* 11
           (1969): 121-26.

1543   Philip Yancey, "Riddles of Pain: Clues from the Book of Job," *CT*
           29/18 (1985): 80.

13:4

1544   Michael B. Walker, "Luke xiii.4," *ET* 75 (1963-1964): 151.

13:6-9

1545   Ulrich Schoenborn, "El Jardinero Audaz: Aspectos Semánticos y
           Pragmáticos en Lucas 13,6-9," *RevB* 52/2 (1990): 65-84.

1546   Jonathan A. Draper, "For the Kingdom is Inside of You and it is
           Outside of You: Contextual Exegesis in South Africa," in
           Patrick J. Hartin and J. H. Petzer, eds., *Text and Interpretation:
           New Approaches in the Criticism of the New Testament.* Leiden:
           Brill, 1991. Pp. 235-57.

13:9

1547 G. Scholz, "Aesthetische Beobachtungen am Gleichnis vom reichen Mann und armen Lazarus und von drei anderen Gleichnissen," *LB* 43 (1978): 67-74.

13:10-21

1548 H. Welzen, "Loosening and Binding: Luke 13.10-21 as Programme and Anti-Programme of the Gospel of Luke," in Spike Draisma, eds., *Intertextuality in Biblical Writings* (festschrift for Bastiaan M. F. van Iersel). Kampen: Kok, 1989. Pp. 175-87.

13:10-17

1549 J. Wilkinson, "The Case of the Bent Woman in Luke 13:10-17," *EQ* 49 (1977): 195-205.

1550 C. Dietzfelbinger, "Vom Sinn der Sabbatheilungen Jesu," *EvT* 38 (1978): 281-97.

1551 A. Steiner and H. Stotzer, "Freiheit befreit: Jesus heilt eine behinderte Frau am Sabbat (Lukas 13:10-17)—Ein Normenwunder," in A. Steiner and V. Weymann, eds., *Wunder Jesu Bibelarbeit in der Gemeinde*. Themen und Materialen #2. Basel: Reinhardt, 1978. Pp. 127-46.

1552 R. C. Wahlberg, *Jesus and the Freed Woman*. New York: Paulist Press, 1978.

1553 J. Duncan M. Derrett, "Positive Perspectives on Two Lucan Miracles," *DR* 104 (1986): 272-87.

1554 Dennis Hamm, "The Freeing of the Bent Woman and the Restoration of Israel: Luke 13:10-17 as Narrative Theology," *JSNT* 31 (1987): 23-44.

1555 Elisabeth Schüssler Fiorenza, "Luke 13:10-17: Interpretation for Liberation and Transformation," *TD* 36 (1989): 303-19.

1556 Joel B. Green, "Jesus and a Daughter of Abraham (Luke 13:10-17): Test Case for a Lucan Perspective on Jesus' Miracles," *CBQ* 51 (1989): 643-54.

1557   Blanqui Otaño, "Nueva identidad de la mujer encorvada," in Irene
       Foulkes, ed., *Teología desde la mujer en Centroamerica*. Costa
       Rica: Sebila, 1989. Pp. 125-32.

1558   Robert F. O'Toole, "Some Exegetical Reflections on Luke
       13:10-17," *Bib* 73 (1992): 84-107.

13:10-13
1559   Gretchen E. Ziegenhals, "This Bridge Called Me Back," *CC* 106
       (1989): 343-44.

13:10
1560   Christoph Burchard, "Fußnoten zum neutestamentlichen Griechisch
       II," *ZNW* 69 (1978): 143-57.

13:11
1561   Günther Schwarz, "καὶ ἦν συγκύπτουσα," *BibN* 20 (1983): 58.

1562   Walter Radl, "Ein 'Doppeltes Leiden' in Lk. 13,11: Zu Einer Notiz
       von Günther Schwarz," *BibN* 31 (1986): 35-36.

13:16
1563   Günther Schwarz, "λυθῆναι απὸ τοῦ δεσμοῦ τούτου," *BibN* 15
       (1981): 47.

13:18-19
1564   O. Kuss, "Zur Senfkornparabel," *TGl* 41 (1951): 40-49.

1565   B. Schultze, "Die ekklesioklogische Bedeutung des Gleichnisses
       vom Senfkorn," *OCP* 27 (1961): 362-86.

1566   H. K. McArthur, "The Parable of the Mustard Seed," *CBQ* 33
       (1971): 198-210.

1567   John Dominic Crossan, "The Seed Parables of Jesus," *JBL* 92
       (1973): 244-66.

13:20-21
1568   Robert W. Funk, "Beyond Criticism in Quest of Literacy: The
       Parable of the Leaven," *Int* 25 (1971): 149-70.

1569   Elizabeth Waller, "The Parable of the Leaven: A Sectarian
       Teaching and the Inclusion of Women," *USQR* 35 (1980): 99-109.

13:22-30
    1570 P. Hoffmann, "Pántes ergátai adikías, Redaktion und Tradition in Lc 13,22-30," *ZNW* 58 (1967): 188-214.

    1571 J. Seynaeve, "La parabole de la porte étroite: l'acceptation 'pratique' du Christ (Lc 13)," *AsSeign* N.S. 52 (1974): 68-77.

    1572 J. C. Sampedro-Forner, "Historia de la sahación o salvación en la historia Estudio exegético-teológico de Lc. 13,22-30," *StudL* 21 (1980): 9-48.

13:22-24
    1573 R. Parrott, "Entering the Narrow Door: Matt 7:13/Luke 13:22-24," *Forum* 5 (1989): 111-20.

13:22
    1574 C. L'Eplattenier, "Lecture d'une séquence lucanienne, Luc 13:22 à 14:24," *ÉTR* 56 (1981): 282-87.

13:23-24
    1575 A. Denaux, "Der Spruch von den zwei Wegen im Rahmen des Epilogs der Bergpredigt (Mt 7,13-14 par. Lk 13,23-24)," in J. Delobel, ed., *Logia: Les paroles de Jésus (The Sayings of Jesus).* BETL #59. Louvain: Peeters Press, 1982. Pp. 305-35.

13:24
    1576 J. Duncan M. Derrett, "The Merits of the Narrow Gate," *JSNT* 15 (1982): 20-29.

    1577 H. Giesen, "Verantwortung des Christen in der Gegenwart und Heilsvollendung: Ethik und Eschatologie nach Lk 13,24 und 16,16," *TGeg* 31 (1988): 218-28.

13:28-29
    1578 Dale C. Allison, "Who Will Come from East and West," *IBS* 11 (1989): 158-70.

13:28
    1579 Dieter Zeller, "Das Logion Mt 8,11f./Lk 13,28f. und das Motiv der 'Völkerwallfahrt'," *BZ* 15 (1971): 222-37; 16 (1972): 84-93.

    1580 W. Grimm, "Zum Hintergrund von Mt 8,11f., Lk 13,28.f," *BZ* 16 (1972): 255-56.

140

BIBLIOGRAPHIES FOR BIBLICAL RESEARCH

13:29-30
1581 Otto E. Strasser, "Letzte Erste, Erste Letzte: Predigt über Luk 13,29.30," in *Das Wort sie sollen lassen stahn* (festschrift for D. Albert Schädelin). Bern: Lang, 1950. Pp. 215-20.

13:31-33
1582 A. Denaux, "L'hypocrisie des Pharisiens et le dessein de Dieu. Analyse de Lc. XIII,31-33," in *L'Évangile de Luc: Problèmes littéraires et théologiques*. Gembloux: Duculot, 1973. Pp. 245-85.

1583 W. Grimm, "Eschatologischer Saul wider eschatologischen David," *NovT* 15 (1973): 114-33.

1584 M. Reese, "Einige Uberlegungen zu Lukas XIII,31-33," in J. DuPont, et al., eds., *Jésus aux origines de la christologie*. Louvain: University Press, 1975. Pp. 201-25.

13:31
1585 B. Prete, "Il testo di Luca 13:31. Unità letteraria ed insegnamento cristologico," *BibO* 24 (1982): 59-79.

13:32
1586 L. H. Bunn, "Herod Antipas and 'That Fox'," *ET* 43 (1931-1932): 380-81.

1587 J. Duncan M. Derrett, "The Lucan Christ and Jerusalem: τελειοῦμαι," *ZNW* 75 (1984): 36-43.

13:33
1588 J. Bishop, "The Power of the Single Purpose," *ET* 93 (1982-1983): 115-16.

13:34-35
1589 F. D. Weinert, "Luke, the Temple, and Jesus' Saying about Jerusalem's Abandoned House (Luke 13:34-35)," *CBQ* 44 (1982): 68-76.

13:34
1590 Dieter Zeller, "Entrückung zur Ankunft als Menschensohn (Lk 13:34f; 11:29f)," in Françios Refoulé, ed., *à cause de l'Evangile: Etudes sur les synoptiques et les Actes* (festschrift for Jacques Dupont). Paris: Cerf, 1985. Pp. 513-30.

13:35

1591   Dale C. Allison, "Matt. 23:39 = Luke 13:35b as a Conditional Prophecy," *JSNT* 18 (1983): 75-84.

14:1-24

1592   J. Ernst, "Gastmahlgespräche: Lk 14,1-24," in Rudolf Schnackenburg, et al., eds., *Die Kirche des Anfangs* (festschrift for H. Schürmann). Freiburg: Herder, 1978. Pp. 57-78.

1593   E. Springs Steele, "Jesus's Table Fellowship with Pharisees: An Editorial Analysis of Luke 7:36-50, 11:37-54, and 14:1-24," doctoral dissertation, University of Notre Dame, Notre Dame IN, 1982.

1594   S. van Tilborg, "De parabel van de grote feestmaaltijd (Lc 14,1-24)," in B. van Iersel, et al., eds., *Parabelverhalen in Lucas: Van semiotiek naar pragmatiek.* TFT-Studies #8. Tilburg: University Press, 1987. Pp. 133-47.

14:1-11

1595   E. Galbiati, "Esegesi degli Evangeli festivi," *BibO* 1 (1959): 20-25.

14:1-10

1596   C. Dietzfelbinger, "Vom Sinn der Sabbatheilungen Jesu," *EvT* 38 (1978): 281-97.

14:1-6

1597   Ben Hemelsoet, "Gezegend hij die komf, de Koning, in de naam des Heren': Rondom Lucas 14,1-6," *ACEBT* 1 (1980): 85-95.

1598   J. Duncan M. Derrett, "Positive Perspectives on Two Lucan Miracles," *DR* 104 (1986): 272-87.

14:5

1599   Matthew Black, "The Aramaic Spoken by Christ and Luke 14,5," *JTS* 1 (1950): 60-62.

1600   H. Riesenfeld, "Anteckning till Luk 14:5," *SEÅ* 49 (1984): 83-88.

14:7-35
   1601 H.-J. Degenhardt, "Gastmahlgespräche und Eintrittsbedingungen für die Jüngerschaft Jesu: Lk 14,7-35," in *Lukas Evangelist der Armen*. Stuttgart: Katholisches Bibelwerk, 1965. Pp. 97-113.

14:7-11
   1602 Erhardt Güttgemanns, "Narrative Analyse Synoptischer Texte," *LB* 25/26 (1973): 50-73.

   1603 Timothy L. Noël, "The Parable of the Wedding Guest: A Narrative-Critical Interpretation," *PRS* 16 (1989): 17-27.

14:8-11
   1604 D. Bivin, "A Measure of Humility," *JeruP* 4 (1991): 13-14.

14:12-24
   1605 Otto Glombitza, "Das Grosse Abendmahl: Luk 14:12-24," *NovT* 5 (1962): 10-16.

   1606 Daniel L. Migliore, "The Open Banquet," *PSB* 6/1 (1985): 8-13.

14:14
   1607 P. Ketter, "Die Auferstehung der Gerechten und der Sünder (Luke 14:14)," *BK* 4 (1949): 10-20.

   1608 Caesarius Cavallin, "Bienheureux seras-tu--à la résurrection des justes: le macarisme de Lc 14:14," in François Refoulé, ed., *à cause de l'Evangile: Etudes sur les synoptiques et les Actes* (festschrift for Jacques Dupont). Paris: Cerf, 1985. Pp. 531-46.

14:15-24
   1609 J. Baker, "Christ's Challenge to Straight Thinking," *ET* 67 (1955-1956): 179-81.

   1610 Eta Linneman, "Überlegungen zur Parabel vom grossen Abendmahl, Lc 14,15-24/Mt 22,1-14," *ZNW* 51 (1960): 246-55.

   1611 J. Duncan M. Derrett, "The Parable of the Great Supper," in *Law in the New Testament*. London: Darton, Longman & Todd, 1970. Pp. 126-55.

1612 F. Hahn, "Das Gleichnis von der Einladung zum Festmahl," in O. Böcher and K. Haacker, eds., *Verborum Veritas* (festschrift for Gustav Stählin). Wuppertal: Brockhaus, 1970. Pp. 51-82.

1613 Dan O. Via, "The Relationship of Form to Content in the Parable: The Wedding Feast," *Int* 25 (1971): 171-84.

1614 A. Vögtle, "Die Einladung zum grossen Gastmahl und zum königlichen Hochzeitsmahl: Ein Paradigma für den Wandel des geschichtlichen Verständnishorizonts," in *Das Evangelium und die Evangelien*. Düsseldorf: Patmos, 1971. Pp. 171-218.

1615 D. Dormeyer, "Literarische und theologische Analyse der Parabel Lukas 14:15-24," *BibL* 15 (1974): 206-19.

1616 J. A. Sanders, "The Ethic of Election in Luke's Great Banquet Parable," in James L. Crenshaw and J. T. Willis, eds., *Essays in Old Testament Ethics* (Philip Hyatt, in memoriam). New York: KTAV, 1974. Pp. 245-71.

1617 E. Pousset, "Les invités au banquet (Luc 14,15-24)," *Chr* 32 (1985): 81-89.

1618 L. Schottroff, "Das Gleichnis vom grossen Gastmahl in der Logienquelle," *EvT* 47 (1987): 192-211.

1619 K. Wegenast, "Freiheit ist lernbar: Lukas 14,15-24 im Unterricht," *EvErz* 40 (1988): 592-600.

1620 Irene Gysel-Nef, "Ein Anderes Fest," *Reformatio* 38 (1989): 178-83.

1621 Victor E. Vine, "Luke 14:15-24 and Anti-Semitism," *ET* 102 (1990-1991): 262-63.

1622 Richard L. Rohrbaugh, "The Pre-Industrial City in Luke-Acts: Urban Social Relations," in Jerome H. Neyrey, ed., *The Social World of Luke-Acts*. Peabody MA: Hendrickson Publishers, 1991. Pp. 125-49.

14:16-30
1623 D. Bauer, "Das fängt ja gut an! Die Ablehnung Jesu in seiner Heimat (Lk 14,16-30)," in P.-G. Müller, ed., *Das Zeugnis des Lukas*. Stuttgart: Katholisches Bibelwerk, 1985. Pp. 46-53.

14:16-24
1624 Rudolf Bultmann, "Lukas 14,16-24," in Rudolf Bultmann, ed., *Marburger Predigten*. Tübingen: Mohr, 1956. Pp. 126-36.

1625 E. Galbiati, "Gli invitati al convito (Luke 14:16-24)," *BibO* 7 (1965): 129-35.

1626 G. Eichholz, "Von grossen Abendmahl und von der königlichen Hochzeit," in *Gleichnisse der Evangelien*. Neukirchen-Vluyn: Neukirchener Verlag, 1971. Pp. 126-47.

1627 Humphrey Palmer, "Just Married, Cannot Come," *NovT* 18/4 (1976): 241-57.

1628 R. W. Resenhöft, "Jesu Gleichnis von den Talenten, ergänzt durch die Lukas-Fassung," *NTS* 26 (1979-1980): 318-31.

1629 A. P. Dominic, "Lucan Source of Religious Life," *ITS* 23 (1986): 273-89.

1630 Rainer Russ, "Das Fest hat soeben begonnen: Uberlegungen zu Lk 14,16-24: Versuch zur Erhellung einer homiletischen Bewusstseinslage," in Johannes J. Degenhardt, ed., *Die Freude an Gott: Unsere Kraft* (festschrift for Otto B. Knoch). Stuttgart: Verlag Katholisches Bibelwerk, 1991. Pp. 357-65.

14:16-23
1631 Olivier Abel, "De l'Obligation de Croire: les Objections de Bayle au Commentaire Augustinien du 'Contrains-les d'Entrer'," *ÉTR* 61/1 (1986): 35-49.

14:21
1632 Pitirim Nechayev, "On the Called and Chosen," *JMP* 12 (1985): 34-36.

14:23
1633 Siegfried Kreuzer, "Der Zwang des Boten: Beobachtungen zu Lk. 14:23 und 1 Kor 9:16," *ZNW* 76/1-2 (1985): 123-28.

14:24

    1634 C. L'Eplattenier, "Lecture d'une séquence lucanienne, Luc 13:22 à 14:24," *ÉTR* 56 (1981): 282-87.

14:25-33

    1635 P. G. Jarvis, "Expounding the Parables: Tower-Builder and King Going to War," *ET* 77 (1965-1966): 196-98.

    1636 J. Seynaeve, "Exigences de la condition chrétienne (Lc 14)," *AsSeign* N.S. 54 (1972): 64-75.

    1637 J. Hempel, "Luk. 14,25-33, eine 'Fall-Studie'," in H. Seidel, ed., *Das lebendige Wort* (festschrift for G. Voigt). Berlin: Evangelische Verlag, 1982. Pp. 255-69.

    1638 Charles E. Wolfe, "All or Nothing," *ChrM* 16/1 (1985): 32-33.

14:26-27

    1639 Leif E. Vaage, "Q and the Historical Jesus: Some Peculiar Sayings," *Forum* 5 (1989): 159-76.

14:26

    1640 Roy A. Harrisville, "Jesus and the Family," *Int* 23/4 (1969): 425-38.

    1641 I. F. Gough, "Study on Luke 14:26: Jesus Calls His Disciples to a Life of Supreme Commitment," *ATB* 3 (1970): 23-30.

    1642 S. A. Panimolle, "Se uno non odia la moglie e ifgli, non puo essere mio discepolo (Lc 14,26)," *ParSpirV* 12 (1984): 143-65.

    1643 Ieuan Ellis, "Jesus and the Subversive Family," *SJT* 38/2 (1985): 173-88.

    1644 Robert H. Stein, "Luke 14:26 and the Question of Authenticity," *Forum* 5 (1989): 187-92.

14:27

    1645 Jan Lambrecht, "Q-influence on Mark 8,34-9,1," in J. Delobel, ed., *Logia: Les paroles de Jésus (The Sayings of Jesus)*. BETL #59. Louvain: Peeters Press, 1982. Pp. 277-304.

1646   J. Duncan M. Derrett, "Taking Up the Cross and Turning the Cheek," in A. E. Harvey, ed., *Alternative Approaches to New Testament Study*. London: Latimer, 1985. Pp. 61-78.

14:28-33
1647   S. Mechie, "The Parables of the Tower-Builder and the King Going to War," *ET* 48 (1936-1937): 235-36.

14:28-32
1648   G. Eichholz, "Vom Bauen und vom Kriegführen (Luk. 14,28-32)," in *Gleichnisse der Evangelien*. Neukirchen-Vluyn: Neukirchener Verlag, 1971. Pp. 192-99.

1649   J. Duncan M. Derrett, *"Nisi dominus aedificaverit domum:* Towers and Wars," *NovT* 19 (1977): 241-61.

1650   C. A. Stock, *Counting the Cost*. Collegeville MN: Liturgical Press, 1977.

14:28
1651   Werner Bieder, "Das Volk Gottes in Erwartung von Licht und Lobpreis," *TZ* 40/2 (1984): 137-48.

14:31-32
1652   Robert S. Alley, "Render to Jesus the Things that are Jesus'," in R. Joseph Hoffmann and Gerald A. Larue, eds., *Jesus in History and Myth*. Buffalo: Prometheus Books, 1986. Pp. 55-77.

14:31
1653   Jim Wallis, "Acting Boldly in the Spirit: A Call to Peace Pentecost 1985," *Soj* 14/4 (1985): 4-5.

14:33
1654   Thomas Schmidt, "Burden, Barrier, Blasphemy: Wealth in Matt. 6:33, Luke 14:33, and Luke 16:15," *TriJ* 9/2 (1988): 171-89.

14:34-35
1655   Oscar Cullmann, "Que signihe le sel dans la parabole de Jésus?" in *La foi et le culte de l'Église primitive*. Neuchâtel: Delachaux & Niestlé, 1963. Pp. 211-20.

14:34

1656   Johannes B. Bauer, "Quod si sal infatuatum fuerit," *VD* 28 (1951): 228-30.

15:1-32

1657   G. Antoine, "Les trois paraboles de la miséricorde: Explication de Lc 15,1-32," in F. Bovon and G. Rouiller, eds., *Exegesis Problèmes de méthode et exercices de lecture (Genèse 22 et Luc 15)*. Neuchâtel-Paris: Delachaux & Niestlé, 1975. Pp. 126-35.

1658   R. Waelkens, "L'analyse structurale des paraboles. Deux essais: Luke 15:1-32 et Matthieu 13:44-46," *RTL* 8 (1977): 160-78.

1659   E. P. Sanders, "Jesus and the Sinners," *JSNT* 19 (1983): 5-36.

1660   R. Krüger, " 'La sustitución del tener por el ser: Lectura semiótica de Lucas 15,1-32," *RevB* 49 (1987): 65-97.

1661   B. D. Chilton, "Jesus and the Repentance of E. P. Sanders," *TynB* 39 (1988): 1-18.

15:1-10

1662   F. Kamphaus, " ' . . . zu suchen, was verloren war.' Homilie zu Luke 15:1-10," *BibL* 8 (1967): 201-203.

1663   H. Sawatzky, "Problem at the Party," *ET* 91 (1979-1980): 270-72.

1664   J. Toy, "The Lost Sheep and the Lost Coin," *ET* 92 (1980-1981): 276-77.

1665   Camille Focant, "La parabole de la brebis perdue: Lecture historico-critique et réflexions théologiques," *FT* 13 (1983): 52-79.

15:1-7

1666   Wilhelm Schmidt, "Der Gute Hirte: Biblische Besinnung über Luke 15:1-7," *EvT* 24/4 (1964): 173-77.

1667   D. Dormeyer, "Textpragmatische Analyse und Unterrichtsplanung zum Gleichnis vom verlorenen Schaf, Lk 15,1-7," *EvErz* 27 (1975): 347-57.

1668   P. Mourlon-Beernaert, "The Lost Sheep: Four Approaches," *TD* 29 (1981): 143-48.

15:1-2
>   **1669**   M. Völkel, " 'Freund der Zöllner und Sünder'," *ZNW* 69 (1978): 1-10.

>   **1670**   A. Viard, "Un homme avait deux fils (Luke 15:1-2, 11-32)," *EV* 83 (1983): 53-55.

>   **1671**   J. M. Casciaro, "Parábola, hipérbola y mashal en los sinópticos," *ScripT* 25 (1993): 15-31.

15:1
>   **1672**   M. Völkel, "Freund der Zöllner und Sünder," *ZNW* 69 (1978): 1-10.

15:2
>   **1673**   Juan J. Bartolome, "Synesthiein en la Obra Lucana: Lc 15,2; Hch 10,41; 11:3," *Sale* 46/2 (1984): 269-88.

15:3-10
>   **1674**   J. Duncan M. Derrett, "Fresh Light on the Lost Sheep and the Lost Coin," *NTS* 26 (1979-1980): 36-60.

15:3-7
>   **1675**   E. F. F. Bishop, "The Parable of the Lost or Wandering Sheep," *ATR* 44 (1962): 44-57.

>   **1676**   S. Arai, "Das Gleichnis vom verlorenen Schaf: Eine traditionsgeschichtliche Untersuchung," *AJBI* 2 (1976): 111-37.

15:3-6
>   **1677**   W. L. Petersen, "The Parable of the Lost Sheep in the Gospel of Thomas and the Synoptics," *NovT* 23 (1981): 128-47.

>   **1678**   Warren Vanhetloo, "Two Ninety and Nines," *CBTJ* 2/1 (1986): 9-22.

15:4-7
>   **1679**   F. Schnider, "Das Gleichnis vom verloreren Schaf und seine Redaktoren," *K* 19 (1977): 146-54.

>   **1680**   R. Favris, "La parabola della pecora perduta," *ParSpirV* 10 (1984): 105-19.

15:4

1681   F. Bussy, "Did a Shepherd Leave Sheep Upon the Mountains or in the Desert?" *ATR* 45 (1963): 93-94.

15:8-10

1682   Heidemarie Langer, "Letting Ourselves Be Found: Stories of a Feminist Spirituality," *EcumRev* 38/1 (1986): 23-28.

1683   Daniel Sheerin, "The Theotokion: Ὁ ΤΗΝ ΕΥΛΟΓΗΜΕΝΗΝ: Its Background in Patristic Exegesis of Luke 15:8-10 and Western Parallels," *VC* 43/2 (1989): 166-87.

1684   David R. Catchpole, "Ein Schaf, eine Drachme und ein Israelit: die Botschaft Jesu in Q," in Johannes J. Degenhardt, ed., *Die Freude an Gott: Unsere Kraft* (festschrift for Otto B. Knoch). Stuttgart: Verlag Katholisches Bibelwerk, 1991. Pp. 89-101.

15:10

1685   Andrew F. Walls, "In the Presence of the Angels," *NovT* 3 (1959): 314-16.

15:11-52

1686   J. Jeremias, "Zum Gleichnis vom verlorenen Sohn, Luk. 15,11-52," *TZ* 5 (1949): 228-31.

15:11-32

1687   J. E. Compton, "The Prodigal's Brother," *ET* 42 (1930-1931): 287.

1688   H. E. Sticker, "The Prodigal's Brother," *ET* 42 (1930-1931): 45-46.

1689   L. R. Fisher, "An Amarna Age Prodigal," *JSS* 3 (1958): 113-22.

1690   Charles E. Carlston, "A Positive Criterion of Authenticity?" *BR* 7 (1962): 33-44.

1691   R. Silva, "La parábola del hijo pródigo," *CuBí* 23 (1966): 259-63.

1692   J. Duncan M. Derrett, "Law in the New Testament: The Parable of the Prodigal Son," *NTS* 14 (1967-1968): 56-74.

1693   Jack T. Sanders, "Tradition and Redaction in Luke xv.11-32," *NTS* 15 (1968-1969): 433-38.

1694   P. Penning de Vries, "Der nie verlorene Vater," *GeistL* 44 (1971): 74-75.

1695   J. J. O'Rourke, "Some Notes on Luke xv.11-32," *NTS* 18 (1971-1972): 431-33.

1696   J. Delgado Sanchez, "Consideraciones sobre la parábola del hijo pródigo," *CuBí* 29 (1972): 338-41.

1697   Gerhard Lohfink, "Das Gleichnis vom gütigen Vater. Eine Predigt zu Luke 15:11-32," *BibL* 13 (1972): 138-46.

1698   Erhardt Güttgemanns, "Narrative Analyse Synoptischer Texte," *LB* 25/26 (1973): 50-73.

1699   Ingo Broer, "Das Gleichnis vom verlorenen Sohn und die Theologie des Lukas," *NTS* 20 (1973-1974): 453-62.

1700   W. Harrington, "The Prodigal Son," *Furrow* 25 (1974): 432-37.

1701   Gerhard Sellin, "Gleichnisstrukturen," *LB* 31 (1974): 89-115.

1702   L. Beirnaert, "La parabole de l'enfant prodigue (Lc 15,11-32) lue par un analyste," in F. Bovon and G. Rouiller, eds., *Exegesis Problèmes de méthode et exercices de lecture (Genèse 22 et Luc 15)*. Neuchâtel-Paris: Delachaux & Niestlé, 1975. Pp. 136-44.

1703   F. Bovon, "La parabole de l'enfant prodigue (Lc 15,11-32)," in F. Bovon and G. Rouiller, eds., *Exegesis Problèmes de méthode et exercices de lecture (Genèse 22 et Luc 15)*. Neuchâtel-Paris: Delachaux & Niestlé, 1975. Pp. 82-85.

1704   Charles E. Carlston, "Reminiscence and Redaction in Luke 15:11-32," *JBL* 94 (1975): 368-90.

1705   C. Senft, "Ferdinand Christian Baur: Apport méthodologique et interprétation de Lc 15,11-32," in F. Bovon and G. Rouiller, eds., *Exegesis: Problèmes de méthode et exercices de lecture* (Genèse 22, et Luc 15). Neuchâtel: Delachaux & Niestlé, 1975. Pp. 56-68.

1706 Y. Tissot, "Allégories patristiques de la parabole lucanienne des deux fils (Lc 15,11-32)," in F. Bovon and G. Rouiller, eds., *Exegesis: Problèmes de méthode et exercises de lecture* (Genèse 22, et Luc 15). Neuchâtel: Delachaux & Niestlé, 1975. Pp. 243-72.

1707 Daniel Patte, "Structural Analysis of the Parable of the Prodigal Son: Toward a Method," in Daniel Patte, ed., *Semiology and Parables: Explorations of Possibilities Offered by Structuralism for Exegesis*. Pittsburgh Theological Monograph Series #9. Pittsburgh: Pickwick, 1976. Pp. 71-149.

1708 Pierre Grelot, "Le père et ses deux fils: Luke 15:11-32," *RB* 84 (1977): 321-48, 538-65.

1709 Rudolf Pesch, "Zur Exegese Gottes durch Jesus von Nazaret: Eine Auslegung des Gleichnisses vom Vater und den beiden Söhnen (Lk 15,11-32)," in B. Casper, ed., *Jesus, Ort der Erfahrung Gottes* (festschrift for B. Welte). 2nd ed. Freiburg: Herder, 1977. Pp. 140-89.

1710 J. L. Price, "Luke 15:11-32," *Int* 31 (1977): 64-69.

1711 Bernard Brandon Scott, "The Prodigal Son: A Structuralist Interpretation," *Semeia* 9 (1977): 45-73.

1712 Mary Ann Tolbert, "The Prodigal Son: An Essay in Literary Criticism from a Psychoanalytic Perspective," *Semeia* 9 (1977): 1-20.

1713 Dan O. Via, "The Prodigal Son: A Jungian Reading," *Semeia* 9 (1977): 21-43.

1714 O. Hofius, "Alttestamentliche Motive im Gleichnis vom verlorenen Sohn," *NTS* 24 (1977-1978): 240-48.

1715 R. G. Crawford, "A Parable of the Atonement," *EQ* 50 (1978): 2-7.

1716 H. Kruse, "The Return of the Prodigal: Fortunes of a Parable on its Way to the Far East," *Orient* 47 (1978): 163-214.

1717   G. Scholz, "Aesthetische Beobachtungen am Gleichnis vom reichen Mann und armen Lazarus und von drei anderen Gleichnissen," *LB* 43 (1978): 67-74.

1718   R. Strunk and M. Mausshardt, "Leistung des Schöpferischen (Lk 15,11-32)," in Y. Spiegel, ed., *Doppeldeutlich.* Münich: Kaiser, 1978. Pp. 59-78.

1719   M. A. Vázquez-Medel, "El perdón libera del odio: Lectura estructural de Lc 15,11-32," *Communio* 11 (1978): 271-312.

1720   R. T. Osborn, "The Father and his Two Sons: A Parable of Liberation," *Dia* 19 (1980): 204-209.

1721   R. R. Rickards, "Some Points to Consider in Translating the Parable of the Prodigal Son," *BT* 31 (1980): 243-45.

1722   M. Roy, "Jugement et sanction. Matthieu 25:31-46; Luc 15:11-32; 16:19-31," *Chr* 28 (1981): 440-49.

1723   J. R. de Witt, *Amazing Love: The Parable of the Prodigal Son.* Edinburgh: Banner of Truth, 1982.

1724   J. J. Alemany, "Lc 15:11-32: Una sugerencia de análisis estructural," *MisCom* 41 (1983): 167-76.

1725   A. Viard, "Un homme avait deux fils (Luke 15:1-2, 11-32)," *EV* 83 (1983): 53-55.

1726   H.-J. Vogel, "Der verlorene Sohn: Lukas 15,11-32," *TexteK* 18 (1983): 27-34.

1727   Jacques Dupont, "Il padre del figliol prodigo (Lc 15,11-32)," *ParSpirV* 10 (1984): 120-34.

1728   G. S. Gibson, "The Sins of the Saints," *ET* 96 (1984-1985): 276-77.

1729   Roger D. Aus, "Luke 15:11-32 and R. Eliezer Ben Hyrcanus's *Rise to Fame,*" *JBL* 104 (1985): 443-69.

1730   Michael R. Austin, "The Hypocritical Son," *EQ* 57 (1985): 307-15.

1731 Allan Boesak and Wolfram Kistner, "Proclamation and Protest: The Lost Sons and Outside the Gate," in Charles Villa-Vicencio and J. de Gruchy, eds., *Resistance and Hope* (festschrift for Beyers Naudé). Grand Rapids: Eerdmans, 1985. Pp. 74-82.

1732 Nancy Corson Carter, "The Prodigal Daughter: A Parable Re-Visioned," *Soundings* 68 (1985): 88-105.

1733 J. G. Lees, "The Parable of the Good Father," *ET* 97/8 (1985-1986): 246-47.

1734 J. Smit Sibinga, "Zur Kompositionstechnik des Lukas in Lk 15:11-32," in J. W. van Henten, ed., *Tradition and Re-Interpretation in Jewish and Early Christian Literature* (festschrift for Jürgen C. H. Lebram). Leiden: Brill, 1986. Pp. 97-113.

1735 W. Zauner, "Busse als Fest: Eine Busspredigt zu Lk 15,11-32 (der barmherzige Vater—der heimgekehrte Sohn—der daheimgebliebene Bruder)," *TPQ* 134 (1986): 280-82.

1736 Vittorio Fusco, "Narrazione e dialogo nella parabola dena del figliol prodigo (Lc 15,11-32)," in G. Galli, ed., *Interpretazione e invenzione: La parabola de Figliol prodigo tra interpretazioni scientifiche e invenzioni artistiche*. Genova: Marietti, 1987. Pp. 17-67.

1737 Patrick J. Casey, "A Parable of God's Love for Sinners," *CBTJ* 5/1 (1989): 28-42.

1738 G. D. Cloete and Dirkie J. Smit, "Rejoicing With God," *JTSA* 66 (1989): 62-73.

1739 P. Pokorny, "Lukas 15,11-32 und die lukanische Soteriologie," in Karl Kertelge, ed., *Christus bezeugen* (festschrift for Wolfgang Trilling). Leipzig: St. Benno-Verlag, 1989. Pp. 179-92.

15:11-24
1740 R. G. Forrest, "I Believe in the Forgiveness of Sins," *ET* 92 (1980-1981): 18-19.

15:11-12
1741 Rudolf Hoppe, "Gleichnis und Situation," *BZ* 28/1 (1984): 1-21.

15:12
> **1742** W. Pöhlmann, "Die Abschichtung des Verlorenen Sohnes (Lk 15:12f.) und die erzählte Welt der Parabel," *ZNW* 70 (1979): 194-213.

15:17
> **1743** I. MacLeod, "Enough and to Spare," *ET* 88 (1976-1977): 114-15.

> **1744** J. C. Kellogg, "Enough to Spare," *ET* 94 (1982-1983): 272-73.

15:18-21
> **1745** Gerhard Lohfink, " 'Ich habe gesundigt gegen den Himmel und gegen dich': Eine Exegese von Lk 15,18.21," *TQ* 15 (1975): 51-52.

> **1746** J. Coppens, "Le péché, offense de Dieu ou du prochain? Note sur le Ps. LI,6 et Luc XV,18-21," in J. Coppens, ed., *La notion biblique de Dieu.* BETL #41. 2nd ed. Gembloux: Duculot, 1985. Pp. 163-67.

15:19-31
> **1747** C. H. Cave, "Lazarus and the Lukan Deuteronomy," *NTS* 15 (1968-1969): 319-25.

15:21-24
> **1748** Dallas Franklin Billington, "The Forgiving Father," *FundJ* 4/6 (1985): 49.

15:24
> **1749** Georg Braumann, "Tot-lebendig, verloren-gefunden (Lk 15,24 und 32)," in W. Haubeck and M. Bachmann, eds., *Wort in der Zeit* (festschrift for K. H. Rengstorf). Leiden: Brill, 1980. Pp. 156-64.

15:30
> **1750** James Custer, "When Is Communion Communion," *GTJ* 6/2 (1985): 403-10.

> **1751** Tom Corlett, "This Brother of Yours," *ET* 100 (1989-1990): 216.

15:32
> **1752** Georg Braumann, "Tot-lebendig, verloren-gefunden (Lk 15,24 und 32)," in W. Haubeck and M. Bachmann, eds., *Wort in der Zeit* (festschrift for K. H. Rengstorf). Leiden: Brill, 1980. Pp. 156-64.

16:1-35

1753 R. G. Lunt, "Expounding the Parables: Parable of the Unjust Steward," *ET* 77 (1965-1966): 132-36.

16:1-17

1754 Paul Scott Wilson, "The Lost Parable of the Generous Landowner and Other Texts for Imaginative Preaching," *QR* 9 (1989): 80-99.

16:1-13

1755 R. B. Y. Scott, "The Parable of the Unjust Steward," *ET* 49 (1937-1938): 234-35.

1756 W. F. Boyd, "The Parable of the Unjust Steward," *ET* 50 (1938-1939): 46.

1757 Lawrence M. Friedel, "The Parable of the Unjust Steward," *CBQ* 3 (1941): 337-48.

1758 D. R. Fletcher, "The Riddle of the Unjust Steward," *JBL* 82 (1963): 15-30.

1759 Joseph A. Fitzmyer, "The Story of the Dishonest Manager," *TS* 25 (1964): 23-42.

1760 Hans Kosmala, "The Parable of the Unjust Steward in the Light of Qumran," *ASTI* 3 (1964): 114-21.

1761 Francis E. Williams, "Is Almsgiving the Point of the 'Unjust Steward'?" *JBL* 83 (1964): 293-97.

1762 L. J. Topel, "On the Injustice of the Unjust Steward: Lk 16:1-13," *CBQ* 35 (1975): 216-27.

1763 Dan O. Via, "The Parable of the Unjust Judge: A Metaphor of the Unrealized Self," in Daniel Patte, ed., *Semiology and Parables: Exploration of the Possibilities Offered by Structuralism for Exegesis*. Pittsburgh: Pickwick Press, 1976. Pp. 1-32.

1764 J. P. Molina, "Luc 16:1 à 13: l'injustice Mamon," *ÉTR* 53 (1978): 311-75.

1765   G. Barth, "The Dishonest Steward and his Lord: Reflections on Luke 16:1-13," in D. Y. Hadidian, ed., *From Faith to Faith* (festschrift for Donald G. Miller). Pittsburgh: Pickwick, 1979. Pp. 65-73.

1766   Camille Focant, "Tromper le Mamon d'iniquité (Lc 16:1-13)," in Françios Refoulé, ed., *à cause de l'Evangile: Etudes sur les synoptiques et les Actes* (festschrift for Jacques Dupont). Paris: Cerf, 1985. Pp. 547-69.

1767   Stanley E. Porter, "The Parable of the Unjust Steward: Irony is the Key," in David J. A. Clines, et al., eds., *The Bible in Three Dimensions: Essays in Celebration of Forty Years of Biblical Studies in the University of Sheffield.* Sheffield: JSOT Press, 1990. Pp. 127-53.

16:1-9

1768   F. Hüttermann, "Stand das Gleichnis vom ungerechten Verwalter in Q?" *TGl* 27 (1935): 739-42.

1769   Charles H. Pickar, "The Unjust Steward," *CBQ* 1 (1939): 250-53.

1770   E. Galbiati, "Esegesi degli Evangeli festivi," *BibO* 3 (1961): 92-96.

1771   H. Zimmermann, "Die Forderung der Gleichnisse Jesu. Das Gleichnis vom ungerechten Verwalter: Lk 16:1-9," *BibL* 2 (1961): 254-61.

1772   F. J. Moore, "The Parable of the Unjust Steward," *ATR* 47 (1965): 103-105.

1773   André Feuillet, "La parabole du mauvais riche et du pauvre Lazare (Luc 16:19-31) antithèse de la parabole de l'intendant astucieux (Luc 16:1-9)," *NRT* 101 (1979): 212-23.

1774   A. Fossion, "Tromper l'argent trompeur: Lecture structurale de la parabole du gérant habile (Luc 16,1-9)," *FT* 13 (1983): 342-60.

16:1-8

1775   J. Maiworm, "Die Verwalter-Parabel," *TGl* 36 (1944): 149-56.

1776   J. Maiworm, "Die Verwalter-Parabel," *BK* 13 (1958): 11-18.

1777   J. Duncan M. Derrett, "Fresh Light on St. Luke 16: I. The Parable of the Unjust Steward," *NTS* 7 (1960-1961): 198-219.

1778   J. Duncan M. Derrett, "Fresh Light on St. Luke 16: II. Dives and Lazarus and the Preceding Sayings," *NTS* 7 (1960-1961): 364-80.

1779   Francis E. Williams, "Is Almsgiving the Point of the 'Unjust Steward'?" *JBL* 83 (1964): 293-97.

1780   Bernard Brandon Scott, "A Master's Praise: Luke 16:1-8," *Bib* 64 (1983): 173-88.

1781   G. Baudler, "Das Gleichnis vom 'betrügerischen Verwalter' (Lk 16,1-8a) als Ausdruck der 'inneren Biographie' Jesu. Beispiel einer existenz-biographischen Gleichnisinterpretation im religionspädagogischer Absicht," *TGeg* 28 (1985): 65-76.

1782   John S. Kloppenborg, "The Dishonoured Master (Luke 16:1-8a)," *Bib* 70/4 (1989): 474-95.

1783   William R. G. Loader, "Jesus and the Rogue in Luke 16:1-8a: The Parable of the Unjust Steward," *RB* 96 (1989): 518-32.

1784   Douglas M. Parrott, "The Dishonest Steward and Luke's Special Parable Collection," *NTS* 37 (1991): 499-515.

1785   Mary Ann Beavis, "Ancient Slavery as an Interpretive Context for the New Testament Servant Parables with Special Reference to the Unjust Steward," *JBL* 111 (1992): 37-54.

16:1-7

1786   H. Preisker, "Lukas 16,1-7," *TLZ* 74 (1949): 85-92.

1787   H. Drexler, "Zu Lukas 16,1-7," *ZNW* 58 (1967): 286-88.

16:1-3

1788   A. King, "The Parable of the Unjust Steward," *ET* 50 (1938-1939): 474-76.

16:1

1789   H. R. Graham, "Once there Was a Rich Man . . . : Five 'Rich Man' Stories in Luke," *BibTo* 26 (1988): 98-103.

16:3-25
    1790   R. P. Casey, "An Early Armenian Fragment of Luke xvi.3-25,"
           JTS 36 (1935): 70-73.

16:5-7
    1791   G. Gander, "Le procédé de l'économe infidèle, décrit Luc 16:5-7,
           est-il répréhensible ou louable?" *VC* 27/28 (1953): 128-41.

16:6
    1792   J. Duncan M. Derrett, "Take Thy Bond . . . and Write Fifty (Luke
           xvi.6): The Nature of the Bond," *JTS* 23 (1972): 438-40.

16:8-53
    1793   Gregorio Ruiz, "El Clamor de las Piedras (Lk. 19:40; Hab 2:11):
           el Reino Choca con la Ciudad Injusta en la Fiesta de Ramos," *EE*
           59/230 (1984): 297-312.

16:8-9
    1794   A. Maillot, "Notules sur Luc 16:8-9," *ÉTR* 44 (1969): 127-30.

16:8
    1795   I. Howard Marshall, "Luke xvi.8: Who Commended the Unjust
           Steward?" *JTS* 19 (1968): 617-19.

    1796   Günther Schwarz, " . . . lobte den betrügerischen Verwalter?
           (Lukas 16,8s)," *BZ* 18 (1974): 94-95.

    1797   J. T. Noonan, "The Devious Employees," *Commonweal* 104
           (1977): 681-83.

    1798   P. Fasst, " 'Und er lobte den ungerechten Verwalter' (Lk 16,8a):
           Komposition und Redaktion in Lk 16," in R. Kilian, et al., eds.,
           Eschatologie (festschrift for E. Neuhäusler). St. Ottilien: EOS,
           1981. Pp. 109-43.

    1799   Michael G. Steinhauser, "Noah in His Generation: An Allusion in
           Luke 16,8b 'εἰς τὴν γενεὰν τὴν ἑαυτῶν'," *ZNW* 79 (1988):
           152-57.

    1800   C. S. Mann, "Unjust Steward or Prudent Manager?" *ET* 102
           (1990-1991): 234-35.

16:9-13

1801 A. Descamps, "La composition littéraire de Luc xvi.9-13," *NovT* 1 (1956): 47-53.

1802 P. Rüger, "*Mamōnas*," *ZNW* 64 (1973): 127-31.

16:9-11

1803 P. Colella, "De Mamona iniquitatis," *RBib* 19 (1971): 427-28.

16:9

1804 J. C. Wansey, "The Parable of the Unjust Steward: An Interpretation," *ET* 47 (1935-1936): 39-40.

1805 O. Hof, "Luthers Auslegung von Lukas 16,9," *EvT* 8 (1948-1949): 151-66.

1806 P. Colella, "Zu Lk 16,9," *ZNW* 64 (1973): 124-26.

1807 H. R. Graham, "Once there Was a Rich Man . . . : Five 'Rich Man' Stories in Luke," *BibTo* 26 (1988): 98-103.

16:13

1808 S. Safrai and D. Flusser, "The Slave of Two Masters," *Immanuel* 6 (1976): 30-33.

1809 Jacques Dupont, "Dieu ou Mammon (Mt 6,24; Lc 16,13)," *CrNSt* 5 (1984): 441-61.

16:15

1810 Thomas Schmidt, "Burden, Barrier, Blasphemy: Wealth in Matt. 6:33, Luke 14:33, and Luke 16:15," *TriJ* 9/2 (1988): 171-89.

16:16-18

1811 Ernst Bammel, "Is Luke 16,16-18 of Baptist Provenience?" *HTR* 51 (1958): 101-106.

16:16

1812 Frederick W. Danker, "Luke 16:16: An Opposition Logion," *JBL* 77 (1958): 231-43.

1813 David R. Catchpole, "On Doing Violence to the Kingdom," *JTSA* 25 (1978): 50-61.

1814   B. E. Thiering, "Are the 'Violent Men' False Teachers?'' *NovT* 21/4 (1979): 293-97.

1815   P. S. Cameron, *Violence and the Kingdom: The Interpretation of Matthew 11:12.* Frankfurt: Lang, 1984.

1816   David R. Catchpole, "The Law and the Prophets in Q,'' in G. F. Hawthorne and O. Betz, eds., *Tradition and Interpretation in the New Testament* (festschrift for E. Earle Ellis). Grand Rapids MI: Eerdmans, 1987. Pp. 95-109.

1817   J. B. Cortés and F. M. Gatti, "On the Meaning of Luke 16:16,'' *JBL* 106 (1987): 247-59.

1818   H. Giesen, "Verantwortung des Christen in der Gegenwart und Heilsvollendung: Ethik und Eschatologie nach Lk 13,24 und 16,16,'' *TGeg* 31 (1988): 218-28.

1819   Ben Witherington, "Jesus and the Baptist: Two of a Kind?'' *SBLSP* 18 (1988): 225-44.

16:18

1820   Gerhard Schneider, "Jesu Wort über die Ehescheidung in der Überlieferung des Neuen Testaments,'' *TTZ* 80 (1971): 65-87.

1821   J. N. M. Wijngaards, "Do Jesus' Words on Divorce (Lc 16,18) Admit No Exception?'' *Je* 6 (1975): 399-411.

1822   A. Descamps, "Les textes évangéliques sur le mariage,'' *RTL* 9 (1978): 259-86.

1823   Augustine Stock, "Matthean Divorce Texts,'' *BTB* 8/1 (1978): 24-33.

1824   Charles C. Ryrie, "Biblical Teaching on Divorce and Remarriage,'' *GTJ* 3/2 (1982): 177-92.

1825   B. N. Wambacq, "Matthieu 5,31-32: Possibilite de Divorce ou Obligation de Rompre une Union Illigitime,'' *NRT* 104/1 (1982): 34-49.

1826 W. R. Stenger, "Zur Rekonstruktion eines Jesusworts anhand der synoptischen Ehescheidungslogien (Mt 5,32; 19,9; Lk 16,18; Mk 10,11f)," *K* 26 (1984): 194-205.

1827 Edward Dobson, "The Teachings of Jesus," *FundJ* 4/11 (1985): 35-36.

16:19-31

1828 J. Maiworm, "Umgekehrte Gleichnisse," *BK* 10 (1955): 82-85.

1829 Henry Joel Cadbury, "A Proper Name For Dives," *JBL* 81 (1962): 399-402.

1830 Kendrick Grobel, "Whose Name Was Neves," *NTS* 10 (1963-1964): 373-82.

1831 W. P. Huie, "The Poverty of Abundance. From Text to Sermon on Luke 16:19-31," *Int* 22 (1968): 403-20.

1832 Otto Glombitza, "Der reiche Mann und der arme Lazarus," *NovT* 12 (1970): 166-80.

1833 A. George, "La parabole du riche et de Lazare (Lc 16)," *AsSeign* N.S. 57 (1971): 80-93.

1834 J. Zmijewski, "Die Eschatologiereden Lk 21 und Lk 17. Überlegungen zum Verständnis und zur Einordnung der lukanischen Eschatologie," *BibL* 14 (1973): 30-40.

1835 Gerhard Sellin, "Gleichnisstrukturen," *LB* 31 (1974): 89-115.

1836 E. Pax, "Der Reiche und der arme Lazarus eine Milieustudie," *SBFLA* 25 (1975): 254-68.

1837 Thorwald Lorenzen, "A Biblical Meditation on Luke 16,19-31," *ET* 87 (1975-1976): 39-45.

1838 E. S. Wehrli, "Luke 16:19-31," *Int* 31 (1977): 276-80.

1839 F. Schnider and W. Stenger, "Die offene Tür und die unüberschreitbare Kluft. Strukturanalytische Überlegungen zum Gleichnis vom reichen Mann und armen Lazarus," *NTS* 25 (1978-1979): 273-83.

1840   André Feuillet, "La parabole du mauvais riche et du pauvre Lazare (Luc 16:19-31) antithèse de la parabole de l'intendant astucieux (Luc 16:1-9)," *NRT* 101 (1979): 212-23.

1841   J. Toy, "The Rich Man and Lazarus," *ET* 91 (1979-1980): 274-75.

1842   H. J. L. Jensen, "Diesseits und Jenseits des Raumes eines Textes: Textsemiotische Bemerkungen zur Erzählung 'Vom reichen Mann und armen Lazarus'," *LB* 47 (1980): 39-60.

1843   M. Roy, "Jugement et sanction. Matthieu 25:31-46; Luc 15:11-32; 16:19-31," *Chr* 28 (1981): 440-49.

1844   J. P. Sauzède, "Une série pour le Carême," *ÉTR* 58 (1983): 59-71.

1845   Vincent Tanghe, "Abraham, Son Fils et Son Envoyé (Luc 16:19-31)," *RB* 91/4 (1984): 557-77.

1846   Jacob Kremer, "Der arme Lazarus: Lazarus, der Freund Jesu: Beobachtungen zur Beziehung zwischen Lk 16:19-31 und Joh 11:1-46," in François Refoulé, ed., *à cause de l'Evangile: Etudes sur les synoptiques et les Actes* (festschrift for Jacques Dupont). Paris: Cerf, 1985. Pp. 571-84.

1847   H. Kvalbein, "Jesus and the Poor: Two Texts and a Tentative Conclusion," *Themelios* 12 (1986-1987): 80-87.

1848   R. F. Hock, "Lazarus and Micyllus: Greco-Roman Backgrounds to Luke 16:19-31," *JBL* 106 (1987): 447-63.

1849   J. Osei-Bonsu, "The Intermediate State in Luke-Acts," *IBS* 9 (1987): 115-30.

1850   Edward G. Mathews, "The Rich Man and Lazarus: Almsgiving and Repentance in Early Syriac Tradition," *Diakonia* 22/2 (1988-1989): 89-104.

1851   Roger L. Omanson, "Lazarus and Simon," *BT* 40 (1989): 416-19.

1852   Eckart Reinmuth, "Ps-Philo, Liber Antiquitatum Biblicarum 33,1-5 und Die Auslegung der Parabel Lk. 16:19-31," *NovT* 31 (1989): 16-38.

1853 Walter Vogels, "Having or Longing: A Semiotic Analysis of Luke 16:19-31," *ÉgT* 20/1 (1989): 27-46.

1854 Richard J. Bauckham, "The Rich Man and Lazarus: The Parable and the Parallels," *NTS* 37 (1991): 225-46.

16:19-26
1855 A. A. Bucher, *Gleichnisse verstehen lernen: Strukturgenetische Untersuchungen zur Rezeption synoptischer Parabeln.* Freiburg: Universitäts-Verlag, 1990.

16:19-25
1856 G. Scholz, "Aesthetische Beobachtungen am Gleichnis vom reichen Mann und armen Lazarus und von drei anderen Gleichnissen," *LB* 43 (1978): 67-74.

16:19-21
1857 Erhardt Güttgemanns, "Narrative Analyse Synoptischer Texte," *LB* 25/26 (1973): 50-73.

16:19
1858 L. T. Lefort, "Le nom du mauvais riche Lc 16,19 et la tradition copte," *ZNW* 37 (1938): 65-72.

1859 Henry Joel Cadbury, "A Proper Name for Dives," *JBL* 81 (1962): 399-402.

1860 Henry Joel Cadbury, "The Name for Dives," *JBL* 84 (1965): 73.

16:22-31
1861 Edward G. Kettner, "Time, Eternity, and the Intermediate State," *CJ* 12/3 (1986): 90-100.

16:22
1862 H. R. Graham, "Once there Was a Rich Man . . . : Five 'Rich Man' Stories in Luke," *BibTo* 26 (1988): 98-103.

16:26
1863 E. F. F. Bishop, "A Yawning Chasm," *EQ* 45 (1973): 3-5.

17:1-19
1864 Eugene C. Kreider, "The Politics of God: The Way to the Cross," *WW* 6/4 (1986): 453-62.

17:1-10
    1865   R. M. Shelton, "Luke 17:1-10," *Int* 31 (1977): 280-85.

17:2
    1866   Jacques Schlosser, "Lk 17,2 und die Logienquelle," *SNTU-A* 8 (1983): 70-78.

17:3-4
    1867   David R. Catchpole, "Reproof and Reconciliation in the Q Community: A Study of the Tradition History of Mt 18,15-17.21-22/Lk 17,3-4," *SNTU-A* 8 (1983): 79-90.

    1868   G. Segalla, "Perdono 'cristiano' e correzione fraterna nella communità di 'Matteo' (Mt 18,15-17.21-35)," *StPa* 38 (1991): 499-518.

17:3
    1869   G. Barth, "Auseinandersetzngen um die Kirchenzucht im Umkreis des Matthäusevangeliums," *ZNW* 69 (1978): 158-77.

    1870   William R. Domeris, "Biblical Perspectives on Forgiveness," *JTSA* 54 (1986): 48-50.

    1871   Robert D. Enright, et al., "Must a Christian Require Repentance Before Forgiving?" *JPsyC* 9 (1990): 16-19.

17:5-10
    1872   A. George, "La foi des apôtres (Lc 17)," *AsSeign* N.S. 58 (1974): 68-77.

    1873   G. Lafon, *Loi, promesse, grâce: Une lecture de Luc 17,5-10.* Paris: Cerf, 1979.

17:6
    1874   J. Zmijewski, "Der Glaube und seine Macht: Eine traditionsgeschichtliche Untersuchung zu Mt 17,20; 21,21; Mk 11,25; Lk 17,6," in J. Zmijewski and E. Nellessen, eds., *Begegnung mit dem Wort* (festschrift for H. Zimmermann). Bonn: Hanstein, 1980. Pp. 81-103.

    1875   Günther Schwarz, "Πίστιν ὡς κόκκον σινάπεως," *BibN* 25 (1984): 27-35.

1876 F. Hahn, "Jesu Wort vom birgeversetzenden Glauben," *ZNW* 76 (1985): 149-69.

1877 J. Duncan M. Derrett, "Moving Mountains and Uprooting Trees," *BibO* 30 (1988): 231-44.

17:7-10

1878 Paul S. Minear, "A Note on Luke 17:7-10," *JBL* 93 (1974): 82-87.

1879 J. Duncan M. Derrett, "The Parable of the Profitable Servant," in *Studies in the New Testament. IV. Midrash, the Composition of Gospels and Discipline.* Leiden: Brill, 1986. Pp. 157-66.

17:10

1880 A. Marcus Ward, "Uncomfortable Words: IV. Unprofitable Servants," *ET* 81/7 (1969-1970): 200-203.

1881 John J. Kilgallen, "What Kind of Servants Are We?" *Bib* 63 (1982): 549-51.

1882 David P. Scaer, "Sanctification in Lutheran Theology," *CTQ* 49/2-3 (1985): 181-97.

17:11-19

1883 J. Bours, "Vom dankbaren Samariter. Eine Meditation über Lk 17:11-19," *BibL* 1 (1960): 193-98.

1884 E. Galbiati, "Esegesi degli Evangeli festivi," *BibO* 2 (1960): 171-73.

1885 Otto Glombitza, "Der dankbare Samariter," *NovT* 11 (1969): 241-46.

1886 Hans Dieter Betz, "The Cleansing of the Ten Lepers (Luke 17:11-19)," *JBL* 90 (1971): 314-28.

1887 É. Charpentier, "L'etranger appelé au salut (Lc 17)," *AsSeign* N.S. 59 (1974): 68-79.

1888 J. W. Drane, "Simon the Samaritan and the Lucan Concept of Salvation History," *EQ* 47 (1975): 131-37.

1889   W. Bruners, *Die Reinigung der zehn Aussätzigen und die Heilung des Samariters, Lk 17,11-19*. Stuttgart: Katholisches Bibelwerk, 1977.

1890   T. McCaughey, "Paradigms of Faith in the Gospel of St. Luke," *ITQ* 45 (1978): 177-84.

1891   M. J. Kingston, "Modern-day Leprosy," *ET* 92 (1980-1981): 371.

17:11
1892   G. Bouwman, "Samaria in Lucas-Handelingen," *Bij* 34 (1973): 40-59.

17:20-18:8
1893   André Feuillet, "La double venue du Règne de Dieu et du Fils de l'homme en Luc 17:20-18:8," *RT* 81 (1981): 5-33.

17:20-37
1894   F. A. Strobel, "In Dieser Nacht (Luk 17:34): Zu Einer älteren Form der Erwartung in Luk 17:20-37," *ZTK* 58/1 (1961): 16-29.

17:20-21
1895   Alexander Rüstow, "*Entos umōn estin*: zur Deutung von Lc 17,20-21," *ZNW* 51 (1960): 197-224.

1896   Franz Mussner, "Wann Kommt das Reich Gottes? Die Antwort Jesu Nach Lk. 17:20b-21," *BZ* 6/1 (1962): 107-11.

1897   K. S. Proctor, "Luke 17,20.21," *BT* 33 (1982): 245.

1898   H. Riesenfeld, "Gudsriket - här eller där, mitt ibland människor eller inom dem? Till Luk 17:20-21," *SEÅ* 47 (1982): 93-101.

1899   H. Greeven, *Jesus und das Danielbuch I: Jesu Einspruch gegen das Offenbarungssystem Daniels (Mt. 11,25-27; Lk 17,20-21)*. Bern: Lang, 1984.

1900   H. Riesenfeld, "Le règne de Dieu, parmi vous ou en vouse?" *RB* 36 (1991): 190-98.

1901   Günther Schwarz, "Οὐκ . . . μετὰ παρατηρήσεως?" *BibN* 59 (1991): 45-48.

17:20

1902 A. Strobel, "Die Passa-Erwartung als unchristlichen Problem in Lc 17,20f.," *ZNW* 49 (1958): 157-96.

1903 A. Strobel, "A Merx über Lc 17:20f," *ZNW* 51/1-2 (1960): 133-34.

1904 A. Strobel, "Zu Lk. 17:20f," *BZ* 7 (1963): 111-13.

1905 H. Hartl, "Die Aktuaatät des Gottesreiches nach Lk 17,20f," in H. Merklein, ed., *Biblische Randbemerkugen* (festschrift for Rudolf Schnackenburg). Warzburg: Echter, 1974. Pp. 25-30.

17:21

1906 G. Smith, "The Kingdom of God is Within You," *ET* 43 (1931-1932): 378-79.

1907 P. M. S. Allen, "Luke 17:21," *ET* 49 (1937-1938): 476-77; 50 (1938-1939): 233-35.

1908 A. Sledd, "The Interpretation of Luke 17,21," *ET* 50 (1938-1939): 235-37.

1909 C. H. Roberts, "The Kingdom of Heaven (Lk. XV11.21)," *HTR* 41 (1948): 1-8.

1910 Richard Sneed, "The Kingdom of God is Within You (Lk. 17:21)," *CBQ* 24 (1962): 363-82.

1911 David H. C. Read, "Christ Comes Unexpectedly," *ET* 98/1 (1986-1987): 21-22.

17:22-37

1912 W. Powell, "The Days of the Son of Man," *ET* 67 (1955-1956): 219.

17:22

1913 E. Ashby, "The Days of the Son of Man," *ET* 67 (1955-1956): 124-25.

1914 E. Leaney, "The Days of the Son of Man (Luke xvii. 22)," *ET* 67 (1955-1956): 28-29.

168 BIBLIOGRAPHIES FOR BIBLICAL RESEARCH

1915 Matthew Black, "The Aramaic Dimension in Q with Notes on Luke 17:22, Matthew 24:26," *JSNT* 40 (1990): 33-41.

17:23-37
1916 David R. Catchpole, "The Law and the Prophets in Q," in G. F. Hawthorne and O. Betz, eds., *Tradition and Interpretation in the New Testament* (festschrift for E. Earle Ellis). Grand Rapids MI: Eerdmans, 1987. Pp. 95-109.

17:25
1917 D. Meyer, "*Polla pathein*," *ZNW* 55 (1964): 132.

17:26-30
1918 Jacques Schlosser, "Les jours de Noé et de Lot: À propos de Luc, xvii,26-30," *RB* 80 (1973): 13-36.

17:26-29
1919 D. Lührmann, "Noah and Lot (Lk 17,26-29): - ein Nachtrag," *ZNW* 63 (1972): 130-32.

17:33
1920 X. Léon-Dufour, "Luc 17:33," *RechSR* 69 (1981): 101-12.

1921 Jan Lambrecht, "Q-influence on Mark 8,34-9,1," in J. Delobel, ed., *Logia: Les paroles de Jésus (The Sayings of Jesus)*. BETL #59. Louvain: Peeters Press, 1982. Pp. 277-304.

17:34-35
1922 Clayton N. Jefford, "The Dangers of Lying in Bed: Luke 17:34-35 and Parallels," *Forum* 5 (1989): 106-10.

17:34
1923 A. Strobel, "In Dieser Nacht (Luk 17:34): Zu Einer älteren Form der Erwartung in Luk 17:20-37," *ZTK* 58/1 (1961): 16-29.

17:37
1924 Ben Hemelsoet, "Jesus en Jerusalem niel gescheiden, niel gedeeld," *ACEBT* 3 (1982): 86-98.

1925 John Pairman Brown, "The Ark of the Covenant and the Temple of Janus," *BZ* 30/1 (1986): 20-35.

1926 Heinz O. Guenther, "When 'Eagles' Draw Together [Q 17:37b],"
Forum 5 (1989): 140-50.

18:1-18

1927 G. Delling, "Das Gleichnis vom gottlosen Richter," *ZNW* 53
(1962): 1-25.

1928 R. Deschryver, "La parabole du juge malveillant," *RHPR* 48
(1968): 355-66.

1929 J. Duncan M. Derrett, "Law in the New Testament: The Parable
of the Unjust Judge," *NTS* 18 (1971-1972): 178-91.

1930 Walther Bindemann, "Die Parabel vom ungerechten Richter," in
Joachim Rogge, et al., eds., *Theologische Versuche.* #13. Berlin:
Evangelisches Verlagsanstalt Berlin, 1983. Pp. 91-97.

18:1-8

1931 H. G. Meecham, "The Parable of the Unjust Judge," *ET* 57
(1945-1946): 300-307.

1932 Ceslaus Spicq, "La Parabole de la Veuve Obstinée et du Juge
Inerte, aux Décisions Impromptues," *RB* 68 (1961): 68-90.

1933 C. E. B. Cranfield, "The Parable of the Unjust Judge and the
Eschatology of Luke-Acts," *SJT* 16 (1963): 297-301.

1934 A. George, "La parabole du juge qui fait attendre le jugement (Lc
18)," *AsSeign* N.S. 60 (1975): 68-79.

1935 H. Paulsen, "Die Witwe und der Richter (Lk 18,1-8)," *TGl* 74
(1984): 13-39.

1936 E. D. Freed, "The Parable of the Judge and the Widow," *NTS* 33
(1987): 38-60.

1937 B. van Iersel, "De rechter en de weduwe (Lc 18,1-8)," in B. van
Iersel, et al., eds., *Parabelverhalen in Lucas: Van semiotiek naar
pragmatiek.* TFT-Studies #8. Tilburg: University Press, 1987. Pp.
168-93.

1938 H. Binder, *Das Gleichnis von dem Richter und der Witwe: Lk
18,1-8.* Neukirchen-Vluyn: Neukirchener Verlag, 1988.

1939 Porcile Santiso, Maria Teresa, and Angelica Ferreira, "The Parable of the Importunate Widow," in Samuel Amirtham, ed., *Stories Make People: Examples of Theological Work in Community.* Geneva: WCC Publications, 1989. Pp. 75-82.

1940 John Mark Hicks, "The Parable of the Persistent Widow," *RQ* 33/4 (1991): 209-23.

18:1

1941 Woodrow M. Kroll, "The Peril of Prayerlessness," *FundJ* 4/7 (1985): 21-22.

18:2-7

1942 Hermann J. Vogt, "Die Witwe als Bild der Seele in der Exegese des Origenes," *TQ* 165/2 (1985): 105-18.

18:7

1943 Herman Ljungvik, "Zur Erklärung Einer Lukas-Stelle," *NTS* 10 (1963-1964): 289-94.

1944 Albert Wifstrand, "Lukas 18:7," *NTS* 11 (1964-1965): 72-74.

1945 Alessandro Sacchi, "Pazienza di Dio e Ritardo Della Parousia," *RBib* 36 (1988): 299-327.

18:8

1946 David R. Catchpole, "The Son of Man's Search for Faith (Luke 18:8)," *NovT* 19 (1977): 81-104.

1947 K. H. Tyson, "Faith on Earth," *ET* 88 (1977): 111-12.

1948 Domingo Muñoz León, "Jesus y la apocaliptica pesimista (a proposito de Lc 18:8b y Mt 24:12)," *EB* 46/4 (1988): 457-95.

18:9-23

1949 J. Kodell, "Luke and the Children: The Beginning and End of the Great Interpolation (Luke 9:46-56; 18:9-23)," *CBQ* 49 (1987): 415-30.

18:9-14

1950 F. F. Bruce, "Justification by Faith in the Non-Pauline Writing of the N.T.," *EQ* 24 (1952): 66-67.

1951   A. Colunga, "El fariseo y el publicano," *CuBí* 13 (1956): 136-38.

1952   E. Galbiati, "Esegesi degli Evangeli festivi," *BibO* 2 (1960): 169-71.

1953   É. Charpentier, "Le chrétien: un homme 'juste' ou 'justifié'? (Lc 18)," *AsSeign* N.S. II/61 (1972): 66-78.

1954   E. Neuhäusler, " 'Anstösse' zur Besinnung über das Gleichnis vom Pharisäer und Zöllner," *BibL* 13 (1972): 293-96.

1955   Erhardt Güttgemanns, "Narrative Analyse Synoptischer Texte," *LB* 25/26 (1973): 50-73.

1956   M. Hengel, "Die ganz andere Gerechtigkeft: Bibelarbeit über Lk 18,9-14," *TBe* 5 (1974): 1-13.

1957   A. Biesinger, "Vorbild und Nachahmung Imitationspsychologische und bibeltheologische Anmerkungen zu Lk 18:9-14," *BK* 32 (1977): 42-45.

1958   H. Merklein, " 'Dieser ging als Gerechter nach Hause . . . ' Das Gottesbild Jesu und die Haltung der Menschen nach Lk 18:9-14," *BK* 32 (1977): 34-42.

1959   H. G. Heimbrock and A. Heimler, "Das Gleichnis wm Pharisäer und Zöllner (Lk 18,9-14)," in Y. Spiegel, ed., *Doppeldeutlich*. Münich: Kaiser, 1978. Pp. 171-88.

1960   M. Völkel, " 'Freund der Zöllner und Sünder'," *ZNW* 69 (1978): 1-10.

1961   André Feuillet, "Le pharisien et le publicain (Luc 18:9-14). La manifestation de la miséricorde divine en Jésus Serviteur souffrant," *EV* 91 (1981): 657-65.

1962   P. Raffin, "Le pharisien et le publicain," *EV* 82 (1982): 260-61.

1963   S. Schmitz, "Psychologische Hilfen zum Verstehen biblischer Texte?" *BK* 38 (1983): 112-18.

1964   Ralph P. Martin, "Two Worshippers, One Way to God," *ET* 96 (1984-1985): 117-18.

1965 Marion C. Barnett, "Graceless Goodness, Forgiven Folly," *ChrM* 16/1 (1985): 25-27.

1966 Peter Fiedler, "Die Tora bei Jesus und in der Jesusüberlieferung," in Karl Kertelge, ed., *Das Gesetz im Neuen Testament*. Freiburg: Herder, 1986. Pp. 71-87.

1967 Thorwald Lorenzen, "The Radicality of Grace: The Pharisee and the Tax Collector as a Parable of Jesus," *FM* 3/2 (1986): 66-75.

1968 John G. Strelan, "The Pharisee Lurking: Reflections on Luke 18:9-14," *LTJ* 20/2-3 (1986): 116-20.

1969 B. van Iersel, "De Farizeeër en de tollenaar (Lc 18,9-14)," in B. van Iersel, et al., eds., *Parabelverhalen in Lucas: Van semiotiek naar pragmatiek*. TFT-Studies #8. Tilburg: University Press, 1987. Pp. 194-216.

1970 R. Krüger, "El desenmascaramiento de un despreciador prestigioso: Lectura semiótica de la parábola del fariseo y del publicano. Lucas 18,9-14," *RevB* 49 (1987): 155-67.

1971 Agnès Gueuret, "Le pharisien et le publicain et son contexte," in Jean Delorme, ed., *Les paraboles évangéliques: perspectives nouvelles*. Paris: Cerf, 1989. Pp. 289-307.

1972 Jacques Schlosser, "Le pharisien et le publicain (Lc 18,9-14)," in Jean Delorme, ed., *Les paraboles évangéliques: perspectives nouvelles*. Paris: Cerf, 1989. Pp. 271-88.

1973 F. Gerald Downing, "The Ambiguity of 'The Pharisee and the Toll-Collector' (Luke 18:9-14) in the Greco-Roman World of Late Antiquity," *CBQ* 54 (1992): 80-99.

18:10-14

1974 Gerhard Sellin, "Gleichnisstrukturen," *LB* 31 (1974): 89-115.

1975 F. Mahr, "Der Antipharisäer. Ein Kapitel 'Bibel verfremdet' zu Lk 18:10-14," *BK* 32 (1977): 47.

1976 F. Schnider, "Ausschließen und ausgeschlossen werden. Beobachtungen zur Struktur des Gleichnisses vom Pharisäer und Zöllner Lk 18:10-14," *BZ* 24 (1980): 42-56.

1977   J. W. Holleran, "The Saint and the Scoundrel," *BibTo* 25 (1987): 375-79.

18:12
1978   F. Böhl, "Das Fasten an Montagen und Donnerstagen: Zur Geschichte einer Pharisdischen Praxis (Lk 18,12)," *BZ* 31 (1987): 247-50.

18:13
1979   Robert George Hoerber, "God Be Merciful to Me a Sinner: A Note on Luke 18:13," *CTM* 33 (1962): 283-86.

18:14
1980   Patrick P. Saydon, "Some Biblico-Liturgical Passages Reconsidered," *MeliT* 18/1 (1966): 10-17.

1981   André Feuillet, "La signification christologique de Luc 18,14 et les références des évangiles au Serviteur souffrant," *NovVet* 55 (1980): 188-229.

1982   J. B. Cortés, "The Greek Text of Luke 18:14a: A Contribution to the Method of Reasoned Eclecticism," *CBQ* 46 (1984): 255-73.

18:15-17
1983   Daniel Patte, "Jesus' Pronouncement about Entering the Kingdom Like a Child: A Structural Exegesis," *Semeia* 29 (1983): 3-42.

18:17
1984   F. A. Schilling, "What Means the Saying about Receiving the Kingdom of God as a Little Child (τὴν βασιλείαν τοῦ θεοῦ ὡς παιδίον)? Mark 10:15; Luke 18:17," *ET* 77 (1965-1966): 56-58.

18:18-30
1985   Richard A. Ward, "Pin-Points and Panoramas: The Preacher's Use of the Aorist," *ET* 71 (1959-1960): 267-70.

1986   B. Celada, "Distribución de los bienes y seguimiento de Jesús, según Lucas 18:18-30," *CuBí* 26 (1969): 337-40.

1987   Claude Coulot, "La structuration de la péricope de l'homme riche et ses différentes lectures (Mc 10:17-31; Mt 19:16-30; Lc 18:18-30)," *RevSR* 56 (1982): 240-52.

1988   C. M. Swezey, "Luke 18:18-30," *Int* 37 (1983): 68-73.

18:18-23
1989   J. Williams, "The Rich Young Ruler and St. Paul," *ET* 41 (1929-1930): 139-40.

1990   Gregory Murray, "The Rich Young Man," *DR* 103 (1985): 144-46.

1991   Reginald H. Fuller, "The Decalogue in the NT," *Int* 43/3 (1989): 243-55.

18:18-19
1992   John W. Wenham, " 'Why Do You Ask Me about the Good?' A Study of the Relation between Text and Source Criticism," *NTS* 28 (1982): 116-25.

18:18
1993   P. Huuhtanen, "Die Perikope vom 'reichen Jüngling' unter Berücksichtigung der Aksentuierungen des Lukas," *SNTU-A* 7 (1976): 79-98.

18:25
1994   B. Celada, "Más acerca del camello y la aguja," *CuBí* 26 (1969): 157-58.

1995   H. R. Graham, "Once there Was a Rich Man . . . : Five 'Rich Man' Stories in Luke," *BibTo* 26 (1988): 98-103.

1996   José O'Callaghan, "Examen critico de Mt 19,24," *Bib* 69 (1988): 401-405.

18:29-30
1997   J. Garcia Burillo, "El ciento por uno (Mc. 10:29-30 par)," *EB* 36 (1977): 173-203.

18:31-22:6
1998   Jan Lambrecht, "Reading and Rereading Luke 18:31-22:6," in Françios Refoulé, ed., *à cause de l'Evangile: Etudes sur les synoptiques et les Actes* (festschrift for Jacques Dupont). Paris: Cerf, 1985. Pp. 585-612.

18:31-43
> **1999** E. Galbiati, "Esegesi degli Evangeli festivi," *BibO* 4 (1962): 57-63.

18:33
> **2000** John M. Perry, "The Three Days in the Synoptic Passion Predictions," *CBQ* 48/4 (1986): 637-54.

18:35-43
> **2001** T. McCaughey, "Paradigms of Faith in the Gospel of St. Luke," *ITQ* 45 (1978): 177-84.

> **2002** Roland Meynet, "Au coeur du texte. Analyse rhétorique de l'aveugle de Jéricho selon saint Luc," *NRT* 103 (1981): 696-710.

19:1-27
> **2003** S. van Tilborg, "De koning en de tien slaven (Lc 19,1-27)," in B. van Iersel, et al., eds., *Parabelverhalen in Lucas: Van semiotiek naar pragmatiek.* TFT-Studies #8. Tilburg: University Press, 1987. Pp. 217-50.

19:1-11
> **2004** W. Hülsbusch, "Begegnung vor Jerusalem," *BibL* 15 (1974): 220-25.

19:1-10
> **2005** W. P. Loewe, "Towards an Interpretation of Lk 19:1-10," *CBQ* 36 (1974): 321-31.

> **2006** C. Bizer, "Geschichte von Zachdus (Lk 19,1-10) - relegionsunterrkhtlich, religionskundlich und alternativisch buchstabiert: Ein durchaus subjektiver Versuch," *EvErz* 28 (1976): 217-24.

> **2007** F. W. Hobbie, "Luke 19:1-10," *Int* 31 (1977): 285-90.

> **2008** V. Weymann, "Vom Zwiespalt befreit im Zwiespalt leben: Biblisch-theologische Beobachtungen zur Erfahrung der Befreiung vom Bosen inmitten des Bösen (Lc 19,1-10; Gen 32,23-33)," *Reformatio* 26 (1977): 333-42.

> **2009** Walter Vogels, "Structural Analysis and Pastoral Work: The Story of Zacchaeus," *LV* 33 (1978): 482-92.

2010   M. Völkel, " 'Freund der Zöllner und Sünder'," *ZNW* 69 (1978): 1-10.

2011   R. C. White, "A Good Word for Zachaeus? Exegetical Comment on Lk 19:1-10," *LexTQ* 14 (1979): 89-96.

2012   R. C. White, "Vindication for Zacchaeus," *ET* 91 (1979-1980): 21.

2013   W. J. Hollenweger, *Besuch bei Lukas: 4 narrative Exegesen zu 2 Mose 14, Lukas 2,1-14, 2 Kor 6,4-11 und Lukas 19,1-10.* Münich: Kaiser, 1981.

2014   J. O'Hanlon, "The Story of Zacchaeus and the Lukan Ethic," *JSNT* 12 (1981): 2-26.

2015   E. A. LaVerdiere, "Zacchaeus," *Emmanuel* 90 (1984): 461-65.

2016   Charlie Garriott, "Land, Sin, and Repentence," *OSide* 21/4 (1985): 22-25.

2017   Paul Kariamadam, *The Zacchaeus Story (Lk 19:1-10): A Redactional-Critical Investigation.* Kerala, India: Pontifical Institute of Theology and Philosophy, 1985.

2018   Jyotsna Chatterji, "Our Struggle for Wholeness: A Bible Study," *RS* 36 (1989): 37-40.

2019   Dennis Hamm, "Zacchaeus Revisited Once More: A Story of Vindication or Conversion?" *Bib* 2 (1991): 248-52.

2020   Robert F. O'Toole, "The Literary Form of Luke 19:1-10," *JBL* 110 (1991): 107-16.

2021   D. A. S. Ravens, "Zacchaeus: The Final Part of a Lucan Triptych," *JSNT* 41 (1991): 19-32.

19:2

2022   B. M. Ahern, "The Zacchaeus Incident," *BibTo* 25 (1987): 348-51.

19:3

2023   Günther Schwarz, "Ὅτι τῇ ἡλικίᾳ μικρὸς ἦν," *BibN* 8 (1979): 23-24.

19:8

2024 N. M. Watson, "Was Zacchaeus Really Reforming?" *ET* 77 (1965-1966): 282-85.

2025 A. P. Salom, "Was Zacchaeus Really Reforming?" *ET* 78 (1966-1967): 87.

2026 A. J. Kerr, "Zacchaeus's Decision to Make Fourfold Restitution," *ET* 98/3 (1986-1987): 68-71.

2027 B. W. Grindlay, "Zacchaeus and David," *ET* 99 (1987-1988): 46-47.

2028 Dennis Hamm, "Luke 19:8 Once Again: Does Zacchaeus Defend or Resolve?" *JBL* 107 (1988): 431-37.

2029 Alan C. Mitchell, "Zacchaeus Revisited: Luke 19:8 as a Defense," *Bib* 71/2 (1990): 153-76.

2030 Alan C. Mitchell, "The Use of *Sykophantein* in Luke 19:8: Further Evidence for Zacchaeus's Defense," *Bib* 72/4 (1991): 546-47.

19:10

2031 D. Howell-Jones, "Lost and Found," *ET* 92 (1980-1981): 371-72.

19:11-28

2032 Ignace de la Potterie, "La parabole du prétendant à la royauté (Lc 19:11-28)," in Françios Refoulé, ed., *à cause de l'Evangile: Etudes sur les synoptiques et les Actes* (festschrift for Jacques Dupont). Paris: Cerf, 1985. Pp. 613-41.

2033 A. Puig i Tàrrech, "La parabole des talents (Mt 25,14-30) ou des mines (Lc 19,11-28)," *RCT* 10 (1985): 269-317.

2034 Jean N. Aletti, "Lc 19,11-28: parabole des mines et/ou parabole du roi: remarques sur l'écriture parabolique de Luc," in Jean Delorme, ed., *Les paraboles évangéliques: perspectives nouvelles*. Paris: Cerf, 1989. Pp. 309-32.

19:11-27

2035 Walter Lüthi, "Das Gleichnis von anvertranten Pfund: Predigt über Lk. 19,11-27," in *Das Wort sie sollen lassen stahn* (festschrift for D. albert Schädelin). Bern: Lang, 1950. Pp. 207-14.

2036   R. W. Resenhöft, "Jesu Gleichnis von den Talenten, ergänzt durch die Lukas-Fassung," *NTS* 26 (1979-1980): 318-31.

2037   Jack T. Sanders, "The Parable of the Pounds and Lucan Anti-Semitism," *TS* 42 (1981): 660-68.

2038   Luke T. Johnson, "The Lukan Kingship Parable," *NovT* 24 (1982): 139-59.

2039   Louis Panier, "La parabole des mines: lecture sémiotique (Lc 19,11-27)," in Jean Delorme, ed., *Les paraboles évangéliques: perspectives nouvelles*. Paris: Cerf, 1989. Pp. 333-47.

19:12-27
2040   Gerhard Sellin, "Gleichnisstrukturen," *LB* 31 (1974): 89-115.

2041   F. D. Weinert, "The Parable of the Throne Claimant Reconsidered," *CBQ* 39 (1977): 505-14.

19:24-40
2042   O. Samuel, "Die Regierungsgewalt des Wortes Gottes," *EvT* 3 (1936): 1-3.

19:26
2043   G. Lindeskog, "Logia-Studien," *ST* 4 (1951-1952): 129-89.

19:27
2044   J. Duncan M. Derrett, "A Horrid Passage in Luke Explained," *ET* 97 (1985-1986): 136-38.

19:28-20:19
2045   J. W. Doeve, "Purification du Temple et Dessèchement du Figuiem," *NTS* 1 (1954-1955): 297-308.

19:28-38
2046   T. L. Davies, "Was Jesus Compelled?" *ET* 42 (1930-1931): 526-27.

2047   R. S. Frayn, "Was Jesus Compelled?" *ET* 43 (1931-1932): 381-82.

2048   J. Meikle, "Was Jesus Compelled?" *ET* 43 (1931-1932): 288.

2049 B. A. Mastin, "The Date of the Triumphal Entry," *NTS* 16 (1969-1970): 76-82.

2050 J. Duncan M. Derrett, "Law in the New Testament: The Palm Sunday Colt," *NovT* 13 (1971): 241-58.

2051 V. Mariadasan, *Le triomphe messianiaue de Jésus et son entrée à Jérusalem. Étude critico-littéraire des traditions évangéliques (Mc 11:1,11; Mt 21:1-11; Lc 19:28-38; Jn 12:12-16)*. Tindivanam, India: Catechetical Centre, 1978.

19:31-34

2052 Randall Buth, "Luke 19:31-34, Mishnaic Hebrew, and Bible Translation: Is *Kyrioi Tou Polou* Singular?" *JBL* 104/4 (1985): 680-85.

19:31

2053 Henry Osborn, "A Quadruple Quote in the Triumphal Entry Account in Warao," *BT* 18/1 (1967): 301-21.

19:35-40

2054 N. Fernández Marcos, "La unción de Salomón y la entrada de Jesús en Jérusalén: 1 Re 1,33-40/Lc 19,35-40," *Bib* 68 (1987): 89-97.

19:38

2055 Heinrich Baarlink, "Friede im Himmel: die Lukanische Redaktion von Lk 19,38 und Ihre Deutung," *ZNW* 76/3 (1985): 170-86.

19:40

2056 Gregorio Ruiz, "El Clamor de las Piedras (Lk. 19:40; Hab 2:11): el Reino Choca con la Ciudad Injusta en la Fiesta de Ramos," *EE* 59/230 (1984): 297-312.

2057 Frédéric Rilliet, "La Louange des Pierres et le Tonnerre: Luc 19,40 Chez Jacques de Saroug et Dans la Patristique Syriaque," *RHR* 117/4 (1985): 293-304.

19:41-44

2058 Ben Hemelsoet, "Tranen over Jerusalem: Luc 19:41-44: teksten rondom een tekst," in Wim Beuken, et al., eds., *Proef en toets: theologie als experiment*. Amersfoort: De Horstink, 1977. Pp. 30-38.

2059 Peter von der Osten-Sacken, "Jesu Weinen über sein Volk: Predigt
      über Lukas 19,41-44," in Erhard Blum, et al., eds., *Die Hebräische
      Bibel und ihre zweifache Nachgeschichte* (festschrift for Rolf
      Rendtorff). Neukirchen-Vluyn: Neukirchener Verlag, 1990. Pp.
      555-59.

19:44
2060 Kairos Theologians, 1985, "The Kairos Document--Challenge to
      the Church: A Theological Comment on the Political Crisis in
      South Africa," *JTSA* 53 (1985): 61-81.

19:45-46
2061 É. Trocmé, "L'expulsion des marchands du Temple," *NTS* 15
      (1968-1969): 1-22.

20:1
2062 Christoph Burchard, "Fußnoten zum neutestamentlichen Griechisch
      II," *ZNW* 69 (1978): 143-57.

20:5
2063 Gerard Mussies, "The Sense of συνελογίσαντο: Luke xx,5," in
      T. Baarda, et al., eds., *Miscellanea Neotestamentica*. Leiden: Brill,
      1978. 2:59-76.

20:9-19
2064 Hans-Josef Klauck, "Das Gleichnis vom Mord im Weinberg (Mk
      12,1-12; Mt 21,33-46; Lk 20,9-19)," *BibL* 11 (1970): 118-45.

2065 J. A. T. Robinson, "The Parable of the Wicked Husbandmen: A
      Test of Synoptic Relationships," *NTS* 21 (1974-1975): 443-61.

2066 Klyne B. Snodgrass, "The Parable of the Wicked Husbandmen: Is
      the Gospel of Thomas Version the Original?" *NTS* 21 (1974-1975):
      142-44.

2067 W. Weren, "De parabel van de wijnbouwers (Lc 20,9-19)," in B.
      van Iersel, et al., eds., *Parabelverhalen in Lucas: Van semiotiek
      naar pragmatiek*. TFT-Studies #8. Tilburg: University Press, 1987.
      Pp. 251-80.

2068 Robert W. Bertram, "The Storyteller Visits the Vineyard," *CC* 106
      (1989): 255-56.

20:9-18
    2069 John Dominic Crossan, "The Parable of the Wicked Husbandmen," *JBL* 90/4 (1971): 451-65.

    2070 Donald L. Jones, "The Title υἱὸς θεοῦ in Acts," *SBLSP* 15 (1985): 451-63.

20:13
    2071 A. Scattolon, "L'agapêtos sinottico nella luce della tradizione giudaica," *RBib* 26 (1978): 2-32.

20:18
    2072 Robert Doran, "Luke 20:18: A Warrior's Boast?" *CBQ* 45 (1983): 61-67.

20:20-26
    2073 James M. Dawsey, "Entre César e Deus (Lc 20,20-26)," *REB* 44 (1984): 391-93.

    2074 H. St. J. Hart, "The Coin of 'Renda unto Caesar . . .' (A Note on Some Aspects of Mark 12:13-17; Matt 22:15-22; Luke 20:20-26)," in E. Bammel and C. F. D. Moule, eds., *Jesus and the Politics of His Day*. Cambridge: University Press, 1984. Pp. 241-48.

20:21
    2075 L. Van Rompay, "The Rendering of *prosôpon lambanein* and Related Expressions in the Early Oriental Versions of the New Testament," *OLoP* 6/7 (1975-1976): 569-75.

20:25
    2076 Charles H. Giblin, " 'The Things of God' in the Questions Concerning Tribute to Caesar," *CBQ* 33/4 (1971): 510-27.

    2077 J. Duncan M. Derrett, "Luke's Perspective on Tribute to Caesar," in R. J. Cassidy and P. J. Scharper, eds., *Political Issues in Luke-Acts*. Maryknoll NY: Orbis, 1983. Pp. 38-48.

20:27-40
    2078 Sebastián Bartina, "Jesús y los saduceos: 'El Dios de Abraham, de Isaac y de Jacob' es 'El que hace existir'," *EB* 21 (1962): 151-60.

    2079 John J. Kilgallen, "The Sadducees and Resurrection From the Dead: Luke 20:27-40," *Bib* 67/4 (1986): 478-95.

20:27-38
 2080   É. Charpentier, "Tous vivent pour lui," *AsSeign* N.S. 63 (1971):
        81-94.

20:34-36
 2081   C. Monanti, "Lc 20,34-36 e la filiazione divina degli uomini,"
        BibO 13 (1971): 255-75.

20:37-38
 2082   Dan M. Cohn-Sherbok, "Jesus' Defence of the Resurrection of the
        Dead," *JSNT* 11 (1981): 64-73.

20:38
 2083   M. Trowitzsch, "Gemeinschaft der Lebenden und der Toten. Lk.
        20:38 als Text der Ekklesiologie," *ZTK* 79 (1982): 212-29.

20:41-44
 2084   Fritz Neugebauer, "Die Davidsohnsfrage (Mark xii.35-7 parr) und
        der Menschensohn," *NTS* 21 (1974-1975): 81-108.

21-24
 2085   Paul Winter, "The Treatment of his Sources by the Third
        Evangelist in Luke XXI-XXIV," *ST* 8 (1954-1955): 138-72.

21:1-4
 2086   A. G. Wright, "The Widow's Mites: Praise or Lament? A Matter
        of Context," *CBQ* 44 (1982): 256-65.

 2087   Gregory Murray, "Did Luke Use Mark?" *DR* 104 (1986): 268-71.

21:5-36
 2088   C. Perrot, "Essai sur le Discours eschatologique (Mc. XIII,1-37;
        Mt. XXIV,1-36; Lc. XXI,5-36)," *RechSR* 47 (1959): 481-514.

 2089   A. del Agua Perez, "Derás Lucano de Mc 13 a la luz de su
        'teologia del Reino' Lc 21,5-36," *EB* 39 (1981): 285-313.

 2090   Frans Neirynck, "Note on the Eschatological Discourse," in
        David L. Dungan, ed., *The Interrelations of the Gospels*. Louvain:
        Peeters Press, 1990. Pp. 77-80.

21:5-35
    2091 Hugo Lattanzi, "Eschatologici Sermonis Domini Logica Interpretatio," *Div* 11/1 (1967): 71-92.

21:12-19
    2092 Bo Reicke, "A Test of Synoptic Relationships: Matthew 10,17-23 and 24,9-14 with Parallels," in William R. Farmer, ed., *New Synoptic Studies*. Macon GA: Mercer University Press, 1983. Pp. 209-29.

21:12-15
    2093 William L. Schutter, "Luke 12:11-12/21:12-15 and the Composition of Luke-Acts," *EGLMBS* 10 (1990): 236-50.

21:14-15
    2094 Matthew Mahoney, "Luke 21:14-15: Editorial Rewriting or Authenticity?" *ITQ* 47/3 (1980): 220-38.

21:20-28
    2095 D. Flusser, "The Liberation of Jerusalem: A Prophecy in the New Testament," *E-I* 10 (1971): 226-36.

21:20-24
    2096 C. H. Dodd, "The Fall of Jerusalem and the 'Abomination of Desolation'," in *Normanno Hebburn Baynes . . . lustrum decimum quintum feliciter auspicanti*. London: Society for the Promotion of Roman Studies, 1947. Pp. 47-54.

    2097 F. Flückiger, "Luk. 21,20-24 und die Zerstorung Jerusalems," *TZ* 28 (1972): 385-90.

    2098 Gordon D. Fee, "A Text-Critical Look at the Synoptic Problem," *NovT* 22/1 (1980): 12-28.

21:20-22
    2099 Craig Koester, "The Origin and Significance of the Flight to Pella Tradition," *CBQ* 51 (1989): 90-106.

21:25-36
    2100 Johann H. Heinz, "The 'Summer That Will Never End': Luther's Longing For the 'Dear Last Day' in His Sermon on Luke 21 (1531)," *AUSS* 23 (1985): 181-86.

21:25-33
    2101 E. Galbiati,"L'avvento liberatore (Lc. 21:25-33)," *BibO* 3 (1961): 222-24.

21:28
    2102 A. Salas, " 'Vuestra liberación está cerca' (Lc 21,28): Dimension liberacionista del acto redentor," *CuBí* 31 (1974): 157-63.

21:29-34
    2103 William H. Willimon, "Take Heed to Yourselves," *CC* 103/37 (1986): 1085-86.

21:29
    2104 Miguel Pérez Fernández, " 'prope est aestas'," *VD* 46 (1968): 361-69.

21:31-34
    2105 William J. Tobin, "The Petrine Primacy Evidence of the Gospels," *LV* 23/1 (1968): 27-70.

21:32
    2106 C. L. Holman, "The Idea of an Imminent Parousia in the Synoptic Gospels," *SBT* 3 (1973): 15-31.

    2107 Vittorio Fusco, "Lc 21,32 alla luce dell'espressione 'questa generazione'," *Asprenas* 31 (1984): 397-424.

21:34-36
    2108 L. Aejmelaeus, *Wachen vor dem Ende: Die traditionsgeschichtlichen Wurzeln von 1. Thess 5:1-11 und Luk 21:34-36.* Helsinki: Finnish Exegetical Society, 1985.

21:34
    2109 Günther Schwarz, "μήποτε βαρηθῶσιν ὑμῶν αἱ καρδίαι," *BibN* 10 (1979): 40.

21:36
    2110 Martino Conti, "La via della beatitudine e della rovina secondo il Salmo I," *Ant* 61/1 (1986): 3-39.

22-24
2111   Roland Meynet, *Quelle est donc cette Parole? Lecture 'rhétorique'*
       de l'évangile de Luc (1-9, 22-24). Lectio divina #99. Paris: Cerf,
       1979.

22-23
2112   A. M. Perry, "Luke's Disputed Passion-Source," *ET* 46
       (1934-1935): 256-60.

2113   M. Kiddle, "The Passion Narrative in St. Luke's Gospel," *JTS* 36
       (1935): 267-80.

2114   V. Monsarrat, "Le récit de la Passion: un enseignement pour le
       disciple fidèle. Luc 22-23," *FV* 81 (1982): 40-47.

22:1-38
2115   X. Léon-Dufour, "Das letzte Mahl Jesu und die testamentarische
       Tradition nach Lk 22," *ZKT* 103 (1981): 33-55.

22:3
2116   Heinrich Baarlink, "Friede im Himmel: die Lukanische Redaktion
       von Lk 19,38 und Ihre Deutung," *ZNW* 76/3 (1985): 170-86.

22:7-38
2117   H. Schürmann, *Jesu Abschiedsrede, Lk 22,21-29: III. Teil einer
       quellenkritischen Untersuchung des lukanischen
       Abendmahlsberichtes, Lk 22,7-38*. 2nd ed. Münster: Aschendorff,
       1977.

2118   H. Schürmann, *Der Paschamahlbericht Lk 22,(7-14) 15-18: Erster
       Teil einer quellenkritischen Untersuchung des lukanischen
       Abendmahlsberichtes 22,7-38*. 3rd ed. Münster: Aschendorff, 1980.

22:7-30
2119   M. Sabbe, "The Footwashing in John 13 and Its Relation to the
       Synoptic Gospels," *ETL* 58 (1982): 279-308.

22:7-14
2120   H. Schürmann, *Der Paschamahlbericht Lk 22,(7-14) 15-18: Erster
       Teil einer quellenkritischen Untersuchung des lukanischen
       Abendmahlsberichtes 22,7-38*. 3rd ed. Münster: Aschendorff, 1980.

22:7-13
  2121 Joel B. Green, "Preparation for Passover: A Question of
        Redactional Technique," *NovT* 29 (1987): 305-19.

22:7
  2122 Arthur G. Arnott, " 'The First Day of the Unleavened . . . ' Mt
        26.17, Mk 14.12, Lk 22.7," *BT* 35 (1984): 235-38.

22:14-38
  2123 Dennis M. Sweetland, "The Lord's Supper and the Lukan
        Community," *BTB* 13 (1983): 23-27.

  2124 William S. Kurz, "Luke 22:14-38 and Greco-Roman and Biblical
        Farewell Addresses," *JBL* 104 (1985): 251-68.

22:14-23
  2125 E. A. LaVerdiere, "Discourse at the Last Supper," *BibTo* 71
        (1974): 1540-48.

22:14-20
  2126 G. J. Bahr, "The Seder of Passover and the Eucharistic Words,"
        NovT 12 (1970): 181-202.

22:14-18
  2127 W. Weren, "The Lord's Supper: An Inquiry into the Coherence in
        Luke 22,14-18," in H. J. Auf der Maur, et al., eds., *Fides
        Sacramenti* (festschrift for P. Smulders). Assen: Van Gorcum,
        1981. Pp. 9-26.

22:15-21
  2128 James Custer, "When Is Communion Communion," *GTJ* 6/2
        (1985): 403-10.

22:15-20
  2129 Henry Chadwick, "The Shorter Text of Luke XXII.15-20," *HTR*
        50 (1957): 249-58.

  2130 Christian Bernard Amphoux, "Le dernier repas de Jésus, Lc
        22/15-20 par," *ÉTR* 56 (1981): 449-54.

  2131 T. Huser, "Les récits de l'institution de la Cène. Dissemblances et
        traditions," *Hokhmah* 21 (1982): 28-50.

2132 Q. Quesnell, "The Women at Luke's Supper," in R. J. Cassidy and P. J. Scharper, eds., *Political Issues in Luke-Acts*. Maryknoll NY: Orbis, 1983. Pp. 59-79.

22:15-18
2133 N. Hook, "The Dominical Cup Saying," *Theology* 77 (1974): 625-30.

2134 H. Schürmann, *Der Paschamahlbericht Lk 22,(7-14) 15-18: Erster Teil einer quellenkritischen Untersuchung des lukanischen Abendmahlsberichtes 22,7-38*. 3rd ed. Münster: Aschendorff, 1980.

22:15
2135 C. K. Barrett, "Luke XXII,15: To Eat the Passover," *JTS* 9 (1958): 305-307.

2136 Ronald W. Graham, "On 'Longing with all Your Heart' to Break Bread," *LexTQ* 20 (1985): 130-34.

22:17-19
2137 B. A. Mastin, "Jesus said Grace," *SJT* 24 (1971): 449-56.

22:17
2138 M. Rese, "Zur Problematik von Kurz- und Langtext in Luk. xxii.17ff.," *NTS* 22 (1975-1976): 15-31.

22:19-28
2139 Bart D. Ehrman, "The Cup, the Bread, and the Salvific Effect of Jesus' Death in Luke-Acts," *SBLSP* 21 (1991): 576-91.

22:19-20
2140 K. Goetz, "Das vorausweisende Demonstrativum in Lc 22,19-20 und 1 Cor 11,24," *ZNW* 38 (1939): 188-90.

2141 Pierre Benoit, "Luc XXII.19b-20," *JTS* 49 (1948): 145-47.

2142 B. H. Throckmorton, "The Longer Reading of Luke 22:19-20," *ATR* 30 (1948): 55-56.

2143 John C. Cooper, "Problem of the Text in Luke 22:19-20," *LQ* 14 (1962): 39-48.

2144   Pierson Parker, "Three Variant Readings in Luke-Acts," *JBL* 83 (1964): 165-70.

2145   Jacobus H. Petzer, "Luke 22:19b-20 and the Structure of the Passage," *NovT* 26 (1984): 249-52.

22:19

2146   M. H. Sykes, "The Eucharist as 'Anamnesis'," *ET* 71 (1959-1960): 115-18.

2147   Hans Kosmala, "Das Tut Zu Meinem Gedächtnis," *NovT* 4 (1960): 81-94.

2148   X. Léon-Dufour, "Do This in Memory of Me," *TD* 26 (1978): 36-39.

2149   D. W. A. Gregg, "Hebraic Antecedents to the Eucharistic Anamnèsis Formula," *TynB* 30 (1979): 165-68.

2150   B. Schwank, "Das ist mein Leib, der für euch hingegeben wird (Lk 22,19)," *ErAu* 59 (1983): 279-90.

2151   Oda Hagemeyer, "Tut dies zu meinem Gedächtnis (1 Kor 11,24f; Lk 22,19)," in Lothar Lies, ed., *Praesentia Christi* (festschrift for Johannes Betz). Düsseldorf: Patmos, 1984. Pp. 101-17.

2152   B. de Margerie, " 'Hoc facite in meam commemorationem' (Lc 22,19b): Les exégeses des Pères préchaícédoniens (150-451)," *Div* 28 (1984): 43-69, 137-49.

2153   Richard D. Patterson, "In Remembrance of Me," *FundJ* 4/5 (1985): 31.

2154   John D. Laurence, "The Eucharist as the Imitation of Christ," *TS* 47/2 (1986): 286-96.

22:20

2155   J. Günther, "Das Becherwort Jesu," *TGl* 45 (1955): 47-49.

22:21-39

2156   A. Vööbus, "A New Approach to the Problem of the Shorter and Longer Text in Luke," *NTS* 15 (1968-1969): 457-63.

22:21-38
    2157   Philip Sellew, "The Last Supper Discourse in Luke 22:21-38," *Forum* 3 (1987): 70-95.

22:21-29
    2158   H. Schürmann, *Jesu Abschiedsrede, Lk 22,21-29: III. Teil einer quellenkritischen Untersuchung des lukanischen Abendmahlsberichtes, Lk 22,7-38.* 2nd ed. Münster: Aschendorff, 1977.

22:22
    2159   Leslie C. Allen, "The Old Testament Background of (Pro)Orizein in the New Testament," *NTS* 17/1 (1970-1971): 104-108.

22:23
    2160   F. G. Untergassmair, "Thesen zur Sinndeutung des Todes Jesu in der lukanischen Passionsgeschichte," *TGl* 70 (1980): 180-93.

22:24-30
    2161   David J. Lull, "The Servant-Benefactor as a Model of Greatness," *NovT* 28/4 (1986): 289-305.

    2162   David L. Tiede, "The King of the Gentiles and the Leader Who Serves: Luke 22:24-30," *WW* 12 (1992): 23-28.

22:24-27
    2163   L. Rasmussen, "Luke 22:24-27," *Int* 37 (1983): 73-76.

    2164   A. W. Swamidoss, "Diakonia as Servanthood in the Synoptics," *IJT* 32 (1983): 37-51.

    2165   Peter K. Nelson, "The Flow of Thought in Luke 22:24-27," *JSNT* 43 (1991): 113-23.

22:25-27
    2166   Jacques Schlosser, "La genèse de Luc XXII,25-27," *RB* 89 (1982): 52-70.

22:25
    2167   K. W. Clark, "The Meaning of [κατα]κυριευειν," in J. K. Elliott, ed., *Studies in New Testament Language and Text* (festschrift for G. D. Kilpatrick). Leiden: Brill, 1976. Pp. 100-105.

2168   R. R. Rickards, "Lk 22:25: They Are Called 'Friends of the People'," *BT* 28 (1977): 445-46.

2169   Frederick W. Danker, "The Endangered Benefactor in Luke-Acts," *SBLSP* 11 (1981): 39-48.

22:27

2170   J. Roloff, "Anfänge der Soteriologischen Deutung des Todes Jesu (Mk. x.45 und Lk. xxii.27)," *NTS* 19 (1972-1973): 38-64.

2171   Tjitze Baarda, " 'Als hij die bedient': Luc 22,27. Marginalia bij een woord van Jezus in het verhaal van het avondmaal in het evangelie van Lucas," in H. H. Grosheide, et al., eds., *De knechtsgestalte van Christus* (festschrift for H. N. Riderbos). Kampen: Kok, 1978. Pp. 11-22.

22:28-30
2172   Harry Fleddermann, "The End of Q," *SBLSP* 20 (1990): 1-10.

22:29

2173   J. Guillet, "Luc 22,29: Une Jormule johannique dans l'évangile de Luc," *RechSR* 69 (1981): 113-22.

22:30

2174   O. Knock, " 'Tut das zu meinem Gedächtnis!' (Lk 22,30; 1 Kor 11,24f.): Die Feier der Eucharistie in den urchristlichen Gemeinden," in J. Schreiner, ed., *Freude arn Gonesdienst* (festschrift for J. G. Plöger). Stuttgart: Katholisches Bibelwerk, 1983. Pp. 31-42.

22:31-34
2175   J. Thompson, "The Odyssey of a Disciple (Luke 22,31-34)," *RQ* 23 (1980): 77-81.

22:31

2176   W. Foerster, "Lukas 22,31f.," *ZNW* 46 (1955): 129-33.

22:32

2177   J. L. Larrabie, "Confirma en la fe a tus hermanos (Lc 22,32), magisterio y teólogos en la Iglesia," *LRSOCE* 31 (1982): 273-99.

22:35-53

2178 T. M. Napier, "The Enigma of the Swords," *ET* 49 (1937-1938): 467-70.

2179 S. K. Finlayson, "The Enigma of the Swords," *ET* 50 (1938-1939): 563.

2180 W. Western, "The Enigma of the Swords," *ET* 50 (1938-1939): 377.

2181 Hans Werner Bartsch, "Jesu Schwertwort, Lukas xxii.35-38: Überlieferungsgeschichtliche Studien," *NTS* 20 (1973-1974): 190-203.

2182 J. F. Gormiley, "The Final Passion Prediction: A Study of Luke 22:35-38," doctoral dissertation, Fordham University, Bronx NY, 1974.

2183 N. B. Steen, "The Interpretation of Jesus' Sword-Saying in Luke 22:35-38," doctoral dissertation, Calvin Theological Seminary, Grand Rapids MI, 1982.

2184 J. Gillman, "A Temptation to Violence: The Two Swords in Luke 22:35-38," *LouvS* 9 (1982-1983): 142-53.

2185 G. W. H. Lampe, "The Two Swords (Luke 22:35-38)," in E. Bammel and C. F. D. Moule, eds., *Jesus and the Politics of His Day*. Cambridge: University Press, 1984. Pp. 335-51.

2186 H. Kruger, "Die twee swaarde (Luk. 22:35-53), 'n poging tot verstaan," *NGTT* 27 (1986): 191-96.

22:36

2187 Paul S. Minear, "Note on Luke 22:36," *NovT* 7/2 (1964): 128-34.

22:37

2188 R. T. France, "The Servant of the Lord in the Teaching of Jesus," *TynB* 19 (1968): 26-52.

22:38

2189 Günther Schwarz, "Κύριε, ἰδοὺ μάχαιραι ὧδε δύο," *BibN* 8 (1979): 22.

2190 J. Duncan M. Derrett, "History and the Two Swords," in *Studies in the New Testament*. III. *Midrash, Naggadah, and the Character of the Community*. Leiden: Brill, 1982. Pp. 193-99.

22:39-49
2191 Jerome H. Neyrey, "The Absence of Jesus' Emotions—The Lucan Redaction of Lk 22,39-49," *Bib* 61/2 (1980): 153-71.

22:39-46
2192 Mario Galizzi, *Gesù nel Getsemani (Mc 14:32-42; Mt 26:36-46; Lc 22:39-46)*. Biblioteca di Scienze Religiose. Zürich: PAS-Verlag, 1972.

2193 André Feuillet, "Le récit lucanien de l'agonie de Gethsémani (Lc 22:39-46)," *NTS* 22 (1975-1976): 397-417.

2194 S. Tostengard, "Luke 22:39-46," *Int* 34 (1980): 283-88.

2195 Joel B. Green, "Jesus on the Mount of Olives (Luke 22:39-46): Tradition and Theology," *JSNT* 26 (1986): 29-48.

22:39
2196 J. Bishop, "The Place of Habit in the Spiritual Life," *ET* 91 (1980-1981): 374-75.

2197 Marion L. Soards, "On Understanding Luke 22:39," *BT* 36/3 (1985): 336-37.

22:40-46
2198 K. G. Kuhn, "Jesus in Gethsemane," *EvT* 12 (1952-1953): 260-85.

2199 J. Héring, "Zwei exegetische Problemein der Periope von Jesus in Gethsemane," in *Neotestamentica et Patristica: eine freundesgabe, herrn Professor Dr. Oscar Cullmann zu seinem 60. Geburtstag überricht*. Novum Testamentum Supplement #6. Leiden: Brill, 1962. Pp. 64-69.

2200 T. Lescow, "Jesus in Gethsemane bei Lukas und im Hebräerbrief," *ZNW* 58 (1967): 215-39.

2201 T. Lescow, "Jesus in Gethsemane," *EvT* 26 (1968): 141-59.

2202   R. S. Barbour, "Gethsemane in the Tradition of the Passion," *NTS* 16 (1969-1970): 231-51.

22:40
2203   H. N. Bate, "Luke xxii.40," *JTS* 36 (1935): 76-77.

22:42-47
2204   Tjitze Baarda, "Luke 22:42-47a: The Emperor Julian as a Witness to the Text of Luke," *NovT* 30 (1988): 289-96.

22:43-44
2205   L. Brun, "Engel und Blutschweiss Lc 22,43-44," *ZNW* 32 (1933): 265-76.

2206   Gerhard Schneider, "Engel und Blutschweiss," *BZ* 20 (1976): 112-16.

2207   W. J. Larkin, "The Old Testament Background of Luke 22:43-44," *NTS* 25 (1978-1979): 250-54.

2208   Bart D. Ehrman and M. A. Plunkett, "The Angel and the Agony: The Textual Problem of Luke 22:43-44," *CBQ* 45 (1983): 401-16.

22:48
2209   P. Maurice Casey, "The Son of Man Problem," *ZNW* 67/3 (1976): 147-54.

22:54-23:25
2210   Jean Delorme, "Le procès de Jésus ou la parole risquée (Lc 22:54-23:25)," *RechSR* 69 (1981): 123-46.

2211   Gerhard Schneider, "Das Verfahren gegen Jesus in der Sicht des dritten Evangeliums (Lk 22,54-23,25): Redaktionskritik und historische Rückfrage," in Karl Kertelge, ed., *Der Prozeß gegen Jesus*. Freiburg: Herder, 1988. Pp. 111-30.

22:54-62
2212   N. J. McEleney, "Peter's Denials—How Many? To Whom?" *CBQ* 52 (1990): 467-72.

22:55-62
2213   Dietfried Gewalt, "Die Verlegnung des Petrus," *LB* 43 (1978): 113-44.

2214   Gregory Murray, "St. Peter's Denials," *DR* 103 (1985): 296-98.

22:57
2215   W. J. P. Boyd, "Peter's Denials—Mark 14:68, Luke 22:57," *ET*
            67 (1955-1956): 341.

22:61
2216   Marion L. Soards, "And the Lord Turned and Looked Straight at
            Peter: Understanding Luke 22:61," *Bib* 67/4 (1986): 518-19.

22:62-66
2217   Michael D. Goulder, "On Putting Q to the Test," *NTS* 24
            (1977-1978): 218-34.

22:63-65
2218   W. C. van Unnik, "Jesu Verhüng vor dem Synedrium," *ZNW* 29
            (1930): 310-11.

2219   Marion L. Soards, "A Literary Analysis of the Origin and Purpose
            of Luke's Account of the Mockery of Jesus," in Earl Richard, ed.,
            New Views on Luke and Acts. Collegeville MN: Liturgical Press,
            1990. Pp. 86-93.

22:63-64
2220   D. L. Miller, "*Empaizein:* Playing the Mock Game (Luke
            22:63-64)," *JBL* 90 (1971): 309-13.

22:64
2221   D. Flusser, " 'Who is it that Struck You'?" *Immanuel* 20 (1986):
            27-32.

2222   Franz Neirynck, "Τίς ἐστιν ὁ παίσας σε. Mt 26,68/Lk 22,64
            (diff. Mk 14,65)," *ETL* 63/1 (1987): 5-47.

22:66-23:25
2223   Bruce J. Malina and Jerome H. Neyrey, "Conflict in Luke-Acts:
            Labeling and Deviance Theory," in Jerome H. Neyrey, ed., *The
            Social World of Luke-Acts*. Peabody MA: Hendrickson Publishers,
            1991. Pp. 87-122.

22:66-71
2224   Paul Winter, "Luke XXII,66b-71," *ST* 9 (1956): 112-15.

2225   R. T. France, "Jésus devant Caiphe," *Hokhmah* 15 (1980): 20-35.

2226   Kurt Schubert, "Biblical Criticism Criticised: With Reference to
       the Markan Report of Jesus's Examination before the Sanhedrin
       [Mk 14:55-64; 15:2-5; Lk 22:66-71]," in Ernst Bammel and
       C. F. D. Moule, eds., *Jesus and the Politics of His Day.*
       Cambridge: University Press, 1984. Pp. 385-402.

2227   John P. Heil, "Reader-Response and the Irony of Jesus Before the
       Sanhedrin in Luke 22:66-71," *CBQ* 51 (1989): 271-84.

2228   Frank J. Matera, "Luke 22:66-71: Jesus Before the Presbyterion,"
       ETL 65/1 (1989): 43-59.

22:67-68
2229   J. Duncan M. Derrett, "Midrash in the New Testament: The Origin
       of Luke 22:67-68," *ST* 29 (1975): 147-56.

22:67
2230   Walter   Radl,   "Sonderüberlieferungen   bei   Lukas?
       Traditionsgeschichtliche Fragen zu Lk 22,67f; 23,2 und 23,6-12,"
       in Karl Kertelge, ed., *Der Prozess gegen Jesus.* Freiburg: Herder,
       1988. Pp. 131-47.

22:69
2231   D. Flusser, "At the Right Hand of the Power," *Immanuel* 14
       (1982): 42-46.

2232   Joseph Plevnik, "Son of Man Seated at the Right Hand of God:
       Luke 22:69 in Lucan Christology," *Bib* 72/3 (1991): 331-47.

22:70
2233   Renatus Kempthorne, "The Marcan Text of Jesus' Answer to the
       High Priest (Mark XIV 62)," *NovT* 19/3 (1977): 197-208.

23:1-25
2234   M. Chico Cano, "Der Prozeß Jesu: Eine literarkritische und
       redaktionsgeschichtliche Untersuchung zu Lk 23,1-25," doctoral
       dissertation, University of Münster, Germany, 1984.

23:1-16
2235   J. Duncan M. Derrett, "Daniel and Salvation History," *DR* 100
       (1982): 62-68.

23:1-7
2236   J. M. Creed, "The Supposed 'Proto-Lucan' Narrative of the Trial before Pilate: A Rejoinder," *ET* 46 (1934-1935): 378-79.

23:1-5
2237   Gerhard Schneider, "The Political Charge against Jesus (Lk 23:2)," in E. Bammel and C. F. D. Moule, eds., *Jesus and the Politics of His Day*. Cambridge: University Press, 1984. Pp. 403-14.

23:2
2238   J. S. Kennard, "Syrian Coin Hoards and the Tribute Question," *ATR* 27 (1945): 248-52.

2239   Gerhard Schneider, "The Political Charge against Jesus (Lk 23:2)," in E. Bammel and C. F. D. Moule, eds., *Jesus and the Politics of His Day*. Cambridge: University Press, 1984. Pp. 403-14.

2240   Walter Radl, "Sonderüberlieferungen bei Lukas? Traditionsgeschichtliche Fragen zu Lk 22,67f; 23,2 und 23,6-12," in Karl Kertelge, ed., *Der Prozess gegen Jesus*. Freiburg: Herder, 1988. Pp. 131-47.

23:3
2241   J. Irmscher, "Su legeis (Mk 15,2; Mt 27,1; Lc 23,3)," *StudC* 2 (1960): 151-58.

23:5
2242   David Hill, "Jesus before the Sanhedrin: On What Charge?" *IBS* 7 (1985): 174-86.

23:6-12
2243   M. Corbin, "Jésus devant Hérode," *Chr* 25 (1978): 190-97.

2244   E. Buck, "The Function of the Pericope 'Jesus before Herod' in the Passion Narrative of Luke," in W. Haubeck and M. Bachmann, eds., *Wort in der Zeit* (festschrift for K. H. Rengstorf). Leiden: Brill, 1980. Pp. 165-78.

2245   Marion L. Soards, "Tradition, Composition, and Theology in Luke's Account of Jesus before Herod Antipas," *Bib* 66/3 (1985): 344-64.

2246 Walter Radl, "Sonderüberlieferungen bei Lukas? Traditionsgeschichtliche Fragen zu Lk 22,67f; 23,2 und 23,6-12," in Karl Kertelge, ed., *Der Prozess gegen Jesus*. Freiburg: Herder, 1988. Pp. 131-47.

2247 Chris U. Manus, "The Universalism of Luke and the Motif of Reconciliation (Lk 23:6-12): The African Cultural Context," *AJT* 3 (1989): 192-205.

23:8

2248 H. Hutchison, "Beware of the Sensational!" *ET* 91 (1979-1980): 117-19.

2249 Marion L. Soards, "Herod Antipas' Hearing in Luke 23:8," *BT* 37/1 (1986): 146-47.

23:9

2250 Marion L. Soards, "The Silence of Jesus Before Herod: An Interpretative Suggestion," *ABR* 33 (1985): 41-45.

23:13

2251 G. Rau, "Das Volk in der lukanischen Passionsgeschichte, eine Konjektur zu Lc 23,13," *ZNW* 56 (1965): 41-51.

23:17-19

2252 M. Herranz Marco, "Un problema de crítica histórica en el relato de la Pasión: la liberación de Barrabás," *EstB* 30 (1971): 137-60.

23:21

2253 J. M. Ford, " 'Crucify Him, Crucify Him' and the Temple Scroll," *ET* 87 (1975-1976): 275-78.

23:25-31

2254 Nicholas T. Wright, "Jesus, Israel and the Cross," *SBLSP* 15 (1985): 75-95.

23:25

2255 W. C. van Unnik, " 'Levensmogelijkheid of doodvonnis," in A. J. Bronkhorst, et al., eds., *Woorden gaan leven: Opstellen van en over W. C. van Unnik, 1910-1978*. Kampen: Kok, 1979. Pp. 127-32.

23:26-49
2256 Vittorio Fusco, "La morte del Messia," in Giovanni Boggio, et al., eds., *Gesù e la sua morte*. Brescia: Paideia, 1984. Pp. 51-73.

2257 John T. Carroll, "Luke's Crucifixion Scene," in Dennis D. Sylva, ed., *Reimaging the Death of the Lukan Jesus*. Frankfurt am Main: Hain, 1990. Pp. 108-24

23:26-34
2258 John V. Taylor, "Weep Not For Me: Meditations on the Cross and the Resurrection," *Risk* 27 (1986): 1-46.

23:26-32
2259 Marion L. Soards, "Tradition, Composition, and Theology in Jesus' Speech to the 'Daughters of Jerusalem' (Luke 23,26-32)," *Bib* 68/2 (1987): 221-44.

23:27-31
2260 Jerome H. Neyrey, "Jesus' Address to the Women of Jerusalem: A Prophetic Judgment Oracle," *NTS* 29 (1983): 74-86.

23:29
2261 Walter Käser, "Exegetische und Theologische Erwägungen zur Seligpreisung der Kinderlosen, Lc 23:29b," *ZNW* 54/3-4 (1963): 240-54.

2262 B. Rinaldi, "Beate le sterili (Lc. 23,29)," *BibO* 15 (1973): 61-64.

23:33
2263 Joseph A. Fitzmyer, "Crucifixion in Ancient Palestine, Qumran Literature, and the New Testament," *CBQ* 40/4 (1978): 493-513.

2264 J. Duncan M. Derrett, "The Two Malefactors (Lk xxiii 33,39-43)," in *Studies in the New Testament. III. Midrash, Naggadah, and the Character of the Community*. Leiden: Brill, 1982. Pp. 200-14.

2265 José O'Callaghan, "Fluctuación textual en Mt 20,21.26,27," *Bib* 71/4 (1990): 553-58.

23:34-46
2266 J. Wilkinson, "The Seven Words from the Cross," *SJT* 17 (1964): 69-82.

23:34

2267   J. Reid, "The Words from the Cross: I. 'Father, Forgive Them',"
       ET 41 (1929-1930): 103-107.

2268   D. Flusser, " 'Sie wissen nicht, was sie tun': Geschichte eines
       Herrenwortes," in P.-G. Müller and W. Stenger, eds., *Kontinuität
       und Einheit* (festschrift for F. Mussner). Freiburg: Herder, 1981.
       Pp. 393-410.

2269   William H. Willimon, "Following Jesus," *CC* 102 (1985): 236-37.

2270   D. A. S. Ravens, "St. Luke and Atonement," *ET* 97 (1985-1986):
       291-94.

2271   Jacobus H. Petzer, "Eclecticism and the Text of the New
       Testament," in Patrick J. Hartin and J. H. Petzer, eds., *Text and
       Interpretation: New Approaches in the Criticism of the New
       Testament.* Leiden: Brill, 1991. Pp. 47-62.

2272   Jacobus H. Petzer, "Anti-Judaism and the Textual Problem of Luke
       23:34," *FilN* 5 (1992): 199-203.

23:35-43

2273   W. Trilling, "Le Christ, roi crucifié (Lc 23)," *AsSeign* 65 (1973):
       56-65.

23:35

2274   P. M. Webb, "Saved," *ET* 85 (1973-1974): 175-76.

23:39-43

2275   W. M. MacGregor, "The Words from the Cross: II. The Penitent
       Thief," *ET* 41 (1929-1930): 151-54.

2276   A. Strobel, "Der Tod Jesu und das Sterben des Uenschen nach Lk
       23,39-43," in A. Strobel, ed., *Der Tod, ungelöstes Rätsel oder
       überwundener Feind?* Stuttgart: Calwer, 1974. Pp. 81-102.

2277   J. Duncan M. Derrett, "The Two Malefactors (Lk xxiii 33,39-43),"
       in *Studies in the New Testament. III. Midrash, Naggadah, and the
       Character of the Community.* Leiden: Brill, 1982. Pp. 200-14.

2278   J. M. García Pérez, "El relato del Buen Ladron (Lc 23,39-43),"
       EB 44 (1986): 263-304.

23:43
> **2279** L. P. Hope, "The King's Garden," *ET* 48 (1936-1937): 471-73.

23:44-49
> **2280** Joel B. Green, "The Death of Jesus and the Rending of the Temple Veil (Luke 23:44-49): A Window into Luke's Understanding of Jesus and the Temple," *SBLSP* 21 (1991): 543-57.

23:44-46
> **2281** Dennis D. Sylva, "The Temple Curtain and Jesus' Death in the Gospel of Luke," *JBL* 105/2 (1986): 239-50.

23:44-45
> **2282** J. F. A. Sawyer, "Why is a Solar Eclipse Mentioned in the Passion Narrative (Luke xxiii.44-45)?" *JTS* 23 (1972): 124-28.

> **2283** R. Grandez, "La tinieblas en la muerte de Jesús: Estudio sobre Lc 23,44-45," doctoral dissertation, Antonianum, Rome, 1987. 2 vols.

> **2284** R. Grandez, "La tinieblas en la muerte de Jesús: Historia de la exégesis de Lc 23,44-45a," *EB* 47 (1989): 177-223.

23:46-48
> **2285** Hartmut Gese, "Psalm 22 und das Neue Testament," *ZTK* 65/1 (1968): 1-22.

23:46
> **2286** T. Yates, "The Words from the Cross - Vll," *ET* 41 (1929-1930): 427-29.

> **2287** L. Abramowski and E. Goodman, "Luke xxiii.46: *paratithemai* in a Rare Syriac Rendering," *NTS* 13 (1966-1967): 290-91.

> **2288** Robert L. Brawley, "Entrusting Your Life to God's Care," *CumSem* 24/1 (1986): 18-20.

23:47
> **2289** George D. Kilpatrick, "A Theme of the Lucan Passion Story and Luke XXIII.47," *JTS* 43 (1942): 34-36.

> **2290** Robert J. Karris, "Luke 23:47 and the Lucan View of Jesus' Death," *JBL* 105/1 (1986): 65-74.

23:50-24:12
   2291 Timothy L. Chafins, "Women and Angels . . . When They Speak, It's Time to Listen!" *ATJ* 22 (1990): 11-17.

23:50-52
   2292 G. Ghiberti, "Sepolcro, sepoltura e panni sepolcrali di Gesù. Riconsiderando i dati biblici relativi alla Sindone di Torino," *RBib* 27 (1979): 123-58.

23:53-55
   2293 George Rice, "Western Non-Interpolations: A Defense of the Apostolate," in Charles H. Talbert, ed., *Luke-Acts.* New York: Crossroads, 1984. Pp. 1-16.

23:53-54
   2294 Michael D. Goulder, "On Putting Q to the Test," *NTS* 24 (1977-1978): 218-34.

23:53
   2295 D. Moody Smith, "Mark 15:46: The Shroud of Turin as a Problem of History and Faith," *BA* 46/4 (1983): 251-54.

23:55
   2296 Richard I. Pervo, "Social and Religious Aspects of the Western Text," in Dennis Groh and Robert Jewett, eds., *The Living Text* (festschrift for Ernest Saunders). Lanham MD: University Press of America, 1985. Pp. 229-41.

24:1-53
   2297 Raymond E. Brown, *A Risen Christ in Eastertime: Essays on the Gospel Narratives of the Resurrection.* Collegeville MN: Liturgical Press, 1991.

24:1-12
   2298 H. Gerits, "Le message pascal au tombeau (Lc 24,1-12): La résurrection selon la présentation théologique de Lc," *EstT* 8/15 (1981): 3-63.

   2299 H. Ritt, "Die Frauen und die Osterbotschaft: Synopse der Grabesgeschichten (Mk 16,1-8; Mt 27,62-28,15; Lk 24,1-12; Joh 20,1-18)," in G. Dautzenberg, et al., eds., *Die Frau im Urchristentum.* Freiburg: Herder, 1983. Pp. 117-33.

2300 Renata Huonker-Jenny, "Feminismus und Theologie: Definierbares und Undefinierbares," *Reformatio* 34/6 (1985): 435-39.

24:1-11
2301 Michael D. Goulder, "Mark 21:1-8 and Parallels," *NTS* 24 (1977-1978): 235-40.

2302 Luke T. Johnson, "Luke 24:1-11," *Int* 46 (1992): 57-61.

24:1-6
2303 George Rice, "Western Non-Interpolations: A Defense of the Apostolate," in Charles H. Talbert, ed., *Luke-Acts*. New York: Crossroads, 1984. Pp. 1-16.

24:1
2304 Michael D. Goulder, "On Putting Q to the Test," *NTS* 24 (1977-1978): 218-34.

2305 Richard I. Pervo, "Social and Religious Aspects of the Western Text," in Dennis Groh and Robert Jewett, eds., *The Living Text* (festschrift for Ernest Saunders). Lanham MD: University Press of America, 1985. Pp. 229-41.

24:3
2306 Mikeal C. Parsons, "A Christological Tendency in P^{75}," *JBL* 105/3 (1986): 463-79.

24:4
2307 Christoph Burchard, "Fußnoten zum neutestamentlichen Griechisch II," *ZNW* 69 (1978): 143-57.

24:6
2308 Richard I. Pervo, "Social and Religious Aspects of the Western Text," in Dennis Groh and Robert Jewett, eds., *The Living Text* (festschrift for Ernest Saunders). Lanham MD: University Press of America, 1985. Pp. 229-41.

2309 Mikeal C. Parsons, "A Christological Tendency in P^{75}," *JBL* 105/3 (1986): 463-79.

2310 Domingo Muñoz León, " 'Iré delante de vosotros a Galilea' (Mt 26,32 y par). Sentido mesiánico y posible sustrato arameo del logion," *EB* 48 (1990): 215-41.

24:7-21

2311   John M. Perry, "The Three Days in the Synoptic Passion Predictions," *CBQ* 48/4 (1986): 637-54.

24:9

2312   R. Oppermann, "Eine Beobachtung in bezug auf das Problem des Markus-Schlusses," *BibN* 40 (1987): 24-29.

24:12-24

2313   W. L. Craig, "The Disciples' Inspection of the Empty Tomb (Lk 24,12.24; Jn 20,2-10)," in Adelbert Denaux, ed., *John and the Synoptics*. BETL #101. Louvain: Peeters Press, 1992. Pp. 614-19.

24:12

2314   J. Muddiman, "A Note on Reading Luke 24:12," *ETL* 48 (1972): 542-48.

2315   Frans Neirynck, "Παρακύψας βλέπει: Lc 24:12 et Jn 20:5," *ETL* 53 (1977): 113-52.

2316   Frans Neirynck, "Lc 24:12. Les temoins du texte occidental," in T. Baarda, et al., eds., *Miscellancea Neotestamentica I.* NovTSupplement #47. Leiden: Brill, 1978. Pp. 45-60.

2317   Frans Neirynck, "Ἀπῆλθεν πρὸς ἑαυτὸν: Lc 24:12 et Jn 20:10," *ETL* 54 (1978): 104-18.

2318   Frans Neirynck, "John and the Synoptics: The Empty Tomb Stories," *NTS* 30/2 (1984): 161-87.

2319   J. M. Ross, "The Genuineness of Luke 24:12," *ET* 98 (1986-1987): 107-108.

24:13-53

2320   J. M. Nielen, "Gestalten des Neuen Testamentes," *BK* 10 (1955): 35-49.

2321   Jacob Kremer, "Die Bezeugung der Auferstehung Christi in Form von Geschichten: Zu Schwierigkeiten und Chancen heutigen Verstehens von Lk 24,13-53," *GeistL* 61 (1988): 172-87.

24:13-35

2322   Arnold Ehrhardt, "Disciples of Emmaus," *NTS* 10 (1963-1964): 182-201.

2323   Joseph A. Grassi, "Emmaus Revisited (Luke 24:13-35 and Acts 8:26-40)," *CBQ* 26 (1964): 463-67.

2324   G. Lazzati, "Les voyageurs d'Emmaüs," *Communion* 100 (1971): 67-76.

2325   J. Wanke, " 'Wie sie ihm beim Brotbrechen erkannten': Zur Auslegung der Emmauserzählung Lk 24,13-35," *BZ* 18 (1974): 180-92.

2326   Soeur Jeanne D'Arc, "Un grand jeu d'inclusions dans les pèlerins d'Emmaüs," *NRT* 99 (1977): 62-76.

2327   P. M. J. Stravinskas, "The Emmaus Pericope: Its Sources, Theology and Meaning for Today," *BB* 3 (1977): 97-115.

2328   André Feuillet, "L'apparition du Christ à Marie-Madeleine, Jean 20:11-18. Comparaison avec l'apparition aux disciples d'Emmaüs Luc 24:13-35," *EV* 88 (1978): 193-204, 209-23.

2329   D. Cerbelaud, "Bribes sur Emmaüs," *VS* 133 (1979): 4-7.

2330   X. Thévenot, "Emmaüs, une nouvelle Genèse? Une lecture psychanalytique de Genèse 2-3 et Luc 24:13-35," *MSR* 37 (1980): 3-18.

2331   P. J. Berry, "The Road to Emmaus," *ET* 91 (1980-1981): 204-206.

2332   O. K. Walther, "A Solemn One Way Trip Becomes a Joyous Roundtrip! A Study of the Structure of Luke 24:13-35," *ATB* 14 (1981): 60-67.

2333   Jacques Dupont, "Les disciples d'Emmaüs (Lc 24,13-35)," in M. Benzerath, et al., eds., *La Psoque du Christ: Mystère de salut* (festschrift for F.-X. Durrwell). Paris: Cerf, 1982. Pp. 167-95.

2334   Antoine Delzant, "Les Disciples d'Emmaüs (Luc 24:13-35)," *RechSR* 73/2 (1985): 177-86.

2335 Jim Forest, "In the Breaking of the Bread: Recognizing the Face of Jesus," *Soj* 14/4 (1985): 34-36.

2336 B.-J. Koet, "Some Traces of a Semantic Field of Interpretation in Luke 24:13-35," *Bij* 46 (1985): 59-73.

2337 Peter Fiedler, "Die Gegenwart als österliche Zeit - erfahrbar im Gottesdienst: Die 'Emmausgeschichte' Lk 24,13-35," in Ingo Broer and Lorenz Oberlinner, eds., *Auferstehung Jesu - Auferstehung der Christen: Deutungen des Osterglaubens*. Freiburg: Herder, 1986. Pp. 124-44.

2338 K. Jockwig, "Erfahrung und Vermittlung von Lebensbedeutsamkeit als Wesensmerkmal der Verkündigung: Homiletische Überlegungen zur Emmaus Perikope (Lk 24,13-35)," *TGeg* 29 (1986): 119-25.

2339 Robert J. Karris, "Luke 24:13-35," *Int* 41 (1987): 57-61.

2340 R. F. Smith, "Did Not Our Hearts Burn Within Us?" *CThM* 15 (1988): 187-93.

2341 François Rousseau, "Un Phénomène Particulier d'Inclusions dans Luc 24:13-35," *SR* 18/1 (1989): 67-79.

2342 Mary Catherine Hilkert, "Retelling the Gospel Story: Preaching and Narrative," *ÉgT* 21/2 (1990): 147-67.

2343 S. J. Nortjé, "On the Road to Emmaus: A Woman's Experience," in Patrick J. Hartin and J. H. Petzer, eds., *Text and Interpretation: New Approaches in the Criticism of the New Testament*. Leiden: Brill, 1991. Pp. 271-80.

24:13-33

2344 John M. Gibbs, "Luke 24:13-33 and Acts 8:26-39: The Emmaus Incident and the Eunuch's Baptism as Parallel Stories," *BTF* 7 (1975): 17-30.

2345 John M. Gibbs, "Canon Cuming's 'Service-Endings in the Epistles': A Rejoinder," *NTS* 24 (1977-1978): 545-47.

2346   Lucien Legrand, "Deux voyages: Lc 2,41-50; 24,13-33," in
           Françios Refoulé, ed., *à cause de l'Evangile: Etudes sur les
           synoptiques et les Actes* (festschrift for Jacques Dupont). Paris:
           Cerf, 1985. Pp. 409-29.

2347   Jean N. Aletti, "Luc 24,13-33: Signes, accomplissement et temps,"
           RechSR 75 (1987): 305-20.

24:13-32
2348   Hans Dieter Betz, "The Origin and Nature of Christian Faith
           According to the Emmaus Legend (Luke 24:13-32)," *Int* 23
           (1969): 32-46.

2349   Bernard P. Robinson, "The Place of the Emmaus Story in
           Luke-Acts," *NTS* 30/4 (1984): 481-97.

24:13-29
2350   Soeur Jeanne D'Arc, "La catéchèse sur la route d'Emmaüs," *LV*
           32 (1977): 7-20.

24:16
2351   Günther Schwarz, "Οἱ δὲ ὀφθαλμοὶ αὐτῶν ἐκρατοῦντο?" *BibN*
           55 (1990): 16-17.

24:18
2352   Ludger Thier, "Christus Peregrinus: Christus als Pilger in der Sicht
           von Theologen, Predigern und Mystikern des Mittelalters Ecclesia
           Peregrinans," in Karl Amon, et al., eds., *Ecclesia peregrinans*.
           Vienna: Verband des Wissenschaftlichen Gesellschaften
           Osterreichs, 1986. Pp. 29-41.

24:22
2353   Richard I. Pervo, "Social and Religious Aspects of the Western
           Text," in Dennis Groh and Robert Jewett, eds., *The Living Text*
           (festschrift for Ernest Saunders). Lanham MD: University Press of
           America, 1985. Pp. 229-41.

24:23-35
2354   Russell J. Asvitt, "On the Road to Emmaus," *FundJ* 5/3 (1986):
           28.

24:28-32
    2355 Soeur Jeanne D'Arc, "Le partage du pain à Emmaüs," *VS* 130 (1976): 896-909.

24:28-31
    2356 Ronald Goetz, "Picturing a Vanishing," *CC* 107 (1990): 395.

24:30-31
    2357 R. Abba, "The Unrecognized Guest," *ET* 92 (1980-1981): 210-12.

24:32-37
    2358 George Rice, "Western Non-Interpolations: A Defense of the Apostolate," in Charles H. Talbert, ed., *Luke-Acts*. New York: Crossroads, 1984. Pp. 1-16.

24:32
    2359 G. Widengren, "Was Not then Our Heart Burning within Us?" in E. C. Polomé, ed., *Essays in Memory of Karl Keréni*. Journal of Indo-European Studies Monographs #4. Washington: Institute for the Study of Man, 1984. Pp. 116-22.

24:33-35
    2360 R. Annand, " 'He Was Seen of Cephas': A Suggestion about the First Resurrection Appearance to Peter," *SJT* 11 (1958): 180-87.

24:33
    2361 Joseph Plevnik, " 'The Eleven and Those with Them' According to Luke," *CBQ* 40 (1978): 205-11.

24:34-35
    2362 P. Nash, "The Emmaus Road Incident," *ET* 85 (1973-1974): 178-79.

24:34
    2363 J. R. Gray, "The Lord is Risen Indeed," *ET* 93 (1981-1982): 179-80.

    2364 Gordon Dalbey, "Does the Resurrection Happen," *CC* 102 (1985): 319-20.

208   BIBLIOGRAPHIES FOR BIBLICAL RESEARCH

2365 Ingo Broer, " 'Der Herr ist wahrhaft auferstanden' (Lk 24,34):
Auferstehung Jesu und historisch-kritische Methode: Erwägungen
zur Entstehung des Osterglaubens," in Ingo Broer and Lorenz
Oberlinner, eds., *Auferstehung Jesu - Auferstehung der Christen:
Deutungen des Osterglaubens*. Freiburg: Herder, 1986. Pp. 39-62.

2366 Ingo Broer, " 'Der Herr ist Simon erschienen' (Lk 24,34): Zur
Entstehung des Osterglaubens," *SNTU-A* 13 (1988): 81-100.

24:35
2367 J. Reid, "Old Texts in Modern Translations: Luke 24,35
(Moffatt)," *ET* 49 (1937-1938): 186-89.

24:36-53
2368 A. Stöger, "Österliche Freude: Meditation über Lk 24,36-53," *BL*
50 (1977): 121-24.

2369 Gerard Mussies, "Variation in the Book of Acts," *FilN* 4 (1991):
165-82.

24:36-49
2370 M.-A. Chevallier, " 'Pentecôtes' lucaniennes et 'Pentecôtes'
johanniques," *RechSR* 69 (1981): 301-13.

2371 A. Dauer, *Johannes und Lukas: Untersuchungen zu den
johanneisch-lukanischen Parallel-Perikopen Joh 4,46-54/Lk 7,1-10;
Joh 12,1-8/Lk 7,36-50, 10,38-42; Joh 20,19-29/Lk 24,36-49*.
Würzburg: Echter, 1984.

24:36-43
2372 Frans Neirynck, "Lc 24,36-43: un récit lucanien [Jn 20:19-20;
Ignatius of Antioch, Smyr 3:1-2]," in Françios Refoulé, ed., *à
cause de l'Evangile: Etudes sur les synoptiques et les Actes*
(festschrift for Jacques Dupont). Paris: Cerf, 1985. Pp. 655-80.

24:36-38
2373 L. Köhler, "Gebratener Fisch und Honigseim," *ZDPV* 54 (1931):
289-307.

2374 G. Dalman, "Nochmals gebratener Fisch und Honigseim," *ZDPV*
55 (1932): 80-81.

24:40

2375   Mikeal C. Parsons, "A Christological Tendency in P^{75}," *JBL* 105/3 (1986): 463-79.

24:42-43

2376   George D. Kilpatrick, "Luke 24:42-43," *NovT* 28/4 (1986): 306-308.

2377   G. O'Collins, "Did Jesus Eat the Fish (Luke 24:42-43)," *Greg* 69 (1988): 65-76.

24:44-49

2378   J. D. Kingsbury, "Luke 24:44-49," *Int* 35 (1981): 170-74.

2379   Jacques Dupont, "La mission de Paul d'après Actes 26,16-23 et la mission des apôtres d'après Luc 24,44-49 et Actes 1,8," in M. D. Hooker and S. G. Wilson, eds., *Paul and Paulinism* (festschrift for C. K. Barrett). London: SPCK, 1982. Pp. 290-301.

24:44

2380   José Antonio Jáuregui, " 'Israel' y la Iglesia en la Teologia de Lucas," *EE* 61/237 (1986): 129-49.

24:46-53

2381   A. Viard, "L'ascension de Jésus et le don de l'Esprit," *EV* 87 (1977): 267-68.

24:46-48

2382   R. Trevijano Etcheverría, "La misión de la iglesia primitiva y los mandatos del Señor en los evangelios," *Salm* 25 (1978): 5-36.

2383   R. J. Dillon, "Easter Revelation and Mission Program in Luke 24:46-48," in D. Durken, ed., *Sin, Salvation, and the Spirit*. Collegeville MN: Liturgical Press, 1979. Pp. 240-70.

24:46-47

2384   Ronald Russell, "The Encounter with the Roman World," *FundJ* 4/10 (1985): 38-40.

24:46

2385   John M. Perry, "The Three Days in the Synoptic Passion Predictions," *CBQ* 48/4 (1986): 637-54.

24:47

2386   Jacques Dupont, "La portée christologique de l'évangélisation des
nations d'après Luc 24,47," in J. Gnilka, ed., *Neues Testament und
Kirche* (festschrift for Rudolf Schnackenburg). Freiburg: Herder,
1974. Pp. 125-43.

24:49

2387   J. H. Sieber, "The Spirit as the 'Promise of My Father' in Luke
24:49," in D. Durken, ed., *Sin, Salvation, and the Spirit*.
Collegeville MN: Liturgical Press, 1979. Pp. 271-78.

24:50-53

2388   P. A. van Stempvoort, "The Interpretation of the Ascension in
Luke and Acts," *NTS* 5 (1958-1959): 30-42.

2389   E. A. LaVerdiere, "The Ascension of the Risen Lord," *BibTo* 95
(1978): 1553-59.

2390   F. Schnider, "Die Himmelfahrt Jesu: Ende oder Anfang? Zum
Verständnis des lukanischen Doppelwerkes," in P.-G. Muller and
W. Stenger, eds., *Kontinuität und Einheit* (festschrift for F.
Mussner). Freiburg: Herder, 1981. Pp. 158-72.

2391   John F. Maile, "The Ascension in Luke-Acts," *TynB* 37 (1986):
29-59.

2392   P. Palatty, "The Ascension of Christ in Luke-Acts: An Exegetical
Critical Study of Luke 24,50-53 and Acts 1,2-3.9-11," *BB* 12
(1986): 100-17, 166-81.

2393   Mikeal C. Parsons, "Narrative Closure and Openness in the Plot of
the Third Gospel: The Sense of an Ending in Luke 24:50-53,"
SBLSP 16 (1986): 201-23.

2394   Mikeal C. Parsons, *The Departure of Jesus in Luke-Acts: The
Ascension Narratives in Context*. Sheffield: JSOT Press, 1987.

2395   Carol L. Stockhausen, "Luke's Stories of the Ascension: The
Background and Function of a Dual Narrative," *EGLMBS* 10
(1990): 251-63.

24:51-52
> **2396** Mikeal C. Parsons, "A Christological Tendency in P^{75}," *JBL* 105/3 (1986): 463-79.

24:51
> **2397** G. Odasso, "L'ascensione nell'evangelo di Luca," *BibO* 13 (1971): 107-18.

PART TWO

Citations by Subjects

advent
2398   H. Spaemann, "Advent der Christen im Gleichnis. Eine Meditation über Lk 12:35-39," *BibL* 1 (1960): 266-70.

2399   C. Küven, "Advent in der Entscheidung nach Lukas 12:35-59," *BK* 16 (1961): 109-12.

almsgiving
2400   Francis E. Williams, "Is Almsgiving the Point of the 'Unjust Steward'?" *JBL* 83 (1964): 293-97.

2401   Edward G. Mathews, "The Rich Man and Lazarus: Almsgiving and Repentance in Early Syriac Tradition," *Diakonia* 22/2 (1988-1989): 89-104.

anti-Semitism
2402   Jack T. Sanders, "The Parable of the Pounds and Lucan Anti-Semitism," *TS* 42 (1981): 660-68.

2403   Lloyd Gaston, "Anti-Judaism and the Passion Narrative in Luke and Acts," in P. Richardson and D. Granskou, eds., *Anti-Judaism in Early Christianity: 1. Paul and the Gospels*. Waterloo: Wilfrid Laurier University Press, 1986. Pp. 127-53.

2404   Victor E. Vine, "Luke 14:15-24 and Anti-Semitism," *ET* 102 (1990-1991): 262-63.

apocalyptic
2405   William J. Crowder, "Jesus' Use of Apocalyptic Language in the Synoptic Gospels," doctoral dissertation, Southern Baptist Theological Seminary, Louisville KY, 1937.

2406   Richard J. Bauckham, "Synoptic Parousia Parables and the Apocalypse," *NTS* 23 (1976-1977): 162-76.

ascension
2407   J. G. Davies, "The Prefigurement of the Ascension in the Third Gospel," *JTS* 6 (1955): 229-33.

2408   P. A. van Stempvoort, "The Interpretation of the Ascension in Luke and Acts," *NTS* 5 (1958-1959): 30-42.

2409   Robert F. O'Toole, "Luke's Understanding of Jesus' Resurrection—Ascension—Exaltation," *BTB* 9 (1979): 106-14.

2410   William Baird, "Ascension and Resurrection: An Intersection of Luke and Paul," in W. E. March, ed., *Texts and Testaments* (festschrift for S. D. Currie). San Antonio TX: Trinity University Press, 1980. Pp. 3-18.

2411   Elton J. Epp, "The Ascension in the Textual Tradition of Luke-Acts," in Elton J. Epps and Gordon D. Fee, eds., *New Testament Textual Criticism* (festschrift for Bruce M. Metzger). Oxford: Clarendon Press, 1981. Pp. 131-45.

2412   F. Schnider, "Die Himmelfahrt Jesu: Ende oder Anfang? Zum Verständnis des lukanischen Doppelwerkes," in P.-G. Muller and W. Stenger, eds., *Kontinuität und Einheit* (festschrift for F. Mussner). Freiburg: Herder, 1981. Pp. 158-72.

2413   Frans Neirynck, "John and the Synoptics: The Empty Tomb Stories," *NTS* 30/2 (1984): 161-87.

2414   Mikeal C. Parsons, "The Ascension Narratives in Luke-Acts," doctoral dissertation, Southern Baptist Theological Seminary, Louisville KY, 1985.

2415   John F. Maile, "The Ascension in Luke-Acts," *TynB* 37 (1986): 29-59.

2416   P. Palatty, "The Ascension of Christ in Luke-Acts: An Exegetical Critical Study of Luke 24,50-53 and Acts 1,2-3.9-11," *BB* 12 (1986): 100-17, 166-81.

2417   Mikeal C. Parsons, *The Departure of Jesus in Luke-Acts: The Ascension Narratives in Context.* Sheffield: JSOT Press, 1987.

2418   Carol L. Stockhausen, "Luke's Stories of the Ascension: The Background and Function of a Dual Narrative," *EGLMBS* 10 (1990): 251-63.

atonement
2419   D. A. S. Ravens, "St. Luke and Atonement," *ET* 97 (1985-1986): 291-94.

audience

2420 R. J. Cassidy, "Luke's Audience, the Chief Priests, and the Motives for Jesus' Death," in R. J. Cassidy and P. J. Scharper, eds., *Political Issues in Luke-Acts*. Maryknoll NY: Orbis, 1983. Pp. 146-67.

authorship

2421 Herbert H. Wernecke, "The Authorship, Date and Characteristics of the Gospel of Luke," doctoral dissertation, Southern Baptist Theological Seminary, Louisville KY, 1927.

2422 B. E. Beck, "The Common Authorship of Luke and Acts," *NTS* 23 (1976-1977): 346-52.

baptism

2423 Bo Reicke, "Die Verkündigung des Täufers nach Lukas," *SNTU-A* 1 (1976): 50-61.

2424 Schuyler Brown, " 'Water-Baptism' and 'Spirit-Baptism' in Luke-Acts," *ATR* 59 (1977): 135-50.

2425 Otto Böcher, "Lukas und Johannes der Täufer," *SNTU-A* 4 (1979): 27-44.

2426 M. Bachmann, "Johannes der Täufer bei Lukas: Nachzügler oder Vorläufer?" in W. Haubeck and M. Bachmann, eds., *Wort in der Zeit* (festschrift for K. H. Rengstorf). Leiden: Brill, 1980. Pp. 123-55.

2427 Robert F. O'Toole, "Christian Baptism in Luke," *RevRel* 39 (1980): 855-66.

2428 J. L. Pretlove, "Baptism ἐν πνεῦμα: A Comparison of the Theologies of Luke and Paul," doctoral dissertation, Southwestern Baptist Theological Seminary, Fort Worth TX, 1980.

2429 Claus P. März, "Feuer auf die Erde zu werfen, bin ich gekommen: Zum Verständnis und zur Entstehung von Lk 12,49," in Françios Refoulé, ed., *à cause de l'Evangile: Etudes sur les synoptiques et les Actes* (festschrift for Jacques Dupont). Paris: Cerf, 1985. Pp. 479-511.

2430   F. Porsch, "Erwählt und erprobt: Die Taufe und Versuchung
       Jesu," in P.-G. Müller, ed., *Das Zeugnis des Lukas*. Stuttgart:
       Katholisches Bibelwerk, 1985. Pp. 36-43.

beatitudes
2431   J. E. Murray, "The Beatitudes," *Int* 1 (1947): 374-76.

2432   P.-E. Jacquemin, "Les Béatitudes selon saint Luc (Lc 6)," *AsSeign*
       N.S. 37 (1971): 80-91.

2433   J. Coppens, "Les Béatitudes," *ETL* 50 (1974): 256-60.

2434   N. J. McEleney, "The Beatitudes of the Sermon on the
       Mount/Plain," *CBQ* 43 (1981): 1-13.

2435   M. Eugene Boring, "Criteria of Authenticity: The Lucan Beatitudes
       as a Test Case," *Forum* 1 (1985): 3-38.

2436   Robert W. Funk, "The Beatitudes and Turn the Other Cheek:
       Recommendations and Polling," *Forum* 2 (1986): 103-28.

2437   M. Eugene Boring, "The Historical-Critical Method's Criteria of
       Authenticity: The Beatitudes in Q and Thomas as a Test Case,"
       Semeia 44 (1988): 9-44.

2438   Adrian M. Leske, "The Beatitudes: Salt and Light in Matthew and
       Luke," *SBLSP* 21 (1991): 816-39.

bibliography
2439   Bruno Corsani, "Bulletin du Nouveau Testament: Études
       lucaniennes," *ETL* 64 (1989): 83-93.

2440   Charles H. Talbert, "Shifting Sands: The Recent Study of the
       Gospel of Luke," *Int* 30 (1976): 381-95.

2441   F. Bovon, "Recent Trends in Lucan Studies," *TD* 25 (1977):
       217-24.

2442   B. E. Beck, "Commentaries on Luke's Gospel," *EpRev* 6 (1979):
       81-85.

2443   M. Cambe, "Bulletin de Nouveau Testament: études lucaniennes,"
       ÉTR 56 (1981): 159-67.

2444 M. Rese, "Neuere Lukas-Arbeiten," *TLZ* 106 (1981): 225-37.

2445 Earl Richard, "Luke—Writer, Theologian, Historian: Research and Orientation of the 1970s," *BTB* 13 (1983): 3-15.

2446 Günter Wagner, *An Exegetical Bibliography of the New Testament.* 3. *Luke-Acts.* Macon GA: Mercer University Press, 1985.

2447 G. Van Belle, *Johannine Bibliography 1966-1985: A Cumulative Bibliography on the Fourth Gospel.* BETL #82. Louvain: Peeters Press, 1988.

2448 Frans van Segbroeck, *The Gospel of Luke: A Cumulative Bibliography 1973-1988.* BETL #88. Louvain: Peeters Press, 1989.

birth narratives
2449 H. T. Kuist, "Sources of Power in the Nativity Hymns. An Exposition of Luke 1 and 2," *Int* 2 (1948): 288-98.

2450 Paul Winter, "Some Observations on the Language in the Birth and Infancy Stories of the Third Gospel," *NTS* 1 (1954-1955): 111-21.

2451 A. R. C. Leaney, "The Birth Narratives in St. Luke and St. Matthew," *NTS* 8 (1961-1962): 158-66.

2452 H. H. Oliver, "The Lucan Birth Stories and the Purpose of Luke-Acts," *NTS* 10 (1963-1964): 202-26.

2453 O. A. Piper, "The Virgin Birth. The Meaning of the Gospel Accounts," *Int* 18 (1964): 131-48.

2454 Paul S. Minear, "Luke's Use of the Birth Stories," in Leander Keck and J. L. Martyn, eds., *Studies in Luke-Acts* (festschrift for Paul Schubert). Nashville: Abingdon Press, 1966. Pp. 111-30.

2455 C. T. Ruddick, "Birth Narratives in Genesis and Luke," *NovT* 12 (1970): 343-48.

2456 J. Duncan M. Derrett, "The Manger at Bethlehem: Light on St. Luke's Technique from Contemporary Jewish Religious Law," *StudE* 6 (1973): 86-94.

2457   R. L. Humenay, "The Place of Mary in Luke: A Look at Modern Biblical Criticism," *AmER* 168 (1974): 291-303.

2458   J. Duncan M. Derrett, "Further Light on the Narratives of the Nativity," *NovT* 17 (1975): 81-108.

2459   M. E. Isaacs, "Mary in the Lucan Infancy Narrative," *Way* Suppl. 25 (1975): 80-95.

2460   J. Neville Birdsall, "Some Names in the Lukan Genealogy of Jesus in the Armenian Biblical Tradition," in M. E. Stone, ed., *Armenian and Biblical Studies*. Jerusalem: St. James, 1976. Pp. 13-16.

2461   Lloyd Gaston, "The Lukan Birth Narratives in Tradition and Redaction," *SBLSP* 6 (1976): 209-18.

2462   Raymond E. Brown, *An Adult Christ at Christmas: Essays on Three Biblical Stories*. Collegeville MN: Liturgical Press, 1978.

2463   Raymond E. Brown, *The Birth of the Messiah*. New York: Doubleday, 1979.

2464   L. Kaufmann, "Geburt des Messias: Text und Kontext einer guten Nachricht," *Orient* 44 (1980): 250-53.

2465   M. R. Mulholland, "The Infancy Narratives in Matthew and Luke: Of History, Theology, and Literature," *BAR* 7/2 (1981): 46-59.

2466   A. Gueuret, *L'engendrement d'un récit: L'évangile de l'enfance selon saint Luc*. Paris: Cerf, 1983.

2467   H. Hendrickx, *The Infancy Narratives*. Studies in the Synoptic Gospels. Rev. ed. San Francisco: Harper & Row, 1984.

2468   M. Boyd, "The Search for the Living Text of the Lukan Infancy Narrative," in D. E. Groh and Robert Jewett, eds., *The Living Text* (festschrift E. W. Saunders). Lanham MD: University Press of America, 1985. Pp. 123-40.

2469   Carlo Buzzetti, "Traducendo κεχαριτωμένη (Lc 1,28)," in M. Angelini, et al., eds., *Testimonium Christi* (festschrift for Jacques Dupont). Brescia: Paideia, 1985. Pp. 111-16.

2470   E. W. Conrad, "The Annunciation of Birth and the Birth of the Messiah," *CBQ* 47 (1985): 656-63.

2471   James M. Dawsey, "The Form and Function of the Nativity Stories in Luke," *MeliT* 36 (1985): 41-48.

2472   Charles T. Knippel, "The Nativity of Our Lord," *CJ* 11 (1985): 228-29.

2473   Lucien Legrand, "Deux voyages: Lc 2,41-50; 24,13-33," in François Refoulé, ed., *à cause de l'Evangile: Etudes sur les synoptiques et les Actes* (festschrift for Jacques Dupont). Paris: Cerf, 1985. Pp. 409-29.

2474   P. Boyd Mather, "The Search for the Living Text of the Lukan Infancy Narrative," in Dennis Groh and Robert Jewett, eds., *The Living Text* (festschrift for Ernest Saunders). Lanham MD: University Press of America, 1985. Pp. 123-40.

2475   Willem S. Vorster, "The Annunciation of the Birth of Jesus in the Protoevangelium of James," in J. H. Petzer and P. J. Hartin, eds., *A South African Perspective on the New Testament* (festschrift for Bruce Metzger). Leiden: Brill, 1986. Pp. 33-53.

2476   J. L. Ottey, "In a Stable Born Our Brother," *ET* 98/3 (1986-1987): 71-73.

2477   Gert J. Steyn, "The Occurrence of 'Kainam' in Luke's Genealogy," *ETL* 65 (1989): 409-11.

2478   Reginald H. Fuller, *He That Cometh: The Birth of Jesus in the New Testament.* Harrisburg PA: Morehouse, 1990.

2479   H. Wayne Merritt, "The Angel's Announcement: A Structuralist Study [Lk 1]," in Theodore W. Jennings and Hendrikus Boers, eds., *Text and Logos: The Humanistic Interpretation of the New Testament.* Atlanta: Scholars Press, 1990. Pp. 97-108.

2480   I. Chappus-Juillard, *Le temps des rencontres. Quand Marie visite Elisabeth.* Aubonne: Editions du Moulin, 1991.

2481   L. Panier, *La Naissance du fils de Dieu.* Paris: Cerf, 1991.

blasphemy
    2482   Eugene W. Daily, "A Study of Blasphemy in the Gospels,"
            doctoral dissertation, Southern Baptist Theological Seminary,
            Louisville KY, 1947.

Caesar
    2483   Charles H. Giblin, " 'The Things of God' in the Question
            Concerning Tribute to Caesar," *CBQ* 33/4 (1971): 510-27.

    2484   J. Duncan M. Derrett, "Luke's Perspective on Tribute to Caesar,"
            in R. J. Cassidy and P. J. Scharper, eds., *Political Issues in
            Luke-Acts*. Maryknoll NY: Orbis, 1983. Pp. 38-48.

Caesar Augustus
    2485   Eugene Seraphin, "The Edict of Caesar Augustus," *CBQ* 7 (1945):
            91-96.

central section
    2486   Carl L. Blomberg, "The Tradition History of the Parables Peculiar
            to Luke's Central Section," doctoral dissertation, University of
            Aberdeen, Aberdeen, UK, 1982.

    2487   Carl L. Blomberg, "Midrash, Chiasmus, and the Outline of Luke's
            Central Section," in Robert T. France and David Wenham, eds.,
            Gospel Perspectives III. Sheffield: JSOT Press, 1983. Pp. 217-61.

children
    2488   Franz Mussner, "Der nicht erkannte Kairos (Mt 11,16-19 = Lk
            7,31-35)," in *Studia Biblica et Orientalia*. 3 vols. Rome: Pontifical
            Institute, 1959. 2:31-44.

    2489   Simon Légasse, "La parabole des enfants sur la place," in *Jésus
            et l'enfant*. Paris: Gabalda, 1969. Pp. 289-317.

    2490   O. Linton, "The Parable of the Children's Game," *NTS* 22/2
            (1975-1976): 159-79.

    2491   C. Siburt, "The Game of Rejecting God: Luke 7:31-35," *RQ* 19
            (1976): 207-10.

    2492   L. Hermans, "De herders in het kindheidsevangelie van Lucas,"
            in M. Menken, et al., eds., *Goede Herders*. HTP Studies #5.
            Averbode: Altiora, 1983. Pp. 62-90.

2493 Wendy J. Cotter, "The Parable of the Children in the Market-Place, Q (Lk) 7:31-35," *NovT* 29 (1987): 289-304.

2494 J. Kodell, "Luke and the Children: The Beginning and End of the Great Interpolation (Luke 9:46-56; 18:9-23)," *CBQ* 49 (1987): 415-30.

2495 Wendy J. Cotter, "Children Sitting in the Agora: Q (Luke) 7:31-35," *Forum* 5 (1989): 63-82.

christology
2496 Robert G. Hamerton-Kelly, *Pre-Existence, Wisdom, and the Son of Man: A Study of the Idea of Pre-Existence in the New Testament.* Cambridge: University Press, 1973.

2497 U. Wilckens, "Das christliche Heilsverständnis nach dem Lukasevangelium," in P. A. Potter, ed., *Das Heil der Welt heute: Ende oder Beginn der Weltmission? Dokwnente der Weltmissionskonferenz Bangkok 1973.* Stuttgart-Berlin: Kreuz, 1973. Pp. 65-74.

2498 Jacques Dupont, "La portée christologique de l'évangélisation des nations d'après Luc 24,47," in J. Gnilka, ed., *Neues Testament und Kirche* (festschrift for Rudolf Schnackenburg). Freiburg: Herder, 1974. Pp. 125-43.

2499 Jacques Dupont, "Les implications christologiques de la parabole de la brebis perdue," in Jacques Dupont, ed., *Jésus aux origines de la christologie.* BETL #40. Louvain: Peeters Press, 1975. Pp. 331-50.

2500 Jacques Dupont, ed., *Jésus aux origines de la christologie.* BETL #40. Louvain: Peeters Press, 1975.

2501 Jacques Dupont, "Le couple parabolique du sénevé et du levain," in G. Strecker, ed., *Jesus Christus in Historie und Theologie* (festschrift for Hans Conzelman). Tübingen: Mohr, 1975. Pp. 331-45.

2502 E. Earle Ellis, "La composition de Luc 9 et les sources de sa christologie," in Jacques Dupont, ed., *Jésus aux origines de la christologie.* BETL #40. Louvain: Peeters Press, 1975. Pp. 193-220.

2503 Gerhard Schneider, " 'Der Menschensohn' in der lukanischen Christologie," in Rudolf Pesch, et al., eds., *Jesus und der Menschensohn* (festschrift for A. Vogtle). Freiburg: Herder, 1975. Pp. 98-113.

2504 J. Berchmans, "Some Aspects of Lukan Christology," *BB* 2 (1976): 5-22.

2505 Silverio Zedda, "La croce nella cristologia della kénosis di Luca 3-24," in B. Rinaldi, ed., *La sapienza della croce oggi*. I. Torino (Leumann): ElleDiCi, 1976. Pp. 86-94.

2506 Jacques Dupont, *Pourquoi des paraboles? La méthode parabolique de Jésus*. Paris: Cerf, 1977.

2507 William S. Kurz, "The Function of Christological Proof from Prophecy for Luke and Justin," doctoral dissertation, Yale University, New Haven CT, 1977.

2508 William S. Kurz, "Hellenistic Rhetoric in the Christological Proof of Luke-Acts," *CBQ* 42 (1980): 171-95.

2509 Johannes M. Nützel, *Jesus als Offenbarer Gottes nach den lukanischen Schriften*. Würzburg: Echter, 1980.

2510 G. W. Grogan, "The Light and the Stone: A Christological Study in Luke and Isaiah," in H. H. Rowdon, ed., *Christ the Lord* (festschrift for Donald Guthrie). Leicester: InterVarsity Press, 1982. Pp. 151-67.

2511 Eduard Schweizer, "Zur lukanischen Christologie," in E. Jüngel, ed., *Verifiikationen* (festschrift for Gerhard Ebeling). Tübingen: Mohr, 1982. Pp. 43-65.

2512 Frederick W. Danker, "Graeco-Roman Cultural Accommodation in the Christology of Luke-Acts," *SBLSP* 13 (1983): 391-414.

2513 André Feuillet, "Deux références évangéliques cachées au Serviteur martyrisé (Is 52,13-53,12)," *NRT* 106 (1984): 549-65.

2514 Joseph G. Kelly, "Lucan Christology and the Jewish-Christian Dialogue," *JES* 21 (1984): 688-708.

2515 M. Wren, "Sonship in Luke: The Advantage of a Literary Approach," *SJT* 37 (1984): 301-11.

2516 M. de Jonge, "The Christology of Luke-Acts," in *Christology in Context: The Earliest Christian Response to Jesus*. Philadelphia: Westminster, 1988. Pp. 97-111.

2517 Lucien Legrand, "The Angel Gabriel and Politics: Messianism and Christology," *ITS* 26 (1989): 1-21.

2518 D. M. Crump, *Jesus the Intercessor. Prayer and Christology in Luke-Acts*. WUNT #49. Tübingen: Mohr-Siebeck, 1992.

coins

2519 J. S. Kennard, "Syrian Coin Hoards and the Tribute Question," *ATR* 27 (1945): 248-52.

2520 N. Heutger, "Münzen im Lukasevangelium," *BZ* 27 (1983): 97-101.

community

2521 Eugene A. La Verdiere and William G. Thompson, "New Testament Communities in Transition: A Study of Matthew and Luke," *TS* 37 (1976): 567-97.

2522 Luke T. Johnson, "On Finding the Lukan Community: A Cautious Cautionary Essay," *SBLSP* 9/1 (1979): 87-100.

2523 A. Rodriguez-Carmona, "La comunidad cristiana a la luz de los escritos de Lucas," *Communio* 14 (1981): 311-34.

compassion

2524 H. Klein, *Barmherzigkeit gegenüber den Elenden und Geächteten: Studien zur Botschaft des lukanischen Sondergutes*. Biblisch-theologische Studien #10. Neukirchen-Vluyn: Neukirchener Verlag, 1987.

conflict

2525 Arland J. Hultgren, *Jesus and His Adversaries: The Form and Function of the Conflict Stories in the Synoptic Tradition*. Minneapolis MN: Augsburg, 1979.

2526   J. D. Kingsbury, *Conflict in Luke: Jesus, Authorities, Disciples.*
       Minneapolis MN: Fortress, 1991.

2527   Bruce J. Malina and Jerome H. Neyrey, "Conflict in Luke-Acts:
       Labeling and Deviance Theory," in Jerome H. Neyrey, ed., *The
       Social World of Luke-Acts.* Peabody MA: Hendrickson Publishers,
       1991. Pp. 87-122.

criticism, literary

2528   B. C. Butler, *The Originality of St. Matthew: A Critique of the
       Two-Documents Hypothesis.* Cambridge: University Press, 1951.

2529   Henry G. Russell, "Which Was Written First, Luke or Acts?" *HTR*
       48 (1955): 167-74.

2530   A. W. Mosley, "Jesus' Audiences in the Gospels of St. Mark and
       St. Luke," *NTS* 10 (1963-1964): 139-49.

2531   J. H. Davies, "The Lucan Prologue (1-3): An Attempt at Objective
       Redaction Criticism," *StudE* 4 (1968): 78-85.

2532   P. R. Baldacci, "The Significance of the Transfiguration Narrative
       in the Gospel of Luke: A Redactional Investigation," doctoral
       dissertation, Marquette University, Milwaukee WI, 1974.

2533   D. Dormeyer, "Literarische und theologische Analyse der Parabel
       Lukas 14:15-24," *BibL* 15 (1974): 206-19.

2534   J. D. Anido, "The Status and Achievement of Luke the Theologian
       in the Light of Contemporary Redaction Criticism," doctoral
       dissertation, McGill University, Montréal, 1975.

2535   Charles E. Carlston, "The Lukan Redaction," in *The Parables in
       the Triple Tradition.* Philadelphia: Fortress, 1975. Pp. 53-94.

2536   D. Dormeyer, "Textpragmatische Analyse und Unterrichtsplanung
       zum Gleichnis vom verlorenen Schaf, Lk 15,1-7," *EvErz* 27
       (1975): 347-57.

2537   F. H. Daniel, "The Transfiguration (Mark 9,2-13 and Parallels): A
       Redaction-Critical and Traditio-Historical Study," doctoral
       dissertation, Vanderbilt University, Nashville TN, 1976.

2538 Helmut L. Egelkraut, *Jesus' Mission to Jerusalem: A Redaction-Critical Study of the Travel Narrative in the Gospel of Luke*. Bern: Lang, 1976.

2539 R. Holst, "The One Anointing of Jesus: Another Application of the Form-Critical Method," *JBL* 95 (1976): 435-46.

2540 F. Schnider, *Die verlorenen Söhne: Strukturanalytische und historisch-kritische Untersuchungen zu Lk 15*. Göttingen: Vandenhoeck, 1977.

2541 Mary Ann Tolbert, "The Prodigal Son: An Essay in Literary Criticism from a Psychoanalytic Perspective," *Semeia* 9 (1977): 1-20.

2542 Jacob W. Elias, "The Beginning of Jesus' Ministry in the Gospel of Luke: A Redaction-Critical Study of Luke 4:14-30," doctoral dissertation, Toronto School of Theology, Toronto, 1978.

2543 Joseph B. Tyson, "Source Criticism of the Gospel of Luke," in Charles H. Talbert, ed., *Perspectives on Luke-Acts*. Macon GA: Mercer University Press, 1978. Pp. 24-39.

2544 Tavares A. Augusto, "Infancy Narratives and Historical Criticism," *TD* 28 (1980): 53-54.

2545 C. M. Fuhrman, "A Redactional Study of Prayer in the Gospel of Luke," doctoral dissertation, Southwestern Baptist Theological Seminary, Fort Worth TX, 1981.

2546 Sharon H. Ringe, "The Jubilee Proclamation in the Ministry and Teaching of Jesus: A Tradition-Critical Study in the Synoptic Gospels and Acts," doctoral dissertation, Union Theological Seminary NY, 1982.

2547 R. M. Shelton, *Filled with the Holy Spirit: A Redactional Motif in Luke's Gospel*. London: British Library, 1982.

2548 John W. Wenham, " 'Why Do You Ask Me about the Good?' A Study of the Relation between Text and Source Criticism," *NTS* 28 (1982): 116-25.

228 · BIBLIOGRAPHIES FOR BIBLICAL RESEARCH

2549 Camille Focant, "La parabole de la brebis perdue: Lecture historico-critique et réflexions théologiques," *FT* 13 (1983): 52-79.

2550 Susan Marie Praeder, "Jesus-Paul, Peter-Paul, and Jesus-Peter Parallelisms in Luke-Acts: A History of Reader Response," *SBLSP* 14 (1984): 23-39.

2551 Victor Saxer, "Anselme et la Madeleine: l'oraison LXXIV, ses sources, son style et son influence," in Raymonde Foreville, ed., *Les mutations socio-Culturelles*. Paris: Editions du Centre national de la recherche scientifique, 1984. Pp. 365-82.

2552 Samuel O. Abogunrin, "The 3 Variant Accounts of Peter's Call: Critical, Theological Examination of the Texts," *NTS* 31 (1985): 587-602.

2553 Oscar H. Hirt, "Interpretation in the Gospels: An Examination of the Use of Redaction Criticism in Mark 8:27-9:32," doctoral dissertation, Dallas Theological Seminary, Dallas TX, 1985.

2554 Paul Kariamadam, *The Zacchaeus Story (Lk 19:1-10): A Redactional-Critical Investigation*. Kerala, India: Pontifical Institute of Theology and Philosophy, 1985.

2555 Timothy L. Noël, "Parables in Context: Developing a Narrative-Critical Approach to Parables in Luke," doctoral dissertation, Southwestern Baptist Theological Seminary, Fort Worth TX, 1986.

2556 J. Smit Sibinga, "Zur Kompositionstechnik des Lukas in Lk 15:11-32," in J. W. van Henten, ed., *Tradition and Re-Interpretation in Jewish and Early Christian Literature* (festschrift for Jürgen C. H. Lebram). Leiden: Brill, 1986. Pp. 97-113.

2557 Willem S. Vorster, "The Annunciation of the Birth of Jesus in the Protoevangelium of James," in J. H. Petzer and P. J. Hartin, eds., *A South African Perspective on the New Testament* (festschrift for Bruce Metzger). Leiden: Brill, 1986. Pp. 33-53.

2558 Gerhard Schneider, "Das Verfahren gegen Jesus in der Sicht des dritten Evangeliums (Lk 22,54-23,25): Redaktionskritik und historische Rückfrage," in Karl Kertelge, ed., *Der Prozeß gegen Jesus.* Freiburg: Herder, 1988. Pp. 111-30.

2559 Jean N. Aletti, "Lc 19,11-28: parabole des mines et/ou parabole du roi: remarques sur l'écriture parabolique de Luc," in Jean Delorme, ed., *Les paraboles évangéliques: perspectives nouvelles.* Paris: Cerf, 1989. Pp. 309-32.

2560 Thomas L. Brodie, "Luke 9:57-62: A Systematic Adaptation of the Divine Challenge to Elijah (1 Kings 19)," *SBLSP* 19 (1989): 237-45.

2561 Jean Delorme, "Récit, parole et parabole," in Jean Delorme, ed., *Les paraboles évangéliques: perspectives nouvelles.* Paris: Cerf, 1989. Pp. 123-50.

2562 Agnès Gueuret, "Le pharisien et le publicain et son contexte," in Jean Delorme, ed., *Les paraboles évangéliques: perspectives nouvelles.* Paris: Cerf, 1989. Pp. 289-307.

2563 Stephen D. Moore, *Literary Criticism and the Gospels.* New Haven: Yale University Press, 1989.

2564 Timothy L. Noël, "The Parable of the Wedding Guest: A Narrative-Critical Interpretation," *PRS* 16 (1989): 17-27.

2565 Barbara Reid, "Voices and Angels: What Were They Talking About at the Transfiguration? A Redaction-Critical Study of Luke 9:28-36," *BR* 34 (1989): 19-31.

2566 Judette M. Kolasny, "An Example of Rhetorical Criticism: Luke 4:16-30," in Earl Richard, ed., *New Views on Luke and Acts.* Collegeville MN: Liturgical Press, 1990. Pp. 67-77.

2567 Joseph V. Kozar, "The Function of the Character of Elizabeth as the Omniscient Narrator's Reliable Vehicle in the First Chapter of the Gospel of Luke," *EGLMBS* 10 (1990): 214-22.

2568 Sherman E. Johnson, *The Griesbach Hypothesis and Redaction Criticism.* Atlanta: Scholars Press, 1991.

crucifixion
   2569   Joseph A. Fitzmyer, "Crucifixion in Ancient Palestine, Qumran
            Literature, and the New Testament," *CBQ* 40/4 (1978): 493-513.

   2570   John T. Carroll, "Luke's Crucifixion Scene," in Dennis D. Sylva,
            ed., *Reimaging the Death of the Lukan Jesus*. Frankfurt am Main:
            Hain, 1990. Pp. 108-24

decalogue
   2571   Reginald H. Fuller, "The Decalogue in the NT," *Int* 43/3 (1989):
            243-55.

demon/demonic
   2572   R. Yates, "Jesus and the Demonic in the Synoptic Gospels," *ITQ*
            44 (1977): 39-57.

disciples
   2573   Bruce M. Metzger, "Seventy or Seventy-Two Disciples," *NTS* 5
            (1958-1959): 299-306.

   2574   Robert F. O'Toole, "Parallels between Jesus and His Disciples in
            Luke-Acts: A Further Study," *BZ* 27 (1983): 195-212.

   2575   Mary Schertz, "Interpretation as Discipleship: Luke 24 as Model,"
            in Harry Huebner, ed., *The Church as Theological Community*
            (festschrift for David Schroeder). Winnipeg: CMBC Publications,
            1990. Pp. 115-39.

   2576   J. D. Kingsbury, *Conflict in Luke: Jesus, Authorities, Disciples*.
            Minneapolis MN: Fortress, 1991.

discipleship
   2577   William T. Smith, "Cross-Bearing in the Synoptic Gospels,"
            doctoral dissertation, Southern Baptist Theological Seminary,
            Louisville KY, 1953.

   2578   S. Freyne, *The Twelve: Disciples and Apostles: A Study in the
            Theology of the First Three Gospels*. London/Sydney: Sheed &
            Ward, 1968.

   2579   Dennis M. Sweetland, "The Understanding of Discipleship in Lk
            12:1-13:9," doctoral dissertation, University of Notre Dame, Notre
            Dame IN, 1978.

2580   Ben Witherington, "On the Road with Mary Magdalene, Joanna, Susanna, and Other Disciples (Luke 8:1-3)," *ZNW* 70 (1979): 243-48.

2581   Paul Kariamadam, "Discipleship in the Lucan Journey Narrative," *Je* 16 (1980): 111-30.

2582   George E. Rice, "Luke's Thematic Use of the Call to Discipleship," *AUSS* 20 (1981): 51-58.

2583   M. Sheridan, "Disciples and Discipleship in Matthew: Dimensions of Lukan Spirituality," *PRS* 9 (1982): 237-49.

2584   M. R. D'Angelo, "Images of Jesus and the Christian Call in the Gospels of Luke and John," *SpirTo* 37 (1985): 196-212.

2585   R. Ryan, "The Women from Galilee and Discipleship in Luke," *BTB* 15 (1985): 56-59.

2586   Charles H. Talbert, "Discipleship in Luke-Acts," in F. F. Segovia, ed., *Discipleship in the New Testament*. Philadelphia: Fortress Press, 1985. Pp. 62-75.

2587   Mary Schertz, "Interpretation as Discipleship: Luke 24 as Model," in Harry Huebner, ed., *The Church as Theological Community* (festschrift for David Schroeder). Winnipeg: CMBC Publications, 1990. Pp. 115-39.

2588   Dennis M. Sweetland, *Our Journey with Jesus: Discipleship in Luke and Acts*. Collegeville MN: Liturgical Press, 1991.

divorce/remarriage
2589   H. G. Coiner, "Those 'Divorce and Remarriage' Passages (Matt. 5:32; 19;9; 1 Cor 7:10-16), with Brief Reference to the Mark and Luke Passages," *CTM* 39 (1958): 367-84.

2590   Charles C. Ryrie, "Biblical Teaching on Divorce and Remarriage," *GTJ* 3/2 (1982): 177-92.

ecclesiology
2591   B. Schultze, "Die ekklesioklogische Bedeutung des Gleichnisses vom Senfkorn," *OCP* 27 (1961): 362-86.

2592 H. Flender, "Die Kirche in den Lukas-Schriften als Frage an ihre heutige Gestalt," in M. Brauman, ed., *Das Lukas-Evangelium: Die redaktions- und kompositions- geschichtliche Forschung.* Darmstadt: Wissenschaftliche Buchgesellschaft, 1974. Pp. 261-86.

2593 P. Zinng, *Das Wachsen der Kirche: Beiträge zur Frage der lukanischen Redaktion und Theologie.* Orbis Biblicus et Orientalis #3. Göttingen: Vandenhoeck, 1974.

2594 F. Bovon, "Évangélisation et unité de l'Église dans la perspective de Luc," in J. Brantschen and P. Selvatico, eds., *Unterwegs zur Einheit* (festschrift for H. Stirnimann). Freiburg: Publications universitaires, 1980. Pp. 188-99.

2595 K. N. Giles, "The Church in the Gospel of Luke," *SJT* 34 (1981): 121-46.

2596 K. N. Giles, "Luke's Use of the Term ἐκκλησία with Special Reference to Acts 20:28 and 9:31," *NTS* 31 (1985): 135-42.

2597 Robert S. Alley, "Render to Jesus the Things that are Jesus'," in R. Joseph Hoffmann and Gerald A. Larue, eds., *Jesus in History and Myth.* Buffalo: Prometheus Books, 1986. Pp. 55-77.

elders, teaching of
2598 William H. Crouch, "Jesus and the Teaching of the Elders in the Synoptic Gospels," master's thesis, Southern Baptist Theological Seminary, Louisville KY, 1954.

Emmaus story
2599 Joseph A. Grassi, "Emmaus Revisited (Luke 24:13-35 and Acts 8:26-40)," *CBQ* 26 (1964): 463-67.

2600 John M. Gibbs, "Luke 24:13-33 and Acts 8:26-39: The Emmaus Incident and the Eunuch's Baptism as Parallel Stories," *BTF* 7 (1975): 17-30.

2601 Bernard P. Robinson, "The Place of the Emmaus Story in Luke-Acts [Lk. 24:13-32]," *NTS* 30/4 (1984): 481-97.

2602 D. McBride, *Emmaus: The Gracious Visit of God According to Luke.* Dublin: Dominican Publications, 1991.

eschatology

2603   C. E. B. Cranfield, "The Parable of the Unjust Judge and the Eschatology of Luke-Acts," *SJT* 16 (1963): 297-301.

2604   Jacques Dupont, "Die individuelle Eschatologie im Lukasevangelium und in der Apostelgeschichte," in P. Hoffmann, et al., eds., *Orientierung an Jesus* (festschrift for J. Schmid). Freiburg: Herder, 1973. Pp. 37-47.

2605   R. Geiger, *Die lukanischen Endzeitreden: Studien zur Eschatologie des Lukas-Evangeliums*. Bern: Lang, 1973.

2606   J. Zmijewski, "Die Eschatologiereden Lk 21 und Lk 17. Überlegungen zum Verständnis und zur Einordnung der lukanischen Eschatologie," *BibL* 14 (1973): 30-40.

2607   R. H. Hiers, "The Problem of the Delay of the Parousia in Luke-Acts," *NTS* 20 (1973-1974): 145-55.

2608   A. Vögtle, "Der 'eschatologische' Bezug der Wir-Binen des Vaterunsers (Lk 11,2c-4; Mt 6, 9b-13)," in E. Earle Ellis and Erich Grässer, eds., *Jesus und Paulus* (festschrift for W. G. Kummel). Göttingen: Vandenhoeck, 1975. Pp. 344-62.

2609   Giuseppe Frizzi, "Mandare-inviare in Luca-Atti: Una chiave importante per la comprensione dell'escatologia di Luca," *RBib* 24 (1976): 359-401.

2610   J. Ernst, *Herr der Geschichte: Perspektiven der lukanischen Eschatologie*. Stuttgart: Katholisches Bibelwerk, 1978.

2611   P. Deterding, "Eschatological and Eucharistic Motifs in Luke 12,35-40," *CJ* 5 (1979): 85-94.

2612   Beverly R. Gaventa, "The Eschatology of Luke-Acts Revisited," *Enc* 43 (1982): 27-42.

2613   Leopold Sabourin, "The Eschatology of Luke," *BTB* 12 (1982): 73-76.

2614   Walther Bindemann, "Die Parabel vom ungerechten Richter," in Joachim Rogge, et al., eds., *Theologische Versuche*. #13. Berlin: Evangelisches Verlagsanstalt Berlin, 1983. Pp. 91-97.

2615 F. J. G. Collison, "Eschatology in the Gospel of Luke," in William R. Farmer, ed., *New Synoptic Studies*. Macon GA: Mercer University Press, 1983. Pp. 363-71.

2616 John W. Wenham, *The Rediscovery of Jesus' Eschatological Discourse*. Gospel Perspectives #4. Sheffield: JSOT Press, 1984.

2617 Caesarius Cavallin, "Bienheureux seras-tu—à la résurrection des justes: le macarisme de Lc 14:14," in Françios Refoulé, ed., *à cause de l'Evangile: Etudes sur les synoptiques et les Actes* (festschrift for Jacques Dupont). Paris: Cerf, 1985. Pp. 531-46.

2618 Dieter Zeller, "Entrückung zur Ankunft als Menschensohn (Lk 13:34f; 11:29f)," in Françios Refoulé, ed., *à cause de l'Evangile: Etudes sur les synoptiques et les Actes* (festschrift for Jacques Dupont). Paris: Cerf, 1985. Pp. 513-30.

2619 Peter Fiedler, "Die Gegenwart als österliche Zeit - erfahrbar im Gottesdienst: Die 'Emmausgeschichte' Lk 24,13-35," in Ingo Broer and Lorenz Oberlinner, eds., *Auferstehung Jesu - Auferstehung der Christen: Deutungen des Osterglaubens*. Freiburg: Herder, 1986. Pp. 124-44.

2620 John T. Carroll, *Response to the End of History: Eschatology and Situation in Luke-Acts*. Atlanta GA: Scholars Press, 1988.

2621 E. Earle Ellis, "La fonction de l'eschatologie dans l'évangile de Luc," in Frans Neirynck, ed., *L'Évangile de Luc, Problèmes littéraires et théologiques* (festschrift for Lucien Cerfaux). BETL #32. 2nd ed. Louvain: Peeters Press, 1989. Pp. 51-65.

2622 M. de Jonge, "The Radical Eschatology of the Fourth Gospel and the Eschatology of the Synoptics. Some Suggestions," in Adelbert Denaux, ed., *John and the Synoptics*. BETL #101. Louvain: Peeters Press, 1992. Pp. 481-87.

ethics

2623 G. R. Osborne, "Luke: Theologian of Social Concern," *TriJ* 7 (1978): 135-48.

2624 J. O'Hanlon, "The Story of Zacchaeus and the Lukan Ethic," *JSNT* 12 (1981): 2-26.

2625   W. E. Pilgrim, *Good News to the Poor: Wealth and Poverty in Luke-Acts*. Minneapolis MN: Augsburg, 1981.

2626   S. Arai, "Individual- und Gemeindeethik bei Lukas," *AJBI* 9 (1983): 88-127.

2627   Robert F. O'Toole, "Luke's Position on Politics and Society in Luke-Acts," in R. J. Cassidy and P. J. Scharper, eds., *Political Issues in Luke-Acts*. Maryknoll NY: Orbis Books, 1983. Pp. 1-17.

2628   W. M. Swartley, "Politics and Peace εἰρήνη in Luke's Gospel," in R. J. Cassidy and P. J. Scharper, eds., *Political Issues in Luke-Acts*. Maryknoll NY: Orbis, 1983. Pp. 18-37.

2629   Charles H. Talbert, "Martyrdom in Luke-Acts and the Lukan Social Ethic," in R. J. Cassidy and P. J. Scharper, eds., *Political Issues in Luke-Acts*. Maryknoll NY: Orbis, 1983. Pp. 99-110.

2630   Romano Penna, "Osservazioni sull'anti-edonismo nel Nuovo Testamento in rapporto al suo ambiente culturale [Lk 8:14; 2 Tim 3:4; Tit 3:3; Jas 4:1-3; 2 Pet 2:13]," in M. Angelini, et al., eds., *Testimonium Christi* (festschrift for Jacques Dupont). Brescia: Paideia, 1985. Pp. 351-77.

2631   William W. Klein, "The Sermon at Nazareth (Luke 4:14-22)," in Kenneth W. M. Wozniak and Stanley J. Grenz, eds., *Christian Freedom* (festschrift for Vernon C. Grounds). Lanham MD: University Press of America, 1986. Pp. 153-72.

2632   Jan Lambrecht, "The Sayings of Jesus on Nonviolence," *LouvS* 12 (1987): 291-305.

2633   Gerhard Schneider, "Imitatio Dei als Motiv der Ethik Jesu," in Helmut Merklein, ed., *Neues Testament und Ethik* (festschrift for Rudolf Schnackenburg). Freiburg: Herder, 1989. Pp. 71-83.

2634   Peter von der Osten-Sacken, "Jesu Weinen über sein Volk: Predigt über Lukas 19,41-44," in Erhard Blum, et al., eds., *Die Hebräische Bibel und ihre zweifache Nachgeschichte* (festschrift for Rolf Rendtorff). Neukirchen-Vluyn: Neukirchener Verlag, 1990. Pp. 555-59.

eucharist
2635 Donald E. Cook, "The Lukan Concept of the Lord's Supper," master's thesis, Southeastern Baptist Theological Seminary, Wake Forest NC, 1958.

2636 M. H. Sykes, "The Eucharist as 'Anamnesis'," *ET* 71 (1959-1960): 115-18.

2637 G. J. Bahr, "The Seder of Passover and the Eucharistic Words," *NovT* 12 (1970): 181-202.

2638 M. A. Smith, "The Lukan Last Supper Narrative," *StudE* 6 (1973): 502-509.

2639 J. Wanke, *Beobachtungen zum Eucharistieverständnis des Lukas.* Leipzig: St. Benno, 1973.

2640 E. A. LaVerdiere, "Discourse at the Last Supper," *BibTo* 71 (1974): 1540-48.

2641 Rudolf Pesch, "Der lukanische Abandmahlstext," in *Wie Jesus das Abendmahl hielt: Der Grund der Eucharistie.* Freiburg: Herder, 1977. Pp. 33-40.

2642 P. Deterding, "Eschatological and Eucharistic Motifs in Luke 12,35-40," *CJ* 5 (1979): 85-94.

2643 D. W. A. Gregg, "Hebraic Antecedents to the Eucharistic Anamnèsis Formula," *TynB* 30 (1979): 165-68.

2644 W. Bösen, *Jesusmahl, eucharistisches Mahl, Endzeitmahl: Ein Beitrag zur Theologie des Lukas.* Stuttgart: Katholisches Bibelwerk, 1980.

2645 Christian Bernard Amphoux, "Le dernier repas de Jésus, Lc 22/15-20 par," *ÉTR* 56 (1981): 449-54.

2646 W. Weren, "The Lord's Supper: An Inquiry into the Coherence in Luke 22,14-18," in H. J. Auf der Maur, et al., eds., *Fides Sacramenti* (festschrift for P. Smulders). Assen: Van Gorcum, 1981. Pp. 9-26.

2647   T. Huser, "Les récits de l'institution de la Cène. Dissemblances et traditions," *Hokhmah* 21 (1982): 28-50.

2648   G. Ghiberti, "L'eucaristia in Lc 24 e negli Atti degli Apostoli," *ParSpirV* 7 (1983): 159-73.

2649   O. Knock, " 'Tut das zu meinem Gedächtnis!' (Lk 22,30; 1 Kor 11,24f.): Die Feier der Eucharistie in den urchristlichen Gemeinden," in J. Schreiner, ed., *Freude arn Gonesdienst* (festschrift for J. G. Plöger). Stuttgart: Katholisches Bibelwerk, 1983. Pp. 31-42.

2650   E. A. LaVerdiere, "The Eucharist in Luke's Gospel," *Emmanuel* 89 (1983): 446-49, 452-53.

2651   Dennis M. Sweetland, "The Lord's Supper and the Lukan Community," *BTB* 13 (1983): 23-27.

2652   Oda Hagemeyer, "Tut dies zu meinem Gedächtnis (1 Kor 11,24f; Lk 22,19)," in Lothar Lies, ed., *Praesentia Christi* (festschrift for Johannes Betz). Düsseldorf: Patmos, 1984. Pp. 101-17.

2653   James Custer, "When Is Communion Communion," *GTJ* 6/2 (1985): 403-10.

2654   William S. Kurz, "Luke 22:14-38 and Greco-Roman and Biblical Farewell Addresses," *JBL* 104 (1985): 251-68.

2655   John D. Laurence, "The Eucharist as the Imitation of Christ," *TS* 47/2 (1986): 286-96.

2656   R. W. Canoy, "Perspectives on Eucharistic Theology: Luke as Paradigm for an Inclusive Invitation to Communion," doctoral dissertation, Southern Baptist Theological Seminary, Louisville KY, 1987.

2657   Philip Sellew, "The Last Supper Discourse in Luke 22:21-38," *Forum* 3 (1987): 70-95.

2658   Bart D. Ehrman, "The Cup, the Bread, and the Salvific Effect of Jesus' Death in Luke-Acts," *SBLSP* 21 (1991): 576-91.

exaltation
    2659 Robert F. O'Toole, "Luke's Understanding of Jesus' Resurrection—Ascension—Exaltation," *BTB* 9 (1979): 106-14.

exodus
    2660 J. Manek, "The New Exodus of the Books of Luke," *NovT* 2 (1957-1958): 8-23.

    2661 Susan R. Garrett, "Exodus from Bondage: Luke 9:31 and Acts 12:1-24," *CBQ* 52 (1990): 656-80.

faith
    2662 W. Schenk, "Glaube im lukanischen Doppelwerk," in F. Hahn and H. Klein, eds., *Glaube im Neuen Testament* (festschrift for H. Binder). Biblisch-theologische Studien #7. Neukirchen-Vluyn: Neukirchener Verlag, 1982. Pp. 69-92.

false prophet
    2663 M. Krämer, "Hütet euch vor den falschen Propheten. Eine überlieferungsgeschichtliche Untersuchung zu Mt 7:15-23/Lk 6:43-46/Mt 12:33-37," *Bib* 57 (1976): 349-77.

father
    2664 J. H. Sieber, "The Spirit as the 'Promise of My Father' in Luke 24:49," in D. Durken, ed., *Sin, Salvation, and the Spirit.* Collegeville MN: Liturgical Press, 1979. Pp. 271-78.

    2665 Martin Cawley, "Health of the Eyes: Gift of the Father: In the Gospel Tradition 'Q'," *WS* 3 (1981): 41-70.

    2666 E. A. LaVerdiere, "God as Father," *Emmanuel* 88 (1982): 545-50.

    2667 S. M. Harris, "My Father's House," *ET* 94 (1982-1983): 84-85.

    2668 Dallas Franklin Billington, "The Forgiving Father," *FundJ* 4/6 (1985): 49.

feeding narratives
    2669 Joseph A. Grassi, *Loaves and Fishes: The Gospel Feeding Narratives.* Collegeville MN: Liturgical Press, 1991.

Galilean ministry

2670   R. E. Baergen, "The Identity of Jesus in the Galilean Ministry of Luke," doctoral dissertation, Union Theological Seminary, Richmond VA, 1987.

genre

2671   G. F. Nuttell, *The Moment of Recognition: Luke as Story-Teller.* London: Athlone, 1978.

2672   Susan Marie Praeder, "Luke-Acts and the Ancient Novel," *SBLSP* 11 (1981): 269-92.

gentiles

2673   P. Zinng, "Die Stellung des Lukas zur Heidenmission," *NZM* 29 (1973): 200-209.

Gethsemane

2674   Robert R. Darby, "A Study of the Variations of the Gethsemane Sayings of Jesus Common to the Synoptics," doctoral dissertation, New Orleans Baptist Theological Seminary, New Orleans LA, 1953.

2675   J. Héring, "Zwei exegetische Problemein der Periope von Jesus in Gethsemane," in *Neotestamentica et Patristica: eine freundesgabe, herrn Professor Dr. Oscar Cullmann zu seinem 60. Geburtstag überricht.* NovTSupp #6. Leiden: Brill, 1962. Pp. 64-69.

2676   T. Lescow, "Jesus in Gethsemane bei Lukas und im Hebräerbrief," *ZNW* 58 (1967): 215-39.

2677   T. Lescow, "Jesus in Gethsemane," *EvT* 26 (1968): 141-59.

2678   R. S. Barbour, "Gethsemane in the Tradition of the Passion," *NTS* 16 (1969-1970): 231-51.

2679   André Feuillet, "Le récit lucanien de l'agonie de Gethsémani (Lc 22:39-46)," *NTS* 22 (1975-1976): 397-417.

grace

2680   P. Bossuyt and J. Radermakers, *Jésus, Parole de la grace selon saint Luc. 1. Texte*; 2. *Lecture continue.* 2 vols. Bruxelles: Institut d'Études Théologiques, 1981.

grammar
2681   John H. Winstead, "The Greek Infinitive in Luke's Gospel," doctoral dissertation, Southern Baptist Theological Seminary, Louisville KY, 1930.

2682   Atley A. Kitchings, "The Greek Participle in Luke's Gospel," doctoral dissertation, Southern Baptist Theological Seminary, Louisville KY, 1933.

2683   John T. Luper, "Aorist Tense in the Writings of Luke," doctoral dissertation, Southwestern Baptist Theological Seminary, Fort Worth TX, 1934.

2684   S. Brock, "The Treatment of Greek Particles in the Old Syriac Gospels, with Special Reference to Luke," in J. K. Eliott, ed., *Studies in New Testament Language and Text* (festschrift for G. D. Kilpatrick). Leiden: Brill, 1976. Pp. 80-86.

2685   D. Davies, "The Position of Adverbs in Luke," in J. K. Elliott, ed., *Studies in New Testament Language and Text* (festschrift for G. D. Kilpatrick). Leiden: Brill, 1976. Pp. 106-21.

2686   Nigel Turner, "The Quality of the Greek of Luke-Acts," in J. K. Elliott, ed., *Studies in New Testament Language and Text* (festschrift for G. D. Kilpatrick). Leiden: Brill, 1976. Pp. 387-400.

2687   F. J. G. Collison, "Linguistic Usages in the Gospel of Luke," doctoral dissertation, Southern Methodist University, Dallas TX, 1977.

2688   F. J. G. Collison, "Linguistic Usages in the Gospel of Luke," in William R. Farmer, ed., *New Synoptic Studies*. Macon GA: Mercer University Press, 1983. Pp. 245-60.

2689   James M. Dawsey, "*Mathetaí (autoû)* and Luke's Concern for the Sound of his Gospel," *MeliT* 40 (1989): 59-62.

Greek
2690   A. W. Argyle, "The Greek of Luke and Acts," *NTS* 20 (1973-1974): 441-45.

heilsgeschichte
2691   Gerhard Schneider, *Lukas, Theologe der Heilsgeschichte: Aufsätze zum lukanischen Doppelwerk.* BBB #59. Konigstein-Bonn: Hanstein, 1985.

historical figures
2692   John A. Darr, " 'Glorified in the Presence of Kings': A Literary-Critical Study of Herod the Tetrarch in Luke-Acts," doctoral dissertation, Vanderbilt University, Nashville TN, 1987.

Holy Spirit
2693   S. S. Smalley, "Spirit, Kingdom, and Prayer in Luke-Acts," *NovT* 15 (1973): 59-71.

2694   H. von Baer, "Der Heilige Geist in den Lukasschriften," in G. Braumann, ed., *Das Lukas-Evangelium: Die redaktions- und kompositions- geschichtliche Forschung.* Darmstadt: Wissenschaftliche Buchgesellschaft, 1974. Pp. 1-6.

2695   E. Rasco, "Jésus y el Espiritu, Iglesia e 'Historia': elementos para una lectura de Lucas," *Greg* 56 (1975): 321-68.

2696   K. Stalder, "Der Heilige Geist in der lukanischen Ekklesiologie," *US* 30 (1975): 287-93.

2697   N. Schultz, "St. Paul Describes the Spirit as *Arrabôn*: Would St. Luke and St. John Have Agreed?" *LTJ* 11 (1977): 112-21.

2698   L. M. Adkins, "An Awareness of the Holy Spirit: Using Luke as a Major Source of Guidance," doctoral dissertation, Drew University, Madison NJ, 1978.

2699   A. George, "L'Esprit Saint dans l'oeuvre de Luc," *RB* 85 (1978): 500-42.

2700   J. L. Pretlove, "Baptism en pneuma ἐν πνεῦμα: A Comparison of the Theologies of Luke and Paul," doctoral dissertation, Southwestern Baptist Theological Seminary, Fort Worth TX, 1980.

2701   M. M. B. Turner, "Luke and the Spirit: Studies in the Significance of Receiving the Spirit in Luke-Acts," doctoral dissertation, Trinity Hall, Cambridge University, UK, 1980.

2702   M. M. B. Turner, "Jesus and the Spirit in Lucan Perspective," *TynB* 32 (1981): 3-42.

2703   M. M. B. Turner, "The Significance of Receiving the Spirit in Luke-Acts: A Survey of Modern Scholarship," *TriJ* 2 (1981): 131-58.

2704   M. M. B. Turner, "Spirit Endowment in Luke-Acts: Some Linguistic Considerations," *VoxE* 12 (1981): 45-63.

2705   M.-A. Chevallier, "Luc et l'Esprit Saint," *RevSR* 56 (1982): 1-16.

2706   Réne Laurentin, "Concepito dallo Spirito santa: La critica, I esegesi e il senso," *ParSpirV* 6 (1982): 74-92.

2707   R. M. Shelton, *Filled with the Holy Spirit: A Redactional Motif in Luke's Gospel*. London: British Library, 1982.

2708   Theo Bell, "Das Magnificat vorteutschet und ausgelegt, 1521: een kommentaar bij het voorwoord," in J. T. Bakker and J. P. Boendermaker, eds., *Luther na 500 jaar*. Kampen: Kok, 1983. Pp. 78-98.

2709   R. Stronstad, *The Charismatic Theology of St. Luke*. Peabody MA: Hendrickson, 1984.

2710   M.-A. Chevallier, "Apparentements entre Luc et Jean en matière de pneumatologie," in *à cause de l'Évangile: Études sur les synoptiques et les Actes* (festschrift for Jacques Dupont). Paris: Cerf, 1985. Pp. 377-408.

2711   Gerhard Schneider, "Die Bitte um das Kommen des Geistes im lukanischen Vaterunser," in Wolfgang Schrage, eds., *Studien zum Text und zur Ethik des Neuen Testaments* (festschrift for Heinrich Greeven). New York: de Gruyter, 1986. Pp. 344-73.

2712   O. Mainville, *L'esprit dans l'oeuvre de Luc*. Montreal: Fides, 1991.

2713   J. B. Shelton, *Mighty in Word and Deed: The Role of the Holy Spirit in Luke-Acts*. Peabody MA: Hendrickson, 1991.

incarnation
2714   S. Brock, "The Lost Old Syriac at Luke 1:35 and the Earliest
       Syriac Terms for the Incarnation," in William L. Petersen, ed.,
       *Gospel Traditions in the Second Century: Origins, Recensions, Text
       and Transmission*. Notre Dame IN: University Press, 1989. Pp.
       117-31.

infancy narrative
2715   J. S. Pedro, "Valor apologético de la infancia de Jesús," *CuBí* 11
       (1954): 39-40.

2716   S. Muñoz Iglesias, "Los Evangelios de la infancia y las infancias
       de los héroes," in *Géneros literanos en los Evangelios*. Madrid:
       Científica Medinaceli, 1958. Pp. 83-113.

2717   S. Muñoz Iglesias, "El Evangelio de la infancia en San Lucas y las
       infancias de los héroes biblicos," in *Teología bíblica sobre el
       pecado: La teología bíblica*. Madrid: Liberaría Científica Medinaceli,
       1959. Pp. 325-74.

2718   S. Muñoz Iglesias, "Midráš y Evangelios de la Infancia," *EE* 47
       (1972): 331-59.

2719   F. Gryglewicz, "Die Herkunft der Hymnen des
       Kindheitsevangeliums des Lucas," *NTS* 21 (1974-1975): 265-73.

2720   C. Perrot, "Les récits de l'enfance de Jésus," *CahÉv* 18 (1977):
       72.

2721   Tavares A. Augusto, "Infancy Narratives and Historical
       Criticism," *TD* 28 (1980): 53-54.

2722   Leopold Sabourin, "Recent Views on Luke's Infancy Narratives,"
       RSB 1/1 (1981): 18-25.

2723   A. Beauduin, "The Infancy Narratives: A Confession of Faith," *LV*
       39 (1984): 167-77.

2724   Gail R. O'Day, "The Praise of New Beginnings: The Infancy
       Hymns in Luke," *JP* 14/1 (1990): 3-8.

introduction
2725   A. E. Breen, *A Harmonized Exposition of the Four Gospels*. 4 vols.
       Rochester NY: Smith, 1908.

2726   C. J. Callan, *The Four Gospels*. New York: Wagner, 1917.

2727   I. Daumoser, *Berufung und Erwählung bei den Synoptikern*.
       Stuttgart: KBW, 1954.

2728   W. Hamilton, *The Modern Reader's Guide to Matthew and Luke*.
       New York: Association, 1959.

2729   William Barclay, *The Gospels and Acts*. 1: *The First Three
       Gospels*. London: SCM Press, 1966.

2730   G. Girardet, et al., *Evangelo secondo Luca*. Verona: Mondadori,
       1973.

2731   E. P. Groenewald, *Die Evangelie van Lukas verklaar*. Kaapstad:
       N.G. Kerkuitgevers, 1973.

2732   Frans Neirynck, ed., *L'Évangile de Luc: Problèmes littéraires et
       théologiques* (festschrift for Lucien Cerfaux). BETL #32.
       Gembloux: Duculot, 1973.

2733   G. Petzke, "Historizität und Bedeutsamkeit von Wunderberichten:
       Möglichkeiten   und   Grenzen   des   religionsgeschichtlichen
       Vergleichs," in Hans D. Betz, ed., *Neues Testament und christliche
       Existenz* (festschrift for H. Braun). Tübingen: Mohr, 1973. Pp.
       367-85.

2734   B.   De   Solages,   *Comment   sont   nés   les   évangiles:
       Marc-Luc-Matthieu*. Toulouse: Privat, 1973.

2735   W. C. van Unnik, "Éléments artistiques dans l'évangile de Luc,"
       in Frans Neirynck, ed., *L'évangile de Luc: Problèmes littéraires et
       théologiques* (festschrift for Lucien Cerfaux). BETL #32.
       Gembloux: Duculot, 1973. Pp. 129-40.

2736   W. C. van Unnik, et al., "Essays on the Gospel of Luke and Acts:
       Proceedings of the Ninth Meeting of *Die Nuwe-Testamentiese
       Werkgemeenskap van Suid-Afrika*," *Neo* 7 (1973): 1-103.

2737   L. E. Wilshire, "Was Canonical Luke Written in the Second
       Century?" *NTS* 20 (1973-1974): 246-53.

2738   Schuyler Brown, "Précis of Eckhard Plümacher's *Lukas als
       hellenistischer Schriftstelle*," *SBLSP* 4/2 (1974): 103-13.

2739   Hans Conzelmann, "Der geschichtliche Ort der lukanischen
       Schriften im Urchristentum," in G. Braumann, ed., *Das
       Lukas-Evangelium: Die redaktions- und kompositions-
       geschichtliche Forschung*. Darmstadt: Wissenschaftliche
       Buchgesellschaft, 1974. Pp. 236-60.

2740   Hans Conzelmann, "Zur Lukasanalyse," in G. Braumann, ed., *Das
       Lukas-Evangelium: Die redaktions- und kompositions-
       geschichtliche Forschung*. Darmstadt: Wissenschaftliche
       Buchgesellschaft, 1974. Pp. 43-63.

2741   Charles H. Talbert, *Literary Patterns, Theological Themes and the
       Genre of Luke-Acts*. Missoula MT: Scholars Press, 1974.

2742   F. Bovon, "L'importance des médiations dans le projet théologique
       de Luc," *NTS* 21 (1974-1975): 23-39.

2743   William Barclay, *Introduction to the First Three Gospels*.
       Philadelphia: Westminster, 1975.

2744   A. Drago, *Gesù uomo di preghiera: Nel vangelo di Luca*. Padova:
       Messaggero, 1975.

2745   Walter Radl, *Paulus und Jesus im lukanischen Doppelwerk:
       Untersuchungen zu Parallelmotiven im Lukasevangelium und in der
       Apostelgeschichte*. Europäische Hochschulschriften, XXIII/49. Bern:
       Lang, 1975.

2746   J. Berchmans, "Lukan Studies," *BB* 2 (1976): 81-90.

2747   F. Bovon, "Orientations actuelles des études lucaniennes," *RTP* 26
       (1976): 161-90.

2748   Frederick W. Danker, "The Shape of Luke's Gospel in
       Lectionaries," *Int* 30 (1976): 339-52.

2749 P. Davids, "The Poor Man's Gospel," *Themelios* N.S. 1 (1976): 37-41.

2750 W. Egger, *Das Programm Jesu: Ein Arbeitsheft zum Lukasevangelium.* Klosterneuburg: Österreichisches Katholisches Bibelwerk, 1976.

2751 B. E. Gärtner, "Der historische Jesus und der Christus des Glaubens: Eine Reflexion über die Bultmannschule und Lukas," *SNTU-A* 2 (1976): 9-18.

2752 Arland J. Hultgren, "Interpreting the Gospel of Luke," *Int* 30 (1976): 353-65.

2753 Robert J. Karris, "The Lukan *Sitz im Leben*: Methodology and Prospects," *SBLSP* 6 (1976): 219-34.

2754 E. A. LaVerdiere and W. G. Thompson, "New Testament Communities in Transition: A Study of Matthew and Luke," *TS* 37 (1976): 567-97.

2755 X. Pikaza, *Leggere Luca: Il terzo vangelo e gli Atti.* Torino: Marietti, 1976.

2756 Rainer Russ, *Keiner glaubt für sich allein: Christusbegegnungen im Lukas-Evangelium.* Düsseldorf: Patmos, 1976.

2757 E. H. Schroeder, "Luke's Gospel through a Systematician's Lens," *CThM* 3 (1976): 337-46.

2758 Ulrich Busse, *Die Wunder des Propheten Jesus: Die Rezeption, Komposition und Interpretation der Wundertradition im Evangelium des Lukas.* Stuttgart: Katholisches Bibelwerk, 1977.

2759 Frederick W. Danker, "Theological Presuppositions of St. Luke," *CThM* 4 (1977): 98-103.

2760 C. Dieterlé, et al., *Manuel du traducteur pour l'évangile de Luc.* Paris: Alliance biblique universelle, 1977.

2761 J. Ernst, *Das Evangelium nach Lukas.* Regensburg: Pustet, 1977.

2762   Gerhard Schneider, "Der Zweck des lukanischen Doppelwerks," *BZ* 21 (1977): 45-66.

2763   B. Stabdaert and T. van den Ende, "Het Evangelie volgens Lucas," *Schrift* 49 (1977): 2-38.

2764   A. Stöger, *The Gospel According to St. Luke*, B. Fahy, trans. London: Sheed, 1977.

2765   Jacques Dupont, "Introducción a las bienaventuranzas," *SelTeol* 17 (1978): 323-29.

2766   A. George, *Études sur l'oeuvre de Luc*. Paris: Gabalda, 1978.

2767   J. D. Quinn, "The Last Volume of Luke: The Relation of Luke-Acts to the Pastoral Epistles," in Charles H. Talbert, ed., *Perspectives on Luke-Acts*. Macon GA: Mercer University Press, 1978. Pp. 62-75.

2768   Charles H. Talbert, ed., *Perspectives on Luke-Acts*. Macon GA: Mercer University Press, 1978.

2769   M. C. Tenney, "Historical Verities in the Gospel of Luke," *BSac* 135 (1978): 126-38.

2770   Wilhelm Wilkens, "Die Theologische Struktur der Komposition des Lukasevangeliums," *TZ* 34 (1978): 1-13.

2771   J. G. Donders, *Jesus the Way: Reflections on the Gospel of Luke*. Maryknoll NY: Orbis, 1979.

2772   Jacques Dupont, "La conclusion des Actes et son rapport à l'ensemble de l'ouvrage de Luc," in J. Kremer, ed., *Les Actes des Apôtres: Traditions, rédaction, théologie*. BETL #48. Gembloux: Duculot, 1979. Pp. 359-404.

2773   Jacques Dupont, "Luc le théologien: Vingt-cinq ans de recherches (1950-1975): A propos d'un ouvrage de François Bovon," *RTL* 10 (1979): 218-25.

2774   Reginald H. Fuller, "Luke and the *Theologia Crucis*," in D. Durken, ed., *Sin, Salvation, and the Spirit*. Collegeville MN: Liturgical Press, 1979. Pp. 214-20.

2775 H. Gollwitzer, *Die Freude Gottes: Einführung in das Lukasevangelium.* Gelnhausen: Burckhardt, 1979.

2776 Benjamin J. Hubbard, "Luke, Josephus and Rome: A Comparative Approach to the Lukan *Sitz im Leben,*" *SBLSP* 9/1 (1979): 59-68.

2777 Robert J. Karris, "Missionary Communities: A New Paradigm for the Study of Luke-Acts," *CBQ* 41 (1979): 80-97.

2778 Robert J. Karris, *What Are They Saying about Luke and Acts? A Theology of the Faithful God.* New York: Paulist, 1979.

2779 Robert J. Karris, "Windows and Mirrors: Literary Criticism and Luke's *Sitz im Leben,*" *SBLSP* 9/1 (1979): 47-58.

2780 S. P. Kealy, *The Gospel of Luke.* Denville NJ: Dimension, 1979.

2781 M. Prior, "Revisiting Luke," *ScrB* 10 (1979): 2-11.

2782 Gerhard Schneider, "Schrift und Tradition in der theologischen Neuinterpretation der lukanischen Schriften," *BK* 34 (1979): 112-15.

2783 Stephen G. Wilson, *Luke and the Pastoral Epistles.* London: SPCK, 1979.

2784 B. Hurault, *Sinopsis Pastoral de Mateo-Marcos-Lucas-(Juan) con notas exegéticas y pastorales.* Madrid: Paulinas, 1980.

2785 J. Jeremias, *Die Sprache des Lukasevangeliums: Redaktion und Tradition im Nicht-Markusstoff des dritten Evangeliums.* Göttingen: Vandenhoeck, 1980.

2786 William S. Kurz, "Luke-Acts and Historiography in the Greek Bible," *SBLSP* 10 (1980): 283-300.

2787 E. A. LaVerdiere, "The Gospel of Luke: What the Exegetes Are Saying," *BibTo* 18 (1980): 226-35.

2788 E. A. LaVerdiere, *Luke.* New Testament Message #5. Wilmington DE: Glazier, 1980.

2789   H. Schreckenberg, "Flavius Josephus und die lukanischen
       Schriften," in W. Haubeck and M. Bachmann, eds., *Wort in der
       Zeit* (festschrift for K. H. Rengstorf). Leiden: Brill, 1980. Pp.
       179-209.

2790   David L. Tiede, *Prophecy and History in Luke-Acts.* Philadelphia:
       Fortress Press, 1980.

2791   F. Bovon, "Évangile de Luc et Actes des Apôtres," in J. Auneau,
       ed., *Évangiles synoptiques et Actes des apôtres.* Petite bibliothèque
       des sciences bibliques. Nouveau Testament #4. Paris: Desclée,
       1981. Pp. 195-283.

2792   F. Bovon, "Luc: portrait et projet," *LV* 153/154 (1981): 9-18.

2793   Édouard Delebecque, "L'Hellenisme de la 'Relative Complese,'
       dans le Nouveau Testament et Principalement chez Saint Luc," *Bib*
       62/2 (1981): 229-38.

2794   Susan Marie Praeder, "Luke-Acts and the Ancient Novel," *SBLSP*
       11 (1981): 269-92.

2795   Vernon K. Robbins, "Laudation Stories in the Gospel of Luke and
       Plutarch's *Alexander*," *SBLSP* 11 (1981): 293-308.

2796   E. V. Barrell and K. G. Barrell, *St. Luke's Gospel: An Introductory
       Study.* London: Murray, 1982.

2797   Robert G. Bratcher, *A Translator's Guide to the Gospel of Luke.*
       New York: American Bible Society, 1982.

2798   T. E. Crane, *The Synoptics: Mark, Matthew and Luke Interpret the
       Gospel.* London: Sheed and Ward, 1982.

2799   David Daube, "Shame Culture in Luke," in M. D. Hooker and
       S. G. Wilson, eds., *Paul and Paulinism* (festschrift for C. K.
       Barrett). London: SPCK, 1982. Pp. 355-72.

2800   F. Gerald Downing, "Common Ground with Paganism in Luke and
       in Josephus," *NTS* 28 (1982): 546-59.

2801   K. N. Giles, "Is Luke an Exponent of 'Early Protestantism'? Church Order in the Lukan Writings," *EQ* 54 (1982): 193-205; 55 (1983): 3-20.

2802   S. J. Kistemaker, "The Structure of Luke's Gospel," *JETS* 25 (1982): 33-39.

2803   S. Rabacchi, "Il vangelo di Luca," *SacD* 27 (1982): 464-87.

2804   E. Rasco, "Estudios lucanos," *Bib* 63 (1982): 266-80.

2805   N. Richardson, *The Panorama of Luke: An Introduction to the Gospel of Luke and the Acts of the Apostles*. London: Epworth, 1982.

2806   F. Bovon, "Chroniques du coté de chez Luc," *RTP* 115 (1983): 175-89.

2807   R. J. Cassidy and P. J. Scharper, eds., *Political Issues in Luke-Acts*. Maryknoll NY: Orbis, 1983.

2808   É. Lamirande, "Enfance et développement spirituel: Le commentaire de saint Ambroise sur saint Luc," *SE* 35 (1983): 103-16.

2809   G. Rouiller and C. Varone, *Il vangelo secondo Luca: Testi e teologla*, U. Cavalieri, trans. Assisi: Cittadella, 1983.

2810   W. J. Barnard and P. van 'T. Riet, *Lukas, de Jood: Een joodse inleiding op het Evangelie van Lukas en de Handelingen der Apostelen*. Kampen: Kok, 1984.

2811   David L. Barr and Judith L. Wentling, "The Conventions of Classical Biography and the Genre of Luke-Acts," in Charles H. Talbert, ed., *Luke-Acts: New Perspectives from the Society of Biblical Literature*. New York: Crossroad, 1984. Pp. 63-88.

2812   Robert L. Brawley, "Paul in Acts: Lucan Apology and Conciliation," in Charles H. Talbert, ed., *Luke-Acts: New Perspectives from the Society of Biblical Literature*. New York: Crossroad, 1984. Pp. 129-47.

2813   Thomas L. Brodie, "Greco-Roman Imitation of Texts as a Partial Guide to Luke's Use of Sources," in Charles H. Talbert, ed., *Luke-Acts: New Perspectives from the Society of Biblical Literature.* New York: Crossroad, 1984. Pp. 17-46.

2814   J. Carmignac, *La naissance des évangiles synoptiques.* Paris: O.E.I.L., 1984.

2815   Jacob Jervell, *The Unknown Paul: Essays on Luke-Acts and Early Christian History.* Minneapolis MN: Augsburg, 1984.

2816   Donald L. Jones, "The Title 'Servant' in Luke-Acts," in Charles H. Talbert, ed., *Luke-Acts: New Perspectives from the Society of Biblical Literature.* New York: Crossroad, 1984. Pp. 148-65.

2817   William S. Kurz, *Following Jesus: A Disciple's Guide to Luke and Acts.* Ann Arbor MI: Servant Books, 1984.

2818   Robert F. O'Toole, *The Unity of Luke's Theology: An Analysis of Luke-Acts.* Good News Studies #9. Wilmington DE: Glazier, 1984.

2819   Philippe Rolland, "L'organisation du Livre des Actes et de l'ensemble de l'oeuvre de Luc," *Bib* 65 (1984): 81-86.

2820   Eduard Schweizer, *The Good News According to Luke,* D. E. Green, trans. Atlanta GA: John Knox Press, 1984.

2821   K. Stock, *Jesus, die Güte Gottes: Betrachtungen zum Lukas-Evangelium.* Innsbruck: Tyrolia, 1984.

2822   Charles H. Talbert, ed., *Luke-Acts: New Perspectives from the Society of Biblical Literature Seminar.* New York: Crossroad, 1984.

2823   Charles H. Talbert, "Promise and Fulfillment in Lucan Theology," in Charles H. Talbert, ed., *Luke-Acts: New Perspectives from the Society of Biblical Literature.* New York: Crossroad, 1984. Pp. 91-103.

2824   John T. Townsend, "The Date of Luke-Acts," in Charles H. Talbert, ed., *Luke-Acts: New Perspectives from the Society of Biblical Literature.* New York: Crossroad, 1984. Pp. 47-62.

2825   Christopher M. Tuckett, "On the Relationship between Matthew and Luke," *NTS* 30 (1984): 130-42.

2826   David Daube, "Neglected Nuances of Exposition in Luke-Acts," *ANRW* II.25.3 (1985): 2329-56.

2827   Morton S. Enslin, "Luke and Matthew: Compilers or Authors?" *ANRW* 11.25.3 (1985): 2357-88.

2828   A. Hecht, "Wer ist dieser? Die Vorgeschichle des Lukas," in P.-G. Müller, ed., *Das Zeugnis des Lukas*. Stuttgart: Katholisches Bibelwerk, 1985. Pp. 27-33.

2829   Judette M. Kolasny, "Pericopes of Confrontation and Rejection as a Plot Device in Luke-Acts," doctoral dissertation, Marquette University, Milwaukee WI, 1985.

2830   Robert F. O'Toole, "Highlights of Luke's Theology," *CThM* 12 (1985): 353-60.

2831   M. Rese, "Das Lukas-Evangelium: Ein Forschungsbericht," *ANRW* 11.25.3 (1985): 2258-28.

2832   Leopold Sabourin, *The Gospel According to St. Luke: Introduction and Commentary*. Bandra, Bombay: Better Yourself Books, 1985.

2833   B. Standaert, "L'art de composer dans l'oeuvre de Luc," in *à cause de l'Évangile: Études sur les synoptiques et les Actes* (festschrift for Jacques Dupont). Paris: Cerf, 1985. Pp. 323-47.

2834   James M. Dawsey, "What's in a Name? Characterization in Luke," *BTB* 16 (1986): 143-47.

2835   J. Duncan M. Derrett, *New Resolutions of Old Conundrums: A Fresh Insight into Luke's Gospel*. Warwickshire: Drinkwater, 1986.

2836   Douglas R. Edwards, "Luke-Acts and the Ancient Romance Chaereas and Callirhoe: A Comparison of their Literary and Social Function," doctoral dissertation, Boston University, Boston MA, 1986.

2837   Joseph A. Grassi, *God Makes Me Laugh: A New Apporoach to Luke*. Wilmington DE: Glazier, 1986.

2838   P. van Linden, *The Gospel of Luke and Acts*. Wilmington DE: Glazier, 1986.

2839   Robert C. Tannehill, *The Narrative Unity of Luke-Acts: A Literary Interpretation*. 1: *The Gospel According to Luke*. Philadelphia: Fortress Press, 1986.

2840   V. S.-K. Yoon, "Did the Evangelist Luke Use the Canonical Gospel of Matthew," doctoral dissertation, Graduate Theological Union, Berkeley CA, 1986.

2841   D. L. Allen, "An Argument for the Lukan Authorship of Hebrews," doctoral dissertation, University of Texas, Arlington TX, 1987.

2842   David L. Balch, "Comparing Literary Patterns in Luke and Lucian," *PJ* 40 (1987): 39-42.

2843   F. Bovon, *L'oeuvre de Luc: Études d'exégèse et de théologie*. Lectio Divina #130. Paris: Cerf, 1987.

2844   Feargus O'Fearghail, "The Introduction to Luke-Acts: A Study of the Role of Lk 1,1-4,44 in the Composition of Luke's Two-Volume Work," doctoral dissertation, Pontifical Biblical Institute, Rome, 1987. 2 vols.

2845   O. Lamar Cope, "On the History of Criticism of the Gospel of Luke," *USQR* 42 (1987-1988): 59-61.

2846   Dale C. Allison, "Was There a 'Lucan Community'?" *IBS* 10 (1988): 62-70.

2847   C. K. Barrett, "Luke/Acts," in D. A. Carson and H. G. M. Williamson, eds., *It Is Written: Scripture Citing Scripture* (festschrift for Barnabas Lindars). Cambridge: University Press, 1988. Pp. 231-44.

2848   Noel S. Donnelly, "The Gospel of Luke: The Pieties of its Sources and Author," doctoral dissertation, University of Edinburgh, UK, 1988.

2849   Camille Focant, "La chute de Jérusalem et la datation des évangiles," *RTL* 19 (1988): 17-37.

2850   K. Haacker, "Verwendung und Vermeidung des Apostelbegriffs im lukanischen Werk," *NovT* 30 (1988): 9-38.

2851   Jacob Kremer, *Lukasevangelium*. Neue Echter Bibel #3. Würzburg: Echter, 1988.

2852   Walter Radl, *Das Lukas-Evangelium*. Erträge der Forschung #261. Darmstadt: Wissenschaftliche Buchgesellschaft, 1988.

2853   J.-L. Vesco, *Jérusalem el son prophète: Une lecture de l'évangile selon saint Luc*. Paris: Cerf, 1988.

2854   James M. Dawsey, "The Literary Unity of Luke-Acts: Questions of Style,"*NTS* 35 (1989): 48-66.

2855   B. Dehandschutter, "L'évangile selon Thomas: témoin d'une tradition prélucanienne?" in Frans Neirynck, ed., *L'Évangile de Luc: Problèmes littéraires et théologiques* (festschrift for Lucien Cerfaux). 2nd ed. BETL #32. Louvain: Peeters Press, 1989. Pp. 197-207.

2856   Michael D. Goulder, *Luke: A New Paradigm*. Sheffield: JSOT Press, 1989.

2857   F. Neirynck, ed., *L'Évangile de Luc. The Gospel of Luke*. BETL #32. Louvain: Peeters, 1989.

2858   Mark Allan Powell, *What Are They Saying about Luke?* New York: Paulist Press, 1989.

2859   Jan Wojcik, *The Road to Emmaus: Reading Luke's Gospel*. West Lafayette IN: Purdue University Press, 1989.

2860   John O. York, "The Rhetorical Function of Bi-Polar Reversal in Luke," doctoral dissertation, Emory University, Atlanta GA, 1989.

2861   W. Dicharry, *Human Authors of the New Testament*. 1: *Mark, Matthew, and Luke*. Collegeville MN: Liturgical Press, 1990.

2862   C. Bussmann and W. Radl, eds., *Der Treue Gottes trauen: Beiträge zum Werke des Lukas* (festschrift for G. Schneider). Freiburg: Herder, 1991.

2863 C. Cook, "The Sense of Audience in Luke: A Literary Examination," *NBlack* 72 (1991): 19-30.

2864 P. Luomanen, *Luke-Acts: Scandinavian Perspectives.* Helsinki: Finnish Exegetical Society, 1991.

2865 Fearghus O'Fearghail, *The Introduction to Luke-Acts: A Study of the Role of Luke 1:1-4:44 in the Composition of Luke's Two-Volume Work.* Rome: Biblical Institute Press, 1991.

2866 J. O. York, *The Last Shall Be First. Rhetoric of Reversal in Luke.* Sheffield: JSOT Press, 1991.

2867 Klaus Berger, "Zur Diskussion um die Gattung Evangelium. Formgeschichtliche Beiträge aus Beobachtungen an Plutarchs 'Leben der zehn Redner'," in F. van Segbroeck, et al., eds., *The Four Gospels 1992* (festschrift for Frans Neirynck). 3 vols. BETL #100. Louvain: Peeters Press, 1992. 1:121-27.

2868 R. Bieringer, "Traditionsgeschichtlicher Ursprung und theologische Bedeutung der ὑπέρ-Aussagen im Neuen Testament," in F. van Segbroeck, et al., eds., *The Four Gospels 1992* (festschrift for Frans Neirynck). 3 vols. BETL #100. Louvain: Peeters Press, 1992. 1:219-48.

2869 J. A. Darr, *On Charcter Building: The Reader and the Rhetoric of Characterization in Luke-Acts.* Louisville KY: Westminster/Knox, 1992.

2870 H. E. Dollar, *A Biblical-Missiological Exploration of the Cross-Cultural Dimensions in Luke-Acts.* San Francisco: Mellen Research University Press, 1993.

2871 G. Strecker, "Schriftlichkeit oder Mündlichkeit der synoptischen Tradition? Anmerkungen zur formgeschichtlichen Problematik," in F. van Segbroeck, et al., eds., *The Four Gospels 1992* (festschrift for Frans Neirynck). 3 vols. BETL #100. Louvain: Peeters Press, 1992. 1:159-72.

2872   F. Vouga, "Formgeschichtliche Überlegungen zu den Gleichnissen
        und zu den Fabeln der Jesus-Tradition auf dem Hintergrund der
        hellenistischen Literaturgeschichte," in F. van Segbroeck, et al.,
        eds., *The Four Gospels 1992* (festschrift for Frans Neirynck). 3
        vols. BETL #100. Louvain: Peeters Press, 1992. 1:173-87.

Jesus, general studies
        2873   T. C. Hall, *The Message of Jesus according to the Synoptists.* The
                Messages of the Bible #9. New York: Scribner, 1901.

        2874   Lemuel Hall, "The Growing Apprehension of Jesus in the
                Synoptics," doctoral dissertation, Southern Baptist Theological
                Seminary, Louisville KY, 1928.

        2875   James L. Hall, "A Study of the Significance of the Appearances of
                Christ after the Resurrection," master's thesis, Southern Baptist
                Theological Seminary, Louisville KY, 1949.

        2876   Walter E. Bundy, *Jesus and the First Three Gospels.* Cambridge:
                Harvard University Press, 1955.

        2877   J. A. Bailey, "The Anointing of Jesus and the Mary-Martha
                Stories: Luke 7.36-50; John 12.1-8," in *The Traditions Common to
                the Gospels of Luke and John.* Leiden: Brill, 1963. Pp. 1-8.

        2878   R. Holst, "The Temptation of Jesus," *ET* 82 (1970-1971): 343-44.

        2879   David Hill, "The Rejection of Jesus at Nazareth: Luke 4:16-30,"
                NovT 13/3 (1971): 161-80.

        2880   James L. Resseguie, "The Lukan Portrait of Christ," *SBT* 4
                (1974): 5-20.

        2881   W. R. Cannon, *A Disciple's Profile of Jesus: From the Gospel of
                Luke.* Nashville TN: Upper Room, 1975.

        2882   G. R. Greene, "The Portrayal of Jesus as Prophet in Luke-Acts,"
                doctoral dissertation, Southern Baptist Theological Seminary,
                Louisville KY, 1975.

        2883   Millar Burrows, *Jesus in the First Three Gospels.* Nashville TN:
                Abingdon Press, 1977.

2884 Joseph B. Tyson, "The Opposition to Jesus in the Gospel of Luke," *PRS* 5 (1978): 144-50.

2885 D. O'Donnell, *Meet Jesus in Luke*. Notre Dame IN: Ave Maria Press, 1980.

2886 M. Bouttier, "L'humanité de Jésus selon saint Luc," *RechSR* 69 (1981): 33-43.

2887 O. C. Edwards, *Luke's Story of Jesus*. Philadelphia: Fortress Press, 1981.

2888 D. Sydnor, *Jesus According to Luke*. New York: Seabury, 1982.

2889 John J. Kilgallen, "Luke 2:41-50: Foreshadowing of Jesus, Teacher," *Bib* 66/4 (1985): 553-59.

2890 James M. Dawsey, "Jesus' Pilgrimage to Jerusalem," *PRS* 14 (1987): 217-32.

2891 Joseph A. Fitzmyer, "Jesus in the Early Church through the Eyes of Luke-Acts," *ScrB* 17 (1987): 26-35.

2892 P. A. Cunningham, *Jesus and the Evangelists: The Ministry of Jesus and Its Portrayal in the Synoptic Gospels*. New York: Paulist Press, 1988.

2893 R. Knopp, *Finding Jesus in the Gospels: A Companion to Mark, Matthew, Luke and John*. Notre Dame IN: Ave Maria, 1989.

Jesus, baptism of

2894 C. Dennison, "How Is Jesus the Son of God? Luke's Baptism Narrative and Christology," *CalTJ* 17 (1982): 6-25.

2895 G. Alencherry, "Le baptême de Jésus dans l'œuvre de Luc et dans la tradition baptismale de l'Église indo-chaldéenne," doctoral dissertation, Catholic Institute, Paris, 1986.

2896 J. Duncan M. Derrett, "Christ's Second Baptism (Lk. 12:50; Mk. 10:38-40)," *ET* 100 (1988-1989): 294-95.

Jesus, death of

2897 R. Zehnle, "The Salvific Character of Jesus' Death in Lucan Soteriology," *TS* 30 (1969): 420-44.

2898 P. W. Walaskay, "The Trial and Death of Jesus in the Gospel of Luke," *JBL* 94 (1975): 81-93.

2899 Frank J. Matera, "The Death of Jesus according to Luke: A Question of Sources," *CBQ* 47 (1985): 469-85.

2900 Robert J. Karris, "Luke 23:47 and the Lucan View of Jesus' Death," *JBL* 105/1 (1986): 65-74.

2901 J. T. Pawlikowski, "The Trial and Death of Jesus: Reflections in Light of an Undersranding of Judaism," *CS* 25 (1986): 79-94.

2902 Joel B. Green, "The Death of Jesus and the Rending of the Temple Veil (Luke 23:44-49): A Window into Luke's Understanding of Jesus and the Temple," *SBLSP* 21 (1991): 543-57.

Jesus, genealogies of

2903 M. J. Moreton, "The Genealogy of Jesus," *StudE* 4 (1964): 219-24.

2904 E. L. Abel, "The Genealogies of Jesus *o Khristos*," *NTS* 20 (1973-1974): 203-10.

2905 R. P. Nettelhorst, "The Geneaology of Jesus," *JETS* 31 (1988): 169-72.

Jesus, life of

2906 W. F. Beck, *The Christ of the Gospels: The Life and Work of Jesus as Told by Matthew, Mark, Luke, and John*. St. Louis MO: Concordia Publishing House, 1959.

2907 H. Schürmann, "Die geistgewirkte Lebensentstehung Jesu: Eine kritische Besinnung auf den Beitrag der Exegese zur Frage," in W. Ernst and K. Feiereis, eds., *Einheit in Vielfalt* (festschrift for H. Aufderbeck). Leipzig: St. Benno, 1974. Pp. 156-69.

Jesus, ministry of

2908   Norman D. Price, "The Place of Galilee in the Ministry of Christ," doctoral dissertation, Southern Baptist Theological Seminary, Louisville KY, 1941.

2909   Sharon H. Ringe, "The Jubilee Proclamation in the Ministry and Teaching of Jesus: A Tradition-Critical Study in the Synoptic Gospels and Acts," doctoral dissertation, Union Theological Seminary NY, 1982.

2910   R. F. Collins, "Jesus' Ministry to the Deaf and Dumb," *MeliT* 35/1 (1984): 12-36.

Jesus, teachings of

2911   Lloyd E. Batson, "A Study of Jesus' Teachings on Possession as Presented in the Gospel of Luke," doctoral dissertation, Southern Baptist Theological Seminary, Louisville KY, 1957.

2912   R. T. France, "The Servant of the Lord in the Teaching of Jesus," *TynB* 19 (1968): 26-52.

2913   R. Geiger, "Gesprächspartner Jesu im Lukas-Evangelium," in H. Merklein and J. Lange, eds., *Biblische Randbemerkungen* (festschrift for Rudolf Schnackenburg). Würzburg: Echter, 1975. Pp. 150-56.

2914   Sharon H. Ringe, "The Jubilee Proclamation in the Ministry and Teaching of Jesus: A Tradition-Critical Study in the Synoptic Gospels and Acts," doctoral dissertation, Union Theological Seminary NY, 1982.

2915   Gerhard Schneider, "Jesu überraschende Antworten: Beobachtungen zu den Apophthegmen des dritten Evangeliums," *NTS* 29 (1983): 321-36.

2916   G. M. Soares-Prahbu, "The Synoptic Love-Commandment: The Dimensions of Love in the Teaching of Jesus," *Je* 13 (1983): 85-103.

2917   Edward Dobson, "The Teachings of Jesus," *FundJ* 4/11 (1985): 35-36.

2918   Marion L. Soards, "Tradition, Composition, and Theology in Jesus' Speech to the 'Daughters of Jerusalem' (Luke 23,26-32)," *Bib* 68/2 (1987): 221-44.

2919   M. D. Hooker, "Traditions about the Temple in the Sayings of Jesus," *BJRL* 70 (1988): 7-19.

2920   John F. O'Grady, *The Four Gospels and the Jesus Tradition.* New York: Paulist, 1989.

Jesus, trial of
2921   Joseph B. Tyson, "The Lukan Version of the Trial of Jesus," *NovT* 3 (1959): 249-58.

2922   P. W. Walaskay, "The Trial and Death of Jesus in the Gospel of Luke," *JBL* 94 (1975): 81-93.

2923   J. T. Pawlikowski, "The Trial and Death of Jesus: Reflections in Light of an Undersranding of Judaism," *CS* 25 (1986): 79-94.

Jewish-gentile relations
2924   L. C. Crockett, "Luke 4:25-27 and Jewish-Gentile Relations in Luke-Acts," *JBL* 88 (1969): 177-83.

John, Gospel of
2925   Edwin D. Johnston, "A Re-Examination of the Relation of the Fourth Gospel to the Synoptics," doctoral dissertation, Southern Baptist Theological Seminary, Louisville KY, 1954.

2926   F. Lamar Cribbs, "A Study of the Contacts that Exist between St. Luke and St. John," *SBLSP* 3/2 (1973): 1-93.

2927   F. Lamar Cribbs, "The Agreements that Exist between Luke and John," *SBLSP* 9/1 (1979): 215-61.

2928   Frans Neirynck, "John and the Synoptics: 1975-1990," in Adelbert Denaux, ed., *John and the Synoptics.* BETL #101. Louvain: Peeters Press, 1992. Pp. 3-61.

2929   D. Moody Smith, "The Problem of John and the Synoptics in Light of the Relation between Apocryphal and Canonical Gospels," in Adelbert Denaux, ed., *John and the Synoptics.* BETL #101. Louvain: Peeters Press, 1992. Pp. 147-62.

John the Baptist

2930 J. A. Bailey, "Speculation about John the Baptist: Luke 3.15, John 1.19,27," in *The Traditions Common to the Gospels of Luke and John*. Leiden: Brill, 1963. Pp. 9-11.

2931 Werner Georg Kümmel, *Jesu Antwort an Johannes den Täufer: Ein Beispiel zum Methodenproblem der Jesusforschung*. Wiesbaden: Steiner, 1974.

2932 E. A. LaVerdiere, "John the Prophet: Jesus' Forerunner in Luke's Theology of History," *BibTo* 77 (1975): 323-30.

2933 J. Ryckmans, "Un parallèle sud-arabe à l'imposition du nom de Jean-Baptiste et de Jésus," in R. G. Stiegmer, ed., *Al-Hudhud* (festschrift for M. Höfner). Graz: Franzens-University Press, 1981. Pp. 28-94.

2934 John J. Kilgallen, "John the Baptist, the Sinful Woman and the Pharisee," *JBL* 104/4 (1985): 675-79.

2935 D. R. Schwartz, "On Quirinius, John the Baptist, the Benedictus, Melchizedek, Qumran and Ephesus," *RevQ* 13 (1988): 635-46.

Judaism, relation to

2936 M. Herranz Marco, "El proceso ante el Sanhedrin y el ministerio publico de Jesus," *EB* 34 (1975): 83-111.

2937 F. Chenderlin, "Distributed Observance of the Passover: A Preliminary Test of the Hypothesis," *Bib* 57 (1976): 1-24.

2938 A. W. Wainwright, "Luke and the Restoration of the Kingdom to Israel," *ET* 89 (1977-1978): 76-79.

2939 Robert L. Brawley, "The Pharisees in Luke-Acts: Luke's Address to Jews and his Irenic Purpose," doctoral dissertation, Princeton Theological Seminary, Princeton NJ, 1978.

2940 J. A. Ziesler, "Luke and the Pharisees," *NTS* 25 (1978-1979): 146-57.

2941 D. A. Carson, "Jesus and the Sabbath in the Four Gospels," in D. A. Carson, ed., *From Sabbath to Lord's Day: A Biblical, Historical and Theological Investigation.* Grand Rapids MI: Zondervan, 1982. Pp. 57-98.

2942 M. M. B. Turner, "The Sabbath, Sunday and the Law in Luke/Acts," in D. A. Carson, ed., *From Sabbath to Lord's Day.* Grand Rapids MI: Zondervan, 1982. Pp. 99-157.

2943 Jack T. Sanders, "The Pharisees in Luke-Acts," in D. E. Groh and Robert Jewett, eds., *The Living Text* (festschrift for E. W. Saunders). Lanham MD: University Press of America, 1985. Pp. 141-88.

2944 É. Trocmé, "The Jews as Seen by Paul and Luke," in Jacob Neusner and E. S. Frerichs, eds., *To See Ourselves as Others See Us.* Chico CA: Scholars Press, 1985. Pp. 145-61.

2945 Jack T. Sanders, "The Jewish People in Luke-Acts," *SBLSP* 16 (1986): 110-29.

2946 David L. Tiede, " 'Glory to Thy People Israel!': Luke-Acts and the Jews," *SBLSP* 16 (1986): 142-51.

2947 Jack T. Sanders, *The Jews in Luke-Acts.* Philadelphia: Fortress Press, 1987.

2948 Joseph B. Tyson, "Scripture, Torah, and Sabbath in Luke-Acts," in E. P. Sanders, ed., *Jesus, the Gospels, and the Church* (festschrift for William R. Farmer). Macon GA: Mercer University Press, 1987. Pp. 89-104.

2949 John T. Carroll, "Luke's Portrayal of the Pharisees," *CBQ* 50 (1988): 604-27.

2950 Joseph B. Tyson, ed., *Luke-Acts and the Jewish People.* Minneapolis MN: Augsburg, 1988.

2951 Jon A. Weatherly, "The Jews in Luke-Acts," *TynB* 40 (1989): 107-17.

2952 J. Bradley Chance, "The Jewish People and the Death of Jesus in Luke-Acts," *SBLSP* 21 (1991): 50-81.

2953 David R. Gowler, *Host, Guest, Enemy and Friend: Portraits of the Pharisees in Luke and Acts.* New York: Lang, 1991.

2954 Joe B. Tyson, *Images of Judaism in Luke-Acts.* Columbia SC: University of South Carolina Press, 1992.

Kingdom of God

2955 Leon Bell Patterson, "A Comparative Study of the Johannine Concept of Eternal Life and the Synoptic Concept of the Kingdom," master's thesis, Southwestern Baptist Theological Seminary, Fort Worth TX, 1958.

2956 S. S. Smalley, "Spirit, Kingdom, and Prayer in Luke-Acts," *NovT* 15 (1973): 59-71.

2957 M. Völkel, "Zur Deutung des 'Reiches Gottes' bei Lukas," *ZNW* 65 (1974): 57-70.

2958 W. W. Glover, "The Kingdom of God in Luke," *BT* 29 (1978): 231-37.

2959 Jacques Schlosser, *Le Règne de Dieu dans les dits de Jésus.* 2 vols. Études Bibliques. Paris: Gabalda, 1980.

2960 Myron Augsburger, "Nonviolence as a Life-Style," in John A. Bernbaum, ed., *Perspectives on Peacemaking.* Ventura CA: Regal Books, 1984. Pp. 147-59.

2961 Chrys C. Caragounis, "Kingdom of God, Son of Man and Jesus' Self-Understanding," *TynB* 40 (1989): 3-23.

2962 Christopher M. Tuckett, "Q, Prayer, and the Kingdom," *JTS* 40 (1989): 367-76.

2963 Chrys C. Caragounis, "The Kingdom of God in John and the Synoptics: Realized or Potential Eschatology?" in Adelbert Denaux, ed., *John and the Synoptics.* BETL #101. Louvain: Peeters Press, 1992. Pp. 473-80.

2964 D. J. Ireland, *Stewardship and the Kingdom of God. An Historical, Exegetical, and Contextual Study of the Parable of the Unjust Steward in Luke 16:1-13.* NovtSupp 70. Leiden: E. J. Brill, 1992.

law

2965 J. Duncan M. Derrett, "Law in the New Testament: Fresh Light on the Parable of the Good Samaritan," *NTS* 11 (1964-1965): 22-37.

2966 J. Duncan M. Derrett, "Law in the New Testament: The Parable of the Prodigal Son," *NTS* 14 (1967-1968): 56-74.

2967 J. Duncan M. Derrett, "The Parable of the Good Samaritan," in *Law in the New Testament*. London: Darton, Longman & Todd, 1970. Pp. 208-27.

2968 J. Duncan M. Derrett, "Law in the New Testament: The Palm Sunday Colt," *NovT* 13 (1971): 241-58.

2969 J. Duncan M. Derrett, "Law in the New Testament: The Parable of the Unjust Judge," *NTS* 18 (1971-1972): 178-91.

2970 J. Duncan M. Derrett, "Law in the New Testament: The Syro-Phoenician Woman and the Centurion of Capernaum," *NovT* 15 (1973): 161-86.

2971 Thomas L. Brodie, "A New Temple and a New Law," *JSNT* 5 (1979): 21-45.

2972 M. M. B. Turner, "The Sabbath, Sunday and the Law in Luke/Acts," in D. A. Carson, ed., *From Sabbath to Lord's Day*. Grand Rapids MI: Zondervan, 1982. Pp. 99-157.

2973 Carl L. Blomberg, "The Law in Luke-Acts," *JSNT* 21 (1984): 53-80.

2974 Stephen G. Wilson, *Luke and the Law*. SNTSMS #50. Cambridge: University Press, 1984.

2975 G. W. Klingsporn, "The Validity of the Law in Luke-Acts," doctoral dissertation, Baylor University, Waco TX, 1985.

2976 F. Gerald Downing, "Freedom from the Law in Luke-Acts," *JSNT* 26 (1986): 49-52.

2977 K. Salo, *Luk'es Treatment of the Law*. Helsinki: Suomalainen Tiedeakatemia, 1991.

Lazarus

2978 R. Dunkerly, "Lazarus," *NTS* 5 (1958-1959): 321-27.

2979 Otto Glombitza, "Der reiche Mann und der arme Lazarus," *NovT* 12 (1970): 166-80.

2980 E. Pax, "Der Reiche und der arme Lazarus eine Milieustudie," *SBFLA* 25 (1975): 254-68.

2981 F. Schnider and W. Stenger, "Die offene Tür und die unüberschreitbare Kluft. Strukturanalytische Überlegungen zum Gleichnis vom reichen Mann und armen Lazarus," *NTS* 25 (1978-1979): 273-83.

2982 André Feuillet, "La parabole du mauvais riche et du pauvre Lazare (Luc 16:19-31) antithèse de la parabole de l'intendant astucieux (Luc 16:1-9)," *NRT* 101 (1979): 212-23.

2983 H. J. L. Jensen, "Diesseits und Jenseits des Raumes eines Textes: Textsemiotische Bemerkungen zur Erzählung 'Vom reichen Mann und armen Lazarus' (Lk 16,19-31)," *LB* 47 (1980): 39-60.

2984 Keith Pearce, "The Lucan Origins of the Raising of Lazarus," *ET* 96 (1984-1985): 359-61.

2985 Jacob Kremer, "Der arme Lazarus: Lazarus, der Freund Jesu: Beobachtungen zur Beziehung zwischen Lk 16:19-31 und Joh 11:1-46," in Françios Refoulé, ed., *à cause de l'Evangile: Etudes sur les synoptiques et les Actes* (festschrift for Jacques Dupont). Paris: Cerf, 1985. Pp. 571-84.

2986 R. F. Hock, "Lazarus and Micyllus: Greco-Roman Backgrounds to Luke 16:19-31," *JBL* 106 (1987): 447-63.

2987 Edward G. Mathews, "The Rich Man and Lazarus: Almsgiving and Repentance in Early Syriac Tradition," *Diakonia* 22/2 (1988-1989): 89-104.

2988 Roger L. Omanson, "Lazarus and Simon," *BT* 40 (1989): 416-19.

lepers

2989 J. Bours, "Vom dankbaren Samariter. Eine Meditation über Lk 17:11-19," *BibL* 1 (1960): 193-98.

2990   Otto Glombitza, "Der dankbare Samariter," *NovT* 11 (1969): 241-46.

2991   J. W. Drane, "Simon the Samaritan and the Lucan Concept of Salvation History," *EQ* 47 (1975): 131-37.

life, Christian
2992   B. E. Beck, "Christian Character in the Gospel of Luke," *EpRev* 6 (1979): 70-77, 86-95.

2993   R. A. Boever, *Good News from Luke: Practical Helps for Christian Living*. Liguori MO: Liguori, 1979.

2994   G. Baudler, "Aspekte für eine christliche Erziehung nach den lukanischen Kindheitserzählungen," *TPQ* 134 (1986): 28-38.

2995   B. E. Beck, *Christian Character in the Gospel of Luke*. London: Epworth, 1989.

Lukan theology
2996   R. W. Canoy, "Perspectives on Eucharistic Theology: Luke as Paradigm for an Inclusive Invitation to Communion," doctoral dissertation, Southern Baptist Theological Seminary, Louisville KY, 1987.

Luke, the individual
2997   J. C. K. Freeborn, "2 Timothy 4,11: 'Only Luke Is with Me'," *StudE* 6 (1973): 128-39.

2998   C. J. Hemer, "Luke the Historian," *BJRL* 60 (1977): 28-51.

2999   W. Bruners, "Lukas, Literat und Theologe: Neue Literatur zum lukanischen Doppelwerk," *BK* 35 (1980): 110-12.

3000   J. P. Claasen, "Lukas as kerkhistorikus," *NGTT* 21 (1980): 217-24.

3001   W. D. Thomas, "Luke, the Beloved Physician (Col 4,5)," *ET* 95 (1983-1984): 279-81.

3002   F. F. Bruce, "The First Church Historian," in C. A. Evans and W. F. Steinspring, ed., *Early Jewish and Christian Exegesis* (festschrift for W. H. Brownlee). Atlanta GA: Scholars Press, 1987. Pp. 1-14.

3003   Joseph A. Fitzmyer, *Luke the Theologian: Aspects of His Teaching*. New York: Paulist Press, 1987.

3004   A. O. Igenoza, "Luke, the Gentile Theologian: A Challenge to the African Theologian," *AfTJ* 16 (1987): 231-41.

Luke/Acts
3005   H. Giesen, "Im Dienst des Glaubens seiner Gemeinde: Zu neueren Arbeiten zum lukanischen Doppelwerk," *TGeg* 26 (1983): 199-208.

3006   P. Luomanen, *Luke-Acts: Scandinavian Perspectives*. Helsinki: Finnish Exegetical Society, 1991.

3007   J. A. Darr, *On Charcter Building: The Reader and the Rhetoric of Characterization in Luke-Acts*. Louisville KY: Westminster/Knox, 1992.

3008   H. E. Dollar, *A Biblical-Missiological Exploration of the Cross-Cultural Dimensions in Luke-Acts*. San Francisco: Mellen Research University Press, 1993.

magnificat
3009   V. Hamp, "Der alttestamentliche Hintergrund des Magnifikat," *BK* 8/3 (1953): 17-23.

3010   P. Gaechter, "Das Magnificat," in P. Gaechter, ed., *Maria im Erdenleben*. 2nd ed. Innsbruck: Marianischen Verlag, 1954. Pp. 127-54.

3011   Paul Winter, "Magnificat and Benedictus: Maccabaean Psalms?" *BJRL* 37 (1954-1955): 328-47.

3012   Paul Winter, "Le Magnificat et le Benedictus sont-ils des Psaumes macchabéens?" *RHPR* 36 (1956): 1-19.

3013   J. G. Davies, "The Ascription of the Magnificat to Mary," *JTS* 15 (1964): 307-308.

3014   Stephen Benko, "The Magnificat: A History of the Controversy," *JBL* 86 (1967): 263-75.

3015   Jacques Dupont, "Note complémentaire sur le Magnificat," in J. DuPont, ed., *Les Béatitudes.* Tome III. *Les évangélistes.* Paris: Gabalda, 1973. 3:186-93.

3016   P.-E. Jacquemin, "Le Magnificat (Lc 1)," *AsSeign* N.S. 66 (1973): 28-40.

3017   P. Schmidt, "Maria in der Sicht des Magnifikat," *GeistL* 46 (1973): 417-30.

3018   Robert C. Tannehill, "The Magnificat as Poem," *JBL* 93 (1974): 263-75.

3019   P. Schmidt, "Maria und das Magnificat," *Cath* 29 (1975): 230-46.

3020   Alberto Ablondi, "Meditando il Magnificat," in P. Visentin, et al., eds., *L'annuncio del regno ai poveri: b atti della XV Sessione di formazione ecumenica organizzata dal Segretariato attivit'a ecumeniche.* Leumann: Elle Di Ci, 1978. Pp. 147-57.

3021   M. Tréves, "Le Magnificat et le Benedictus (Lc 1,46-55.68-79)," *CCER* 27 (1979): 105-10.

3022   Jacques Dupont, "Le Magnificat comme discours sur Dieu," *NRT* 102 (1980): 321-43.

3023   D. Minguez, "Poética generativa del Magnificat," *Bib* 61 (1980): 55-77.

3024   Jacques Dupont, "The Magnificat as God-talk," *TD* 29 (1981): 153-54.

3025   I. Gomá Civit, *El Magnificat: Cántico de la salvación.* Madrid: Editorial católica, 1982.

3026   Theo Bell, "Das Magnificat vorteutschet und ausgelegt, 1521: een kommentaar bij het voorwoord," in J. T. Bakker and J. P. Boendermaker, eds., *Luther na 500 jaar.* Kampen: Kok, 1983. Pp. 78-98.

3027   Robert J. Karris, "Mary's Magnificat and Recent Study," *RevRel* 42 (1983): 903-908.

3028   A. Salas, ed., "Magnificat," *BibFe* 9 (1983): 1-98.

3029   B. Grigsby, "Compositional Hypotheses for the Lucan 'Magnifcat': Tensions for the Evangelical," *EQ* 56 (1984): 159-72.

3030   E. R. Obbard, *Magnificat: The Journey and the Song*. Mahwah NJ: Paulist Press, 1985.

3031   Alberto Valentini, "Magnifcat e lopera lucana," *RBib* 33 (1985): 395-423.

3032   P. Bemile, *The Magnificat within the Context and Framework of Lukan Theology: An Exegetical Theological Study of Luke 1:46-55*. Bern: Lang, 1986.

3033   David M. Scholer, "The Magnificat (Luke 1:46-55): Reflections on its Hermeneutical History," in Mark I. Branson and C. René Padilla, eds., *Conflict and Context*. Grand Rapids MI: Eerdmans, 1986. Pp. 210-19.

3034   Jean Delorme, "Le Magnificat: Laforme et le sens," in H. Cazelles, ed., *La vie de la parole* (festschrift for P. Grelot). Paris: Desclée, 1987. Pp. 175-94.

3035   Alberto Valentini, *Il Magnificat, Genere letterario, struttura, esegesi*. Bologna: Dehoniane, 1987.

3036   Heribert Schützeichel, "Das berühmte und denkwürdige Lied der heiligen Jungfrau: Calvins Auslegung des Magnificat," in Thomas Franke, et al., eds., *Creatio ex amore: Beiträge zu einer Theologie der Liebe* (festschrift for Alexandre Ganoczy). Würzburg: Echter, 1989. Pp. 300-11.

Mary and Martha stories

3037   J. A. Bailey, "The Anointing of Jesus and the Mary-Martha Stories: Luke 7.36-50; John 12.1-8," in *The Traditions Common to the Gospels of Luke and John*. Leiden: Brill, 1963. Pp. 1-8.

3038   Raymond E. Brown, et al., eds., *Mary in the New Testament*. Philadelphia: Fortress Press, 1978.

3039   J. Pétrin, *Le sens de l'oeuvre de S. Luc et le mystère marial*. Ottawa: Éditions Universitaires, 1979.

3040   Dennis M. Sweetland, "The Good Samaritan and Martha and
       Mary," *BibTo* 21 (1983): 325-30.

3041   M.-L. Gubler, "Selig, die geglaubt hat: Das Marienbild des
       Lukas," *TPQ* 136 (1988): 130-39.

3042   Adele Reinhartz, "From Narrative to History: The Resurrection of
       Mary and Martha," in Amy-Jill Levine, ed., *"Women Like This":*
       A New Perspective on Jewish Women in the Greco-Roman World.
       Atlanta: Scholars Press, 1991. Pp. 161-84.

Matthew, Gospel of
3043   William Baird, "Luke's Use of Matthew: Griesbach Revisited," *PJ*
       40 (1987): 35-38.

messiah
3044   Vittorio Fusco, "La morte del Messia," in Giovanni Boggio, et al.,
       eds., *Gesù e la sua morte.* Brescia: Paideia, 1984. Pp. 51-73.

3045   Heinrich Baarlink, *Vrede op aarde: De messiaanse vrede in bijbels*
       perspectief. Kampen: Kok, 1985.

Micyllus
3046   R. F. Hock, "Lazarus and Micyllus: Greco-Roman Backgrounds to
       Luke 16:19-31," *JBL* 106 (1987): 447-63.

miracles
3047   Rudolf Bultmann, "Lukas 5,1-11," in Rudolf Bultmann, ed.,
       Marburger Predigten. Tübingen: Mohr, 1956. Pp. 137-47.

3048   J. A. Bailey, "Miraculous Catch of Fish: Luke 5.1-ll, John
       21.1-14," in *The Traditions Common to the Gospels of Luke and*
       John. Leiden: Brill, 1963. Pp. 12-17.

3049   Rudolf Pesch, *Der Reiche Fischfang. Lk 5,1-11, Jo 21,1-14.*
       Wundergeschichte - Berufungserzählung - Erscheinungsbericht.
       Düsseldorf: Patmos, 1969.

3050   K.-H Crumbach, "Der 'reiche Fischzug' als Berufungsgeschichte.
       Eine Meditation zu Lk 5,1-11," *GeistL* 47 (1974): 228-31.

3051   Paul J. Achtemeier, "The Lukan Perspective on the Miracles of
       Jesus: A Preliminary Sketch," *JBL* 94 (1975): 547-62.

3052   A. George, "Le miracle dans l'oeuvre de Luc," in X. Léon-Dufour, ed. *Les miracles de Jésus selon le Nouveau Testament*. Paris: Seuil, 1977. Pp. 249-68.

3053   J. Duncan M. Derrett, "Positive Perspectives on Two Lucan Miracles," *DR* 104 (1986): 272-87.

3054   M. J. Harris, " 'The Dead are Restored to Life': Miracles of Revivification in the Gospels," in David Wenham and Carl Blomberg, eds., *Gospel Perspectives VI*. Sheffield: JSOT Press, 1986. Pp. 295-326.

3055   H. Hendrickx, *The Miracle Stories of the Synoptic Gospels*. Studies in the Synoptic Gospels. San Francisco: Harper & Row, 1987.

3056   H. Welzen, "Loosening and Binding: Luke 13.10-21 as Programme and Anti-Programme of the Gospel of Luke," in Spike Draisma, ed., *Intertextuality in Biblical Writings* (festschrift for Bastiaan M. F. van Iersel). Kampen: Kok, 1989. Pp. 175-87.

3057   Joseph A. Grassi, *Loaves and Fishes: The Gospel Feeding Narratives*. Collegeville MN: Liturgical Press, 1991.

3058   L. P. Pherigo, *The Great Physician. Luke: The Healing Stories*. Nashville: Abingdon Press, 1991.

missiology

3059   Edgar S. Mizell, "The Missionary Idea in the Synoptic Gospels," doctoral dissertation, Midwestern Baptist Theological Seminary, Kansas City KS, 1946.

3060   Jacob Kremer, "Weltweites Zeugnis für Christus in der Kraft des Geistes: Zur lukanischen Sicht der Mission," in Karl Kertelge, ed., *Mission im Neuen Testament*. Freiburg: Herder, 1982. Pp. 145-63.

3061   Giuseppe Frizzi, "La 'missioné' in Luca-Atti: Semantica, critica e apologia lucana," *RBib* 32 (1984): 395-423.

3062   Donald Senior, "The Mission Perspective of Luke-Acts," in Donald Senior and C. Stuhlmueller, eds., *The Biblical Foundations of Mission*. 2nd ed. London: SCM, 1984. Pp. 255-79.

3063   W. E. Pilgrim, "Luke: History and Mission," in W. C. Sturme, ed., *Bible and Mission*. Minneapolis MN: Augsburg, 1986. Pp. 31-46.

motifs

3064   Walter R. Edwards, "The Doctrine of Stewardship in the Synoptic Gospels," doctoral dissertation, Midwestern Baptist Theological Seminary, Kansas City KS, 1945.

3065   Emanuel A. Dahunsi, "The Significance of the Account of the Nazareth Episode in the Gospel of Luke," doctoral dissertation, Southern Baptist Theological Seminary, Louisville KY, 1957.

3066   George L. Balentine, "The Concept of the New Exodus in the Gospels," doctoral dissertation, Southern Baptist Theological Seminary, Louisville KY, 1961.

3067   Robert H. Taylor, "Jesus' Conception of Man in the Synoptics," doctoral dissertation, Southwestern Baptist Theological Seminary, Fort Worth TX, 1961.

3068   V. E. McEachern, "Dual Witness and Sabbath Motif in Luke," *CJT* 12 (1966): 267-80.

3069   R. T. France, "The Servant of the Lord in the Teaching of Jesus," *TynB* 19 (1968): 26-52.

3070   W. P. Huie, "The Poverty of Abundance. From Text to Sermon on Luke 16:19-31," *Int* 22 (1968): 403-20.

3071   J. Duncan M. Derrett, "Law in the New Testament: The Palm Sunday Colt," *NovT* 13 (1971): 241-58.

3072   Dieter Zeller, "Das Logion Mt 8,11f./Lk 13,28f. und das Motiv der 'Völkerwallfahrt'," *BZ* 15 (1971): 222-37; 16 (1972): 84-93.

3073   P. J. Bernadicou, "The Lukan Theology of Joy," *SE* 25 (1973): 75-98.

3074   T. R. Carruth, "The Jesus-as-Prophet Motif in Luke-Acts," doctoral dissertation, Baylor University, Waco TX, 1973.

3075 J. Navone, "Three Aspects of the Lucan Theology of History," *BTB* 3 (1973): 115-32.

3076 M. Völkel, "Der Anfang Jesu in Galiläa: Bemerkungen zum Gebrauch und zur Funktion Galiläas in den lukanischen Schriften," *ZNW* 64 (1973): 222-32.

3077 Stephen G. Wilson, *The Gentiles and the Gentile Mission in Luke-Acts*. SNTSMS #23. Cambridge: University Press, 1973.

3078 C. van der Waal, "The Temple in the Gospel according to Luke," *Neo* 7 (1973): 49-59.

3079 R. Glöckner, *Die Verkündigung des Heils beim Evangelisten Lukas*. Mainz: Grünewald, 1975.

3080 J. K. Elliott, "Jerusalem in Acts and the Gospels," *NTS* 23 (1976-1977): 462-69.

3081 Benjamin J. Hubbard, "Commissioning Stories in Luke-Acts: A Study of Their Antecedents, Form and Content," *Semeia* 8 (1977): 103-26.

3082 P. J. Bernadicou, "The Lukan Theology of Joy (Revisited)," *SE* 30 (1978): 57-80.

3083 F. X. Reitzel, "St. Luke's Use of the Temple Image," *RevRel* 38 (1979): 520-39.

3084 F. D. Weinert, "The Meaning of the Temple in the Gospel of Luke," doctoral dissertation, Fordham University, Bronx NY, 1979.

3085 J. Duncan M. Derrett, "The Iscariot, Mesira, and the Redemption," *JSNT* 8 (1980): 2-23.

3086 Morton S. Enslin, "The Samaritan Ministry and Mission," *HUCA* 51 (1980): 29-38.

3087 R. I. Garrett, "The Inaugural Addresses of Luke-Acts," doctoral dissertation, Southern Baptist Theological Seminary, Louisville KY, 1980.

3088 Jacques Dupont, "La prière et son efficacité dans l'évangile de Luc," *RechSR* 69 (1981): 45-55.

3089 F. D. Weinert, "The Meaning of the Temple in Luke-Acts," *BTB* 11 (1981): 85-89.

3090 B. Prete, "Le epoche o i tempi della 'storia della salvezza'," *PV* 27 (1982): 426-34.

3091 B. Prete, "Luca teologo della 'storia della salvezza'," *PV* 27 (1982): 404-25.

3092 R. M. Shelton, *Filled with the Holy Spirit: A Redactional Motif in Luke's Gospel.* London: British Library, 1982.

3093 Donald H. Juel, *Luke-Acts: The Promise of History.* Atlanta GA: John Knox Press, 1983.

3094 M. Trainor, "Luke's Story of the Word," *BibTo* 21 (1983): 34-38.

3095 Joseph B. Tyson, "Conflict as a Literary Theme in the Gospel of Luke," in William R. Farmer, ed., *New Synoptic Studies.* Macon GA: Mercer University Press, 1983. Pp. 303-27.

3096 Arthur G. Arnott, " 'The First Day of the Unleavened . . . ' Mt 26.17, Mk 14.12, Lk 22.7," *BT* 35 (1984): 235-38.

3097 L. Doohan, "Images of God in Luke-Acts," *MillSt* 13 (1984): 17-35.

3098 Vincent Tanghe, "Abraham, Son Fils et Son Envoyé (Luc 16:19-31)," *RB* 91/4 (1984): 557-77.

3099 H. M. Conn, "Lucan Perspectives and the City," *Miss* 13 (1985): 409-28.

3100 Christopher C. Conver, "The Portrayal of Joy in the Gospel of Luke," doctoral dissertation, Southern Baptist Theological Seminary, Louisville KY, 1985.

3101 Larry K. Drake, "The Reversal Theme in Luke's Gospel," doctoral dissertation, St. Louis University, St. Louis MO, 1985.

3102   Martin Forward, "Pilgrimage: Luke-Acts and the World of Religions," *KCTR* 8 (1985): 9-11.

3103   Charles H. Giblin, *The Destruction of Jerusalem according to Luke's Gospel: A Historical-Typological Moral.* AnBib #107. Rome: Biblical Institute Press, 1985.

3104   Paul Kariamadam, "India and Luke's Theology of the Way," *BB* 11 (1985): 47-60.

3105   K. Kliesch, " 'Den Armen eine gute Nachricht': Die Botschaft des Lukas," in P.-G. Müller, ed., *Das Zeugnis des Lukas.* Stuttgart: Katholisches Bibelwerk, 1985. Pp. 10-17.

3106   J. W. Watts, "Narrative Tune in Luke's Gospel," *Para* 1 (1985): 65-80.

3107   E. Asante, "The Theological Jerusalem of Luke-Acts," *AfTJ* 15 (1986): 172-82.

3108   James A. Berquist, "Good News to the Poor: Why Does This Lucan Motif Appear to Run Dry in the Book of Acts?" *BTF* 18/1 (1986): 1-16.

3109   Dennis Hamm, "Sight to the Blind: Vision as Metaphor in Luke," *Bib* 67 (1986): 457-77.

3110   Hans-Josef Klauck, "Die heilige Stadt Jerusalem bei Philo und Lukas," *K* 28 (1986): 129-51.

3111   David L. Tiede, " 'Glory to Thy People Israel!' Luke-Acts and the Jews," *SBLSP* 16 (1986): 142-51.

3112   James M. Dawsey, "The Unexpected Christ: The Lucan Image," *ET* 98 (1986-1987): 296-300.

3113   Otto Betz, "The Kerygma of Luke," in *Jesus, der Messias Israels: Aufsätze zur biblischen Theologie.* WUNT #42. Tübingen: Mohr, 1987. Pp. 257-72.

3114   Robert L. Brawley, *Luke-Acts and the Jews: Conflict, Apology, and Conciliation.* SBLMS #33. Atlanta GA: Scholars Press, 1987.

3115   James M. Dawsey, *The Lukan Voice: Confusion and Irony in the Gospel of Luke*. Macon GA: Mercer University Press, 1987.

3116   James M. Dawsey, "The Temple Theme in Luke," *MeliT* 38 (1987): 26-32.

3117   Gerhard Schneider, "Das Vaterunser: Oratio dominica et judaica?" in W. Baier, et al., eds. *Weisheit Gottes - Weisheit der Welt* (festschrift for J. Ratzinger). St. Ottilien: EOS, 1987. Pp. 405-17.

3118   Dennis E. Smith, "Table Fellowship as a Literary Motif in the Gospel of Luke," *JBL* 106 (1987): 613-38.

3119   F. D. Weinert, "Luke, Stephen and the Temple in Luke-Acts," *BTB* 17 (1987): 88-90.

3120   J. Bradley Chance, *Jerusalem, the Temple, and the New Age in Luke-Acts*. Macon GA: Mercer University Press, 1988.

3121   M. Klinghardt, *Gesetz und Volk Gottes: Das lukanische Verständnis des Gesetzes nach Herkunft, Funktfon und seinem Ort in der Geschichte des Urchristentums*. WUNT #II/32. Tübingen: Mohr, 1988.

3122   D. A. S. Ravens, "The Setting of Luke's Account of the Anointing: Luke 7.2-8.3," *NTS* 34 (1988): 282-92.

3123   J.-N. Aletti, *L'art de raconter Jésus-Christ: l'écriture narrative de l'Évangile de Luc*. Paris: Seuil, 1989.

3124   France Beydon, *En danger de richesse: le chrétien et les biens de ce monde selon Luc*. Aubonne: Moulin, 1989.

3125   J. A. Crampsey, "Jesus and Discernment," *Way* Suppl. 64 (1989): 19-28.

3126   Brigid C. Frein, "The Literary Significance of the Jesus-as-Prophet Motif in the Gospel of Luke and the Acts of the Apostles," doctoral dissertation, St. Louis University, St. Louis MO, 1989.

3127   Susan R. Garrett, *The Demise of the Devil: Magic and the Demonic in Luke's Writings*. Minneapolis MN: Fortress Press, 1989.

3128 J. J. Kilgallen, " 'Peace' in the Gospel of Luke and Acts of the Apostles," *SM* 38 (1989): 55-79.

3129 G. L. Klein, "The Challenge of Luke's Gospel," *Emmanuel* 95 (1989): 250-55.

3130 Chris U. Manus, "The Universalism of Luke and the Motif of Reconciliation (Lk 23:6-12): The African Cultural Context," *AJT* 3 (1989): 192-205.

3131 J. Irigoin, "La composition rythmique des cantiques de Luc," *RB* 36 (1991): 5-50.

3132 Jacob Jervell, "Retrospect and Prospect in Luke-Acts Interpretation," *SBLSP* 21 (1991): 383-404.

3133 Richard E. Oster, "Supposed Anachronism in Luke-Acts' Use of συναγωή: A Rejoinder to H. C. Kee," *NTS* 39/2 (1993): 178-208.

narratology
3134 Paul J. Achtemeier, "Enigmatic Bible Passages: It's the Little Things that Count," *BA* 46 (1983): 30-31.

3135 William S. Kurz, "Narrative Approaches to Luke-Acts," *Bib* 68 (1987): 195-220.

3136 S. McA. Sheeley, "Narrative Asides in Luke-Acts," doctoral dissertation, Southern Baptist Theological Seminary, Louisville KY, 1987.

3137 S. McA. Sheeley, "Narrative Asides and Narrative Authority in Luke-Acts," *BTB* 18 (1988): 102-107.

3138 David R. Gowler, "Characterization in Luke: A Socio-Narratological Approach," *BibTo* 19 (1989): 54-62.

3139 David R. Gowler, "A Socio-Narratological Character Anaylsis of the Pharisees in Luke-Acts," doctoral dissertation, Southern Baptist Theological Seminary, Louisville KY, 1989.

OT, relation to
3140 T. R. Carruth, "The Jesus-as-Prophet Motif in Luke-Acts," doctoral dissertation, Baylor University, Waco TX, 1973.

3141   J. A. Sanders, "From Isaiah 61 to Luke 4," in Jacob Neusner, ed., *Christianity Judaism and Other Greco-Roman Cults* (festschrift for Morton Smith). Part 1. Leiden: Brill, 1975. Pp. 75-106.

3142   G. Bleickert, "Ostern und Pfingsten: Lukanische und johanneische Schau," *WoAnt* 17 (1976): 33-37.

3143   N. A. Dahl, "The Story of Abraham in Luke-Acts," in *Jesus in the Memory of the Early Church.* Minneapolis MN: Augsburg, 1976. Pp. 66-86.

3144   P. B. Decock, "Isaiah in Luke-Acts," doctoral dissertation, Pontifical University Gregorium, Rome, 1977.

3145   W. J. Larkin, "Luke's Use of the Old Testament as a Key to his Soteriology," *JETS* 20 (1977): 325-35.

3146   F. Bovon, "La figure de Moïse dans l'oeuvre de Luc," in R. Martin-Achard, ed., *La figure de Moïse: Écriture et relectures.* Genève: Publications universitairs, 1978. Pp. 47-65.

3147   F. F. Bruce, "The Davidic Messiah in Luke-Acts," in G. A. Tuttle, ed., *Biblical and Near Eastern Studies* (festschrift for W. S. LaSor). Grand Rapids: Eerdmans, 1978. Pp. 7-17.

3148   K. E. Bailey, "The Song of Mary: Vision of a New Exodus (Luke 1,46-55)," *NESTTR* 2 (1979): 29-35.

3149   P.-É. Bonnard, "De la Sagesse personnifiée dans l'Ancien Testament à la Sagesse en personne dans le Nouveau," in M. Gilbert, ed., *La Sagesse de l'Ancien Testament.* BETL #51. Gembloux: Duculot, 1979. Pp. 117-49.

3150   R. Heerspink, "The Use of Psalm Citations in the Gospel of Luke and the Book of Acts," doctoral dissertation, Calvin Theological Seminary, Grand Rapids MI, 1979.

3151   S. T. Lachs, "Hebrew Elements in the Gospels and Acts," *JQR* 71 (1980-1981): 31-43.

3152   D. Seccombe, "Luke and Isaiah," *NTS* 27 (1980-1981): 252-59.

3153 P.-É. Bonnard, "Le Psaume 72: Ses relectures, ses traces dans l'oeuvre de Luc?" *RechSR* 69 (1981): 259-78.

3154 D. A. Carson, "Jesus and the Sabbath in the Four Gospels," in D. A. Carson, ed., *From Sabbath to Lord's Day: A Biblical, Historical and Theological Investigation.* Grand Rapids MI: Zondervan, 1982. Pp. 57-98.

3155 J. A. Sanders, "Isaiah in Luke," *Int* 36 (1982): 144-55.

3156 F. Bovon, "Israel, die Kirche und die Völker im lukanischen Doppelwerk," *TLZ* 108 (1983): 403-14.

3157 Randall Buth, "Hebrew Poetic Tenses and the Magnificat," *JSNT* 21 (1984): 67-83.

3158 F. Bovon, "Effet de réel et flou prophétique dans l'oeuvre de Luc," in *à cause de l'Évangile: Études sur les synoptiques et les Actes* (festschrift for Jacques Dupont). Paris: Cerf, 1985. Pp. 349-59.

3159 Edna Brocke, "Die Hebräische Bibel im Neuen Testament: Fragen anhand von Lk 4,14-30," in Edna Brocke and Jürgen Seim, eds., *Gottes Augapfel: Beiträge zur Erneuerung des Verhältnisses von Christen und Juden.* Neukirchen-Vluyn: Neukirchener Verlag, 1986. Pp. 113-19.

3160 Thomas L. Brodie, "Towards Unravelling Luke's Use of the Old Testament: Luke 7:11-17 as an Imitation of 1 Kings 17:17-24," *NTS* 32/2 (1986): 247-67.

3161 P. F. Feiler, "Jesus the Prophet: The Lucan Portrayal of Jesus as the Prophet like Moses," doctoral dissertation, Princeton Theological Seminary, Princeton NJ, 1986.

3162 Helmer Ringgren, "Luke's Use of the Old Testament," *HTR* 79/1-3 (1986): 227-35.

3163 Darrell L. Bock, *Proclamation from Prophecy and Pattern: Lucan Old Testament Christology.* Sheffield: JSOT Press, 1987.

3164 Thomas L. Brodie, "Luke the Literary Interpreter: Luke-Acts as a Systematic Rewriting and Updating of the Elijah-Elisha Narrative in 1 and 2 Kings," doctoral dissertation, University of St. Thomas Aquinas, Rome, 1987.

3165 Jack T. Sanders, "The Prophetic Use of the Scriptures in Luke-Acts," in C. A. Evans and William F. Stinespring, eds., *Early Jewish and Christian Exegesis* (festschrift for W. H. Brownlee). Atlanta GA: Scholars Press, 1987. Pp. 191-98.

3166 Richard D. Nelson, "David: A Model for Mary in Luke?" *BTB* 18 (1988): 138-42.

3167 Feargus O'Fearghail, "Israel in Luke-Acts," *PIBA* 11 (1988): 23-43.

parables
3168 A. T. Cadoux, *The Parables of Jesus*. London: Clarke, 1930.

3169 Harold S. Songer, "A Study of the Background of the Concepts of Parable in the Synoptic Gospels," doctoral dissertation, Southern Baptist Theological Seminary, Louisville KY, 1962.

3170 R. L. Cargill, *All the Parables of Jesus*. Nashville: Broadman, 1970.

3171 Charles E. Carlston, "The Lukan Redaction," in *The Parables in the Triple Tradition*. Philadelphia: Fortress, 1975. Pp. 53-94.

3172 K. E. Bailey, *Poet and Peasant: A Literary Cultural Approach to the Parables in Luke*. Grand Rapids MI: Eerdmans, 1976.

3173 R. Waelkens, "L'analyse structurale des paraboles. Deux essais: Luke 15:1-32 et Matthieu 13:44-46," *RTL* 8 (1977): 160-78.

3174 W. Pöhlmann, "Die Abschichtung des Verlorenen Sohnes (Lk 15:12f.) und die erzählte Welt der Parabel," *ZNW* 70 (1979): 194-213.

3175 K. E. Bailey, *Through Peasant Eyes. More Lucan Parables: Their Culture and Style*. Grand Rapids MI: Eerdmans, 1980.

3176 G. Diamond, "Reflections upon Recent Developments in the Study of Parables in Luke," *ABR* 29 (1981): 1-9.

3177 Carl L. Blomberg, "The Tradition History of the Parables Peculiar to Luke's Central Section," doctoral dissertation, University of Aberdeen, Aberdeen, UK, 1982.

3178 Richard J. Bauckham, "Synoptic Parousia Parables Again," *NTS* 29 (1983): 129-34.

3179 Camille Focant, "La parabole de la brebis perdue: Lecture historico-critique et réflexions théologiques," *FT* 13 (1983): 52-79.

3180 Carl L. Blomberg, "When Is a Parallel Really a Parallel? A Test Case: The Lucan Parables," *WesTJ* 46 (1984): 78-103.

3181 D. Beyer, *Parables for Christian Living: Seeing Ourselves as Jesus Sees Us—Parables from Luke*. Valley Forge PA: Judson Press, 1985.

3182 Jacob Kremer, "Der arme Lazarus: Lazarus, der Freund Jesu: Beobachtungen zur Beziehung zwischen Lk 16:19-31 und Joh 11:1-46," in Françios Refoulé, ed., *à cause de l'Evangile: Etudes sur les synoptiques et les Actes* (festschrift for Jacques Dupont). Paris: Cerf, 1985. Pp. 571-84.

3183 Timothy L. Noël, "Parables in Context: Developing a Narrative-Critical Approach to Parables in Luke," doctoral dissertation, Southwestern Baptist Theological Seminary, Fort Worth TX, 1986.

3184 W. Weren, "De parabel van het zaad (Lc 8,1-21)," in B. van Iersel, et al., eds., *Parabelverhalen in Lucas: Van semiotiek naar pragmatiek*. TFT-Studies #8. Tilburg: University Press, 1987. Pp. 22-54.

3185 W. Weren, "De parabel van de wijnbouwers (Lc 20,9-19)," in B. van Iersel, et al., eds., *Parabelverhalen in Lucas: Van semiotiek naar pragmatiek*. TFT-Studies #8. Tilburg: University Press, 1987. Pp. 251-80.

3186 C. W. Schnell, "Historical Context in Parable Interpretation: A Criticism of Current Tradition-Historical Interpretations of Luke 12:35-48," *Neo* 22 (1988): 269-82.

3187 James Champion, "The Parable as an Ancient and a Modern Form," *LT* 3 (1989): 16-39.

3188 Martin C. McDaniel, "Parables in Context: Luke's Parables of the Minas and the Wicked Tenants and Their Literary Contexts," doctoral dissertation, Vanderbilt University, Nashville TN, 1989.

3189 Eckart Reinmuth, "Ps-Philo, Liber Antiquitatum Biblicarum 33,1-5 und Die Auslegung der Parabel Lk. 16:19-31," *NovT* 31 (1989): 16-38.

3190 Doris Stam, "Qué mujer - no - busca - hasta encontrar?" in Irene Foulkes, ed., *Teología desde la mujer en Centroamerica*. Costa Rica: Sebila, 1989. Pp. 147-53.

3191 J. M. Casciaro, "Parábola, hipérbola y mashal en los sinópticos," *ScripT* 25 (1993): 15-31.

parable, children
3192 Franz Mussner, "Der nicht erkannte Kairos (Mt 11,16-19 = Lk 7,31-35)," in *Studia Biblica et Orientalia*. 3 vols. Rome: Pontifical Institute, 1959. 2:31-44.

3193 Simon Légasse, "La parabole des enfants sur la place," in *Jésus et l'enfant*. Paris: Gabalda, 1969. Pp. 289-317.

3194 O. Linton, "The Parable of the Children's Game," *NTS* 22/2 (1975-1976): 159-79.

3195 C. Siburt, "The Game of Rejecting God: Luke 7:31-35," *RQ* 19 (1976): 207-10.

3196 Wendy J. Cotter, "The Parable of the Children in the Market-Place, Q (Lk) 7:31-35," *NovT* 29 (1987): 289-304.

3197 Wendy J. Cotter, "Children Sitting in the Agora: Q (Luke) 7:31-35," *Forum* 5 (1989): 63-82.

parable, feeding multitude

3198 Ernst Bammel, "The Feeding of the Multitude," in E. Bammel and C. F. D. Moule, eds., *Jesus and the Politics of His Day.* Cambridge: University Press, 1984. Pp. 211-40.

3199 Randel Helms, "Fiction in the Gospels," in R. Joseph Hoffmann and Gerald A. Larue, eds., *Jesus in History and Myth.* Buffalo: Prometheus Books, 1986. Pp. 135-42.

parable, friend at midnight

3200 W. Ott, "Vergleich mit der Parabel vom mit- ternachts bittenden Freund Lk 11,5-8," in *Gebet und Heil.* Münich: Kösel, 1965. Pp. 23-31.

3201 J. Duncan M. Derrett, "The Friend at Midnight: Asian Ideas in the Gospel of St. Luke," in E. Bammel, ed., *Donum Gentiliaum* (festschrift for David Daube). New York: Clarendon Press, 1978. Pp. 78-87.

3202 E. W. Hubbard, "The Parable of the Friend at Midnight: God's Honor or Man's Persistence?" *RQ* 21 (1978): 154-60.

3203 A. F. Johnson, "Assurance for Man: The Fallacy of Translating *anaideia* by 'Persistence' in Luke 11:5-8," *JETS* 22 (1979): 123-31.

3204 David R. Catchpole, "Q and 'The Friend at Midnight'," *JTS* 34 (1983): 407-24.

3205 K. Haacker, "Mut zum Bitren: Ein Auslegung von Lukas 11,5-8," *TBe* 17 (1986): 1-6.

3206 Christopher M. Tuckett, "Q, Prayer, and the Kingdom," *JTS* 40 (1989): 367-76.

parable, gold coins

3207 Walter Lüthi, "Das Gleichnis von anvertranten Pfund: Predigt über Lk. 19,11-27," in *Festschrift für D. Albert Schädelin. Das Wort sie sollen lassen stahn.* Bern: Lang, 1950. Pp. 207-14.

3208 Ignace de La Potterie, "La parabole du prétendant à la royauté (Lc 19:11-28)," in Françios Refoulé, ed., *à cause de l'Evangile: Etudes sur les synoptiques et les Actes* (festschrift for Jacques Dupont). Paris: Cerf, 1985. Pp. 613-41.

3209 A. Puig i Tárrech, "La parabole des talents (Mt 25,14-30) ou des mines (Lc 19,11-28)," *RCT* 10 (1985): 269-317.

3210 Jean N. Aletti, "Lc 19,11-28: parabole des mines et/ou parabole du roi: remarques sur l'écriture parabolique de Luc," in Jean Delorme, ed., *Les paraboles évangéliques: perspectives nouvelles*. Paris: Cerf, 1989. Pp. 309-32.

3211 Louis Panier, "La parabole des mines: lecture sémiotique (Lc 19,11-27)," in Jean Delorme, ed., *Les paraboles évangéliques: perspectives nouvelles*. Paris: Cerf, 1989. Pp. 333-47.

parable, good Samaritan
3212 W. J. Masson, "The Parable of the Good Samaritan," *ET* 48 (1936-1937): 179-81.

3213 F. J. Leenhardt, "La parabole du Samaritain; schéma d'une exégèse existentialiste," in *Aux sources de la tradition chrétienne*. Paris: Delachaux & Niestlé, 1950. Pp. 132-38.

3214 F. H. Wilkinson, "Oded: Proto-Type of the Good Samaritan," *ET* 69 (1957-1958): 94.

3215 B. Gerhardsson, *The Good Samaritan, The Good Shepherd?* Lund: Gleerup, 1958.

3216 H. Binder, "Das Gleichnis vom barmherzigen Samariter," *TZ* 15 (1959): 176-94.

3217 J. Bours, "Vom dankbaren Samariter. Eine Meditation über Lk 17:11-19," *BibL* 1 (1960): 193-98.

3218 C. H. Lindijer, "Oude en Nieuwe Visies op de Gelijkenis van de Barmhartige Samaritaan," *NedTT* 15 (1960): 11-23.

3219 J. Duncan M. Derrett, "Law in the New Testament: Fresh Light on the Parable of the Good Samaritan," *NTS* 11 (1964-1965): 22-37.

3220 C. Daniel, "Les Esséniens et l'arrière-fond historique de la parabole du Bon Samaritain," *NovT* 11 (1969): 71-104.

3221 J. Duncan M. Derrett, "The Parable of the Good Samaritan," in *Law in the New Testament*. London: Darton, Longman & Todd, 1970. Pp. 208-27.

3222 Bo Reicke, "Der barmherzige Samariter," in O. Böcher and K. Haacker, eds., *Verborum Veritas* (festschrift for Gustav Stählin). Wuppertal: Brockhaus, 1970. Pp. 103-109.

3223 H. Zimmermann, "Das Gleichnis vom barmherzigen Samariter: Lk 10,25-37," in E. Lohse, et al., eds., *Der Ruf Jesu und die Antwort der Gemeinde*. Göttingen: Vandenhoeck & Ruprecht, 1970. Pp. 58-69.

3224 G. Eichholz, "Vom barmherzigen Samariter (Luk. 10,25-37)," in *Gleichnisse der Evangelien*. Neukirchen-Vluyn: Neukirchener Verlag, 1971. Pp. 147-78.

3225 G. Crespy, "La Parabole dite: 'Le bon Samaritain'. Recherches structurales," *ÉTR* 48 (1973): 61-79.

3226 Erhardt Güttgemanns, "Narrative Analyse Synoptischer Texte," *LB* 25/26 (1973): 50-73.

3227 G. Crespy, "The Parable of the Good Samaritan: An Essay in Structural Research," trans. John Kirby. *Semeia* 2 (1974): 27-50

3228 John Dominic Crossan, "The Good Samaritan: Towards a Generic Definition of Parable," *Semeia* 2 (1974): 82-112.

3229 Robert W. Funk, "The Good Samaritan as Metaphor," *Semeia* 2 (1974): 74-81.

3230 Jan Lambrecht, "The Message of the Good Samaritan," *LouvS* 5 (1974): 121-35.

3231 Daniel Patte, "An Analysis of Narrative Structure and the Good Samaritan," *Semeia* 2 (1974): 1-26.

3232 Gerhard Sellin, "Lukas als Gleichniserzählen: Die Erzählung vom barmherzigen Samariter (Lk 10,25-37)," *ZNW* 65 (1974): 166-89.

3233   P. Ternant, "Le bon Samaritain (Lc 10)," *AsSeign* N.S. 46 (1974): 66-77.

3234   Daniel Patte, "Structural Network in Narrative: The Good Samaritan," *Soundings* 58 (1975): 221-42.

3235   L. Ramaroson, "Comme 'Le Bon Samaritain' ne chercher qu'à aimer (Lc 10,29-37)," *Bib* 56 (1975): 533-36.

3236   D. O. Ellsworth, "Confronting Christian Responsibility: Exegesis and Application of Luke 10:29-37, the Good Samaritan Example Story," doctoral dissertation, Claremont School of Theology, Claremont CA, 1976.

3237   W. Bruners, *Die Reinigung der zehn Aussätzigen und die Heilung des Samariters, Lk 17,11-19.* Stuttgart: Katholisches Bibelwerk, 1977.

3238   Dietfried Gewalt, "Der 'Barmherzige Samariter': Zu Lukas 10:25-37," *EvT* 38 (1978): 403-17.

3239   Robert H. Stein, "The Interpretation of the Parable of the Good Samaritan," in W. W. Gasque, ed., *Scripture, Tradition, and Interpretation* (festschrift for E. F. Harrison). Grand Rapids MI: Eerdmans, 1978. Pp. 278-95.

3240   Walter Wink, "The Parable of the Compassionate Samaritan: A Communal Exegesis Approach," *RevExp* 76 (1979): 199-217.

3241   André Feuillet, "Le bon Samaritain (Luc 10,25-37): Sa signification christologique et l'universalisme de Jésus," *EV* 90 (1980): 337-51.

3242   N. Heutger, "Die lukanischen Samaritanererzählungen in religionspädagogischer Sicht," in W. Haubeck and M. Bachmann, eds., *Wort in der Zeit* (festschrift for K. H. Rengstorf). Leiden: Brill, 1980. Pp. 275-87.

3243   Robert W. Funk, "The Prodigal Samaritan," *JAAR* 48 (1981): 83-97.

3244   Dennis M. Sweetland, "The Good Samaritan and Martha and Mary," *BibTo* 21 (1983): 325-30.

3245 N. H. Young, "The Commandment to Love Your Neighbour as Yourself and the Parable of the Good Samaritan," *AUSS* 21 (1983): 265-72.

3246 Peter R. Jones, "The Compassionate Samaritan," in James C. Barry, ed., *Preaching in Today's World*. Nashville: Broadman Press, 1984. Pp. 83-89.

3247 F. S. Spencer, "Chronicles 28:5-15 and the Parable of the Good Samaritan," *WTJ* 46 (1984): 317-49.

3248 R. Fabris, "La parabola del buon samaritano," *ParSpirV* 11 (1985): 126-41.

3249 Medardo Gómez, "Forbidden to be a Samaritan," *TSR* 7/1 (1985): 14-17.

3250 W. R. Stenger, "The Parable of the Good Samaritan and Leviticus 18:5," in D. E. Groh and Robert Jewett, eds., *The Living Text* (festschrift for E. W. Saunders). Lanham MD: University Press of America, 1985. Pp. 27-38.

3251 Patrick Tishel, "The Parable of the Good Samaritan," *Epi* 6/2 (1985): 6-9.

3252 M. Gourgues, "L'autre dans le récit exemplaire du Bon Samaritain (Lc 10,29-37)," in M. Gourgues and G.-D. Mailhiot, eds., *L'altérité vivre ensemble differents*. Montréal: Bellarmin, 1986. Pp. 257-68.

3253 A. van Schaik, "De barmhartige Samaritaan (Lc 10,25-37)," in B. van Iersel, et al., eds., *Parabelverhalen in Lucas: Van semiotiek naar pragmatiek*. TFT-Studies #8. Tilburg: University Press, 1987. Pp. 55-82.

3254 R. A. Cooke, "What Is a Person Worth? The Good Samaritan Problem Reconsidered," *List* 23/3 (1988): 198-213.

3255 Stephen Hoyer and Patrice McDaniel, "From Jericho to Jerusalem: The Good Samaritan From a Different Direction," *JPT* 18 (1990): 326-33.

3256   Stephen F. Noll, "The Good Samaritan and Justification by Faith,"
       MM 8 (1990): 36-37.

3257   Pamela Thimmes, "The Language of Community: Metaphors,
       Systems of Convictions, Ethnic, and Gender Issues in Luke
       10:25-37 and 10:38-42," *SBLSP* 21 (1991): 698-713.

parable, great supper
3258   J. Baker, "Christ's Challenge to Straight Thinking," *ET* 67
       (1955-1956): 179-81.

3259   Eta Linneman, "Überlegungen zur Parabel vom grossen
       Abendmahl, Lc 14,15-24/Mt 22,1-14," *ZNW* 51 (1960): 246-55.

3260   J. Duncan M. Derrett, "The Parable of the Great Supper," in *Law
       in the New Testament*. London: Darton, Longman & Todd, 1970.
       Pp. 126-55.

3261   F. Hahn, "Das Gleichnis von der Einladung zum Festmahl," in O.
       Böcher and K. Haacker, eds., *Verborum Veritas* (festschrift for
       Gustav Stählin). Wuppertal: Brockhaus, 1970. Pp. 51-82.

3262   Dan O. Via, "The Relationship of Form to Content in the Parable:
       The Wedding Feast," *Int* 25 (1971): 171-84.

3263   A. Vögtle, "Die Einladung zum grossen Gastmahl und zum
       königlichen Hochzeitsmahl: Ein Paradigma für den Wandel des
       geschichtlichen Verständnishorizonts," in *Das Evangelium und die
       Evangelien*. Düsseldorf: Patmos, 1971. Pp. 171-218.

3264   D. Dormeyer, "Literarische und theologische Analyse der Parabel
       Lukas 14:15-24," *BibL* 15 (1974): 206-19.

3265   J. A. Sanders, "The Ethic of Election in Luke's Great Banquet
       Parable," in James L. Crenshaw and J. T. Willis, eds., *Essays in
       Old Testament Ethics* (Philip Hyatt, in memoriam). New York:
       KTAV, 1974. Pp. 245-71.

3266   Q. Quesnell, "The Women at Luke's Supper," in R. J. Cassidy
       and P. J. Scharper, eds., *Political Issues in Luke-Acts*. Maryknoll
       NY: Orbis, 1983. Pp. 59-79.

3267 L. Schottroff, "Das Gleichnis vom grossen Gastmahl in der Logienquelle," *EvT* 47 (1987): 192-211.

3268 K. Wegenast, "Freiheit ist lernbar: Lukas 14,15-24 im Unterricht," *EvErz* 40 (1988): 592-600.

3269 Peter Dschulnigg, "Positionen des Gleichnisverstandnisses im 20. Jahrhundert," *TZ* 45/4 (1989): 335-51.

3270 Irene Gysel-Nef, "Ein Anderes Fest," *Reformatio* 38 (1989): 178-83.

3271 Victor E. Vine, "Luke 14:15-24 and Anti-Semitism," *ET* 102 (1990-1991): 262-63.

3272 Richard L. Rohrbaugh, "The Pre-Industrial City in Luke-Acts: Urban Social Relations," in Jerome H. Neyrey, ed., *The Social World of Luke-Acts*. Peabody MA: Hendrickson Publishers, 1991. Pp. 125-49.

3273 Rainer Russ, "Das Fest hat soeben begonnen: Uberlegungen zu Lk 14,16-24: Versuch zur Erhellung einer homiletischen Bewusstseinslage," in Johannes J. Degenhardt, ed., *Die Freude an Gott: Unsere Kraft* (festschrift for Otto B. Knoch). Stuttgart: Verlag Katholisches Bibelwerk, 1991. Pp. 357-65.

parable, king going to war

3274 J. Louw, "The Parables of the Tower-Builder and the King Going to War," *ET* 48 (1936-1937): 478.

3275 S. Mechie, "The Parables of the Tower-Builder and the King Going to War," *ET* 48 (1936-1937): 235-36.

3276 P. G. Jarvis, "Expounding the Parables: Tower-Builder and King Going to War," *ET* 77 (1965-1966): 196-98.

3277 J. Duncan M. Derrett, "*Nisi dominus aedificaverit domum:* Towers and Wars," *NovT* 19 (1977): 241-61.

parable, Lazarus and rich man

3278 A. George, "La parabole du riche et de Lazare (Lc 16)," *AsSeign* N.S. 57 (1971): 80-93.

3279   J. Toy, "The Rich Man and Lazarus," *ET* 91 (1979-1980): 274-75.

parable, leaven
3280   Robert W. Funk, "Beyond Criticism in Quest of Literacy: The Parable of the Leaven," *Int* 25 (1971): 149-70.

3281   Elizabeth Waller, "The Parable of the Leaven: A Sectarian Teaching and the Inclusion of Women," *USQR* 35 (1980): 99-109.

parable, lost sheep
3282   E. F. F. Bishop, "The Parable of the Lost or Wandering Sheep," *ATR* 44 (1962): 44-57.

3283   J. Duncan M. Derrett, "Fresh Light on the Lost Sheep and the Lost Coin," *NTS* 26 (1979-1980): 36-60.

3284   J. Toy, "The Lost Sheep and the Lost Coin," *ET* 92 (1980-1981): 276-77.

3285   P. Mourlon-Beernaert, "The Lost Sheep: Four Approaches," *TD* 29 (1981): 143-48.

3286   W. L. Petersen, "The Parable of the Lost Sheep in the Gospel of Thomas and the Synoptics," *NovT* 23 (1981): 128-47.

3287   K. E. Bailey, *Finding the Lost: Cultural Keys to Luke 15*. St. Louis MO: Concordia, 1992.

parable, Pharisee
3288   Erhardt Güttgemanns, "Narrative Analyse Synoptischer Texte," *LB* 25/26 (1973): 50-73.

3289   Thorwald Lorenzen, "The Radicality of Grace: The Pharisee and the Tax Collector as a Parable of Jesus," *FM* 3/2 (1986): 66-75.

3290   F. Gerald Downing, "The Ambiguity of 'The Pharisee and the Toll-Collector' (Luke 18:9-14) in the Greco-Roman World of Late Antiquity," *CBQ* 54 (1992): 80-99.

parable, pounds
3291   Jack T. Sanders, "The Parable of the Pounds and Lucan Anti-Semitism," *TS* 42 (1981): 660-68.

parable, prodigal son

3292   J. E. Compton, "The Prodigal's Brother," *ET* 42 (1930-1931): 287.

3293   H. E. Sticker, "The Prodigal's Brother," *ET* 42 (1930-1931): 45-46.

3294   L. R. Fisher, "An Amarna Age Prodigal," *JSS* 3 (1958): 113-22.

3295   Charles E. Carlston, "A Positive Criterion of Authenticity?" *BR* 7 (1962): 33-44.

3296   R. Silva, "La parábola del hijo pródigo," *CuBí* 23 (1966): 259-63.

3297   J. Duncan M. Derrett, "Law in the New Testament: The Parable of the Prodigal Son," *NTS* 14 (1967-1968): 56-74.

3298   Jack T. Sanders, "Tradition and Redaction in Luke xv.11-32," *NTS* 15 (1968-1969): 433-38.

3299   P. Penning de Vries, "Der nie verlorene Vater," *GeistL* 44 (1971): 74-75.

3300   J. J. O'Rourke, "Some Notes on Luke xv.11-32," *NTS* 18 (1971-1972): 431-33.

3301   J. Delgado Sanchez, "Consideraciones sobre la parábola del hijo pródigo," *CuBí* 29 (1972): 338-41.

3302   Gerhard Lohfink, "Das Gleichnis vom gütigen Vater. Eine Predigt zu Luke 15:11-32," *BibL* 13 (1972): 138-46.

3303   K. E. Bailey, *The Cross and the Prodigal: The 15th Chapter of Luke Seen through the Eyes of Middle Eastern Peasants.* St. Louis MO: Concordia, 1973.

3304   Erhardt Güttgemanns, "Narrative Analyse Synoptischer Texte," *LB* 25/26 (1973): 50-73.

3305   Ingo Broer, "Das Gleichnis vom verlorenen Sohn und die Theologie des Lukas," *NTS* 20 (1973-1974): 453-62.

3306   W. Harrington, "The Prodigal Son," *Furrow* 25 (1974): 432-37.

3307   Gerhard Sellin, "Gleichnisstrukturen," *LB* 31 (1974): 89-115.

3308   G. Antoine, "Les trois paraboles de la miséricorde: Explication de
Lc 15,1-32," in F. Bovon and G. Rouiller, eds., *Exegesis
Problèmes de méthode et exercices de lecture (Genèse 22 et Luc
15)*. Neuchâtel-Paris: Delachaux & Niestlé, 1975. Pp. 126-35.

3309   L. Beirnaert, "La parabole de l'enfant prodigue (Lc 15,11-32) lue
par un analyste," in F. Bovon and G. Rouiller, eds., *Exegesis
Problèmes de méthode et exercices de lecture (Genèse 22 et Luc
15)*. Neuchâtel-Paris: Delachaux & Niestlé, 1975. Pp. 136-44.

3310   F. Bovon, "La parabole de l'enfant prodigue (Lc 15,11-32)," in F.
Bovon and G. Rouiller, eds., *Exegesis Problèmes de méthode et
exercices de lecture (Genèse 22 et Luc 15)*. Neuchâtel-Paris:
Delachaux & Niestlé, 1975. Pp. 82-85.

3311   Charles E. Carlston, "Reminiscence and Redaction in Luke
15:11-32," *JBL* 94 (1975): 368-90.

3312   C. Senft, "Ferdinand Christian Baur: Apport méthodologique et
interprétation de Lc 15,11-32," in F. Bovon and G. Rouiller, eds.,
Exegesis: Problèmes de méthode et exercises de lecture (Genèse
22, et Luc 15). Neuchâtel: Delachaux & Niestlé, 1975. Pp. 56-68.

3313   Y. Tissot, "Allégories patristiques de la parabole lucanienne des
deux fils (Lc 15,11-32)," in F. Bovon and G. Rouiller, eds.,
Exegesis: Problèmes de méthode et exercises de lecture (Genèse
22, et Luc 15). Neuchâtel: Delachaux & Niestlé, 1975. Pp. 243-72.

3314   Daniel Patte, "Structural Analysis of the Parable of the Prodigal
Son: Toward a Method," in Daniel Patte, ed., *Semiology and
Parables: Explorations of Possibilities Offered by Structuralism for
Exegesis*. Pittsburgh Theological Monograph Series #9. Pittsburgh:
Pickwick, 1976. Pp. 71-149.

3315   Pierre Grelot, "Le père et ses deux fils: Luke 15:11-32," *RB* 84
(1977): 321-48, 538-65.

3316 Rudolf Pesch, "Zur Exegese Gottes durch Jesus von Nazaret: Eine Auslegung des Gleichnisses vom Vater und den beiden Söhnen (Lk 15,11-32)," in B. Casper, ed., *Jesus, Ort der Erfahrung Gottes* (festschrift for B. Welte). 2nd ed. Freiburg: Herder, 1977. Pp. 140-89.

3317 J. L. Price, "Luke 15:11-32," *Int* 31 (1977): 64-69.

3318 Bernard Brandon Scott, "The Prodigal Son: A Structuralist Interpretation," *Semeia* 9 (1977): 45-73.

3319 Mary Ann Tolbert, "The Prodigal Son: An Essay in Literary Criticism from a Psychoanalytic Perspective," *Semeia* 9 (1977): 1-20.

3320 Dan O. Via, "The Prodigal Son: A Jungian Reading," *Semeia* 9 (1977): 21-43.

3321 O. Hofius, "Alttestamentliche Motive im Gleichnis vom verlorenen Sohn," *NTS* 24 (1977-1978): 240-48.

3322 R. G. Crawford, "A Parable of the Atonement," *EQ* 50 (1978): 2-7.

3323 H. Kruse, "The Return of the Prodigal: Fortunes of a Parable on its Way to the Far East," *Orient* 47 (1978): 163-214.

3324 G. Scholz, "Aesthetische Beobachtungen am Gleichnis vom reichen Mann und armen Lazarus und von drei anderen Gleichnissen," *LB* 43 (1978): 67-74.

3325 R. Strunk and M. Mausshardt, "Leistung des Schöpferischen (Lk 15,11-32)," in Y. Spiegel, ed., *Doppeldeutlich*. Münich: Kaiser, 1978. Pp. 59-78.

3326 M. A. Vázquez-Medel, "El perdón libera del odio: Lectura estructural de Lc 15,11-32," *Communio* 11 (1978): 271-312.

3327 R. T. Osborn, "The Father and his Two Sons: A Parable of Liberation," *Dia* 19 (1980): 204-209.

3328 R. R. Rickards, "Some Points to Consider in Translating the Parable of the Prodigal Son," *BT* 31 (1980): 243-45.

3329   M. Dumais, "Approche historico-critique d'un texte: La parabole du père et de ses deux fils," *SE* 33 (1981): 191-214.

3330   M. Roy, "Jugement et sanction. Matthieu 25:31-46; Luc 15:11-32; 16:19-31," *Chr* 28 (1981): 440-49.

3331   J. R. de Witt, *Amazing Love: The Parable of the Prodigal Son.* Edinburgh: Banner of Truth, 1982.

3332   J. J. Alemany, "Lc 15:11-32: Una sugerencia de análisis estructural," *MisCom* 41 (1983): 167-76.

3333   A. Viard, "Un homme avait deux fils (Luke 15:1-2, 11-32)," *EV* 83 (1983): 53-55.

3334   H.-J. Vogel, "Der verlorene Sohn: Lukas 15,11-32," *TexteK* 18 (1983): 27-34.

3335   Jacques Dupont, "Il padre del figliol prodigo (Lc 15,11-32)," *ParSpirV* 10 (1984): 120-34.

3336   G. S. Gibson, "The Sins of the Saints," *ET* 96 (1984-1985): 276-77.

3337   Roger D. Aus, "Luke 15:11-32 and R. Eliezer Ben Hyrcanus's *Rise to Fame*," *JBL* 104 (1985): 443-69.

3338   Michael R. Austin, "The Hypocritical Son," *EQ* 57 (1985): 307-15.

3339   Allan Boesak and Wolfram Kistner, "Proclamation and Protest: The Lost Sons and Outside the Gate," in Charles Villa-Vicencio and J. de Gruchy, eds., *Resistance and Hope* (festschrift for Beyers Naudé). Grand Rapids: Eerdmans, 1985. Pp. 74-82.

3340   J. G. Lees, "The Parable of the Good Father," *ET* 97/8 (1985-1986): 246-47.

3341   J. Smit Sibinga, "Zur Kompositionstechnik des Lukas in Lk 15:11-32," in J. W. van Henten, ed., *Tradition and Re-Interpretation in Jewish and Early Christian Literature* (festschrift for Jürgen C. H. Lebram). Leiden: Brill, 1986. Pp. 97-113.

3342   W. Zauner, "Busse als Fest: Eine Busspredigt zu Lk 15,11-32 (der barmherzige Vater—der heimgekehrte Sohn—der daheimgebliebene Bruder)," *TPQ* 134 (1986): 280-82.

3343   Vittorio Fusco, "Narrazione e dialogo nella parabola dena del figliol prodigo (Lc 15,11-32)," in G. Galli, ed., *Interpretazione e invenzione: La parabola de Figliol prodigo tra interpretazioni scientifiche e invenzioni artistiche*. Genova: Marietti, 1987. Pp. 17-67.

3344   Patrick J. Casey, "A Parable of God's Love for Sinners," *CBTJ* 5/1 (1989): 28-42.

3345   G. D. Cloete and Dirkie J. Smit, "Rejoicing With God," *JTSA* 66 (1989): 62-73.

3346   P. Pokorny, "Lukas 15,11-32 und die lukanische Soteriologie," in Karl Kertelge, ed., *Christus bezeugen* (festschrift for Wolfgang Trilling). Leipzig: St. Benno-Verlag, 1989. Pp. 179-92.

3347   K. E. Bailey, *Finding the Lost: Cultural Keys to Luke 15*. St. Louis MO: Concordia, 1992.

parable, rich fool
3348   Erhardt Güttgemanns, "Narrative Analyse Synoptischer Texte," *LB* 25/26 (1973): 50-73.

3349   J. Duncan M. Derrett, "The Rich Fool: A Parable of Jesus Concerning Inheritance," *HeyJ* 18 (1977): 131-51.

parable, rich man
3350   A. George, "La parabole du riche et de Lazare (Lc 16)," *AsSeign* N.S. 57 (1971): 80-93.

3351   André Feuillet, "La parabole du mauvais riche et du pauvre Lazare (Luc 16:19-31) antithèse de la parabole de l'intendant astucieux (Luc 16:1-9)," *NRT* 101 (1979): 212-23.

3352   J. Toy, "The Rich Man and Lazarus," *ET* 91 (1979-1980): 274-75.

3353   M. Roy, "Jugement et sanction. Matthieu 25:31-46; Luc 15:11-32; 16:19-31," *Chr* 28 (1981): 440-49.

3354 Gregory Murray, "The Rich Young Man," *DR* 103 (1985): 144-46.

3355 H. R. Graham, "Once there Was a Rich Man . . .: Five 'Rich Man' Stories in Luke," *BibTo* 26 (1988): 98-103.

3356 H. R. Graham, "Once there Was a Rich Man . . . : Five 'Rich Man' Stories in Luke," *BibTo* 26 (1988): 98-103.

3357 Richard J. Bauckham, "The Rich Man and Lazarus: The Parable and the Parallels," *NTS* 37 (1991): 225-46.

parable, seed

3358 O. Kuss, "Zur Senfkornparabel," *TGl* 41 (1951): 40-49.

3359 B. Schultze, "Die ekklesioklogische Bedeutung des Gleichnisses vom Senfkorn," *OCP* 27 (1961): 362-86.

3360 H. K. McArthur, "The Parable of the Mustard Seed," *CBQ* 33 (1971): 198-210.

3361 John Dominic Crossan, "The Seed Parables of Jesus," *JBL* 92 (1973): 244-66.

parable, servant(s)

3362 E. Lövestam, "The Parable of the Waiting Servants," in *Spiritual Wakefulness in the New Testament*. Lund: Gleerup, 1963. Pp. 92-95.

3363 A. Marcus Ward, "Uncomfortable Words: IV. Unprofitable Servants," *ET* 81/7 (1969-1970): 200-203.

3364 Paul S. Minear, "A Note on Luke 17:7-10," *JBL* 93 (1974): 82-87.

3365 John J. Kilgallen, "What Kind of Servants Are We?" *Bib* 63 (1982): 549-51.

3366 Jacques Dupont, "Le Maître et Son Serviteur," *ETL* 60/4 (1984): 233-51.

3367   J. Duncan M. Derrett, "The Parable of the Profitable Servant," in *Studies in the New Testament: IV. Midrash, the Composition of Gospels and Discipline*. Leiden: Brill, 1986. Pp. 157-66.

3368   Harry Fleddermann, "The Householder and the Servant Left in Charge," *SBLSP* 16 (1986): 17-26.

3369   Patrick J. Hartin, "Angst in the Household: A Deconstructive Reading of the Parable of the Supervising Servant," *Neo* 22 (1988): 373-90.

3370   Mary Ann Beavis, "Ancient Slavery as an Interpretive Context for the New Testament Servant Parables with Special Reference to the Unjust Steward," *JBL* 111 (1992): 37-54.

parable, sower
3371   David Wenham, "The Interpretation of the Parable of the Sower," *NTS* 20 (1973-1974): 299-319.

3372   J. Toy, "The Parable of the Sower and its Interpretation," *ET* 92 (1980-1981): 116-18.

3373   Craig Westendorf, "The Parable of the Sower in the Seventeenth Century," *LQ* 3 (1989): 49-64.

parable, tax collector
3374   Thorwald Lorenzen, "The Radicality of Grace: The Pharisee and the Tax Collector as a Parable of Jesus," *FM* 3/2 (1986): 66-75.

3375   F. Gerald Downing, "The Ambiguity of 'The Pharisee and the Toll-Collector' (Luke 18:9-14) in the Greco-Roman World of Late Antiquity," *CBQ* 54 (1992): 80-99.

parable, threshing floor
3376   James S. Alexander, "A Note on the Interpretation of the Parable of the Threshing Floor at the Conference at Carthage of A.D. 411," *JTS* 24/2 (1973): 512-19.

parable, tower builder
3377   J. Louw, "The Parables of the Tower-Builder and the King Going to War," *ET* 48 (1936-1937): 478.

3378 S. Mechie, "The Parables of the Tower-Builder and the King Going to War," *ET* 48 (1936-1937): 235-36.

3379 P. G. Jarvis, "Expounding the Parables: Tower-Builder and King Going to War," *ET* 77 (1965-1966): 196-98.

3380 J. Duncan M. Derrett, *"Nisi dominus aedificaverit domum:* Towers and Wars," *NovT* 19 (1977): 241-61.

parable, unjust steward
3381 F. Hüttermann, "Stand das Gleichnis vom ungerechten Verwalter in Q?" *TGl* 27 (1935): 739-42.

3382 J. C. Wansey, "The Parable of the Unjust Steward: An Interpretation," *ET* 47 (1935-1936): 39-40.

3383 R. B. Y. Scott, "The Parable of the Unjust Steward," *ET* 49 (1937-1938): 234-35.

3384 A. King, "The Parable of the Unjust Steward," *ET* 50 (1938-1939): 474-76.

3385 Charles H. Pickar, "The Unjust Steward," *CBQ* 1 (1939): 250-53.

3386 Lawrence M. Friedel, "The Parable of the Unjust Steward," *CBQ* 3 (1941): 337-48.

3387 J. Maiworm, "Die Versalter-Parabel," *TGl* 36 (1944): 149-56.

3388 H. Preisker, "Lukas 16,1-7," *TLZ* 74 (1949): 85-92.

3389 J. Maiworm, "Die Verwalter-Parabel," *BK* 13 (1958): 11-18.

3390 J. Duncan M. Derrett, "Fresh Light on St. Luke 16: I. The Parable of the Unjust Steward," *NTS* 7 (1960-1961): 198-219.

3391 E. Galbiati, "Esegesi degli Evangeli festivi," *BibO* 3 (1961): 92-96.

3392 H. Zimmermann, "Die Forderung der Gleichnisse Jesu. Das Gleichnis vom ungerechten Verwalter: Lk 16:1-9," *BibL* 2 (1961): 254-61.

3393 D. R. Fletcher, "The Riddle of the Unjust Steward," *JBL* 82 (1963): 15-30.

3394 Hans Kosmala, "The Parable of the Unjust Steward in the Light of Qumran," *ASTI* 3 (1964): 114-21.

3395 Francis E. Williams, "Is Almsgiving the Point of the 'Unjust Steward'?" *JBL* 83 (1964): 293-97.

3396 F. J. Moore, "The Parable of the Unjust Steward," *ATR* 47 (1965): 103-105.

3397 R. G. Lunt, "Expounding the Parables: Parable of the Unjust Steward," *ET* 77 (1965-1966): 132-36.

3398 H. Drexler, "Zu Lukas 16,1-7," *ZNW* 58 (1967): 286-88.

3399 I. Howard Marshall, "Luke xvi.8: Who Commended the Unjust Steward?" *JTS* 19 (1968): 617-19.

3400 Jacques Dupont, "L'exemple de l'intendant débrouillard (Lc 16)," *AsSeign* N.S. 56 (1974): 67-78.

3401 L. J. Topel, "On the Injustice of the Unjust Steward: Lk 16:1-13," *CBQ* 35 (1975): 216-27.

3402 Dan O. Via, "The Parable of the Unjust Judge: A Metaphor of the Unrealized Self," in Daniel Patte, ed., *Semiology and Parables: Exploration of the Possibilities Offered by Structuralism for Exegesis*. Pittsburgh: Pickwick Press, 1976. Pp. 1-32.

3403 J. P. Molina, "Luc 16:1 à 13: l'injustice Mamon," *ÉTR* 53 (1978): 311-75.

3404 G. Barth, "The Dishonest Steward and His Lord: Reflections on Luke 16:1-13," in D. Y. Hadidian, ed., *From Faith to Faith* (festschrift for Donald G. Miller). Pittsburgh: Pickwick Press, 1979. Pp. 65-73.

3405 Walther Bindemann, "Die Parabel vom ungerechten Richter," in Joachim Rogge, et al., eds., *Theologische Versuche*. #13. Berlin: Evangelisches Verlagsanstalt Berlin, 1983. Pp. 91-97.

3406 K.-G. Essig, "Anmerkungen zur Bildebene des Gleichnisses vom ungerechten Verwalter," in L. Schottroff and W. Schottroff, eds., *Die Auslegung Gottes durch Jesus* (festschrift for H. Braun). Mainz: N.p., 1983. Pp. 116-41.

3407 A. Fossion, "Tromper l'argent trompeur: Lecture structurale de la parabole du gérant habile (Luc 16,1-9)," *FT* 13 (1983): 342-60.

3408 Bernard Brandon Scott, "A Master's Praise: Luke 16:1-8," *Bib* 64 (1983): 173-88.

3409 Camille Focant, "Tromper le Mamon d'iniquité (Lc 16:1-13)," in Françios Refoulé, ed., *à cause de l'Evangile: Etudes sur les synoptiques et les Actes* (festschrift for Jacques Dupont). Paris: Cerf, 1985. Pp. 547-69.

3410 Dennis J. Ireland, "A History of Recent Interpretation of the Parable of the Unjust Steward," *WTJ* 51 (1989): 293-318.

3411 John S. Kloppenborg, "The Dishonoured Master (Luke 16:1-8a)," *Bib* 70/4 (1989): 474-95.

3412 William R. G. Loader, "Jesus and the Rogue in Luke 16:1-8a: The Parable of the Unjust Steward," *RB* 96 (1989): 518-32.

3413 Stanley E. Porter, "The Parable of the Unjust Steward: Irony is the Key," in David J. A. Clines, et al., eds., *The Bible in Three Dimensions: Essays in Celebration of Forty Years of Biblical Studies in the University of Sheffield*. Sheffield: JSOT Press, 1990. Pp. 127-53.

3414 C. S. Mann, "Unjust Steward or Prudent Manager?" *ET* 102 (1990-1991): 234-35.

3415 Douglas M. Parrott, "The Dishonest Steward and Luke's Special Parable Collection," *NTS* 37 (1991): 499-515.

3416 Mary Ann Beavis, "Ancient Slavery as an Interpretive Context for the New Testament Servant Parables with Special Reference to the Unjust Steward," *JBL* 111 (1992): 37-54.

3417   D. J. Ireland, *Stewardship and the Kingdom of God. An Historical, Exegetical, and Contextual Study of the Parable of the Unjust Steward in Luke 16:1-13.* NovtSupp 70. Leiden: E. J. Brill, 1992.

parable, wedding
3418   Dan O. Via, "The Relationship of Form to Content in the Parable: The Wedding Feast," *Int* 25 (1971): 171-84.

3419   Erhardt Güttgemanns, "Narrative Analyse Synoptischer Texte," *LB* 25/26 (1973): 50-73.

3420   Timothy L. Noël, "The Parable of the Wedding Guest: A Narrative-Critical Interpretation," *PRS* 16 (1989): 17-27.

parable, wicked husbandmen
3421   John Dominic Crossan, "The Parable of the Wicked Husbandmen," *JBL* 90/4 (1971): 451-65.

3422   J. A. T. Robinson, "The Parable of the Wicked Husbandmen: A Test of Synoptic Relationships," *NTS* 21 (1974-1975): 443-61.

3423   Klyne B. Snodgrass, "The Parable of the Wicked Husbandmen: Is the Gospel of Thomas Version the Original?" *NTS* 21 (1974-1975): 142-44.

parable, widow and unjust judge
3424   H. G. Meecham, "The Parable of the Unjust Judge," *ET* 57 (1945-1946): 300-307.

3425   C. E. B. Cranfield, "The Parable of the Unjust Judge and the Eschatology of Luke-Acts," *SJT* 16 (1963): 297-301.

3426   J. Duncan M. Derrett, "Law in the New Testament: The Parable of the Unjust Judge," *NTS* 18 (1971-1972): 178-91.

3427   A. George, "La parabole du juge qui fait attendre le jugement (Lc 18)," *AsSeign* N.S. 60 (1975): 68-79.

3428   Dan O. Via, "The Parable of the Unjust Judge: A Metaphor of the Unrealized Self," in Daniel Patte, ed., *Semiology and Parables: Exploration of the Possibilities Offered by Structuralism for Exegesis.* Pittsburgh: Pickwick Press, 1976. Pp. 1-32.

3429 E. D. Freed, "The Parable of the Judge and the Widow," *NTS* 33 (1987): 38-60.

3430 Porcile Santiso, Maria Teresa, and Angelica Ferreira, "The Parable of the Importunate Widow," in Samuel Amirtham, ed., *Stories Make People: Examples of Theological Work in Community.* Geneva: WCC Publications, 1989. Pp. 75-82.

3431 John Mark Hicks, "The Parable of the Persistent Widow," *RQ* 33/4 (1991): 209-23.

parousia
3432 C. L. Holman, "The Idea of an Imminent Parousia in the Synoptic Gospels," *SBT* 3 (1973): 15-31.

3433 R. H. Hiers, "The Problem of the Delay of the Parousia in Luke-Acts," *NTS* 20 (1973-1974): 145-55.

3434 Gerhard Schneider, *Parusiegleichnisse im Lukas-Evangelium.* Stuttgart: Katholisches Bibelwerk, 1975.

3435 Henry G. Waterman, "The Sources of Paul's Teaching on the Second Coming of Christ in 1 and 2 Thessalonians," *JETS* 18/2 (1975): 105-13.

3436 Richard J. Bauckham, "Synoptic Parousia Parables and the Apocalypse," *NTS* 23 (1976-1977): 162-76.

3437 George R. Beasley-Murray, "The Parousia in Mark," *RevExp* 75/4 (1978): 565-81.

3438 Alessandro Sacchi, "Pazienza di Dio e Ritardo Della Parousia," *RBib* 36 (1988): 299-327.

passion
3439 A. M. Perry, "Luke's Disputed Passion-Source," *ET* 46 (1934-1935): 256-60.

3440 E. Osty, "Les points de contact entre le récit de la Passion dans saint Luc et saint Jean," *RechSR* 39 (1951): 146-54.

3441 G. Rau, "Das Volk in der lukanischen Passionsgeschichte, eine Konjektur zu Lc 23,13," *ZNW* 56 (1965): 41-51.

3442 André Feuillet, "La coupe et le baptême de la Passion (Mc x,35-40; cf. Mt xx,20-23; Lc xii,50)," *RB* 74 (1967): 356-91.

3443 J. Blinzler, "Passionsgeschehen und Passionsbericht des Lukasevangeliums," *BK* 24 (1969): 1-4.

3444 A. Stöger, "Eigenart und Botschaft der lukanischen Passionsgeschichte," *BK* 24 (1969): 4-8.

3445 R. S. Barbour, "Gethsemane in the Tradition of the Passion," *NTS* 16 (1969-1970): 231-51.

3446 H. Grosch, " 'Andere hat er gerettet . . . ' Exegetische und didaktische Besinnung uber zwei lukanische Passionstexte," *EvErz* 22 (1970): 233-47.

3447 A. George, "Le sens de la mort de Jésus pour Luc," *RB* 80 (1973): 186-217.

3448 F. Janssen, "Die synoptischen Passionsberichte: Ihre theologische Konzeption und literarische Komposition," *BibL* 14 (1973): 40-57.

3449 P. W. Walaskay, "The Trial and Death of Jesus in the Gospel of Luke," *JBL* 94 (1975): 81-93.

3450 H. Klein, "Die lukanisch-johanneische Passionstradition," *ZNW* 67 (1976): 155-86.

3451 André Feuillet, *L'agonie de Gethsémani: Enquête exégétique et théologique suivie d'une étude du 'Mystère de Jésus' de Pascal.* Paris: Gabalda, 1977.

3452 O. Genest, *Le Christ de la passion: Perspective structurale. Analyse de Mc 14,53-15,47, des parallèles bibliques et extra-bibliques.* Toumai: Desclée, 1978.

3453 Gerhard Schneider, "Die theologische Sicht des Todes Jesu in den Kreuzigungsberichten der Evangelien," *TPQ* 126 (1978): 14-22.

3454 C. A. Blaising, "Gethsemane: A Prayer of Faith," *JETS* 22 (1979): 333-43.

3455 H. Gollwitzer, *Jesu Tod und Auferstehung nach dem Bericht des Lukas.* 6th ed. Münich: Kaiser, 1979.

3456 G. R. Osborne, "Redactional Trajectories in the Crucifixion Narrative," *EQ* 51 (1979): 80-96.

3457 D. M. Stanley, *Jesus in Gethsemane: The Early Church Reflects on the Suffering of Jesus.* New York: Paulist, 1980.

3458 M. Cambe, "Les récits de la passion en relation avec différents textes du IIe siècle," *FV* 81 (1982): 12-24.

3459 G. Jankowski, "Passah und Passion. Die Einleitung der Passiongeschichte bei Lukas," *TexteK* 13 (1982): 40-60.

3460 V. Monsarrat, "Le récit de la Passion: un enseignement pour le disciple fidèle. Luc 22-23," *FV* 81 (1982): 40-47.

3461 Walter Radl, "Der Tod Jesu in der Darstellung der Evangelien," *TGl* 72 (1982): 432-44.

3462 R. J. Cassidy, "Luke's Audience, the Chief Priests, and the Motives for Jesus' Death," in R. J. Cassidy and P. J. Scharper, eds., *Political Issues in Luke-Acts.* Maryknoll NY: Orbis, 1983. Pp. 146-67.

3463 B. S. Finnel, "The Significance of the Passion in Luke," doctoral dissertation, Baylor University, Waco TX, 1983.

3464 Michael M. Goulder, "From Ministry to Passion in John and Luke," *NTS* 29 (1983): 561-68.

3465 É. Trocmé, "The Passion Narrative in Luke," in *The Passion as Liturgy: A Study in the Origin of the Passion Narratives in the Four Gospels.* London: SCM, 1983. Pp. 27-37.

3466 E. Jane Via, "According to Luke: Who Put Jesus to Death?" in R. J. Cassidy and P. J. Scharper, eds., *Political Issues in Luke-Acts.* Maryknoll NY: Orbis Books, 1983. Pp. 122-45.

3467 Vittorio Fusco, "La morte del Messia," in Giovanni Boggio, et al., eds., *Gesù e la sua morte.* Brescia: Paideia, 1984. Pp. 51-73.

3468   H. Hendrickx, *The Passion Narratives of the Synoptic Gospels.*
        Rev. ed. Studies in the Synoptic Gospels. San Francisco: Harper &
        Row, 1984.

3469   W. Schenk, "Der derzeitige Stand der Auslegung der
        Passionsgeschichte," *EvErz* 36 (1984): 527-43.

3470   Robert J. Karris, *Luke: Artist and Theologian—Luke's Passion
        Account as Literature.* New York: Paulist, 1985.

3471   Jerome H. Neyrey, *The Passion according to Luke: A Redaction
        Study of Luke's Soteriology.* New York: Paulist, 1985.

3472   J. Ponthot, "Vers l'historicisation lucanienne de la séquence
        pascale," in *à cause de l'Évangile: Études sur les synoptiques et
        les Actes* (festschrift for Jacques Dupont). Paris: Cerf, 1985. Pp.
        643-54.

3473   P. Ricoeur, "Le récit interprétatif Exégèse et théologie dans les
        récits de la passion," *RechSR* 73 (1985): 17-38.

3474   Raymond E. Brown, "The Passion According to Luke," *Worship*
        60/1 (1986): 2-9.

3475   Lloyd Gaston, "Anti-Judaism and the Passion Narrative in Luke
        and Acts," in P. Richardson and D. Granskou, eds., *Anti-Judaism
        in Early Christianity: 1. Paul and the Gospels.* Waterloo: Wilfrid
        Laurier University Press, 1986. Pp. 127-53.

3476   J. T. Pawlikowski, "The Trial and Death of Jesus: Reflections in
        Light of an Undersranding of Judaism," *CS* 25 (1986): 79-94.

3477   John M. Perry, "The Three Days in the Synoptic Passion
        Predictions," *CBQ* 48/4 (1986): 637-54.

3478   Joseph B. Tyson, *The Death of Jesus in Luke-Acts.* Columbia:
        University of South Carolina Press, 1986.

3479   Marion L. Soards, *The Passion According to Luke: The Special
        Material of Luke 22.* Sheffield: JSOT Press, 1987.

3480   John Dominic Crossan, *The Cross That Spoke. The Origins of the
        Passion Narrative.* San Francisco: Harper & Row, 1988.

3481   Marion L. Soards, "A Literary Analysis of the Origin and Purpose of Luke's Account of the Mockery of Jesus," in Earl Richard, ed., *New Views on Luke and Acts*. Collegeville MN: Liturgical Press, 1990. Pp. 86-93.

3482   J. Bradley Chance, "The Jewish People and the Death of Jesus in Luke-Acts: Some Implications of an Inconsistent Narrative Role," *SBLSP* 21 (1991): 50-81.

passion narrative
3483   Harold Reed, "The Narrative of Christ's Passion in Mark and Luke," doctoral dissertation, Southern Baptist Theological Seminary, Louisville KY, 1929.

3484   George D. Kilpatrick, "A Theme of the Lucan Passion Story and Luke XXIII.47," *JTS* 43 (1942): 34-36.

3485   Richard G. Waggener, "The Passion Predictions of Christ according to Luke: A Study in Luke's Use of the Prediction Sayings of Christ with Conclusions about Luke's Christology in the Light of his Use of These Sayings," master's thesis, Southern Theological Seminary, Louisville KY, 1959.

3486   Ivor Buse, "St. John and the Passion Narratives of St. Matthew and St. Luke," *NTS* 7 (1960-1961): 65-76.

3487   J. L. Blevins, "The Passion Narrative," *RevExp* 64 (1967): 513-22.

3488   J. F. A. Sawyer, "Why is a Solar Eclipse Mentioned in the Passion Narrative (Luke xxiii.44-45)?" *JTS* 23 (1972): 124-28.

3489   R. H. Smith, "Paradise Today: Luke's Passion Narrative," *CThM*3 (1976): 323-36.

3490   W. A. Smalley, "Translating Luke's Passion Story from the TEV," *BT* 28 (1977): 231-35.

3491   B. E. Beck, " 'Imitatio Christi' and the Lucan Passion Narrative," in W. Horbury and B. McNeil, eds., *Suffering and Martyrdom in the New Testament* (festschrift for G. M. Styler). Cambridge: University Press, 1981. Pp. 28-47.

3492   Lloyd Gaston, "Anti-Judaism and the Passion Narrative in Luke and Acts," in P. Richardson and D. Granskou, eds., *Anti-Judaism in Early Christianity: 1. Paul and the Gospels*. Waterloo: Wilfrid Laurier University Press, 1986. Pp. 127-53.

Passover

3493   C. K. Barrett, "Luke XXII,15: To Eat the Passover," *JTS* 9 (1958): 305-307.

3494   G. J. Bahr, "The Seder of Passover and the Eucharistic Words," *NovT* 12 (1970): 181-202.

3495   F. Chenderlin, "Distributed Observance of the Passover: A Preliminary Test of the Hypothesis," *Bib* 57 (1976): 1-24.

3496   H. Schürmann, *Jesu Abschiedsrede, Lk 22,21-29: III. Teil einer quellenkritischen Untersuchung des lukanischen Abendmahlsberichtes, Lk 22,7-38*. 2nd ed. Münster: Aschendorff, 1977.

3497   H. Schürmann, *Der Paschamahlbericht Lk 22,(7-14) 15-18: Erster Teil einer quellenkritischen Untersuchung des lukanischen Abendmahlsberichtes 22,7-38*. 3rd ed. Münster: Aschendorff, 1980.

3498   S. Brock, "Passover, Annunciation and Epiclesis: Some Remarks on the Term *Aggen* in the Syriac Versions of Luke 1:35," *NovT* 24 (1982): 222-33.

3499   Arthur G. Arnott, " 'The First Day of the Unleavened . . . ' Mt 26.17, Mk 14.12, Lk 22.7," *BT* 35 (1984): 235-38.

3500   Joel B. Green, "Preparation for Passover: A Question of Redactional Technique," *NovT* 29 (1987): 305-19.

Paul

3501   A. W. Argyle, "Parallels between the Pauline Epistles and Q," *ET* 60 (1948-1949): 318-20.

3502   W. Argyle, "St. Paul and the Mission of the Seventy," *JTS* 1 (1950): 63.

3503   Otto Bauernfeind, "Zur Erage nach der Entscheidung zwischen Paulus und Lukas," *ZST* 23 (1954): 59-88.

3504 D. R. Adams, "The Suffering of Paul and the Dynamics of Luke-Acts," doctoral dissertation, Yale University, New Haven CT, 1979.

3505 William Baird, "Ascension and Resurrection: An Intersection of Luke and Paul," in W. E. March, ed., *Texts and Testaments* (festschrift for S. D. Currie). San Antonio TX: Trinity University Press, 1980. Pp. 3-18.

3506 J.-W. Taeger, "Paulus und Lukas über den Menschen," *ZNW* 71 (1980): 96-108.

3507 S. Dockx, "Luc a-t-il été le compagnon d'apostolat de Paul?" *NRT* 103 (1981): 385-400.

3508 Michael D. Goulder, "Did Luke Know Any of the Pauline Letters?" *PRS* 13 (1986): 97-112.

3509 Don Jackson, "Luke and Paul: A Theology of One Spirit from Two Perspectives," *JETS* 32 (1989): 335-44.

3510 C.-J. Thornton, *Der Zeuge des Zeugen: Lukas als Historiker der Paulusreisen.* WUNT #56. Tübingen: mOHR-sIEBECK, 1991.

Peter

3511 W. J. P. Boyd, "Peter's Denials—Mark 14:68, Luke 22:57," *ET* 67 (1955-1956): 341.

3512 R. Annand, " 'He Was Seen of Cephas': A Suggestion about the First Resurrection Appearance to Peter," *SJT* 11 (1958): 180-87.

3513 H. Schürmann, "Die Verheissung an Simon Petrus. Auslegung von Luke 5:1-11," *BibL* 5 (1964): 18-24.

3514 K. Zillessen, "Das Schiffdes Petrus und die Gefährten vom andern Schiff (Lc 5,1-11)," *ZNW* 57 (1966): 137-39.

3515 Günter Klein, "Die Berufung des Petrus," *ZNW* 58 (1967): 1-44.

3516 H. Schürmann, "La promesse à Simon-Pierre: Lc 5,1-11," *AsSeign* 36 (1974): 63-70.

3517 Dietfried Gewalt, "Das 'Petrusbild' der lukanischen Schriften als Problem einer ganzheitlichen Exegese," *LB* 34 (1975): 1-22.

3518 A. Viard, "La Parole de Dieu et la mission de Pierre," *EV* 87 (1977): 8.

3519 N. Walter, "Die Verleugnung des Petrus," *TheoV* 8 (1977): 45-61.

3520 Rudolf Pesch, *Simon-Petrus: Geschichte und geschichtliche Bedeutung des ersten Jüngers Jesu Christi*. Päpste und Papsttum #15. Stuttgart: Hiersemann, 1980.

3521 Samuel O. Abogunrin, "The 3 Variant Accounts of Peter's Call: Critical, Theological Examination of the Texts," *NTS* 31 (1985): 587-602.

3522 Claude Coulot, "Les figures du maître et de ses disciples dans les premières communautés chrétiennes," *RevSR* 59/1 (1985): 1-11.

3523 Raymond E. Brown, et al., eds., *Peter in the New Testament*. Minneapolis MN: Augsburg, 1986.

3524 G. Claudel, *La confession de Pierre: Trajectoire d'une péricope évangélique*. Paris: Gabalda, 1988.

3525 N. J. McEleney, "Peter's Denials—How Many? To Whom?" *CBQ* 52 (1990): 467-72.

Pharisee(s)

3526 A. Colunga, "El fariseo y el publicano," *CuBí* 13 (1956): 136-38.

3527 C. J. A. Hickling, "A Tract on Jesus and the Pharisees? A Conjecture about the Redaction of Luke 16," *HeyJ* 16 (1975): 253-65.

3528 Robert L. Brawley, "The Pharisees in Luke-Acts: Luke's Address to Jews and his Irenic Purpose," doctoral dissertation, Princeton Theological Seminary, Princeton NJ, 1978.

3529 J. A. Ziesler, "Luke and the Pharisees," *NTS* 25 (1978-1979): 146-57.

3530   André Feuillet, "Le pharisien et le publicain (Luc 18:9-14). La manifestation de la miséricorde divine en Jésus Serviteur souffrant," *EV* 91 (1981): 657-65.

3531   P. Raffin, "Le pharisien et le publicain," *EV* 82 (1982): 260-61.

3532   E. Springs Steele, "Jesus's Table Fellowship with Pharisees: An Editorial Analysis of Luke 7:36-50, 11:37-54, and 14:1-24," doctoral dissertation, University of Notre Dame, Notre Dame IN, 1982.

3533   John J. Kilgallen, "John the Baptist, the Sinful Woman and the Pharisee," *JBL* 104/4 (1985): 675-79.

3534   Jack T. Sanders, "The Pharisees in Luke-Acts," in D. E. Groh and Robert Jewett, eds., *The Living Text* (festschrift for E. W. Saunders). Lanham MD: University Press of America, 1985. Pp. 141-88.

3535   John G. Strelan, "The Pharisee Lurking: Reflections on Luke 18:9-14," *LTJ* 20/2-3 (1986): 116-20.

3536   R. Krüger, "El desenmascaramiento de un despreciador prestigioso: Lectura semiótica de la parábola del fariseo y del publicano. Lucas 18,9-14," *RevB* 49 (1987): 155-67.

3537   B. van Iersel, "De Farizeeër en de tollenaar (Lc 18,9-14)," in B. van Iersel, et al., eds., *Parabelverhalen in Lucas: Van semiotiek naar pragmatiek*. TFT-Studies #8. Tilburg: University Press, 1987. Pp. 194-216.

3538   Leif E. Vaage, "The Woes in Q (and Matthew and Luke): Deciphering the Rhetoric of Criticism," *SBLSP* 18 (1988): 582-607.

3539   David R. Gowler, "A Socio-Narratological Character Analysis of the Pharisees in Luke-Acts," doctoral dissertation, Southern Baptist Theological Seminary, Louisville KY, 1989.

3540   Agnès Gueuret, "Le pharisien et le publicain et son contexte," in Jean Delorme, ed., *Les paraboles évangéliques: perspectives nouvelles*. Paris: Cerf, 1989. Pp. 289-307.

3541   Jacques Schlosser, "Le pharisien et le publicain (Lc 18,9-14)," in Jean Delorme, ed., *Les paraboles évangéliques: perspectives nouvelles*. Paris: Cerf, 1989. Pp. 271-88.

3542   David R. Gowler, *Host, Guest, Enemy and Friend: Portraits of the Pharisees in Luke and Acts*. New York: Lang, 1991.

politics

3543   J.-Y. Thériault, "Les dimensions sociales, économiques et politiques dans l'oeuvre de Luc," *SE* 26 (1974): 205-31.

3544   G. Girardet, *Il vangelo della liberazione: Lettura politica di Luca*. Torino: Claudiana, 1975.

3545   R. J. Cassidy and P. J. Scharper, eds., *Jesus, Politics, and Society: A Study of Luke's Gospel*. Maryknoll NY: Orbis, 1978.

3546   R. Barraclough, "A Re-assessment of Luke's Political Perspective," *RTR* 38 (1979): 10-18.

3547   R. J. Cassidy and P. J. Scharper, eds., *Political Issues in Luke-Acts*. Maryknoll NY: Orbis, 1983.

3548   Robert F. O'Toole, "Luke's Position on Politics and Society in Luke-Acts," in R. J. Cassidy and P. J. Scharper, eds., *Political Issues in Luke-Acts*. Maryknoll NY: Orbis Books, 1983. Pp. 1-17.

3549   P. W. Walaskay, *"And So We Came to Rome": The Political Perspective of St. Luke*. SNTSMS #49. Cambridge: University Press, 1983.

3550   Frederick W. Danker, "Politics of the New Age According to St. Luke," *CThM* 12 (1985): 338-45.

3551   P. F. Esler, *Community and Gospel in Luke-Acts: The Social and Political Motivations of Lukan Theology*. Cambridge: University Press, 1987.

3552   David L. Balch, "Comments on the Genre and a Political Theme of Luke-Acts: A Preliminary Comparison of Two Hellenistic Historians," *SBLSP* 19 (1989): 343-61.

3553 Lucien Legrand, "The Angel Gabriel and Politics: Messianism and Christology," *ITS* 26 (1989): 1-21.

possessions
3554 Lloyd E. Batson, "A Study of Jesus' Teachings on Possession as Presented in the Gospel of Luke," doctoral dissertation, Southern Baptist Theological Seminary, Louisville KY, 1957.

3555 J. Gillman, *Possessions and the Life of Faith: A Reading of Luke-Acts*. Collegeville MN: Liturgical Press, 1991.

poverty
3556 W. P. Huie, "The Poverty of Abundance. From Text to Sermon on Luke 16:19-31," *Int* 22 (1968): 403-20.

3557 H. Klein, *Barmherzigkeit gegenüber den Elenden und Geächteten: Studien zur Botschaft des lukanischen Sondergutes*. Biblisch-theologische Studien #10. Neukirchen-Vluyn: Neukirchener Verlag, 1987.

prayer
3558 P. T. O'Brien, "Prayer in Luke-Acts," *TynB* 24 (1973): 111-27.

3559 S. S. Smalley, "Spirit, Kingdom, and Prayer in Luke-Acts," *NovT* 15 (1973): 59-71.

3560 M. Vellanickal, "Prayer-Experience in the Gospel of Luke," *BB* 2 (1976): 23-43.

3561 Allison A. Trites, "Some Aspects of Prayers in Luke-Acts," *SBLSP* 7 (1977): 59-78.

3562 J. Ashton, "Our Father," *Way* 18 (1978): 83-91.

3563 Allison A. Trites, "The Prayer Motif in Luke-Acts," in Charles H. Talbert, ed., *Perspectives on Luke-Acts*. Macon GA: Mercer University Press, 1978. Pp. 168-86.

3564 C. A. Blaising, "Gethsemane: A Prayer of Faith," *JETS* 22 (1979): 333-43.

3565 P. Edmonds, "The Lucan 'Our Father': A Summary of Luke's Teaching on Prayer?" *ET* 91 (1979-1980): 140-43.

3566 B. Buby, "The Biblical Prayer of Mary," *RevRel* 39 (1980): 577-81.

3567 C. M. Fuhrman, "A Redactional Study of Prayer in the Gospel of Luke," doctoral dissertation, Southwestern Baptist Theological Seminary, Fort Worth TX, 1981.

3568 S. A. Panimolle, "Gesù modello e maestro di preghiera, nel evangelo secondo Luca," *ParSpirV* 3 (1981): 122-39.

3569 R. F. Collins, " 'Lord, Teach Us to Pray': A Reflection on the Prayer of Petition," *LouvS* 10 (1984-1985): 354-71.

3570 Steven F. Plymale, "The Prayer Texts of Luke-Acts," doctoral dissertation, Northwestern University, Evanston IL, 1986.

3571 Christopher M. Tuckett,"Q, Prayer, and the Kingdom," *JTS* 40 (1989): 367-76.

3572 S. F. Plymale, *The Prayer Texts of Luke-Acts.* New York: Lang, 1991.

3573 D. M. Crump, *Jesus the Intercessor. Prayer and Christology in Luke-Acts.* WUNT #49. Tübingen: Mohr-Siebeck, 1992.

prayer, Lord's
3574 T. W. Manson, "The Lord's Prayer," *BJRL* 38 (1955-1956): 99-113, 436-48.

3575 Ernst Bammel, "A New Text of the Lord's Prayer," *ET* 73 (1961-1962): 54.

3576 Gerhard Schneider, "Die Bitte um das Kommen des Geistes im lukanischen Vaterunser," in Wolfgang Schrage, eds., *Studien zum Text und zur Ethik des Neuen Testaments* (festschrift for Heinrich Greeven). New York: de Gruyter, 1986. Pp. 344-73.

3577 J. C. De Moor, "The Reconstuction of the Aramaic Original of the Lord's Prayer," in P. Van der Meer and J. C. De Moor, eds., *The Structural Analysis of Biblical and Canaanite Poetry.* Sheffield: JSOT Press, 1988. Pp. 397-422.

3578   Robert J. Miller, "The Lord's Prayer and Other Items from the
        Sermon on the Mount," *Forum* 5 (1989): 177-86.

3579   D. Baumgardt, "Kaddish and the Lord's Prayer," *JewBibQ* 19
        (1991): 164-69.

3580   N. Ayo, *The Lord's Prayer: A Survey Theological and Literary*.
        Notre Dame IN: University Press, 1992.

preface/prologue
3581   P. Alfaric, "Les Prologues de Luc," *RHR* 115 (1937): 37-52.

3582   B. Sussarellu, "De praevia sanctificatione Praecursoris," *SBFLA*
        3 (1952-1953): 37-110.

3583   W. C. van Unnik, "Remarks on the Purpose of Luke's Historical
        Writing (Luke 1:1-4)," *NedTT* 9 (1955): 323-31.

3584   D. E. Nineham, "Eyewitness Testimony and the Gospel
        Tradition," *JTS* 9 (1958): 13-25, 243-52.

3585   J. Bauer, "*Polloi* Lk 1,1," *NovT* 4 (1960-1961): 263-66.

3586   H. Schürmann, "Evangelienschrift und kirchliche Unterweisung:
        Die repräsentative Funktion der Schrift nach Lk 1,1-4," in E.
        Kleineidam and H. Schürmann, eds., *Miscellanea Erfordiana*.
        Leipzig: St. Benno-Verlag, 1962. Pp. 48-73.

3587   Günter Klein, "Lukas 1,1-4 als theologisches Programm," in E.
        Dinkler, ed., *Zeit und Geschichte* (festschrift for Rudolf Bultmann).
        Tübingen: Mohr, 1964. Pp. 193-216.

3588   J. H. Davies, "The Lucan Prologue (1-3): An Attempt at Objective
        Redaction Criticism," *StudE* 4 (1968): 78-85.

3589   John M. Gibbs, "Mk 1,1-15, Mt 1,1-4,16, Lk 1,1-4,30, Jn 1,1-51:
        The Gospel Prologues and Their Function," *StudE* 4 (1968):
        154-88.

3590   F. W. Goodman, "Ἐπειδήπερ πολλοὶ ἐπεχείρησαν (Luke 1,1):
        A Proposed Ementation," *StudE* 4 (1968): 205-208.

3591 M. Völkel, "Exegetische Erwägungen zum Verständnis des Begriffs κατεκσῆς im Lukanischen Prolog," *NTS* 20 (1973-1974): 289-99.

3592 I. J. Du Plessis, "Once More: The Purpose of Luke's Prologue," *NovT* 16 (1974): 259-71.

3593 Schuyler Brown, "The Prologues of Luke-Acts in Their Relation to the Purpose of the Author," *SBLSP* 5 (1975): 1-14.

3594 Franz Mussner, "Καθεξῆς im Lukasprolog," in E. Earle Ellis and Erich Grässer, eds., *Jesus und Paulus* (festschrift for W. G. Kümmel). Göttingen: Vandenhoeck, 1975. Pp. 253-55.

3595 L. C. A. Alexander, "Luke-Acts in its Contemporary Setting with Special Reference to the Prefaces (Luke 1:1-4 and Acts 1:1)," doctoral dissertation, Oxford University, UK, 1977.

3596 Jean-Daniel Dubois, "Le prologue de Luc (Luke 1:1-4)," *ÉTR* 52 (1977): 542-47.

3597 G. Menestrina, "L'incipit dell'espitola 'Ad Diognetum,' Luca 1:1-4 et Atti 1:1-2," *BibO* 19 (1977): 215-18.

3598 Schuyler Brown, "The Role of the Prologues in Determining the Purpose of Luke-Acts," in Charles H. Talbert, ed., *Perspectives on Luke-Acts.* Macon GA: Mercer University Press, 1978. Pp. 99-111.

3599 Vernon K. Robbins, "Prefaces in Greco-Roman Biography and Luke-Acts," *SBLSP* 8/2 (1978): 193-208.

3600 Roger L. Omanson, "A Note on Luke 1.1-4," *BT* 30 (1979): 446-47.

3601 R. J. Dillon, "Previewing Luke's Project from his Prologue (Luke 1:1-4)," *CBQ* 43 (1981): 205-27.

3602 Peter Fiedler, "Geschichten als Theologie und Verkündigung: Die Prologe des Matthäus- und Lukas-Evangeliums," in Rudolf Pesch, ed., *Zur Theologie der Kindheitsgeschichten: Der heutige Stand der Exegese.* Münich: Schnell, 1981. Pp. 11-26.

3603 Franz Mussner, "Die Gemeinde des Lukasprologs," *SNTU-A* 6/7 (1981-1982): 113-30.

3604 Erhardt Güttgemanns, "In welchem Sinne ist Lukas 'Historiker'? Die Beziehungen von Luk 1,1-4 und Papias zur antiken Rhetotik," *LB* 54 (1983): 9-26.

3605 Robert H. Stein, "Luke 1:1-4 and Traditionsgeschichte," *JETS* 26 (1983): 421-30.

3606 Franz Mussner, "Die Gemeinde des Lukasprologs," in William C. Weinrich, ed., *The New Testament Age.* 2 vols. Macon GA: Mercer University Press, 1984. 2:201-206.

3607 Terrance Callan, "The Preface of Luke-Acts and Historiography," *NTS* 31 (1985): 576-81.

3608 P. Gibert, "Les évangiles et l'histoire (Luc 1,1-4; Jean 20,30-31)," *LVie* 175 (1985): 19-26.

3609 Jaroslav B. Stanek, "Lukas: Theologie der Heilgeschichte," *CVia* 28/1-2 (1985): 9-31.

3610 Loveday Alexander, "Luke's Preface in the Context of Greek Preface-Writing," *NovT* 28/1 (1986): 48-74.

3611 Roland Kany, "Der Lukanische Bericht von Tod und Auferstehung Jesu aus der Sicht eines hellenistischen Romanlesers," *NovT* 28/1 (1986): 75-90.

3612 J. W. Scott, "Luke's Preface and the Synoptic Problem," doctoral dissertation, St. Andrews University, UK, 1986.

3613 Feargus O'Fearghail, "The Introduction to Luke-Acts: A Study of the Role of Lk 1,1-4,44 in the Composition of Luke's Two-Volume Work," doctoral dissertation, Pontifical Biblical Institute, Rome, 1987. 2 vols.

3614 James M. Dawsey, "The Origin of Luke's Positive Perception of the Temple," *PRS* 18 (1991): 5-22.

publicans

3615 Thomas Leary Cashwell, "The Publicans in the Synoptic Gospels," doctoral dissertation, Southern Baptist Theological Seminary, Louisville KY, 1953.

purpose

3616 N. A. Dahl, "The Purpose of Luke-Acts," in *Jesus in the Memory of the Early Church*. Minneapolis MN: Augsburg, 1976. Pp. 87-98.

3617 E. Franklin, *Christ the Lord: A Study in the Purpose and Theology of Luke-Acts*. London: SPCK, 1976.

3618 K. P. Donfried, "Attempt at Understanding the Purpose of Luke-Acts: Christology and the Salvation of the Gentiles," in R. F. Berkey and S. A. Edwards, eds., *Christological Perspectives* (festschrift for H. K. McArthur). New York: Pilgrim Press, 1982. Pp. 112-22.

3619 J. L. Houlden, "The Purpose of Luke," *JSNT* 21 (1984): 53-65.

Q

3620 F. Hüttermann, "Stand das Gleichnis vom ungerechten Verwalter in Q?" *TGl* 27 (1935): 739-42.

3621 A. W. Argyle, "Parallels between the Pauline Epistles and Q," *ET* 60 (1948-1949): 318-20.

3622 R. A. Edwards, *The Sign of Jonah: In the Theology of the Evangelists and Q*. London: SCM, 1971.

3623 E. P. Sanders, "The Overlaps of Mark and Q and the Synoptic Problem," *NTS* 19 (1972-1973): 453-65.

3624 Giuseppe Frizzi, "Carattere originale e rilevanza degli 'apostoli inviati' in Q," *RBib* 21 (1973): 401-12.

3625 F. Schulz, " 'Die Gottesherrschaft ist nahe herbeigekommen': Der kerygmatische Entwurf der Q-Gemeinde Syriens," in H. Balz and S. Schulz, eds., *Das Wort und die Wörter* (festschrift for G. Friedrich). Stuttgart: Kohlhammer, 1973. Pp. 57-68.

3626 William R. Farmer, "A Fresh Approach to Q," in Jacob Neusner, ed., *Christianity, Judaism and Other Greco-Roman Cults*. 1: *New*

Testament (festschrift for Morton Smith). Leiden: Brill, 1975.
1:39-50.

3627   R. A. Edwards, *A Theology of Q: Eschatology, Prophecy, and Wisdom.* Philadelphia: Fortress Press, 1976.

3628   Santos Sabugal, "La embajada mesiánica del Bautista. IV. La fuente (Q) de Mt y Lc," *AugR* 17 (1977): 395-424.

3629   Michael D. Goulder, "On Putting Q to the Test," *NTS* 24 (1977-1978): 218-34.

3630   Albert Fuchs, "Die Überschneidungen von Mk und 'Q' nach B. H. Streeter und E. P. Sanders und ihre wahre Bedeutung (Mk 1,1-8 par.)," in W. Haubeck and M. Bachmann, eds., *Wort in der Zeit* (festschrift for K. H. Rengstorf). Leiden: Brill, 1980. Pp. 28-81.

3631   Martin Cawley, "Health of the Eyes: Gift of the Father: In the Gospel Tradition 'Q'," *WS* 3 (1981): 41-70.

3632   Jacques Dupont, "La transmission des paroles de Jésus sur la lampe et la mesure dans Marc 4,21-25 et dans la tradition Q," in J. Delobel, ed., *Logia: Les paroles de Jésus (The Sayings of Jesus).* BETL #59. Louvain: Peeters Press, 1982. Pp. 259-94.

3633   Arland D. Jacobson, "The Literary Unity of Q," *JBL* 101 (1982): 365-89.

3634   Arland D. Jacobson, "The Literary Unity of Q: Lc 10,2-16 and Parallels as a Test Case," in J. Delobel, ed., *Logia: Les paroles de Jésus (The Sayings of Jesus).* BETL #59. Louvain: Peeters Press, 1982. Pp. 419-23.

3635   Jan Lambrecht, "Q-influence on Mark 8,34-9,1," in J. Delobel, ed., *Logia: Les paroles de Jésus (The Sayings of Jesus).* BETL #59. Louvain: Peeters Press, 1982. Pp. 277-304.

3636   David R. Catchpole, "Q and 'The Friend at Midnight'," *JTS* 34 (1983): 407-24.

3637   David R. Catchpole, "Reproof and Reconciliation in the Q Community: A Study of the Tradition History of Mt 18,15-17.21-22/Lk 17,3-4," *SNTU-A* 8 (1983): 79-90.

3638 James M. Robinson, "The Sermon on the Mount/Plain: Work Sheets for the Reconstruction of Q," *SBLSP* 13 (1983): 451-54.

3639 Ronald D. Worden, "The Q Sermon on the Mount/Plain: Variants and Reconstruction," *SBLSP* 13 (1983): 455-71.

3640 John S. Kloppenborg, "Tradition and Redaction in the Synoptic Sayings Source," *CBQ* 46 (1984): 34-62.

3641 James M. Robinson, "The Preaching of John: Work Sheets for the Reconstruction of Q 3," *SBLSP* 14 (1984): 305-46.

3642 Harry Fleddermann, "The Beginning of Q," *SBLSP* 15 (1985): 153-59.

3643 Claus P. März, "Feuer auf die Erde zu werfen, bin ich gekommen: Zum Verständnis und zur Entstehung von Lk 12,49," in Françios Refoulé, ed., *à cause de l'Evangile: Etudes sur les synoptiques et les Actes* (festschrift for Jacques Dupont). Paris: Cerf, 1985. Pp. 479-511.

3644 Dieter Zeller, "Entrückung zur Ankunft als Menschensohn (Lk 13:34f; 11:29f)," in Françios Refoulé, ed., *à cause de l'Evangile: Etudes sur les synoptiques et les Actes* (festschrift for Jacques Dupont). Paris: Cerf, 1985. Pp. 513-30.

3645 David R. Catchpole, "Jesus and the Community of Israel: The Inaugural Discourse in Q," *BJRL* 68 (1985-1986): 296-316.

3646 John S. Kloppenborg, "Blessing and Marginality: The 'Persecution Beatitude' in Q, Thomas, and Early Christianity," *Forum* 2 (1986): 36-56.

3647 David R. Catchpole, "The Law and the Prophets in Q," in G. F. Hawthorne and O. Betz, eds., *Tradition and Interpretation in the New Testament* (festschrift for E. Earle Ellis). Grand Rapids MI: Eerdmans, 1987. Pp. 95-109.

3648 Wendy J. Cotter, "The Parable of the Children in the Market-Place, Q (Lk) 7:31-35," *NovT* 29 (1987): 289-304.

3649 Harry Fleddermann, "The Q Sayings on Confessing and Denying," *SBLSP* 17 (1987): 606-16.

3650 M. Eugene Boring, "A Proposed Reconstruction of Q: 10:23-24,"
SBLSP 18 (1988): 456-71.

3651 Leif E. Vaage, "The Woes in Q (and Matthew and Luke):
Deciphering the Rhetoric of Criticism," *SBLSP* 18 (1988):
582-607.

3652 Thomas L. Brodie, "Luke 9:57-62: A Systematic Adaptation of the
Divine Challenge to Elijah (1 Kings 19)," *SBLSP* 19 (1989):
237-45.

3653 L. Cerfaux, "L'utilisation de la Source Q par Luc," in Frans
Neirynck, ed., *L'Évangile de Luc: Problèmes littéraires et
théologiques* (festschrift for Lucien Cerfaux). BETL #32. 2nd ed.
Louvain: Peeters Press, 1989. Pp. 285-93.

3654 Wendy J. Cotter, "Children Sitting in the Agora: Q (Luke)
7:31-35," *Forum* 5 (1989): 63-82.

3655 Arthur J. Dewey, "A Prophetic Pronouncement: Q 12:42-46,"
Forum 5 (1989): 99-108.

3656 John S. Kloppenborg, "The Q Sayings on Anxiety (Q 12:2-7),"
Forum 5 (1989): 83-98.

3657 Claus P. März, "Zur Vorgeschichte von Lk 12,35-48:
Beobachtungen zur Komposition der Logientradition in der
Redequelle," in Karl Kertelge, ed., *Christus bezeugen* (festschrift
for Wolfgang Trilling). Leipzig: St. Benno-Verlag, 1989. Pp.
166-78.

3658 Christopher M. Tuckett,"Q, Prayer, and the Kingdom," *JTS* 40
(1989): 367-76.

3659 Leif E. Vaage, "Composite Texts and Oral Myths: The Case of the
'Sermon' (6:20b-49)," *SBLSP* 19 (1989): 424-39.

3660 Harry Fleddermann, "The End of Q," *SBLSP* 20 (1990): 1-10.

3661 David R. Catchpole, "Ein Schaf, eine Drachme und ein Israelit: die
Botschaft Jesu in Q," in Johannes J. Degenhardt, ed., *Die Freude
an Gott: Unsere Kraft* (festschrift for Otto B. Knoch). Stuttgart:
Verlag Katholisches Bibelwerk, 1991. Pp. 89-101.

3662 David R. Catchpole, "Temple traditions in Q," in William Horbury, ed., *Templum amicitiae*. Sheffield: JSOT Press, 1991. Pp. 305-29.

3663 M. Eugene Boring, "The Synoptic Problem, 'Minor' Agreements and the Beelzebul Pericope," in F. van Segbroeck, et al., eds., *The Four Gospels 1992* (festschrift for Frans Neirynck). 3 vols. BETL #100. Louvain: Peeters Press, 1992. 1:587-619.

3664 David R. Catchpole, "The Centurion's Faith and its Function in Q," in F. van Segbroeck, et al., eds., *The Four Gospels 1992* (festschrift for Frans Neirynck). 3 vols. BETL #100. Louvain: Peeters Press, 1992. 1:517-40.

3665 Joseph A. Fitzmyer, "A Palestinian Collection of Beatitudes," in F. van Segbroeck, et al., eds., *The Four Gospels 1992* (festschrift for Frans Neirynck). 3 vols. BETL #100. Louvain: Peeters Press, 1992. 1:509-15.

3666 P. Hoffmann, "QR und der Menschensohn. Eine vorläufige Skizze," in F. van Segbroeck, et al., eds., *The Four Gospels 1992* (festschrift for Frans Neirynck). 3 vols. BETL #100. Louvain: Peeters Press, 1992. 1:421-56.

3667 Arland D. Jacobson, "Apocalyptic and the Synoptic Sayings Source Q," in F. van Segbroeck, et al., eds., *The Four Gospels 1992* (festschrift for Frans Neirynck). 3 vols. BETL #100. Louvain: Peeters Press, 1992. 1:403-19.

3668 James M. Robinson, "The Sayings Gospel Q," in F. van Segbroeck, et al., eds., *The Four Gospels 1992* (festschrift for Frans Neirynck). 3 vols. BETL #100. Louvain: Peeters Press, 1992. 1:361-88.

3669 Christopher M. Tuckett, "The Temptation Narrative in Q," in F. van Segbroeck, et al., eds., *The Four Gospels 1992* (festschrift for Frans Neirynck). 3 vols. BETL #100. Louvain: Peeters Press, 1992. 1:479-507.

3670 N. Walter, "Mk 1,1-8 und die 'agreements' von Mt 3 und Lk 3. Stand die Predigt Johannes des Täufers in Q?" in F. van Segbroeck, et al., eds., *The Four Gospels 1992* (festschrift for Frans Neirynck). 3 vols. BETL #100. Louvain: Peeters Press, 1992. 1:457-78.

3671 Dieter Zeller, "Eine weisheitliche Grundschrift in der Logienquelle?" in F. van Segbroeck, et al., eds., *The Four Gospels 1992* (festschrift for Frans Neirynck). 3 vols. BETL #100. Louvain: Peeters Press, 1992. 1:389-401.

3672 David R. Catchpole, *The Quest for Q.* Edinburgh: T. & T. Clark, 1993.

Qumran

3673 Hans Kosmala, "The Parable of the Unjust Steward in the Light of Qumran," *ASTI* 3 (1964): 114-21.

3674 R. T. Beckwith, "St. Luke, the Date of Christmas and the Priestly Courses at Qumran," *RevQ* 19 (1977): 73-94.

3675 D. R. Schwartz, "On Quirinius, John the Baptist, the Benedictus, Melchizedek, Qumran and Ephesus," *RevQ* 13 (1988): 635-46.

3676 Maurya P. Horgan and Paul J. Kobelski, "The Hodayot (1QH) and New Testament Poetry," in M. P. Horgan and P. J. Kobelski, eds., *To Touch the Text: Biblical and Related Studies in Honor of Joseph A. Fitzmyer.* New York: Crossroad, 1989. Pp. 179-93.

reconciliation

3677 J. M. Ford, "Reconciliation and Forgiveness in Luke's Gospel," in R. J. Cassidy and P. J. Scharper, eds., *Political Issues in Luke-Acts.* Maryknoll NY: Orbis Books, 1983. Pp. 80-98.

redaction

3678 Jack T. Sanders, "Tradition and Redaction in Luke xv.11-32," *NTS* 15 (1968-1969): 433-38.

3679 Jean Delorme, "Luc v.1-11: Analyse Structurale et Histoire de la Rédaction," *NTS* 18 (1971-1972): 331-50.

3680 W. Nicol, "Tradition and Redaction in Luke 21," *Neo* 7 (1973): 61-71.

3681   Jerome H. Neyrey, "The Absence of Jesus' Emotions—The Lucan Redaction of Lk 22,39-49," *Bib* 61/2 (1980): 153-71.

3682   Jerome H. Neyrey, *The Passion according to Luke: A Redaction Study of Luke's Soteriology*. New York: Paulist, 1985.

remarriage/divorce
3683   H. G. Coiner, "Those 'Divorce and Remarriage' Passages (Matt. 5:32; 19;9; 1 Cor 7:10-16), with Brief Reference to the Mark and Luke Passages," *CTM* 39 (1958): 367-84.

3684   Charles C. Ryrie, "Biblical Teaching on Divorce and Remarriage," *GTJ* 3/2 (1982): 177-92.

repentance
3685   Edward G. Mathews, "The Rich Man and Lazarus: Almsgiving and Repentance in Early Syriac Tradition," *Diakonia* 22/2 (1988-1989): 89-104.

resurrection
3686   R. Annand, " 'He Was Seen of Cephas': A Suggestion about the First Resurrection Appearance to Peter," *SJT* 11 (1958): 180-87.

3687   Raymond E. Brown, *The Virginal Conception and Bodily Resurrection of Jesus*. London: Chapman, 1973.

3688   G. R. Brunk, "The Concept of the Resurrection according to the Emmaus Account in Luke's Gospel," doctoral dissertation, Union Theological Seminary, Richmond VA, 1975.

3689   Norman Perrin, "The Resurrection Narratives in the Gospel of Luke," in *The Resurrection Narratives: A New Approach*. London: SCM, 1977. Pp. 61-79.

3690   R. J. Dillon, "Easter Revelation and Mission Program in Luke 24:46-48," in D. Durken, ed., *Sin, Salvation, and the Spirit*. Collegeville MN: Liturgical Press, 1979. Pp. 240-70.

3691   J.-M. Guillaume, *Luc interprète des anciennes traditions sur la résurrection de Jésus*. Paris: Gabalda, 1979.

3692   Robert F. O'Toole, "Luke's Understanding of Jesus' Resurrection—Ascension—Exaltation," *BTB* 9 (1979): 106-14.

3693 William Baird, "Ascension and Resurrection: An Intersection of Luke and Paul," in W. E. March, ed., *Texts and Testaments* (festschrift for S. D. Currie). San Antonio TX: Trinity University Press, 1980. Pp. 3-18.

3694 H. Gerits, "Le message pascal au tombeau (Lc 24,1-12): La résurrection selon la présentation théologique de Lc," *EstT* 8/15 (1981): 3-63.

3695 Robert F. O'Toole, "Activity of the Risen Jesus in Luke-Acts," *Bib* 62 (1981): 471-98.

3696 C. Perrot, "Emmaus oder die Begegnung mit dem Herrn," *TGeg* 26 (1983): 19-25.

3697 T. Radcliffe, "The Emmaus Story: Necessity and Freedom," *NBlack* 64 (1983): 483-93.

3698 R. H. Smith, *Easter Gospels: The Resurrection of Jesus according to the Four Gospels*. Minneapolis MN: Augsburg, 1983.

3699 H. Hendrickx, *The Resurrection Narratives of the Synoptic Gospels*. Studies in the Synoptic Gospels. Rev ed. San Francisco: Harper & Row, 1984.

3700 Frans Neirynck, "John and the Synoptics: The Empty Tomb Stories," *NTS* 30/2 (1984): 161-87.

3701 Johannes M. Nützel, "Vom Hören zum Glauben: Der Weg zum Osterglauben in der Sicht des Lukas," in Lothar Lies, ed., *Praesentia Christi* (festschrift for Johannes Betz). Düsseldorf: Patmos, 1984. Pp. 37-49.

3702 G. R. Osborne, *The Resurrection Narratives: A Redactional Study*. Grand Rapids MI: Baker, 1984.

3703 Pheme Perkins, *Resurrection: New Testament Witness and Contemporary Reflection*. Garden City NY: Doubleday, 1984.

3704 Caesarius Cavallin, "Bienheureux seras-tu—à la résurrection des justes: le macarisme de Lc 14:14," in François Refoulé, ed., *à cause de l'Evangile: Etudes sur les synoptiques et les Actes* (festschrift for Jacques Dupont). Paris: Cerf, 1985. Pp. 531-46.

3705   Jacob Kremer, "Der arme Lazarus: Lazarus, der Freund Jesu: Beobachtungen zur Beziehung zwischen Lk 16:19-31 und Joh 11:1-46," in Françios Refoulé, ed., à cause de l'Evangile: Etudes sur les synoptiques et les Actes (festschrift for Jacques Dupont). Paris: Cerf, 1985. Pp. 571-84.

3706   Frans Neirynck, "Lc 24,36-43: un récit lucanien [Jn 20:19-20; Ignatius of Antioch, Smyr 3:1-2]," in Françios Refoulé, ed., à cause de l'Evangile: Etudes sur les synoptiques et les Actes (festschrift for Jacques Dupont). Paris: Cerf, 1985. Pp. 655-80.

3707   James Swetnam, "No Sign of Jonah," Bib 66/1 (1985): 126-30.

3708   Ingo Broer, " 'Der Herr ist wahrhaft auferstanden' (Lk 24,34): Auferstehung Jesu und historisch-kritische Methode: Erwägungen zur Entstehung des Osterglaubens," in Ingo Broer and Lorenz Oberlinner, eds., Auferstehung Jesu - Auferstehung der Christen: Deutungen des Osterglaubens. Freiburg: Herder, 1986. Pp. 39-62.

3709   John J. Kilgallen, "The Sadducees and Resurrection From the Dead: Luke 20:27-40," Bib 67/4 (1986): 478-95.

3710   E. A. LaVerdiere, "The Passion-Resurrection of Jesus according to St. Luke," CS 25 (1986): 35-50.

3711   Joseph Plevnik, "The Eyewitnesses of the Risen Jesus in Luke 24," CBQ 49 (1987): 90-103.

3712   H. Rusche, "Gastfreundschaft in Emmaus," BK 42 (1987): 65-67.

rich man and Lazarus

3713   Otto Glombitza, "Der reiche Mann und der arme Lazarus," NovT 12 (1970): 166-80.

3714   E. Pax, "Der Reiche und der arme Lazarus eine Milieustudie," SBFLA 25 (1975): 254-68.

3715   F. Schnider and W. Stenger, "Die offene Tür und die unüberschreitbare Kluft. Strukturanalytische Überlegungen zum Gleichnis vom reichen Mann und armen Lazarus," NTS 25 (1978-1979): 273-83.

3716 Edward G. Mathews, "The Rich Man and Lazarus: Almsgiving and Repentance in Early Syriac Tradition," *Diakonia* 22/2 (1988-1989): 89-104.

3717 J. Hintzen, *Verkündigung und Wahrnehmung: Über das Verhältnis von Evangelium und Leser am Beispiel Lk 16,19-31 im Rahmen des lukanischen Doppelwerkes*. Frankfurt: Hain, 1991.

rich/poor
3718 T. Hoyt, "The Poor in Luke-Acts," doctoral dissertation, Duke University, Durham NC, 1975.

3719 Stanley Hauerwas, "The Politics of Charity," *Int* 31 (1977): 251-62.

3720 Luke T. Johnson, *The Literary Function of Possessions in Luke-Acts*. Missoula MT: Scholars Press, 1977.

3721 P. B. Decock, "Poverty and Riches in the Theology of Luke," in K. Nürnberger, ed., *Affluence, Poverty and the Word of God*. Durban: Lutheran Publishing House, 1978. Pp. 153-62.

3722 Robert J. Karris, "Poor and Rich: The Lukan *Sitz im Leben*," in Charles H. Talbert, ed., *Perspectives on Luke-Acts*. Macon GA: Mercer University Press, 1978. Pp. 112-25.

3723 D. B. Kraybill and D. M. Sweetland, "Possessions in Luke-Acts: A Sociological Perspective," *PRS* 10 (1983): 215-39.

3724 J. S. Galligan, "The Tension between Poverty and Possessions in the Gospel of Luke," *SpirTo* 37 (1985): 4-12.

3725 M. V. Abraham, "Good News to the Poor: Luke's Gospel," *BB* 14 (1988): 65-77.

3726 S. Hemraj, "Having Nothing as One's Own," *BB* 14 (1988): 50-64.

sabbath
3727 D. A. Carson, "Jesus and the Sabbath in the Four Gospels," in D. A. Carson, ed., *From Sabbath to Lord's Day: A Biblical, Historical and Theological Investigation*. Grand Rapids MI: Zondervan, 1982. Pp. 57-98.

3728   Joël Delobel, "Luke 6,5 in Codex Bezae: The Man Who Worked on Sabbath," in Françios Refoulé, ed., *à cause de l'Evangile: Études sur les synoptiques et les Actes* (festschrift for Jacques Dupont). Paris: Cerf, 1985. Pp. 453-77.

salvation/salvation history

3729   J. W. Drane, "Simon the Samaritan and the Lucan Concept of Salvation History," *EQ* 47 (1975): 131-37.

3730   B. Prete, "Luca teologo della 'storia della salvezza'," *PV* 27 (1982): 404-25.

3731   B. Prete, "Le epoche o i tempi della 'storia della salvezza'," *PV* 27 (1982): 426-34.

3732   Gerhard Schneider, "Der Missionsauftrag Jesu in der Darstellung der Evangelien," in Karl Kertelge, ed., *Mission im Neuen Testament*. Freiburg: Herder, 1982. Pp. 71-92.

3733   K. N. Giles, "Salvation in Lukan Theology," *RTR* 42 (1983): 10-16.

scribes

3734   P. M. Head, "Observations on Early Papyri of the Synoptic Gospels, especially on the 'Scribal Habits'," *Bib* 71/2 (1990): 240-47.

sermon on plain

3735   J. Manek, "On the Mount, On the Plain (Mt. 5:1, Lk. 6:17)," *NovT* 9 (1967): 124-31.

3736   N. J. McEleney, "The Beatitudes of the Sermon on the Mount/Plain," *CBQ* 43 (1981): 1-13.

3737   James M. Robinson, "The Sermon on the Mount/Plain: Work Sheets for the Reconstruction of Q," *SBLSP* 13 (1983): 451-54.

3738   Ronald D. Worden, "The Q Sermon on the Mount/Plain: Variants and Reconstruction," *SBLSP* 13 (1983): 455-71.

servant in
> **3739** Donald L. Jones, "The Title 'Servant' in Luke-Acts," in Charles H. Talbert, ed., *Luke-Acts: New Perspectives from the Society of Biblical Literature.* New York: Crossroad, 1984. Pp. 148-65.

> **3740** David J. Lull, "The Servant-Benefactor as a Model of Greatness," *NovT* 28/4 (1986): 289-305.

servanthood
> **3741** A. W. Swamidoss, "Diakonia as Servanthood in the Synoptics," *IJT* 32 (1983): 37-51.

Simon
> **3742** J. W. Drane, "Simon the Samaritan and the Lucan Concept of Salvation History," *EQ* 47 (1975): 131-37.

> **3743** Roger L. Omanson, "Lazarus and Simon," *BT* 40 (1989): 416-19.

sociology
> **3744** Elias R. Callahan, "Social Problems in the Gospel of Luke," doctoral dissertation, New Orleans Baptist Theological Seminary, New Orleans LA, 1938.

> **3745** J. Ernst, "Das Evangelium nach Lukas: kein soziales Evangelium," *TGl* 67 (1977): 415-21.

> **3746** Gary T. Meadows, "The Poor in Luke's Gospel: An Analysis of Lukan Emphasis on the Poor in Light of Contemporary Evangelical Social Ethics," doctoral dissertation, Grace Theological Seminary, Winona IN, 1983.

> **3747** L. Noble, "A Sociological Analysis of the Gospel of Luke," *JASA* 35 (1983): 177-80.

> **3748** Stephen C. Mott, "The Use of the Bible in Social Ethics: 2. The Use of the New Testament [2 pts.]," *Trans* 1/2 (1984): 21-26; 3 (1984): 19-26.

> **3749** B. C. P. Aymer, "A Socio-Religious Revolution: A Sociological Exegesis of the 'Poor' and 'Rich' in Luke-Acts," doctoral dissertation, Boston University, Boston MA, 1987.

3750 David R. Gowler, "Characterization in Luke: A Socio-Narratological Approach," *BibTo* 19 (1989): 54-62.

3751 David R. Gowler, "A Socio-Narratological Character Anaylsis of the Pharisees in Luke-Acts," doctoral dissertation, Southern Baptist Theological Seminary, Louisville KY, 1989.

3752 J. H. Neyrey, ed., *The Social World of Luke-Acts: Models for Interpretation.* Peabody MA: Hendrickson, 1991.

son of man
3753 E. Ashby, "The Days of the Son of Man," *ET* 67 (1955-1956): 124-25.

3754 P. Maurice Casey, "The Son of Man Problem," *ZNW* 67/3 (1976): 147-54.

3755 David R. Catchpole, "The Son of Man's Search for Faith (Luke 18:8)," *NovT* 19 (1977): 81-104.

3756 M. Sabbe, "The Son of Man Saying in Acts 7,56," in J. Kremer, ed., *Les Actes des Apôtres.* BETL #48. Louvain: University Press, 1979. Pp. 241-79.

3757 David R. Catchpole, "The Angelic Son of Man in Luke 12:8," *NovT* 2 (1982): 255-65.

3758 P. Maurice Casey, "The Jackals and the Son of Man (Matt. 8.20//Luke 9.58)," *JSNT* 23 (1985): 3-22.

3759 Dieter Zeller, "Entrückung zur Ankunft als Menschensohn (Lk 13:34f; 11:29f)," in François Refoulé, ed., *à cause de l'Evangile: Etudes sur les synoptiques et les Actes* (festschrift for Jacques Dupont). Paris: Cerf, 1985. Pp. 513-30.

3760 J. R. Donahue, "Recent Studies on the Origin of 'Son of Man' in the Gospels," *CBQ* 48 (1986): 484-98.

3761 Chrys C. Caragounis, "Kingdom of God, Son of Man and Jesus' Self-Understanding," *TynB* 40 (1989): 3-23.

3762 A. Dagron, *Aux jours du Fils de l'Homme. Essai sur le service de la parole.* Lyon: CADIR-PROFAC, 1990.

3763 B. D. Chilton, "The Son of Man: Human and Heavenly," in
      F. van Segbroeck, et al., eds., *The Four Gospels 1992* (festschrift
      for Frans Neirynck). 3 vols. BETL #100. Louvain: Peeters Press,
      1992. 1:203-18.

3764 M. D. Hooker, "The Son of Man and the Synoptic Problem," in
      F. van Segbroeck, et al., eds., *The Four Gospels 1992* (festschrift
      for Frans Neirynck). 3 vols. BETL #100. Louvain: Peeters Press,
      1992. 1:189-201.

soteriology

3765 J. Roloff, "Anfänge der Soteriologischen Deutung des Todes Jesu
      (Mk. x.45 und Lk. xxii.27)," *NTS* 19 (1972-1973): 38-64.

3766 F. Bovon, "Le salut dans les écrits de Luc. Essai," *RTP* 105
      (1973): 296-307.

3767 H. Flender, "Salut et histoire dans la théologie de Luc," *FV* 72
      (1973): 90-92.

3768 K. N. Giles, "The Community of Salvation in the Theology of St.
      Luke," doctoral dissertation, Duke University, Durham NC, 1973.

3769 L. Persson, "Theology of Conversion: A Study in the Concept of
      Repentance and Conversion in the Lukan Writings," doctoral
      dissertation, South East Asia Graduate School of Theology,
      Singapore, 1973.

3770 A. George, "L'emploi chez Luc du vocabulaire de salut," *NTS* 23
      (1976-1977): 308-20.

3771 D. Flusser, "The Crucifed One and the Jews," *Immanuel* 7 (1977):
      25-37.

3772 W. J. Larkin, "Luke's Use of the Old Testament as a Key to his
      Soteriology," *JETS* 20 (1977): 325-35.

3773 R. Swaeles, "L'évangile du salut: S. Luc (Pastorale)," *CL* 58
      (1977): 45-70.

3774 N. M. Flanagan, "The What and How of Salvation in Luke-Acts,"
      in D. Durken, ed., *Sin, Salvation, and the Spirit*. Collegeville MN:
      Liturgical Press, 1979. Pp. 203-13.

3775 J. Irik, "Lukas, evangelie voor de volken, evangelie voor Israël?"
KerkT 33 (1982): 278-90.

3776 Jack T. Sanders, "The Salvation of the Jews in Luke-Acts,"
SBLSP 12 (1982): 467-83.

3777 Robert J. Karris, "Luke's Soteriology of With-ness," *CThM* 12
(1985): 346-52.

3778 Jerome H. Neyrey, *The Passion according to Luke: A Redaction
Study of Luke's Soteriology*. New York: Paulist, 1985.

3779 G. E. Witte, "Salvation and the Law in Luke-Acts," doctoral
dissertation, Union Theological Seminary in Virginia, Richmond
VA, 1985.

3780 A. P. Athyal, "Towards a Soteriology for the Indian Society:
Guidelines from Luke-Acts," *BB* 14 (1988): 132-48.

3781 P. Pokorny, "Lukas 15,11-32 und die lukanische Soteriologie," in
Karl Kertelge, ed., *Christus bezeugen* (festschrift for Wolfgang
Trilling). Leipzig: St. Benno-Verlag, 1989. Pp. 179-92.

sources
3782 J. Vernon Bartlett, "The Sources of St. Luke's Gospel," in
William Sanday, ed., *Studies in the Synoptic Problem by Members
of the University of Oxford*. Oxford: Clarendon Press, 1911. Pp.
315-66.

3783 M. Perry, "A Judaeo-Christian Source in Luke," *JBL* 49 (1930):
181-94.

3784 A. M. Perry, "Luke's Disputed Passion-Source," *ET* 46
(1934-1935): 256-60.

3785 Pierre Benoit and M.-É. Boismard, *Synopse des quatre Évangiles
avec parallèles des apocryphes et des Pères*. Paris: Cerf, 1972.

3786 B. de Solages, *La composition des évangiles de Luc et de Matthieu
et leurs sources*. Leiden: Brill, 1973.

3787 J. J. Rourke, "The Construction with a Verb of Saying as an
Indication of Sources in Luke," *NTS* 21 (1974-1975): 421-23.

3788   Joseph B. Tyson, "The Sources of Luke: A Proposal for the
       Consultation on the Relationships of the Gospels," *SBLSP* 6
       (1976): 279-86.

3789   Franz Neirynck, "The Matthew-Luke Agreements in Matt 14:13-14
       and Lk 9:10-11 (Par. Mk 6:30-34): The Two-Source Theory Behind
       the Impasse," *ETL* 60/1 (1984): 25-44.

3790   Noel S. Donnelly, "The Gospel of Luke: The Pieties of its Sources
       and Author," doctoral dissertation, University of Edinburgh,
       Edinburgh, 1988.

3791   D. Kosch, "Q and Jesus," *BZ* 36/1 (1992): 30-38.

spirit/spirituality
3792   P. J. Bernadicou, "Luke-Acts and Contemporary Spirituality,"
       SpirTo 31 (1979): 137-48.

3793   E. Rasco, "Spirito e istituzione nell'opera lucana," *RivBib* 30
       (1982): 301-22.

3794   Odette Mainville, *L'Esprit dan l'oeuvre de Luc*. Héritage et projet
       45. Saint-Laurent: Fides, 1991.

structuralism
3795   G. Crespy, "The Parable of the Good Samaritan: An Essay in
       Structural Research," trans. John Kirby *Semeia* 2 (1974): 27-50

3796   Daniel Patte, "An Analysis of Narrative Structure and the Good
       Samaritan," *Semeia* 2 (1974): 1-26.

3797   Daniel Patte, "Structural Network in Narrative: The Good
       Samaritan," *Soundings* 58 (1975): 221-42.

3798   Stephen D. Moore, *Mark and Luke in Poststructuralist
       Perspectives*. New Haven: Yale University Press, 1992.

synoptic problem
3799   Henry L. Jackson, "The Present State of the Synoptic Problem,"
       in Henry B. Sweet, ed., *Essays on Some Biblical Questions of the
       Day*. London: Macmillan, 1909. Pp. 421-60.

3800 W. E. Addis, "The Criticism of the Hexateuch Compared with that of the Synoptic Gospels," in William Sanday, ed., *Studies in the Synoptic Problem by Members of the University of Oxford.* Oxford: Clarendon Press, 1911. Pp. 367-88.

3801 W. C. Allen, "The Book of Sayings Used by the Editor of the First Gospel," in William Sanday, ed., *Studies in the Synoptic Problem by Members of the University of Oxford.* Oxford: Clarendon Press, 1911. Pp. 235-86.

3802 John C. Hawkins, "Probabilities as to the So-Called Double Tradition of St. Matthew and St. Luke," in William Sanday, ed., *Studies in the Synoptic Problem by Members of the University of Oxford.* Oxford: Clarendon Press, 1911. Pp. 95-140.

3803 John C. Hawkins, "Three Limitations to St. Luke's Use of St. Mark's Gospel," in William Sanday, ed., *Studies in the Synoptic Problem by Members of the University of Oxford.* Oxford: Clarendon Press, 1911. Pp. 29-94.

3804 William Sanday, "The Conditions Under Which the Gospels Were Written," in William Sanday, ed., *Studies in the Synoptic Problem by Members of the University of Oxford.* Oxford: Clarendon Press, 1911. Pp. 3-28.

3805 B. H. Streeter, "The Literary Evolution of the Gospels," in William Sanday, ed., *Studies in the Synoptic Problem by Members of the University of Oxford.* Oxford: Clarendon Press, 1911. Pp. 209-28.

3806 B. H. Streeter, "On the Original Order of Q," in William Sanday, ed., *Studies in the Synoptic Problem by Members of the University of Oxford.* Oxford: Clarendon Press, 1911. Pp. 141-64.

3807 B. H. Streeter, "The Original Extent of Q," in William Sanday, ed., *Studies in the Synoptic Problem by Members of the University of Oxford.* Oxford: Clarendon Press, 1911. Pp. 185-208.

3808 B. H. Streeter, "St. Mark's Knowledge and Use of Q," in William Sanday, ed., *Studies in the Synoptic Problem by Members of the University of Oxford.* Oxford: Clarendon Press, 1911. Pp. 165-208.

3809   B. H. Streeter, "Synoptic Criticism and the Eschatological Problem," in William Sanday, ed., *Studies in the Synoptic Problem by Members of the University of Oxford*. Oxford: Clarendon Press, 1911. Pp. 425-36.

3810   N. P. Williams, "A Recent Theory of the Origin of St. Mark's Gospel," in William Sanday, ed., *Studies in the Synoptic Problem by Members of the University of Oxford*. Oxford: Clarendon Press, 1911. Pp. 389-424.

3811   H. G. Wood, "Some Characteristics of the Synoptic Writers," in F. J. Foakes Jackson, ed., *The Parting of the Roads: Studies in the Development of Judaism and Early Christianity*. London: Edward Arnold, 1912. Pp. 133-71.

3812   Paul Fiebig, "Die Mündliche Überlieferung als Quelle der Syoptiker," in Hans Windisch, ed., *Neutestamentliche Studien Georg Heinrici zu seinem 70. Geburtstag*. Leipzig: Hinrichs'sche, 1914. Pp. 79-91.

3813   Reinhold Hartstock, "Visionsberichte in den synoptischen Evangelien," in *Festgabe für D. Dr. Julius Kaftan zu seinem 70. Geburtstage*. Tübingen: Mohr, 1920. Pp. 130-45.

3814   C. A. Bernoulli, "Queleques difficultés non résolues du problème synoptique et leur interprétation psychologique," in P.-L. Counchoud, ed., *Congrès d'historie du Christianisme: Jubilé Alfred Loisy*. Paris: Rieder, 1928. 1:178-87.

3815   J. Rezevskis, "Wie haben Matthäus und Lukas den Markus benutzt?" in *Voldemaro Maldonis . . . septuagenario dedicant collegae amici discipuli*. Rīgā: Studentu Padomes Grāmatrīca, 1940. Pp. 117-34.

3816   A. W. Argyle, "Agreements between Matthew and Luke," *ET* 73 (1961-1962): 19-22.

3817   William R. Farmer, "The Two-Document Hypothesis as a Methodological Criterion in Synoptic Research," *ATR* 48 (1966): 380-96.

3818   A. W. H. Moule, "The Pattern of the Synoptists," *EQ* 43/3 (1971): 162-71.

3819   E. P. Sanders, "The Overlaps of Mark and Q and the Synoptic Problem," *NTS* 19 (1972-1973): 453-65.

3820   Frans Neirynck, "The Argument from Order and St. Luke's Transpositions," *ETL* 49 (1973): 784-815.

3821   Frans Neirynck, "La matière marcienne dans l'évangile de Luc," in Frans Neirynck, ed., *L'Évangile de Luc: Problèmes littéraires et théologiques* (festschrift for Lucien Cerfaux). BETL #32. Gembloux: Duculot, 1973. Pp. 157-201.

3822   David R. Catchpole, "The Synoptic Divorce Material as a Traditio-Historical Problem," *BJRL* 57/1 (1974): 92-127.

3823   R. Banks, *Jesus and the Law in the Synoptic Tradition.* Cambridge: University Press, 1975.

3824   E. Burrows, "The Use of Textual Theories to Explain Agreements of Matthew and Luke against Mark," in J. K. Elliott, ed. *Studies in New Testament Language and Text* (festschrift for G. D. Kilpatrick). Leiden: Brill, 1976. Pp. 87-99.

3825   R. A. Edwards, *A Theology of Q: Eschatology, Prophecy, and Wisdom.* Philadelphia: Fortress Press, 1976.

3826   Bernard Orchard, *Matthew, Luke and Mark.* The Griesbach Solution to the Synoptic Question #1. Manchester: Koinonia, 1976.

3827   R. L. Thomas, "An Investigation of the Agreements between Matthew and Luke against Mark," *JETS* 19 (1976): 103-12.

3828   Santos Sabugal, "La embajada mesiánica del Bautista. IV. La fuente (Q) de Mt y Lc," *AugR* 17 (1977): 395-424.

3829   Hans Conzelmann, "Literaturbericht zu den synoptischen Evangelien," *TR* 43 (1978): 3-51, 321-27.

3830   Albert Fuchs, "Die Behandlung der mt/lk Übereinstimmungen gegen Mk durch S. McLoughlin und ihre Bedeutung für die synoptische Frage," *SNTU-A* 3 (1978): 24-57.

3831   Albert Fuchs, "Die Überschneidungen von Mk und 'Q' nach B. H. Streeter und E. P. Sanders und ihre wahre Bedeutung (Mk 1,1-8 par.)," in W. Haubeck and M. Bachmann, eds., *Wort in der Zeit* (festschrift for K. H. Rengstorf). Leiden: Brill, 1980. Pp. 28-81.

3832   Frans Neirynck, "Deuteromarcus et les accords Matthieu-Luc," *ETL* 56 (1980): 397-408.

3833   William R. Stegner, "The Priority of Luke: An Exposition of Robert Lindsey's *Solution to the Synoptic Problem*," *BR* 27 (1982): 26-38.

3834   David R. Catchpole, "Reproof and Reconciliation in the Q Community: A Study of the Tradition History of Mt 18,15-17.21-22/Lk 17,3-4," *SNTU-A* 8 (1983): 79-90.

3835   T. Friedrichsen, "The Minor Agreements of Matthew and Luke against Mark," doctoral dissertation, University of Louvain, 1984.

3836   H. B. Green, "The Credibility of Luke's Transformation of Matthew," in C. M. Tuckett, ed., *Synoptic Studies*. Sheffield: JSOT Press, 1984. Pp. 131-55.

3837   John S. Kloppenborg, "Tradition and Redaction in the Synoptic Sayings Source," *CBQ* 46 (1984): 34-62.

3838   Richard B. Vinson, "The Significance of the Minor Agreements as an Argument against the Two-Document Hypothesis," doctoral dissertation, Duke University, Durham NC, 1984.

3839   A. W. Argyle, "Evidence for the View that St. Luke Used St. Matthew's Gospel," in Arthur J. Bellinzoni, ed., *The Two-Source Hypothesis: A Critical Appraisal*. Macon GA: Mercer University Press, 1985. Pp. 371-79.

3840   F. Wheeler, "Textual Criticism and the Synoptic Problem: A Textual Commentary on the Minor Agreements of Matthew and Luke against Mark," doctoral dissertation, Baylor University, Waco TX, 1985.

3841   David R. Catchpole, "Jesus and the Community of Israel: The Inaugural Discourse in Q," *BJRL* 68 (1985-1986): 296-316.

3842   J. W. Scott, "Luke's Preface and the Synoptic Problem," doctoral dissertation, St. Andrews University, 1986.

3843   William Baird, "Luke's Use of Matthew: Griesbach Revisited," *PJ* 40 (1987): 35-38.

3844   C. Niemand, "Studien zu den Minor Agreements der synoptischen Verklärungsperikopen: Eine Untersuchung der literarkritischen Relevanz der gemeinsamen Abweichungen des Matthäus und Lukas von Markus 9,2-10 für die synoptische Frage," doctoral dissertation, University of Linz, 1987.

3845   Bernard Orchard, "Some Reflections on the Relationship of Luke to Matthew," in E. P. Sanders, ed., *Jesus, the Gospels and the Church* (festschrift for William R. Farmer). Macon GA: Mercer University Press, 1987. Pp. 33-46.

3846   Bernard Orchard and Harold Riley, *The Order of the Synoptics: Why Three Synoptic Gospels?*. Macon GA: Mercer University Press, 1987.

3847   M. Eugene Boring, "A Proposed Reconstruction of Q: 10:23-24," *SBLSP* 18 (1988): 456-71.

3848   L. Cerfaux, "L'utilisation de la Source Q par Luc," in Frans Neirynck, ed., *L'Évangile de Luc: Problèmes littéraires et théologiques* (festschrift for Lucien Cerfaux). BETL #32. 2nd ed. Louvain: Peeters Press, 1989. Pp. 285-93.

3849   J. J. McDonnell, *Acts to Gospels: A New Testament Path*. Lanham MD: University Press of America, 1989.

3850   E. P. Sanders and M. Davies, *Studying the Synoptic Gospels*. London: SCM, 1989.

3851   Harry Fleddermann, "The End of Q," *SBLSP* 20 (1990): 1-10.

3852   Frans Neirynck, "Note on the Eschatological Discourse," in David L. Dungan, ed., *The Interrelations of the Gospels*. Louvain: Peeters Press, 1990. Pp. 77-80.

3853   Marion L. Soards, "A Literary Analysis of the Origin and Purpose
        of Luke's Account of the Mockery of Jesus," in Earl Richard, ed.,
        New Views on Luke and Acts. Collegeville MN: Liturgical Press,
        1990. Pp. 86-93.

3854   Joel B. Green, "The Death of Jesus and the Rending of the Temple
        Veil (Luke 23:44-49): A Window into Luke's Understanding of
        Jesus and the Temple," *SBLSP* 21 (1991): 543-57.

3855   Sherman E. Johnson, *The Griesbach Hypothesis and Redaction
        Criticism*. Atlanta: Scholars Press, 1991.

3856   John W. Wenham, *Redating Matthew, Mark and Luke: A Fresh
        Assault on the Synoptic Problem*. London: Hodder & Stoughton,
        1991.

3857   F. Gerald Downing, "A Paradigm Perplex: Luke, Matthew and
        Mark," *NTS* 38/1 (1992): 15-36.

3858   J. K. Elliott, "Printed Editions of Greek Synopses and their
        Influence on the Synoptic Problem," in F. van Segbroeck, et al.,
        eds., *The Four Gospels 1992* (festschrift for Frans Neirynck). 3
        vols. BETL #100. Louvain: Peeters Press, 1992. 1:337-57.

3859   M. D. Hooker, "The Son of Man and the Synoptic Problem," in
        F. van Segbroeck, et al., eds., *The Four Gospels 1992* (festschrift
        for Frans Neirynck). 3 vols. BETL #100. Louvain: Peeters Press,
        1992. 1:189-201.

3860   John S. Kloppenborg, "The Theological Stakes in the Synoptic
        Problem," in F. van Segbroeck, et al., eds., *The Four Gospels 1992*
        (festschrift for Frans Neirynck). 3 vols. BETL #100. Louvain:
        Peeters Press, 1992. 1:93-120.

3861   John W. Wenham, *Redating Matthew, Mark and Luke: A Fresh
        Assault on the Synoptic Problem*. Downers Grove: InterVarsity,
        1992.

3862   David R. Catchpole, *The Quest for Q*. Edinburgh: T. & T. Clark,
        1993.

synoptic text
3863 Erhardt Güttgemanns, "Narrative Analyse Synoptischer Texte," *LB* 25/26 (1973): 50-73.

synoptics
3864 D. B. J. Campbell, *The Synoptic Gospels*. New York: Seabury, 1969.

3865 J. A. T. Robinson, "The Parable of the Wicked Husbandmen: A Test of Synoptic Relationships," *NTS* 21 (1974-1975): 443-61.

3866 Michael Warren Baird, "Jesus's Use of the Decalogue in the Synoptics: An Exegetical Study," doctoral dissertation, Southwestern Baptist Theological Seminary, Fort Worth TX, 1982.

temple, cleansing of
3867 Ivor Buse, "The Cleansing of the Temple in the Synoptics and in John," *ET* 70 (1959-1960): 22-24.

3868 V. Eppstein, "The Historicity of the Gospel Account of the Cleansing of the Temple (Mc 11, Mt 21, Lc 19)," *ZNW* 55 (1964): 42-58.

temple, expulsion from
3869 É. Trocmé, "L'expulsion des marchands du Temple," *NTS* 15 (1968-1969): 1-22.

temptation narrative
3870 G. S. Freeman, "The Temptation," *ET* 48 (1936-1937): 45.

3871 J. M. Bover, "Diferente género literario de los evangelistas en la narración de las tentaciones de Jesus en el Desierto," in *En torno al problema de la escatología individual del Antiguo Testamento*. Madrid: Científica Medinaceli, 1955. Pp. 213-19.

3872 André Feuillet, "Le récit lucanien de la tentation (Lc 4,1-13)," in *Studia Biblica et Orientalia*. 3 vols. Rome: Pontifical Institute, 1959. 2:45-63.

3873 G. H. P. Thompson, "Called-Proved-Obedient: A Study in the Baptism and Temptation Narratives of Matthew and Luke," *JTS* 11 (1960): 1-12.

3874   Jacques Dupont, "Les Tenations de Jésus dans le Récit de Luc," *SE* 14/1 (1962): 7-29.

3875   B. Gerhardsson, *The Testing of God's Son (Matt 4:1-11, Par.): An Analysis of an Early Christian Midrash.* Lund: Gleerup, 1966.

3876   H. Swanston, "The Lukan Temptation Narrative," *JTS* 17 (1966): 71.

3877   E. Smyth-Florentin, "Jésus, le Fils du Père, vainqueur de Satan. Mt 4,1-11; Mc 1,12-15; Lc 4,1-13," *AsSeign* 14 (1973): 56-75.

3878   P. Pokorn , "The Temptation Stories and Their Intention," *NTS* 20 (1973-1974): 115-27.

3879   Wilhelm Wilkens, "Die Versuchungsgeschichte, Luk. 4,1-13, und die Komposition des Evangeliums," *TZ* 30 (1974): 262-72.

3880   D. C. Hester, "Luke 4:1-13," *Int* 31 (1977): 53-59.

3881   R. Yates, "Jesus and the Demonic in the Synoptic Gospels," *ITQ* 44 (1977): 39-57.

3882   A. Knockaert and C. Van Der Plancke, "Catéchèses de la tentation," *LV* 34 (1979): 123-53.

3883   Dieter Zeller, "Die Versuchungen Jesu in der Logienquelle," *TTZ* 89 (1980): 61-73.

3884   J. A. Davidson, "The Testing of Jesus," *ET* 94 (1982-1983): 113-15.

3885   S. C. Glickman, "The Temptation Account in Matthew and Luke," doctoral dissertation, University of Basel, 1983.

3886   F. Gerald Downing, "Cynics and Christians," *NTS* 30/4 (1984): 584-93.

3887   Albert Fuchs, "Versuchung Jesu," *SNTU-A* 9 (1984): 95-159.

3888   Elliott J. Bush, "A Fruitful Wilderness," *ChrM* 16/2 (1985): 24-26.

3889   Bill Kellermann, "A Confusion Before the Cross: Confronting
        Temptation [Pt 2 of 6]," *Soj* 14/2 (1985): 32-35.

3890   Klaus-Peter Koppen, "The Interpretation of Jesus' Temptations by
        the Early Church Fathers," *PatByzR* 8/1 (1989): 41-43.

3891   William R. Stegner, "Early Jewish Christianity—A Lost Chapter?"
        ATJ 44/2 (1989): 17-29.

3892   Christopher M. Tuckett, "The Temptation Narrative in Q," in
        F. van Segbroeck, et al., eds., *The Four Gospels 1992* (festschrift
        for Frans Neirynck). 3 vols. BETL #100. Louvain: Peeters Press,
        1992. 1:479-507.

3893   N. Walter, "Mk 1,1-8 und die 'agreements' von Mt 3 und Lk 3.
        Stand die Predigt Johannes des Täufers in Q?" in F. van
        Segbroeck, et al., eds., *The Four Gospels 1992* (festschrift for
        Frans Neirynck). 3 vols. BETL #100. Louvain: Peeters Press, 1992.
        1:457-78.

temptations
3894   Mark McVann, "Rituals of Status Transformation in Luke-Acts:
        The Case of Jesus the Prophet," in Jerome H. Neyrey, ed., *The
        Social World of Luke-Acts*. Peabody MA: Hendrickson Publishers,
        1991. Pp. 333-60.

textual criticism
3895   G. Erdmann, *Die Vorgeschichten des Lukas- und
        Matthäus-Evangeliums und Vergils vierte Ekloge*. Göttingen:
        Vandenhoeck & Ruprecht, 1932.

3896   H. Zamora, "Un interesante fragmento del evangelio Griego de
        Lucas en el Monasterio de Guadalupe," *EB* 32 (1973): 271-82.

3897   George E. Rice, "The Alteration of Luke's Tradition by the
        Textual Variants in Codex Bezae," doctoral dissertation, Case
        Western Reserve University, Cleveland OH, 1974.

3898   J. Neville Birdsall, "Rational Eclecticism and the Oldest
        Manuscripts: A Comparative Study of the Bodmer and Chester
        Beatty Papyri of the Gospel of Luke," in J. K. Elliott, ed., *Studies
        in New Testament Language and Text* (festschrift for G. D.
        Kilpatrick). Leiden: Brill, 1976. Pp. 39-51.

3899   S. Brock, "The Treatment of Greek Particles in the Old Syriac Gospels, with Special Reference to Luke," in J. K. Eliott, ed., *Studies in New Testament Language and Text* (festschrift for G. D. Kilpatrick). Leiden: Brill, 1976. Pp. 80-86.

3900   E. Burrows, "The Use of Textual Theories to Explain Agreements of Matthew and Luke against Mark," in J. K. Elliott, ed. *Studies in New Testament Language and Text* (festschrift for G. D. Kilpatrick). Leiden: Brill, 1976. Pp. 87-99.

3901   Édouard Delebecque, *Évangile de Luc: Texte traduit et annoté.* Paris: Les Belles Lettres, 1976.

3902   R. G. Bailey, "A Study of the Lukan Text of Manuscript 2533 of the Gospels," *NTS* 23 (1976-1977): 212-30.

3903   F. Schnider, *Die verlorenen Söhne: Strukturanalytische und historisch-kritische Untersuchungen zu Lk 15.* Göttingen: Vandenhoeck, 1977.

3904   Frank Stagg, "Establishing a Text for Luke-Acts," *SBLSP* 7 (1977): 45-58.

3905   Frank Stagg, "Textual Criticism for Luke-Acts," *PRS* 5 (1978): 152-65.

3906   Gordon D. Fee, "A Text-Critical Look at the Synoptic Problem," *NovT* 22/1 (1980): 12-28.

3907   George E. Rice, "The Anti-Judaic Bias of the Western Text in the Gospel of Luke," *AUSS* 18 (1980): 51-57.

3908   George E. Rice, "Some Further Examples of Anti-Judaic Bias in the Western Text of the Gospel of Luke," *AUSS* 18 (1980): 149-56.

3909   W. L. Richards, "An Examination of the Claremont Profile Method in the Gospel of Luke: A Study in Text-Critical Methodology," *NTS* 27 (1980-1981): 52-63.

3910 Elton J. Epp, "The Ascension in the Textual Tradition of Luke-Acts," in Elton J. Epps and Gordon D. Fee, eds., *New Testament Textual Criticism* (festschrift for Bruce M. Metzger). Oxford: Clarendon Press, 1981. Pp. 131-45.

3911 Gordon D. Fee, " 'One Thing Is Needful'? Luke 10:42," in Elton J. Epps and Gordon D. Fee, eds., *New Testament Textual Criticism* (festschrift for Bruce M. Metzger). Oxford: Clarendon Press, 1981. Pp. 61-75.

3912 J. M. Alexanian, "The Armenian Version of Luke and the Question of the Caesarean Text," doctoral dissertation, University of Chicago, Chicago IL, 1982.

3913 Joël Delobel, "The Sayings of Jesus in the Textual Tradition: Variant Readings in the Greek Manuscripts of the Gospels," in J. Delobel, ed., *Logia: Les paroles de Jésus (The Sayings of Jesus).* BETL #59. Louvain: Peeters Press, 1982. Pp. 431-57.

3914 John W. Wenham, " 'Why Do You Ask Me about the Good?' A Study of the Relation between Text and Source Criticism," *NTS* 28 (1982): 116-25.

3915 F. Wisse, *The Profile Method for the Classification and Evaluation of Manuscript Evidence as Applied to the Continuous Greek Text of the Gospel of Luke.* Grand Rapids MI: Eerdmans, 1982.

3916 J. K. Elliott, "The International Project to Establish a Critical Apparatus to Luke's Gospel," *NTS* 29 (1983): 531-38.

3917 Joël Delobel, "Luke 6,5 in Codex Bezae: The Man Who Worked on Sabbath," in François Refoulé, ed., *à cause de l'Evangile: Études sur les synoptiques et les Actes* (festschrift for Jacques Dupont). Paris: Cerf, 1985. Pp. 453-77.

3918 Frans Neirynck, "Papynus Egerton 2 and the Healing of the Leper," *ETL* 61 (1985): 153-60.

3919 Richard I. Pervo, "Social and Religious Aspects of the Western Text," in Dennis Groh and Robert Jewett, eds., *The Living Text* (festschrift for Ernest Saunders). Lanham MD: University Press of America, 1985. Pp. 229-41.

3920   F. Wheeler, "Textual Criticism and the Synoptic Problem: A
       Textual Commentary on the Minor Agreements of Matthew and
       Luke against Mark," doctoral dissertation, Baylor University, Waco
       TX, 1985.

3921   Homer Heater, "A Textual Note on Luke 3:33," *JSNT* 28 (1986):
       25-29.

3922   A. J. B. Higgins, "The Arabic *Diatessaron* in the New Oxford
       Edition of *The Gospel according to St. Luke in Greek*," *JTS* 37
       (1986): 415-19; 38 (1987): 135.

3923   Gerhard Schneider, "Die Bitte um das Kommen des Geistes im
       lukanischen Vaterunser," in Wolfgang Schrage, eds., *Studien zum
       Text und zur Ethik des Neuen Testaments* (festschrift for Heinrich
       Greeven). New York: de Gruyter, 1986. Pp. 344-73.

3924   J. K. Elliott, "The Arabic *Diatessaron* in the New Oxford Edition
       of the Gospel According to St. Luke in Greek: Additional Note,"
       JTS 38 (1987): 135.

3925   L. A. Jackson, "The Textual Character of the Gospels Luke and
       John in Codex," doctoral dissertation, Southwestern Baptist
       Theological Seminary, Fort Worth TX, 1987.

3926   Toshio Hirunuma, *The Praxis of New Testament Textual Studies:
       How to Use Apparatus Criticus. 1. Luke.* Osaka:
       Shin-Yaku-Kenkyu-Sya, 1989.

3927   Daniel Sheerin, "The Theotokion: Ὀ ΤΗΝ ΕΥΛΟΓΗΜΕΝΗΝ: Its
       Background in Patristic Exegesis of Luke 15:8-10 and Western
       Parallels," *VC* 43/2 (1989): 166-87.

3928   W. F. Wisselink, *Assimilation as a Criterion for the Establishment
       of the Text: A Comparative Study on the Basis of Passages from
       Matthew, Mark and Luke.* Kampen: Kok, 1989.

3929   Jacobus H. Petzer, "Eclecticism and the Text of the New
       Testament," in Patrick J. Hartin and J. H. Petzer, eds., *Text and
       Interpretation: New Approaches in the Criticism of the New
       Testament.* Leiden: Brill, 1991. Pp. 47-62.

3930 Jacobus H. Petzer, "Anti-Judaism and the Textual Problem of Luke 23:34," *FilN* 5 (1992): 199-203.

theodicy
3931 Eben Scheffler, "Suffering in Luke's Gospel," doctoral dissertation, University of Pretoria, Pretoria, South Africa, 1989.

theology
3932 A. Stöger, "Die Theologie des Lukasevangeliums," *BL* 46 (1973): 227-36.

3933 M. Wilcock, *The Savior of the World: The Message of Luke's Gospel.* Leicester: InterVarsity Press, 1979.

3934 J. Severino Croatto, "Persecución y perseverancia en la teología lucana: Un estudio sobre la 'hupomoné'," *RevBib* 42 (1980): 21-30.

3935 Eduard Schweizer, *Luke: A Challenge to Present Theology.* Atlanta GA: John Knox Press, 1982.

3936 P. Bemile, *The Magnificat within the Context and Framework of Lukan Theology: An Exegetical Theological Study of Luke 1:46-55.* Bern: Lang, 1986.

3937 P. van Staden, *The Essence of Life: A Social-Scientific Study of the Religious Symbolic Universe Reflected in the Ideology/Theology of Luke.* Pretoria: Kerk, 1991.

Thomas, Gospel of
3938 J. Neville Birdsall, "Luke 12:16ff. and the Gospel of Thomas," *JTS* 13 (1962): 332-36.

time
3939 T. Pasqualetti, "Note sulle determinazioni temporali del vangelo secondo Luca," *RivBib* 23 (1975): 399-412.

tradition
3940 Jack T. Sanders, "Tradition and Redaction in Luke xv.11-32," *NTS* 15 (1968-1969): 433-38.

transfiguration
3941   R. Silva, "El relato de la transfiguración. Problemas de crítica
        literaria y motivos teológicos en Mc 9,2-10; Mt 17,1-9; Lc
        9,28-37," *Comp* 10 (1965): 5-26.

3942   M. Coune, "Radieuse Transfiguration. Mt 17,1-9; Mc 9,2-10; Lc
        9,28-36," *AsSeign* 15 (1973): 44-84.

3943   P. R. Baldacci, "The Significance of the Transfiguration Narrative
        in the Gospel of Luke: A Redactional Investigation," doctoral
        dissertation, Marquette University, Milwaukee WI, 1974.

3944   R. H. Gause, "The Lukan Transfiguration Account (Luke 9:27-36):
        Luke's Pre-Crucifixion Presentation of the Exalted Lord in the
        Story of the Kingdom of God," doctoral dissertation, Emory
        University, Atlanta GA, 1975.

3945   F. H. Daniel, "The Transfiguration (Mark 9,2-13 and Parallels): A
        Redaction-Critical and Traditio-Historical Study," doctoral
        dissertation, Vanderbilt University, Nashville TN, 1976.

3946   Ronald Lynn Farmer, "The Significance of the Transfiguration for
        the Synoptic Accounts of the Ministry of Jesus," doctoral
        dissertation, Southwestern Baptist Theological Seminary, Fort
        Worth TX, 1982.

3947   Daniel H. Pokorny, "The Transfiguration of Our Lord," *CJ* 11
        (1985): 17-18.

3948   M. Coune, "Saint Luc et le mystère de la Transfiguration," *NRT*
        108 (1986): 3-12.

3949   Allison A. Trites, "The Transfiguration in the Theology of Luke:
        Some Redactional Links," in L. D. Hurst and N. T. Wright, eds.,
        The Glory of Christ in the New Testament (festschrift for G. B.
        Caird). Oxford: Clarendon Press, 1987. Pp. 71-81.

3950   Barbara Reid, "The Transfiguration: An Exegetical Study of Luke
        9:28-36," doctoral dissertation, Catholic University of America,
        Washington DC, 1988.

3951   Barbara Reid, "Voices and Angels: What Were They Talking About at the Transfiguration? A Redaction-Critical Study of Luke 9:28-36," *BR* 34 (1989): 19-31.

3952   Michael Rogness, "The Transfiguration of Our Lord: Luke 9:28-36," *WW* 9 (1989): 71-75.

travel narrative
3953   Bo Reicke, "Instruction and Discussion in the Travel Narrative," *StudE* 1 (1959): 206-16.

3954   P. J. Bernadicou, "The Spirituality of Luke's Travel Narrative," *RevRel* 36 (1977): 455-66.

3955   Paul Kariamadam, "Discipleship in the Lucan Journey Narrative," *Je* 16 (1980): 111-30.

3956   John W. Wenham, "Synoptic Independence and the Origin of Luke's Travel Narrative," *NTS* 27 (1980-1981): 507-15.

3957   Paul Kariamadam, "The Composition and Meaning of the Lucan Travel Narrative (Luke 9,51-19,46)," *BB* 13 (1987): 179-98.

Twelve, the
3958   Clarence B. Burke, "The Attitude of the Synoptic Writers Towards the Twelve," master's thesis, Southern Baptist Theological Seminary, Louisville KY, 1955.

violence
3959   J. Gillman, "A Temptation to Violence: The Two Swords in Luke 22:35-38," *LouvS* 9 (1982-1983): 142-53.

3960   J. M. Ford, *My Enemy Is My Guest: Jesus and Violence in Luke.* Maryknoll NY: Orbis Books, 1984.

virgin birth
3961   William H. Cook, "A Comparative Evaluation of the Place of the Virgin Birth in Twentieth-Century Literature," doctoral dissertation, Southwestern Baptist Theological Seminary, Fort Worth TX, 1960.

3962   Raymond E. Brown, *The Virginal Conception and Bodily Resurrection of Jesus.* London: Chapman, 1973.

3963   Joseph A. Fitzmyer, "The Virginal Conception of Jesus in the New Testament," *TS* 34 (1973): 541-75.

3964   Raymond E. Brown, "Luke's Description of the Virginal Conception," *TS* 35 (1974): 360-62.

3965   C. E. B. Cranfield, "Some Reflections on the Subject of the Virgin Birth," *SJT* 41 (1988): 177-89.

wealth

3966   John P. Allison, "The Concept of Wealth in Luke-Acts," doctoral dissertation, New Orleans Baptist Theological Seminary, New Orleans LA, 1960.

3967   J. Gillman, *Possessions and the Life of Faith: A Reading of Luke-Acts*. Collegeville MN: Liturgical Press, 1991.

women

3968   Horace E. Coker, "Women and the Gospel in Luke-Acts," doctoral dissertation, Southern Baptist Theological Seminary, Louisville KY, 1954.

3969   Elizabeth Waller, "The Parable of the Leaven: A Sectarian Teaching and the Inclusion of Women," *USQR* 35 (1980): 99-109.

3970   Jerome H. Neyrey, "Jesus' Address to the Women of Jerusalem: A Prophetic Judgment Oracle," *NTS* 29 (1983): 74-86.

3971   Sister Philsy, "Diakonia of Women in the New Testament," *IJT* 32 (1983): 110-18.

3972   Q. Quesnell, "The Women at Luke's Supper," in R. J. Cassidy and P. J. Scharper, eds., *Political Issues in Luke-Acts*. Maryknoll NY: Orbis, 1983. Pp. 59-79.

3973   M. Kassel, "Weibliche Aspekte im lukanischen Kindheitsevangelium," *Diakonia* 15 (1984): 391-97.

3974   Gail R. O'Day, "Singing Woman's Song: A Hermeneutic of Liberation," *CThM* 12 (1985): 203-10.

3975   R. Ryan, "The Women from Galilee and Discipleship in Luke," *BTB* 15 (1985): 56-59.

3976   E. Jane Via, "Women, the Discipleship of Service, and the Early Christian Ritual Meal in the Gospel of Luke," *SLJT* 29 (1985): 37-60.

3977   T. Bernhard, "Women's Ministry in the Church: A Lukan Perspective," *SLJT* 29 (1986): 261-63.

3978   Bernadine G. McRipley, "Racial-Ethnic Presbyterian Women: In Search for Community," *ChS* 76/4 (1986): 47-53.

3979   Priscilla Padolina, "Our Presence among the Poor," in J. S. Pobee and Bärbel von Wartenberg-Potter, eds., *New Eyes for Reading: Biblical and Theological Reflections by Women from the Third World.* Geneva: WCC Publications, 1986. Pp. 37-40.

3980   J. Kopas, "Jesus and Women: Luke's Gospel," *TT* 43 (1986-1987): 192-202.

3981   E. Jane Via, "Women in the Gospel of Luke," in U. King, ed., *Women in the World's Religions Past and Present.* New York: Paragon, 1987. Pp. 38-55.

3982   Ben Witherington, "Woman and the Third Evangelist," in B. Witherington, *Women in the Earliest Churches.* SNTS MS #58. Cambridge: University Press, 1988. Pp. 128-57.

3983   David C. Sim, "The Women Followers of Jesus: The Implications of Luke 8:1-3," *HeyJ* 30 (1989): 51-62.

3984   Kerry M. Craig and Margret A. Kristjansson, "Women Reading as Men/Women Reading as Women: A Structural Analysis for the Historical Project," *Semeia* 51 (1990): 119-36.

3985   C. M. Martini, *Women in the Gospels.* New York: Crossroad, 1990.

3986   Alberto Casalegno, "Maria e algumas figuras femininas nos escritos lucanos," *PerT* 23 (1991): 191-206.

3987   John J. Kilgallen, "A Consideration of Some of the Women in the Gospel of Luke," *SM* 40 (1991): 27-55.

3988   Tina Pippin, "The Politics of Meeting: Women and Power in the New Testament," in Michael Downey, ed., *That They Might Live: Power, Empowerment, and Leadership in the Church.* New York: Crossroad, 1991. Pp. 13-24.

3989   Adele Reinhartz, "From Narrative to History: The Resurrection of Mary and Martha," in Amy-Jill Levine, ed., *"Women Like This":* *A New Perspective on Jewish Women in the Greco-Roman World.* Atlanta: Scholars Press, 1991. Pp. 161-84.

3990   Wendy Robins, "Woman's Place: Jesus Reverses Traditional Understanding," *ChS* 82 (1992): 85-88.

word studies
3991   Richard C. Nevius, "*Kyrios* and *Iesous* in St. Luke,"*ATR* 48 (1966): 75-77.

3992   É. Samain, "La notion de ἀρχή dans l'oeuvre lucanienne," in Frans Neirynck, ed., *L'Évangile de Luc: Problèmes littéraires et théologiques* (festschrift for Lucien Cerfaux). BETL #32. Gembloux: Duculot, 1973. Pp. 209-38.

3993   B. H. Throckmorton, "Σῶζειν, σωτηρία in Luke-Acts," *StudE* 6 (1973): 515-26.

3994   A. V. Cernuda, "El paralelismo de γεννω y τικτω en Lc 1-2," *Bib* 55 (1974): 260-64.

3995   Donald L. Jones "The Title κύριος in Luke-Acts," *SBLSP* 4/2 (1974): 85-101.

3996   Franz Mussner, "Καθεξῆς im Lukasprolog," in E. Earle Ellis and Erich Grässer, eds., *Jesus und Paulus* (festschrift for W. G. Kümmel). Göttingen: Vandenhoeck, 1975. Pp. 253-55.

3997   J. Carmignac, "The Meaning of παρθενος in Lk 1,27: A Reply to C. H. Dodd," *BT* 28 (1977): 327-30.

3998   Gerhard Schneider, "Zur Bedeutung von καθεξῆς im lukanischen Doppelwerk," *ZNW* 68 (1977): 128-31.

3999 J. L. Pretlove, "Baptism ἐν πνεῦμα: A Comparison of the Theologies of Luke and Paul," doctoral dissertation, Southwestern Baptist Theological Seminary, Fort Worth TX, 1980.

4000 Ignace de la Potterie, "Les deux noms de Jérusalem dans l'évangile de Luc," RechSR 69 (1981): 57-70.

4001 Carlo Buzzetti, "Κεχαριτωμένη, 'favoured' (Lk 1:28), and the Italian Common Language New Testament," BT 33 (1982): 243.

4002 Donald L. Jones "The Title ΠΑΙΣ in Luke-Acts," SBLSP 12 (1982): 217-26.

4003 W. Schenk, "Die makrosyntaktische Signalfunktion des lukanischen Textems ὑποστεφειν," StudE 7 (1982): 443-50.

4004 Silverio Zedda, "Il χαῖρε di Lc 1,28 in luce di un triplice contesto anticotestamentario," in C. Marcheselli Casale, ed., Parola e Spirito (festschrift for S. Cipriani). Brescia: Paideia, 1982. Pp. 273-92.

4005 Dennis D. Sylva, "Ierousalèm and Hierosoluma in Luke-Acts," ZNW 74 (1983): 207-21.

4006 Charles H. Cosgrove, "The Divine δει in Luke-Acts: Investigations into the Lukan Understanding of God's Providence," NovT 26 (1984): 168-90.

4007 J. Duncan M. Derrett, "The Lucan Christ and Jerusalem: τελειουμαι," ZNW 75 (1984): 36-43.

4008 Donald L. Jones, "The Title υἱὸς θεοῦ in Acts," SBLSP 15 (1985): 451-63.

4009 John L. Nolland, "Luke's Use of χάρις," NTS 32 (1986): 614-20.

4010 P. Haudebert, "La metanoia des Seplanle à Saint Luc," in H. Cazelles, ed., La vie de la parole (festschrift for P. Grelot). Paris: Desclée, 1987. Pp. 355-66.

4011 Gert J. Steyn, "The Occurrence of 'Kainam' in Luke's Genealogy," ETL 65 (1989): 409-11.

Zaccheus
4012 A. P. Salom, "Was Zaccheus Really Reforming?" *ET* 78 (1966-1967): 87.

4013 J. O'Hanlon, "The Story of Zaccheus and the Lukan Ethic," *JSNT* 12 (1981): 2-26.

4014 Paul Kariamadam, *The Zaccheus Story (Lk 19:1-10): A Redactional-Critical Investigation.* Kerala, India: Pontifical Institute of Theology and Philosophy, 1985.

4015 B. M. Ahern, "The Zaccheus Incident," *BibTo* 25 (1987): 348-51.

4016 Alan C. Mitchell, "Zaccheus Revisited: Luke 19:8 as a Defense," *Bib* 71/2 (1990): 153-76.

4017 Alan C. Mitchell, "The Use of *Sykophantein* in Luke 19:8: Further Evidence for Zaccheus's Defense," *Bib* 72/4 (1991): 546-47.

4018 D. A. S. Ravens, "Zaccheus: The Final Part of a Lucan Triptych," *JSNT* 41 (1991): 19-32.

PART THREE

Commentaries

4019 G. Marchesi, *Il vangelo della misericordia: Commento biblico-teologico alle letture delle domeniche e delle feste*. Rome: Città Nuova, n.d.

4020 Adolf Harnack, *The Expansion of Christianity in the First Three Centuries*, trans. James Moffatt. 1. *Luke the Physician*. New York: Putnam's Sons, 1907.

4021 Alfred Plummer, *A Critical and Exegetical Commentary on the Gospel of Luke*. ICC. Edinburgh: T. & T. Clark, 1922.

4022 Burton S. Easton, *The Gospel According to Luke*. New York: Scribners, 1926.

4023 Erich Klostermann, *Das Evangelium nach Lukas*. 2nd ed. HNT #5. Tübingen: Mohr, 1929.

4024 John M. Creed, *The Gospel According to Saint Luke*. London: Macmillan, 1930.

4025 William Manson, *The Gospel of Luke*. MNTC. New York: Harper, 1930.

4026 J. Chapman, *Matthew, Mark and Luke*. London: Longmans & Green, 1937.

4027 K. H. Rengstorf, *Das Evangelium nach Lukas*. 5th ed. NTD #3. Göttingen: Vandenhoeck, 1949.

4028 Henry J. Cadbury, *The Making of Luke-Acts*. 2nd ed. London: SPCK, 1958.

4029 George B. Caird, *Saint Luke*. Pelican New Testament Commentaries. New York: Penguin Books, 1963

4030 F. Earle, *Matthew, Mark, Luke*. Beacon Bible Commentary #6. Kansas City MO: Beacon Hill, 1964.

4031 E. J. Tinsley, *The Gospel According to Luke*. CBC. Cambridge: University Press, 1965.

4032 A. R. C. Leaney, *The Gospel According to Saint Luke*. Black's New Testament Commentaries. London: Black, 1966.

4033 Frederick W. Danker, *Jesus and the New Age. A Commentary on St. Luke's Gospel*. Rev. ed. St. Louis MO: Clayton, 1972.

4034   Jacob Jervell, *Luke and the People of God: A New Look at Luke-Acts*. Minneapolis MN: Augsburg, 1972.

4035   J. Drury, *Luke*. Phillips Commentaries. London: Collins, 1973.

4036   G. Girardet, et al., *Evangelo secondo Luca*. Verona: Mondadori, 1973.

4037   E. P. Groenewald, *Die Evangelie van Lukas verklaar*. Kaapstad: N.G. Kerkuitgevers, 1973.

4038   Ray Summers, *Commentary on Luke: Jesus the Universal Savior*. Waco TX: Word Books, 1973.

4039   William Barclay, *The Gospel of Luke: Translation, Introduction, and Interpretation*. Philadelphia: Westminster, 1975.

4040   M. E. Klostermann, *Das Lukasevangelium*. Handbuch zum Neuen Testament #5. 3rd ed. Tübingen: Mohr, 1975.

4041   Adolf Schlatter, *Das Evangelium des Lukas aus seinen Quellen erklärt*. 3rd ed. Stuttgart: Calwer, 1975.

4042   Rudolf Pesch and R. Kratz, *So liest man synoptisch: Anleitung und Kiommentar zum Studium der synoptischen Evangelien*. 7 vols. Frankfurt: Knecht, 1975-1980.

4043   G. Bouwman, *Met Lukas op weg*. Averbode: Altiora, 1976.

4044   Édouard Delebecque, *Évangile de Luc: Texte traduit et annoté*. Paris: Les Belles Lettres, 1976.

4045   W. Egger, *Das Programm Jesu: Ein Arbeitsheft zum Lukasevangelium*. Klosterneuburg: Österreichisches Katholisches Bibelwerk, 1976.

4046   X. Pikaza, *Leggere Luca: Il terzo vangelo e gli Atti*. Torino: Marietti, 1976.

4047   F. Rienecker, *Das Evangelium des Lukas erklärt*. 6th ed. Wuppertal: Brockhaus, 1976.

4048   F. Schaeffer and E. Schaeffer, *L'évangile de Luc expliqué à tous.* Lausanne: Ligue pour la lecture de la Bible, 1976.

4049   Raymond E. Brown, *The Birth of the Messiah: A Commentary on the Infancy Narratives in Matthew and Luke.* Garden City: Doubleday, 1977.

4050   C. Dieterlé, et al., *Manuel du traducteur pour l'évangile de Luc.* Paris: Alliance biblique universelle, 1977.

4051   E. Earle Ellis, *The Gospel of Luke.* New Century Bible Commentary. Greenwood SC: Attic Press, 1977.

4052   J. Ernst, *Das Evangelium nach Lukas.* Regensburg: Pustet, 1977.

4053   Robert J. Karris, *Invitation to Luke: A Commentary on the Gospel of Luke with Complete Text from the Jerusalem Bible.* New York: Doubleday, 1977.

4054   A. Stöger, *The Gospel According to St. Luke*, B. Fahy, trans. London: Sheed, 1977.

4055   G. Coppa, *S. Ambrogio, Esposizione del vangelo secondo Luca: Introduzione traduzione, note e indici.* Rome: Città Nuova, 1978.

4056   W. Hendriksen, *Exposition of the Gospel according to Luke.* New Testament Commentaries. Grand Rapids MI: Baker, 1978.

4057   I. H. Marshall, *The Gospel of Luke: A Commentary on the Greek Text.* The New International Greek Testament Commentary. Grand Rapids: Eerdmans, 1978.

4058   D. J. Fox, ed., *The Matthew-Luke Commentary of Philoxenus.* SBLDS 43. Atlanta: Scholars Press, 1979.

4059   S. P. Kealy, *The Gospel of Luke.* Denville NJ: Dimension, 1979.

4060   A. J. Mattill, *Luke and Last Things: A Perspective for the Understanding of Lukan Thought.* Dillsboro NC: Western North Carolina Press, 1979.

4061   R. Meynet, *Quelle est donc cette parole? Lecture ''rhétorique'' de l'évangile de Luc.* 2 vols. Paris: Cerf, 1979.

4062 M. Wilcock, *The Savior of the World: The Message of Luke's Gospel.* Leicester: InterVarsity Press, 1979.

4063 Ulrich Busse, et al., *Jesus zwischen Arm und Reich: Lukas-Evangelium.* Stuttgart: Katholisches Bibelwerk, 1980.

4064 E. A. LaVerdiere, *Luke.* New Testament Message #5. Wilmington DE: Glazier, 1980.

4065 Walter Schmithals, *Das Evangelium nach Lukas.* Zurich: Theologischen Verlag, 1980.

4066 W. Grundmann, *Das Evangelium nach Lukas.* THNT. 9th ed. Berlin: Evangelische Verlagsanstalt, 1981.

4067 Joseph A. Fitzmyer, *The Gospel According to Luke: Introduction, Translation and Notes.* 2 vols. Anchor Bible Commentary. Garden City NY: Doubleday, 1981/1985.

4068 B. Aland, *Monophysitismus und Schriftauslegung. Der Kommentar zum Matthäus- und Lukasevangelium des Philoxenus von Mabbug.* Göttingen: Vandenhoeck, 1982.

4069 Robert L. Maddox, *The Purpose of Luke-Acts.* Edinburgh: T. & T. Clark, 1982.

4070 O. da Spinetoli, *Luca: Il vangelo dei poveri.* Assisi: Cittadella, 1982.

4071 D. McBride, *The Gospel of Luke: A Reflective Commentary.* Northfort NY: Castello, 1982.

4072 H. Schürmann, *Das Lukasevangelium: Erster Teil: Kommentar zu Kap. 1,1-9,50.* Herders theologischer Kommentar zum Neuen Testament #3. 2nd ed. Freiburg: Herder, 1982.

4073 Charles H. Talbert, *Reading Luke: A Literary and Theological Commentary on the Third Gospel.* New York: Crossroad, 1982.

4074 R. J. Dean, *Luke.* Layman's Bible Book Commentary. Nashville TN: Broadman Press, 1983.

4075 D. J. Harrington, *The Gospel according to Luke: An Access Guide for Scripture Study*. New York: Sadlier, 1983.

4076 J. Kodell, *The Gospel according to Luke*. Collegeville Bible Commentary #3. Collegeville MN: Liturgical Press, 1983.

4077 B. Larson, *Luke*. Communicator's Commentary #3. Waco TX: Word Books, 1983.

4078 J. T. Nielsen, *Het evangelie naar Lucas* 2 vols, Nijkerk: Callenbach, 1983.

4079 G. Rouiller and C. Varone, *Il vangelo secondo Luca: Testi e teologla*, U. Cavalieri, trans. Assisi: Cittadella, 1983.

4080 S. Benetti, *Una alegre noticia*. Madrid: Paulinas, 1984.

4081 William S. Kurz, *Following Jesus: A Disciple's Guide to Luke and Acts*. Ann Arbor MI: Servant Books, 1984.

4082 P.-G. Müller, *Lukas-Evangelium*. Stuttgart: Katholisches Bibelwerk, 1984.

4083 J. Reuss, *Lukas-Kommentare aus der griechischen Kirche: Aus Katenenhandschriften gesammelt und herausgegeben*. TU #130. Berlin: Akademie Verlag, 1984.

4084 G. Schneider, *Das Evangelium nach Lukas*. 2 vols. 2nd ed. Würzburg: Echter, 1984.

4085 Eduard Schweizer, *The Good News According to Luke*, D. E. Green, trans. Atlanta GA: John Knox Press, 1984.

4086 Thomas Reist, ed., *Saint Bonaventure as a Biblical Commentator: A Translation and Analysis of his Commentary on Luke 18:34-19:42*. Lanham MD: University Press of America, 1985.

4087 Leopold Sabourin, *The Gospel According to St. Luke: Introduction and Commentary*. Bandra, Bombay: Better Yourself Books, 1985.

4088 Gerhard Schneider, *Lukas, Theologe der Heilsgeschichte: Aufsätze zum lukanischen Doppelwerk*. BBB #59. Königstein: Hanstein, 1985.

4089 H. Mulder, *Lucas I-II. Een praktische bijbelverklaring.* 2 vols. Kampen: Kok, 1985-1988.

4090 J. Duncan M. Derrett, *New Resolutions of Old Conundrums: A Fresh Insight into Luke's Gospel.* Warwickshire: Drinkwater, 1986.

4091 S. Jeanne d'Arc, *Évangile selon Luc.* Paris: Les Belles Lettres, 1986.

4092 P. van Linden, *The Gospel of Luke and Acts.* Wilmington DE: Glazier, 1986.

4093 R. E. Obach and A. Kirk, *A Commentary on the Gospel of Luke.* Mahwah NJ: Paulist Press, 1986.

4094 Robert C. Tannehill, *The Narrative Unity of Luke-Acts: A Literary Interpretation.* 1: *The Gospel According to Luke.* Philadelphia: Fortress Press, 1986.

4095 Frederick W. Danker, *Luke.* Proclamation Commentaries. 2nd ed. Philadelphia: Fortress Press, 1987.

4096 D. Gooding, *According to Luke: A New Exposition of the Third Gospel.* Grand Rapids MI: Eerdmans, 1987.

4097 S. T. Lachs, *A Rabbinic Commentary on the New Testament: The Gospels of Matthew, Mark, and Luke.* Hoboken NJ: KTAV, 1987.

4098 H. Mentz, *Das Lukas-Evangelium neu erzählt.* Göttingen: Vandenhoeck, 1987

4099 J. J. Kilgallen, *A Brief Commentary on the Gospel of Luke* Mahwah NJ: Paulist Press, 1988.

4100 Jacob Kremer, *Lukasevangelium.* Neue Echter Bibel #3. Würzburg: Echter, 1988.

4101 M. Masini, *Luca: Il vangelo del discepolo.* Brescia: Queriniana, 1988.

4102 R. Meynet, *L'évangile selon saint Luc. Analyse rhétorique.* 2 vols. Paris: Cerf, 1988.

4103 Leon Morris, *The Gospel according to Saint Luke: An Introduction and Commentary*. Tyndale New Testament Commentaries #3. Rev. ed. Grand Rapids: Eerdmans, 1988.

4104 David L. Tiede, *Luke*. Augsburg Commentary on the New Testament. Minneapolis MN: Augsburg, 1988.

4105 J.-L. Vesco, *Jérusalem el son prophète: Une lecture de l'évangile selon saint Luc*. Paris: Cerf, 1988.

4106 W. Wiefel, *Das Evangelium nach Lukas*. THNT #3. Berlin: Evangelische Verlagsanstalt, 1988.

4107 T. Zahn, *Das Evangelium des Lukas ausgelegt*. Wuppertal: Brockhaus, (reprinted) 1988.

4108 F. Bovon, *Das Evangelium nach Lukas (1:1-9:50)*. Neukirchen: Neukirchener Verlag, 1989.

4109 Michael D. Goulder, *Luke: A New Paradigm*. Sheffield: JSOT Press, 1989.

4110 John L. Nolland, *Luke 1-9:20*. Word Book Commentary. Dallas: Word, 1989.

4111 Joseph A. Grassi, *God Makes Me Laugh: A New Approach to Luke*. Wilmington DE: Glazier, 1986.

4112 J. Nolland, *Luke 1-9:20*. Word Biblical Commentary #34a. Dallas: Word, 1989.

4113 K. Bittleston, *The Gospel of Luke*. Edinburgh: Floris, 1990.

4114 A. Chouraqui, *Les Evangiles. Matthieu - Marc - Luc - Jean*. Turnhout: Brepols, 1990.

4115 C. A. Evans, *Luke*. New International Biblical Commentary #3. Peabody MA: Hendrickson, 1990.

4116 C. F. Evans, *Saint Luke*. TPI New Testament Commentaries. London: SCM, 1990.

4117   G. P. Weber and R. Miller, *Breaking Open the Gospel of Luke*. Cincinnati OH: St. Anthony Messenger, 1990.

4118   F. Bovon, *L'Évangile selon Saint Luc (1,1-9,50)*. Geneba: Labor et Fides, 1991.

4119   J. Ruis-Camps, *El éxodo del hombre libre: Catequesis sobre el Evangelio de Lucas*. Córdoba: Ediciónes El Almendro, 1991.

4120   Luke T. Johnson, *The Gospel of Luke*. Sacra Pagina #3. Collegeville MN: Liturgical Press, 1991.

4121   S. Zedda, *Teologia della salvezza nel Vangelo di Luca*. Bologna: Dehoniane, 1991.

4122   Robert H. Stein, *Luke*. New American Commentary #24. Nashville TN: Broadman Press, 1993.

Author Index

Hamm, Dennis, 1554, 2019, 2028, 3109
Hamp, V., 0235, 3009
Hann, Robert R., 0358
Hansack, E., 0382
Harbarth, A., 0861
Harnack, Adolf, 4020
Harrington, D. J., 4075
Harrington, Patricia A., 0251
Harrington, W., 1700, 3306
Harris, J. R., 0222, 0223
Harris, J. W., 0818
Harris, M. J., 3054
Harris, S. M., 0469, 2667
Harrisville, Roy A., 1287, 1640
Hart, H. St. J., 2074
Hartin, Patrick J., 1515, 3369
Hartl, H., 1905
Hartstock, Reinhold, 3813
Harvey, A. E., 1146
Haslam, J. A. G., 0854
Haudebert, P., 4010
Hauerwas, Stanley, 3719
Hawkins, John C., 3802, 3803
Hawthorn, T., 0993
Head, P. M., 3734
Healey, J. F., 1489
Heater, Homer, 0496, 0546, 3921
Hecht, A., 2828
Heer, Josef, 0787
Heerspink, R., 3150
Heffner, Blake R., 1275
Heggen, F. J., 0356
Heil, John P., 2227
Heimbrock, H. G., 1959
Heimler, A., 1959
Heinz, Johann H., 2100
Helbling, H., 1152
Helms, Randel, 0831, 3199
Hemelsoet, Ben, 1597, 1924, 2058

Hemer, C. J., 2998
Hempel, J., 1637
Hemraj, S., 3726
Hendrickx, H., 2467, 3055, 3468, 3699
Hendriksen, W., 4056
Hengel, M., 1956
Héring, J., 2199, 2675
Hermann, I., 1366
Hermans, L., 0313, 2492
Hermant, Dominique, 0701, 1003, 1074
Herzog, William R., 1225
Hester, D. C., 0558, 3880
Heutger, N., 1211, 2520, 3242
Hickling, C. J. A., 3527
Hicks, John Mark, 1940, 3431
Hiers, R. H., 2607, 3433
Higgins, A. J. B., 0071, 1439, 3922
Hilkert, Mary Catherine, 2342
Hill, David, 0597, 2242, 2879
Hills, Julian V., 1158
Hintzen, J., 3717
Hirt, Oscar H., 1033, 2553
Hirunuma, Toshio, 3926
Hobbie, F. W., 2007
Hock, R. F., 1848, 2986, 3046
Hodgson, Robert, 0572, 0637
Hoerber, Robert George, 1979
Hof, O., 1805
Hoffmann, P., 0875, 1167, 1487, 1570, 3666
Hofius, O., 1714, 3321
Hogg, W. Richey, 0434
Hollenbach, Paul W., 0501, 0506
Hollenweger, W. J., 0322, 2013
Holleran, J. W., 1977
Holman, C. L., 1052, 2106, 3432
Holst, R., 0926, 2539, 2878
Hook, N., 2133
Hooker, M. D., 2919, 3764, 3859

Wansey, J. C., 1804, 3382
Ward, A. Marcus, 1880, 3363
Ward, Richard A., 1985
Ware, Browning, 1186
Waterman, Henry G., 3435
Watson, N. M., 2024
Watts, J. W., 3106
Weatherly, Jon A., 2951
Webb, P. M., 2274
Weber, G. P., 4117
Wegenast, K., 1619, 3268
Wegner, Uwe, 0856, 1251
Wehrli, E. S., 1838
Weinert, F. D., 0466, 1589, 2041, 3084, 3089, 3119
Weiser, A., 0850, 1511, 1516, 1520
Weiss, K., 0961
Welzen, H., 1469, 1548, 3056
Wendland, Ioann, 0362
Wenham, David, 0973, 1072, 3371
Wenham, John W., 1102, 1992, 2548, 2616, 3856, 3861, 3914, 3956
Wentling, Judith L., 2811
Weren, W., 0764, 0964, 0965, 2067, 2127, 2646, 3184, 3185
Wernecke, Herbert H., 2421
Westendorf, Craig, 0975, 3373
Westermann, C., 0308
Western, W., 2180
Weymann, V., 2008
Wheeler, F., 3840, 3920
White, L. Michael, 1387
White, R. C., 2011, 2012
Widengren, G., 2359
Wiefel, W., 4106
Wifstrand, Albert, 1944
Wijngaards, J. N. M., 1821
Wilckens, U., 0154, 0923, 2497
Wilcock, M., 3933, 4062

Wilkens, Wilhelm, 0557, 1010, 2770, 3879
Wilkinson, F. H., 1235, 3214
Wilkinson, J., 1549, 2266
Willaert, B., 1038
Williams, A. L., 0366
Williams, Francis E., 1761, 1779, 2400, 3395
Williams, J., 1989
Williams, J. G., 1449
Williams, N. P., 3810
Willimon, William H., 2103, 2269
Willis, G. G., 1302
Willmington, Harold L., 0124
Wilshire, L. E., 2737
Wilson, Paul Scott, 1754
Wilson, R. McLean, 0029
Wilson, Stephen G., 2783, 2974, 3077
Wink, Walter, 0039, 0884, 1208, 3240
Winstead, John H., 2681
Winter, Paul, 0018, 0019, 0021, 0025, 0026, 0133, 0225, 0267, 0280, 0284, 0420, 0462, 1175, 2085, 2224, 2450, 3011, 3012
Wirt, Edgar, 0785
Wiseman, T. P., 0335
Wiskirchen, W., 0436
Wisse, F., 3915
Wisselink, W. F., 3928
Witherington, Ben, 0476, 0876, 0966, 1819, 2580, 3982
Witte, G. E., 3779
Wojcik, Jan, 2859
Wolfe, Charles E., 1638
Wolff, A. M., 0326
Wood, H. G., 3811
Worden, Ronald D., 0760, 3639, 3738
Wrege, T. H., 1457
Wren, M., 2515